An Officer in MacArthur's Court

An Officer in MacArthur's Court

The Memoir of the first Headquarters Commandant for
General Douglas MacArthur
in Australia

World War II
November 1941 – August 1945

A 39-month Wartime Odyssey through the Southwest Pacific Area from
San Francisco through Java, Australia, New Guinea, and the Philippines

Based on the true diary, letters, and oral history of
Col. John F. Day Jr., USA

By
John F. Day III

2014

An Officer in MacArthur's Court

ISBN13: 978-1-61170-176-0
ISBN10: 1-61170-176-7
Library of Congress Control Number: 2014940844

Disclaimer

The information contained in this book is accurate insofar as the author knows. However, it is based upon a contemporaneous diary, contemporary letters, an oral history recorded 25 years after the events described, and a lifetime of dinner-table family stories. The book retains the language and slang of the period (i.e. Japs, nigger, bitch) which may not be politically correct in modern discourse but which was common in the period. The story has been assembled in good faith as a best effort and is accurate as far as the author is aware. However, the author bears no responsibility for the truth or validity of any statement included in this document.

Published in the USA .

 Robertson Publishing™
www.RobertsonPublishing.com

Printed in the USA, UK and Australia on acid-free paper.
To purchase additional copies of this book go to:
amazon.com
barnesandnoble.com

"If anyone wants to know, I am keeping this diary for my wife and son, my mother and father and all other loved ones I know. There is nothing I could write at this time that could express all of my feelings.

With a big hug, John"

John F. Day Jr.
10 Jan 1942

"Everyone experiences their own war. Everyone has their own job to do, and that is the war to him. Your job depends on everybody else doing their job; and everybody else depends on you. It is a collective effort. Each person had their own experiences, and those experiences were the war to him. These are my experiences.

"I was lucky. I was in some good places. I got through some tight places. Every night when the Japanese came over dropping bombs or strafing, you got in a hole. Any bomb could get you. It was just a matter of chance if you got hit or if the fellow next to you got hit. I was lucky and did not get hit. Many others got hit."

John F. Day Jr.
18 Feb 1988

Col. John F. Day Jr.

In Memoriam

1909 - 2000

Dedication

My father, Col. John F. Day Jr., was a military man. The military is endowed with discipline, determination, honor, loyalty, integrity, and independence. The mission was always clear. There was never any equivocation. The world was black or white, good or evil, right or wrong. Yet this book can only be written because my father disobeyed the Army rules and maintained a daily diary during some of the defining moments of the Twentieth Century.

The relationship between a father and a son is a complex thing. It is grounded in shared blood, but nurtured by a lifetime of shared experiences. The bond can sometimes be strong and at other times weak, a balance between independence and obedience. In adulthood, it can be a conflict between strong male egos grounded with mutual respect and admiration.

Years after the war, my father and I lived on opposite coasts, 3,000 miles apart. On my periodic visits to his home, we would sit across the kitchen table late into the night with a shared bottle of scotch. In the privacy of the night, he would open his life experiences to me. I got to know a man I had never known, a younger man trying to make his way in an uncertain world. Those were special moments that I will treasure the rest of my life. A bond was forged between us that is one of the reasons this book is dedicated to him.

John F. Day III

Acknowledgement

In the preparation of this book, I am indebted to many people. Certainly, I am indebted to my wife who tolerated my endless hours on the computer and who read the early drafts. There were family members who saved the documents during the war and who supplied those documents to me – my two grandmothers, Flora Gray Day and Lucille Hackley, and my aunt, Hazel Dawn Day. There were many who helped me with the basic research – Karen Nunan, the Archivist at the MacArthur Memorial Museum in Brisbane, Australia, Peter Dunn of Australia@war and www.oz@war.com for an unforgettable tour of the Brisbane of World War II, James Tobias, the Archivist at the U.S. Army Center of Military History at Ft. McNair. William (Billy) Huston, who served as a staff officer in MacArthur's GHQ during WWII, gave me access to his personal collection of original GHQ documents and pointed me to other source materials.

I am indebted to the members of my Memoirs Class at the Los Altos Senior Center who listened to endless rewrites and guided me through the English language. Our instructor, Sylvia Hallaron, and especially Gail Ballinger, have constantly corrected my grammar and poor punctuation. In the end, however, I am responsible for the final product with all its imperfections.

Foreword

Much has been written about Gen. MacArthur and the Southwest Pacific Area from the point of view of the allied generals and admirals. In contrast, this is a memoir written from the perspective of a young U.S. Army officer who is swept up in the swirl of war, a victim of the "Europe First" policy of Churchill and Roosevelt, but consumed by the mystique of MacArthur's charisma.

In February 1988 during one of my visits to my father's home in Florida, I took my video camera and recorded his oral history of World War II. At the time, my father, Col. John F. Day Jr., was 79. His mind was clear and his sense of humor very much intact. Over a three-day period, I recorded eight hours of my father's memoirs of Java, Australia, New Guinea, and the Philippines. When I returned to California, the recording rested on a closet shelf until after his death, almost 12 years later. When my father died, I came into possession of two diaries he maintained during his deployment in the Southwest Pacific. I also received his military personnel file covering a 30-year military career along with the family photo album. My aunt learned of my interests and sent me 70 original letters written by my father to his mother during the war, many still in their original envelopes. Leave it to a mother to save everything from her son at war.

I retired two years later and embarked on a personal journey of discovery. I transcribed the faded and water-stained script of the diaries and letters. The video was digitized and transcribed. To understand the events and emotions of the period, I became an avid reader of military history and memoirs of the Southwest Pacific. I traveled to Australia, New Guinea, and the Philippines to visit the wartime sites described in the diary. I visited a number of libraries and repositories of military documents in both the United States and Australia, where I talked with historians in both countries. A California acquaintance, who served in GHQ with my father, guided me through his personal collection of official government reports and steered me to the Stanford University Hoover Institute Library. I received special assistance from the Archivists of the MacArthur Memorial Museum in Brisbane, Australia. The Archivist of the U.S. Army Center of Military History at Ft. McNair, D.C. graciously allowed me to copy the faded flimsy onion-skin carbon copies of draft manuscripts prepared by U.S. Army historians in 1946 for military histories of ASCOM and USASOS that were never published.

As I wrote this book, I endeavored to record the sources of the information. In addition to footnotes and bibliography, I used three different font types. Material from the diary and the oral history is presented in standard Book Antigua font. Original letters and personal notes from my father are enclosed in a box and presented in Calibri font. *Historical material added from outside sources is presented in Book Antigua Italics font.* Comments and observations added by me are placed in [*brackets in italics*]. Section subtitles are added to ease navigation through this odyssey.

The diary has been used as the principal timeline of this story. Oral history and letters have been blended primarily to add color and texture to the descriptions of the events from historical records. The book is not a literal transcription of the diary, but has been edited for grammar, spelling, and punctuation. Some dialog has been added where it was alluded to in the diary or quoted in the oral history. The colonial Dutch spelling of locations in Java (for example, Soerabaja and Tjilatjap) has been used rather than modern Malay spelling (Surabaya and Cilachap). Extensive use of military abbreviations was necessary, but a special listing of these abbreviations has been provided as an aide to the reader.

This book is not intended as a definitive history of Southwest Pacific Area. Rather, this is a chronicle of the experiences and observations of a specific American officer who served as the first Headquarters Commandant for Gen. Douglas MacArthur. Discrepancies between the diary and sources made available since the war have appeared, and I have endeavored to identify those discrepancies where I am aware of them. However, my intent is to be faithful to the knowledge of the diarist at the time of his writing.

I hope the reader and my grandchildren enjoy the story.

John F. Day III
July 14, 2014

Table of Contents

Table of Figures

Abbreviations

ABDACOM – Australia, British Dutch American Command

AIF – Australian Imperial Forces (the Army of Australia)

ASCOM – Army Services Command (attached to the Sixth Army)

FEAF – U.S. Far East Air Force

GHQ – General Headquarters (Gen. Douglas MacArthur's Headquarters)

HQ - Headquarters

KNIL - (Koninklijk Nederlands Indisch Leger) - Royal Netherlands East Indies Army.

LST – Landing Ship, Tank, an amphibious landing craft

NEI – Netherlands East Indies

SOC – Scout-Observation-Craft, cruiser launched seaplane called Seagull

SWPA – South-West Pacific Area

USAAF – U.S. Army Air Force

USAFFE – U.S. Armed Forces Far East

USAFIA - U.S. Army Forces in Australia

USASOS – United States Army Services of Supply – Services consist of the seven technical branches of the Army, including the Corps of Engineers, Signal Corps, Ordinance Corps, Chemical Warfare, Medical Corps, Quartermaster Corps, and Transportation Corps

USAT – U.S. Army Transport

USS – United States Ship

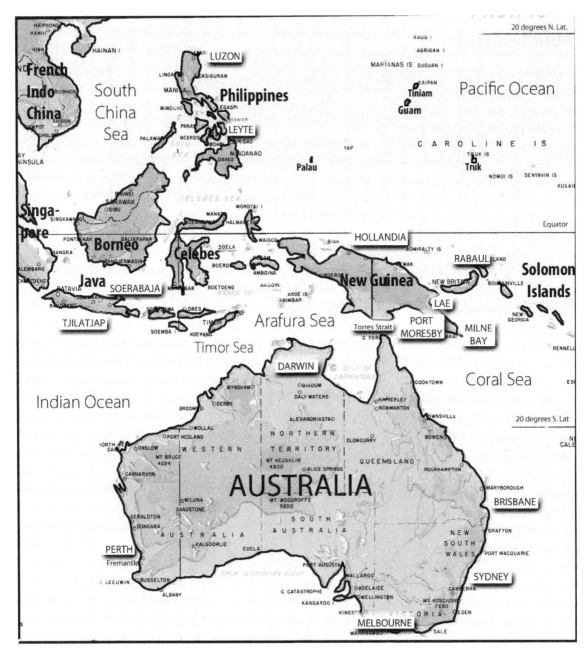

SOUTH WEST PACIFIC AREA
World War II

Part I - The Diary

1.   ORDERS TO THE PACIFIC – 23 Oct 1941

1.1.   The Red Bordered "Immediate Action" Order – 23 Oct 1941

The brown manila envelope arrived at 2nd Division Headquarters in the Quadrangle of Fort Sam Houston, Texas on 27 Oct 1941. It was addressed to First Lieutenant John F. Day, Jr., Field Artillery, and contained a Red Letter Order. In military terms, Red Letter Orders demand IMMEDIATE ACTION. The package had been expected for two months. Ever since we returned from the largest peacetime maneuvers in U.S. history, we knew we would be shipped out. The question was "Europe or the Pacific"?

About 400,000 soldiers spent August and September of 1941 in northwest Louisiana fighting a simulated war over navigation rights along the Mississippi River. Nazi Germany had invaded Poland the previous year, and Japan had captured Shanghai and Nanking. The U.S. military was greatly concerned over how to deal with a German *blitzkrieg*. The Louisiana maneuvers were intended to explore alternative tactics to deal with an invading tank force supported by strong air power. The leadership of the Red and Blue armies included men who would later become household names – Omar Bradley, Mark Clark, Dwight D. Eisenhower, George Patton, Walter Krueger, and Leslie McNair. The Army Air Corps included George C. Kenney.[1]

As a First Lieutenant, I was Battery Commander of Headquarters Battery, 38th Field Artillery, 2nd Infantry Division. Our division was one of the pawns in the great Louisiana chess game. We learned a lot of things to not do in war.

Figure 1 - 2nd Infantry Division Shoulder Patch

San Antonio weather in October was still in the low 80's, but the thick limestone walls of the Quadrangle headquarters provided a comfortable year-around environment. Without air conditioning, the ventilation was based entirely upon open windows and the available breeze. In 1876 when the building was built, it was designed for storage of grain and military supplies. However, its most famous use was as a jail for the Apache warrior, Geronimo, when he was captured in 1886. The

---

[1] Both Kruger and Kenny reappear on MacArthur's staff in GHQ in Australia in 1942. Brigadier General George C. Kenny, a pilot who flew 75 combat missions in World War I, had two confirmed "kills." One "kill" was reputed to be Hermann Göring, the head of the German Luftwaffe.

building had been in continuous use for the 65 years following its construction.

I still had not received the orders for my promotion to Captain. I was very upset. The papers for my Recommendation for Promotion had been returned from Washington for the third time because of either incomplete paper work at Corps or changing rules in Washington. I wanted to protest, so I marched into the Quadrangle that housed Corps Headquarters and up to second floor to the Adjutant General's office. I bypassed the division headquarters since they had approved the matter three times. I explained my story to a sympathetic Colonel, who said he would investigate the matter. West Pointers have their own networks, and after a single call to Washington by the Colonel, I had my promotion in three days. I returned to his office the next week to express my gratitude for his assistance. He was most gracious as he congratulated me on my new promotion. It was the last time I met with Col. Dwight David Eisenhower.

Figure 2 - Lt. John F Day Jr. with Johnnie, Fort Sam Houston, Texas 1941

When I arrived back at the Battalion Headquarters, I was given the brown manila envelope. I was ordered to the Philippine Department and given one month to clear Fort Sam Houston. I was to arrive in San Francisco ready to board a ship on November 20, 1941. My adventures for the next four years in the Pacific had begun.

1.2.   San Francisco, Here We Come

Preparing to ship out for war is not trivial. A myriad of decisions had to be made. I had to transfer my Field Artillery Battery to my replacement. There was a medical exam, shots, a will, life insurance, and lots of papers to be completed. There was the relocation of my wife, our 5-year-old son, and our German shepherd. We had to vacate our apartment at 223 Funston Place, San Antonio, Texas, and say goodbye to relatives. And then there was the trip to San Francisco. It all takes time.

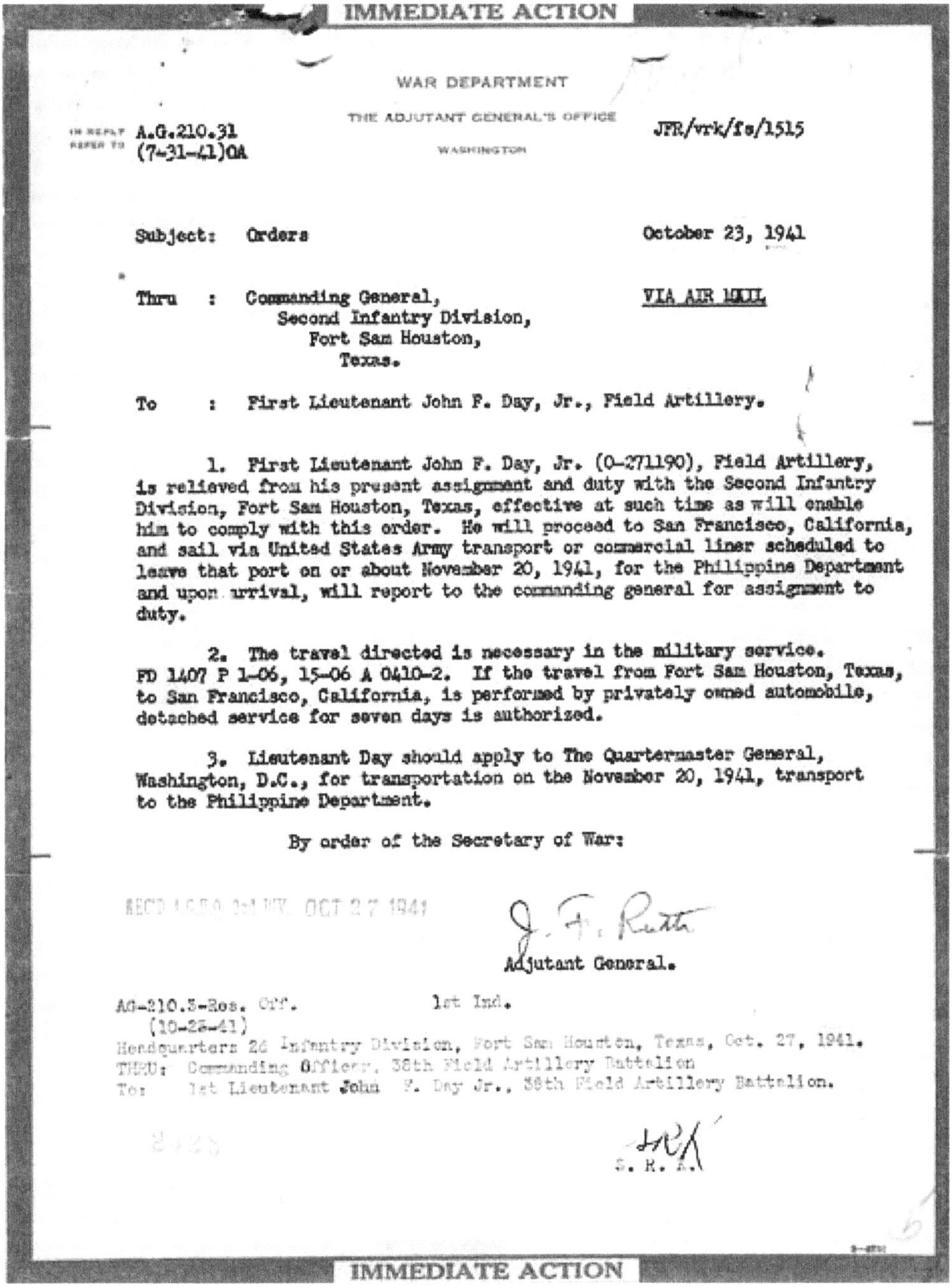

IMMEDIATE ACTION

WAR DEPARTMENT

THE ADJUTANT GENERAL'S OFFICE

WASHINGTON

IN REPLY REFER TO A.G.210.31
(7-31-41)OA

JFR/vrk/fs/1515

Subject: Orders   October 23, 1941

Thru   :   Commanding General,   VIA AIR MAIL
           Second Infantry Division,
           Fort Sam Houston,
           Texas.

To   :   First Lieutenant John F. Day, Jr., Field Artillery.

     1. First Lieutenant John F. Day, Jr. (O-271190), Field Artillery,
is relieved from his present assignment and duty with the Second Infantry
Division, Fort Sam Houston, Texas, effective at such time as will enable
him to comply with this order. He will proceed to San Francisco, California,
and sail via United States Army transport or commercial liner scheduled to
leave that port on or about November 20, 1941, for the Philippine Department
and upon arrival, will report to the commanding general for assignment to
duty.

     2. The travel directed is necessary in the military service.
FD 1407 P 1-06, 15-06 A 0410-2. If the travel from Fort Sam Houston, Texas,
to San Francisco, California, is performed by privately owned automobile,
detached service for seven days is authorized.

     3. Lieutenant Day should apply to The Quartermaster General,
Washington, D.C., for transportation on the November 20, 1941, transport
to the Philippine Department.

                    By order of the Secretary of War:

RECD AGRA 2d INV. OCT 27 1941

                              J. F. Ruttr

                         Adjutant General.

AG-210.3-Res. Off.   1st Ind.
    (10-23-41)
Headquarters 2d Infantry Division, Fort Sam Houston, Texas, Oct. 27, 1941.
THRU: Commanding Officer, 38th Field Artillery Battalion
To: 1st Lieutenant John F. Day Jr., 38th Field Artillery Battalion.

                                        S. R. A.

IMMEDIATE ACTION

Figure 3 - Orders to 1st Lt. John F Day Jr. to the Philippine Islands
October 23, 1941

Fortunately, I had leave accrued, and the Army gave me an extra seven days to travel by personal car. Cile, Johnnie, and I could say goodbye to Papa and Mama in New Mexico on the way to San Francisco.

Cile and I had been married for six years. We had lived in four different mill towns across Texas, so we knew how to move. We met in Bonham the summer of 1930 after I

graduated from Texas A&M, when I was working at the Bonham Cotton Mill. A big strike closed the Bonham Mill in 1935, so we moved to the cotton mill in New Braunfels, where Johnnie was born. For the next four years we moved from one cotton mill to another. After New Braunfels, it was Post, Texas, and then Brenham, Texas. In Brenham I had been promoted to plant superintendent, but the winds of war in 1940 changed everything. I had been in the Reserve Army since A&M graduation and knew I would be called to duty. I went on active duty on 20 Nov 1940. I was 31 years old.

Cile and I decided that for the duration of the war she and Johnnie should return to her childhood home in

Figure 4 – Cile & John Day – 1941 Bonham, Texas

Bonham. They could move in and live with her parents, the Hackleys. She had a strong support network of relatives and high school friends to help her. Johnnie could start school there in September. The Hackleys loved dogs, so Prince would fit right in. Prince was a full-size German shepherd and Johnnie's protector. With only a 6 months age difference between Johnnie and Prince, they were inseparable. I could never spank Johnnie outdoors because Prince would always intervene, gently putting my wrist in his jaws without biting. I knew when to stop.

For the car trip to San Francisco, Cile did not want to make the return trip to Texas alone with Johnnie. I asked my brother, Carl, who lived in New Mexico, to accompany Cile on the trip and he agreed. Carl lived on Papa's sheep ranch in New Mexico, and that would be one of our stops going to and returning from San Francisco.

We made a short trip to Kerrville to say good-bye to Cile's

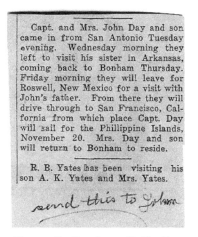

Capt. and Mrs. John Day and son came in from San Antonio Tuesday evening. Wednesday morning they left to visit his sister in Arkansas, coming back to Bonham Thursday. Friday morning they will leave for Roswell, New Mexico for a visit with John's father. From there they will drive through to San Francisco, California from which place Capt. Day will sail for the Phillippine Islands, November 20. Mrs. Day and son will return to Bonham to reside.

R. B. Yates has been visiting his son A. K. Yates and Mrs. Yates.

send this to John

Figure 5 - Bonham Daily Favorite, Nov 1941

Aunt Hopie and Uncle Oscar Hackley. There were two trips from San Antonio to Bonham to haul clothes and household goods, and deliver Prince. We made a brief detour to say goodbye to my sister, Alta Pearl, in Arkansas. She was two years older than me, and had married the druggist in Eden. By 1941, she had two children, John Charles and Pat.

Finally, after about ten days we were clear of Fort Sam Houston and ready to head for California. The trip to California was a great adventure, a vacation in disguise. None of us had ever been west of New Mexico, so everything was new.

1.3.   The Ranch

Papa and Mama lived on a 17-section[2] ranch about 27 miles south of Roswell, New Mexico. The first ten miles of the road from Roswell were paved. Then the road turned into a gravel rut across open range with arroyo crossings that were subject to flash floods in the summer and impassable creeks in the rainy winter. The ranch was at a 3,800-foot elevation, an arid high plateau that was hot in the summer and cold in the winter. The wind blew all the time. The main house was a one-bedroom adobe structure with thick mud walls and a large shaded front porch. It was cool in the summer and retained the heat in the winter. There was no electricity, no telephone, and no indoor plumbing. The oil hurricane lamp in the living room dimly illuminated the wood stove and two large bookcases with glass doors against one wall. With seasonal dust storms, books had to be kept behind glass doors to protect them. The privy, or outhouse, was a "two-holer" out beyond the orchard – the scene of

Figure 6 - John F Day Sr. & Flora Gray Day, New Mexico 1941

many serious family discussions. A tall windmill pumped water for a small tank reservoir that watered the horse corral, the sheep trough, a small garden, and a few fruit trees. The nearest neighbor was about 11 miles away. My Australian friends always compared the ranch to a sheep station in the Outback.

---

[2] A section is a unit of land that is one square mile in area. Seventeen sections are 17 square miles.

Papa had been a school teacher, a successful merchant, and the elected school board chairman in Eden, Texas in the 1920s. Papa and Mama had three sons and one daughter. I was the third child and the second son.

Mama was the "Iron Hand" that ruled the family. A former school teacher, she was a strong-willed woman who demanded great things of her children and her grandchildren. Education was very important to her – books, reading, and history. She demanded independence, resourcefulness, and self-confidence – all part of her persona. When Audna, the wife of my oldest brother, Gilbert, was killed in a tragic car-train accident, she left a two-year-old baby daughter without a mother. Mama demanded "possession" of Jo Ann. Jo Ann lived with Mama on the ranch until she was eleven and entering the fifth grade. Only then was she allowed to rejoin her father, Gilbert, and his new wife, Louise.

In the middle of the Dust Bowl and the Great Depression, about 1935, Papa's hardware, clothing, and drug businesses collapsed when the local farmers lost their crops and were unable to pay their debts to the merchants who had supplied them on credit. Papa traded a small farm outside of Eden to buy the New Mexico ranch and 800 head of sheep that were still in Texas. My younger brother, Carl with one Basque shepherd and two sheep dogs drove the 800 head across 350 miles of desolate West Texas range to reach the new ranch in New Mexico. The Basque had come into New Mexico in the 1600's with the Spanish Conquistadores to care for their sheep. They were legendary as the best shepherds in the world.

Carl, his wife, Hazel Dawn, and their 10-month-old son, Carl Edward, lived on the ranch in a trailer about 25 yards from the main house. Carl was the foreman of the ranch. He was three years younger than I was. Carl had had scarlet fever as a child. Papa once said he was afraid to let Carl go to college because he was not physically strong enough to survive the intense physical hazing that was common for freshmen on most college campuses, especially Texas A&M. So Carl never made it to college like his three older siblings. His weak heart also caused the Draft Board to declare him "4F", not eligible for military service. When Papa's businesses collapsed, there also was no college money for Carl, so Carl agreed to stay home and work Papa's farm. In the long term, Carl made far more money farming than anyone else in the family.

1.4.   Parting Words

The first morning I was at the ranch Papa and I saddled up two horses and took off to ride the south fence. Riding the fence was one of the regular chores on a ranch to make sure you keep the sheep in and the predators out. The coyote traps were inspected to see if any critters had been caught. Dead coyote were strung up from the fence posts as a warning to the next predator. The real purpose of the ride was that Papa wanted to talk to me alone – no mother, no wife, no other ears. Fathers have a special way of talking to sons that works better when they are alone and working together on a task. Two men never talk face to face, but usually shoulder to shoulder. When you are riding the fence, you are alone with the jack rabbits, the prairie dogs, and an occasional snake.

Papa had the usual check list: Is Cile going to be OK? Do you have enough money? What can I do to help? I asked him to buy some cattle for me and let them run on the ranch. I would cable him money from time to time, and I wanted him to invest it in livestock for me. That was my savings account for after the war.

The conversation eventually worked its way around to "What do you want me to do if something happens to you at war?" I had my checklist to share with him too.

Finally, he got to his sermon "John Frank, go do your duty, make us proud, but don't do anything foolish. Above all, come home safe."

1.5.   Road Trip

After a few days at the ranch Carl and I packed up the car and headed west. The drive to San Francisco was formidable in 1941. There were

Figure 7 - 1941 Buick 2-door Super, Grand Canyon, - November 1941

no freeways – only narrow country roads that passed through every small town. The Army allowed seven days to travel from Texas by personal car.

We had a 1941 two-door Buick Super that had a radio – a luxury in that day – but no air-conditioning. I picked up two spare tires and a canvas water bag to get us safely across the desert. Somehow we managed to fit three adults and one child inside and stow everyone's luggage with the two spare tires in the trunk. Fortunately, the Army shipped my luggage directly to San Francisco.

After our stop at the Grand Canyon, we drove across Boulder Dam[3], which had been completed only five years earlier in 1936, and took a boat ride on Lake Mead.

Our car pulled into San Francisco after dark on Monday night, 17 Nov 1941. It was too late to check into Fort Mason, so we took a room at the William Penn Hotel. The next morning we drove to Fort Mason, where I signed in.

I was scheduled to sail on Friday, November 21, 1941, at 12 noon aboard the *USS Republic* in Cabin #148. Officers had to pay a per diem food allowance for meals aboard the ship. My luggage, which included a wardrobe trunk, footlocker, and golf clubs, had been lost in transit between Texas and San Francisco. I spent two anxious days searching before everything finally turned up.

Figure 8 - Capt. John F Day Jr. and Johnnie
On Lake Mead, Nevada,
Carl Day in background

The USS Republic had been built in 1907 as a German passenger liner, "U.S. Grant." Sometime before World War I, she became American property as the USS Grant and was used as a troop carrier from 1917 to 1920. After the Great War[4], she again became a commercial passenger liner for the United States Lines until 1931, when she was re-

Figure 9 - Pier 7, San Francisco, CA
November 1941

Figure 10 - Cile's photo of USS Republic at
Pier 7, San Francisco, CA November 1941

[3] There was great political controversy over the name of the dam. Originally, Boulder Canyon Dam, the name was not officially changed to Hoover Dam until 1947.
[4] World War I

claimed by the Army as a U.S. Army Transport (USAT). Sometime in mid-1941 the ship was transferred to the US Navy and became the USS Republic. At 635 feet, the Republic was the seventh longest ship in the U.S. fleet and the thirteenth longest ship in the world in 1941.

The length of the ship meant that she would not rock as much at sea, which made me very happy. After we sailed, we learned there were 3,160 soldiers on board.

Cile, Carl, and Johnnie became San Francisco tourists while I started my processing. I joined them to visit the Japanese Tea Garden and to ride on a cable car. Carl and Cile were only allowed on the dock for 30 minutes before we departed, so I thought they should leave for home. Instead, they wanted to wait until I was off. They drove out along the Marina and watched my ship go underneath the Golden Gate Bridge on Friday, 21 Nov 1941. I was off to the Philippines.

USS Republic passenger manifest identified 281 officers, 2,385 enlisted men, and 18 flying cadets. The senior Commander of Troops in the convoy was Brigadier General Julian F. Barnes. The Captain of the USS Republic was Commander Guy Clerk, USN. [5]

The *USS Republic* was carrying the personnel and equipment of a number of military units including:

Figure 11 – My baggage Tag for Pensacola Convoy

- 131st Field Artillery Battalion
- 26th Field Artillery Brigade Headquarters
- 453rd Ordnance Company
- 3rd Chemical Company
- Company "B" of 3rd Signal Regiment
- Company "A" of the 91st Quartermaster Battalion
- 35th Signal Platoon
- 7th Bomb Group (including 88th Reconnaissance Squadron and the 8th Matériel Squadron)

---

[5] Military History of the US Army Services of Supply in the Southwest Pacific, Office of the Chief of Military History, 1941-1946, Unpublished Manuscripts, File 8-5.8, Vol. 1 p. 77. A separate source reported 3,160 which must have included the ship crew.

The *USAT Holbrook* carried the 26th Field Artillery Brigade including the 147th and 148th Field Artillery Regiments.

Photo # NH 105094   USAT Republic underway

Figure 12 - U.S.A.T. Republic - Official Navy Archives

**Figure 13 - USS Republic sailing under Golden Gate Bridge
21 Nov 1941 – Cile's Photo**

2.   THE PACIFIC JOURNEY – 21 NOV 1941

2.1.   The Philippine Islands and Gen. Douglas MacArthur

*In 1934 the U.S. Congress passed **The Philippine Independence Act**[6] which established the intent of the federal government to make the Philippine Islands an independent nation in 10 years. This Act authorized a Philippine Constitutional Convention and the first elections to be held in 1935. That first election adopted a Constitution that created the Commonwealth of the Philippine Islands. Under the new Constitution, the Filipinos freely elected a National Assembly and a President.*

In parallel, as a Territory of the United States, the U.S. President appointed a civilian High Commissioner for the Philippines, who reported to the Secretary of the Interior.[7] The civilian High Commissioner was responsible for the administration and budget of the Commonwealth, but the U.S. Army was responsible for its military defense.

The Philippine Department was an element of the U.S. Army Forces Far East (USAFFE) headquartered in Manila. The Philippine Department served as a training and leadership command for the Philippine Army. The defense strategy for the Commonwealth was predicated upon a military force using American officers and conscripted Filipino troops.

Gen. Douglas A. MacArthur retired from active duty with the U.S. Army in 1937 after a distinguished 34-year military career. A 1903 graduate of West Point, he had been nominated twice for the Congressional Medal of Honor, first in 1914 for Valor in Veracruz, Mexico, and second in 1918 for his action during World War I taking Cote-de-Chatillion as Commander of the 42nd Rainbow Division. Afterward, he was recommended for promotion to Major General by General Pershing. In 1924 MacArthur was assigned to the Philippine Islands where his father had played an important role in the Spanish American War. By 1930 Douglas MacArthur had been promoted to Chief of Staff of the U.S. Army in Washington, the highest ranking officer in the U.S. military. While Chief of Staff, he was called upon by President Herbert Hoover to quell domestic riots in 1932 by World War I veterans. His role in maintaining public order gained him modest political visibility within the Republican Party.

After retirement, MacArthur accepted an appointment as Military Advisor to the Commonwealth of the Philippines. He was given the rank of Field Marshal of the Philippine Army with duties to advise the Commonwealth on defense preparations and security of the islands. In 1935,

---

[6] The Tydings-McDuffie Act (officially the Philippine Independence Act; Public Law 73-127) approved on March 24, 1934.

[7] Harold L. Ickes served as Secretary of the Interior from 1933-1946.

MacArthur was en route to Manila on board the S.S. President Hoover on the long trans-Pacific voyage when he met Jean Marie Faircloth, a wealthy 37-year-old woman (18 years his junior) who was traveling the world. Jean became his friend, companion, and two years later, his second wife. She was the mother of his only child, Arthur MacArthur IV[8], and was always at his side.[9].

In 1938, Gen. MacArthur realigned his staff in Manila by replacing his previous Chief of Staff, Col. Dwight D. Eisenhower, with Lt. Col. Richard K. Sutherland. Col. Sutherland was reassigned from an infantry position in China and would remain MacArthur's Chief of Staff for the duration of the War. [10] Sutherland was the son of a U.S. Senator, a graduate of Philips Andover Academy and Yale University. Sutherland was 13 years younger than MacArthur and known for a brilliant mind with extreme powers of concentration. Fluent in French, he had graduated from the Ecole Supérieure de Guerre and had served as U.S. Military Attaché to France.

Japan had invaded China in 1937. By 1941, Japan controlled Shanghai, Nanking, and the major cities of the eastern seaboard of China. In January 1941, an alarmed U.S. military decided to recall 61-year-old Gen. MacArthur to Active Duty to become Commander of USAFFE[11] in Manila.

In February 1941, MacArthur submitted his first formal request for reinforcements for the Philippine Department to Gen. George Marshall, Chief of Staff in Washington. MacArthur requested more American troops, specifically artillery and air corps. His requests were approved with qualifications in July 1941.[12] The difference of opinion between MacArthur and Washington continued into November 1941.

During the first half of 1941, unescorted transport ships were crossing the Pacific from San Francisco to Manila making the one-month-plus voyage on a routine basis at a frequency of one or two per month. These ships were rotating military personnel and dependents while carrying replacement matériel to the Philippine Department. Beginning in late August, the Navy started escorting many of these ships. In October and November, there were four escorted convoys. Additionally, some slower ships were dispatched unescorted. After Washington made the decision to reinforce the Philippines in November, the pace of escorted shipping increased. Plans for the Pen-

---

[8] Arthur MacArthur was born in 1938.

[9] Jean Marie Faircloth MacArthur died in 2000 at the age of 101. She is buried next to Gen. MacArthur in Norfolk, Virginia, the home of Douglas MacArthur's mother.

[10] Paul P. Rogers, *The Good Years: MacArthur and Sutherland*, Praeger Publishing (New York) 1990, p36.

[11] United States Army Forces Far East

[12] Paul P. Rogers, Ibid. p.43.

sacola Convoy (No. 4002) were already in place for November, but the number of convoys planned for December was increased to four and January was also be increased. [13]

2.2.   The Pensacola Convoy and PLUM

The Pensacola Convoy (Convoy No. 4002) was a collection of eight ships, including troop transports and freighters destined for Manila. The convoy was named after its escort, the USS Pensacola, a heavy cruiser of the US Navy line. The transports and freighters sailed individually from California to Hawaii where they were joined by the military ships to form a convoy. The route ordered by the Navy from Hawaii was south to Suva Bay, Fiji Islands, west to Port Moresby, New Guinea, through Torres Strait and the Molucca and Simutu Passage to Manila, P.I.[14] The plan was to depart Hawaii on 29 Nov 1941 and to arrive in Manila on 4 Jan 1942. The 36 day passage would move with an average of 9-10 knots. The Captain of the USS Pensacola was Commander Scott, USN.

The military used code words for confidential locations in their correspondence. Some names were only location, for example, COPPER (Oahu), BOBCAT (Bora Bora), and X (Australia). Others appear to tie to specific military organizations. PLUM and PEACH represented two different military organizations both in Manila. PLUM stood for the U.S. Army Far East, while PEACH stood for the newly conscripted Filipino military called the Army of the Philippines.

The literature since the war has perpetuated the controversy over the meaning of the word "PLUM." There was no "Operation PLUM" in the same sense that there was Operation Overlord at Normandy, Operation Cartwheel in Rabaul, or Operation King II in Leyte. There also appears to be no official military use of the acronym for PLUM: **Philippines-LU**zon-**M**anila.

2.3.   San Francisco Sailing – Friday, 21 Nov 1941

The *USS Republic* departed on schedule about noon. Our next stop would be Honolulu in seven days where we would join the Pensacola Convoy. We were less than three hours beyond the Golden Gate Bridge when I got seasick. It took three days before I felt normal. It seemed like the ship was rolling and bucking all the time. "There is no gambling or drinking aboard ship, which makes it very nice, much more pleasant than it would be if we had [*drunks*]. On Sunday, I made my first purchase from the ship com-

---

[13] Glen M. Williford, *Racing the Sunrise,* Reinforcing America's Pacific Outposts, 1941-1942, Naval Institute Press, Annapolis, Maryland, 2010

[14] USN Operation Order, dated 27 Nov 1941, From The Commandant, Fourteenth Naval District, To The Convoy Commander

missary – one large tube shaving cream (8-inch-long Colgate), one carton Camel cigarettes, one box of Fig Newton's, and one box Ritz cakes – all for $1.10.

When I was not sick, reading became my escape. I found myself consumed by William
Shirer's Berlin Diary. This book had just been published (*June 1941*)[15], and was on all the
charts. It is the diary of a Berlin correspondent from 1934 to 1940 describing the rise of
Hitler in Germany. I found this book a most interesting and timely read.

By Wednesday, I moved on to my second book, Burma Road, a 1940 publication by Nic-
ol Smith describing a 700-mile car trip from Yun-Nam-Fu in China to Lashio in Burma.
This book was at least about Asia, although much less serious.

On Thursday, we had 30-foot waves that washed the deck. It was hard just to stay in my
bunk.

2.4.   A Casual Officer

I was classified as a "Casual Officer" assigned to the Philippine Department, which
meant I would be assigned to a specific unit as a replacement upon arrival in Manila. As
a Casual Officer, I had a lot of extra military forms to complete. G-1 (Personnel) wanted
my life history, my schooling (both military and civilian), special training, and industrial
experience to help them decide where to assign me after arrival. Casuals were a group
unto themselves and were assigned a special table at the second feeding in the mess hall.
We were independent of the 2nd Battalion of the 131st Field Artillery Regiment, the 26th
Field Artillery Brigade Headquarters, or the pilots that were also being transported on
the ship.

2.5.   The Diary Begins

In the evenings, movies were shown on deck. Early in the week I could not watch more
than about five minutes due to the motion of the ship, but after about four days, the
rocking slowed, and I managed to sit through the entire show.

After the first day at sea, the order came down that all cameras would be collected. Our
mission was classified Secret, and the military did not want any uncontrolled information released. Everything was to be censored. We received a lecture on what we could

---

[15] This was Shirer's first book and established his reputation. In later years, he would publish
other books including *The Rise and Fall of the Third Reich*, 1960.

and could not write home. About all we could say was "I am alive." My Kodak film camera was confiscated.

Maintaining a diary was forbidden for fear a diary could fall into enemy hands. All diaries were subject to confiscation. That troubled me, because I did not feel my personal experiences would help the Japanese. I had already started my diary and was not inclined to surrender it. While in Fort Sam Houston, Texas, in 1941, I decided to keep a diary of my coming deployment. I

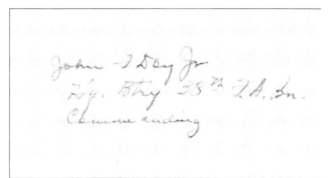

Figure 14 – Inscription inside the cover of Volume I of the Diary.

bought a small "Record" book, for which I paid 50 cents. On maneuvers in Louisiana in October 1941, I took the book along, inscribing my name and unit inside the cover.

Figure 15 – Diary Volume I – Record Begins 21 Nov 1941 to 11 Jan 1942

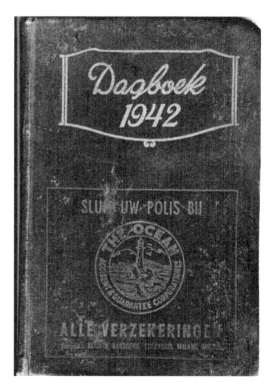

Figure 16 - Diary Volume II - Dagboek 1942

When my ship sailed from San Francisco on 21 Nov 1941, I began a daily routine of making entries in my diary. I concealed my diary in the bottom of my footlocker. Two months later, on 11 Jan 1942, when I was stationed in Malang, Java, Dutch East Indies, I was able to ship a wardrobe trunk, including this first Record Book with 89 completed pages and a footlocker back to Cile in Texas.[16] Immediately, I purchased a Dutch *Dagboek* from a Malang book store in which I continued my daily record until 3 Dec 1942

Onboard the ship when the rocking settled down, I passed time by walking from bow to stern. It was my only exercise. Onboard the ship I was given more booster shots. The typhoid booster made me sick, and the smallpox vaccination itched like crazy.

After five days I ate my first shipboard meal – two bowls of soup. Honolulu radio came into range, so we were able to pick up the Texas A&M football game. I addressed ten postcards to mail when we docked in Honolulu.

I found a pick-up game of bridge. On Wednesday, I managed to win a quarter. Then on Thursday night, we played until the ungodly hour of 12:20 AM, and I managed to lose twenty cents – a net gain of five cents for two days of bridge.

2.6.   Honolulu Arrival and Shore Leave – Friday, 28 Nov 1941

Friday, 28 Nov 1941
I was up at 7:40 AM to watch as we came around Oahu and passed Diamond Head. It was a beautiful harbor and a clear day for a change. This was one of the first times I was able to see most of the other ships that would be joining our convoy. In addition to the troop ships, there were four or five freighters loaded with army trucks and equipment. One of the other ships had crates of airplanes piled on its deck.

A group of airplanes flew out from Pearl Harbor to greet us. They seemed to be having fun flying low and "buzzing" the ships.

The *USS Republic* docked near downtown Honolulu very close to the Aloha Clock Tower. This tower is a ten-story structure that housed the Harbor Master. It was the site of the traditional Lei greetings for the arriving tour ships, but we were military, so we did not receive the tourist welcome. While the troop ships docked at the commercial piers, the military warships were in the Naval Base at Pearl Harbor.

---

[16] The wardrobe trunk and footlocker took more than six months to go from Java to Brooklyn, New York to Bonham, Texas, but both did arrive safely.

Everyone was eager to put their feet on firm soil. Finally, about noon the orders came down that we could go ashore for the afternoon. Officers were allowed to remain ashore until 11 PM. We were sailing the next morning. Honolulu was a short visit.

After lunch in the mess hall, my roommates (Capt. Steffey and Capt. Smith) and I walked to town rather than taking a cab. Our first stop was the Post Office, which turned out to be farther away than we expected. After mailing a stack of postcards, Smith left us to visit some relatives. Steffey and I went downtown, looking in curio shops to see what we could find. I was after something for Johnnie but could find nothing for a long time. Eventually I found a toy steam shovel.

Photo # USAF 38381 A.C.   USAT Republic at Honolulu, 22 November 1937

(O-618-917-C-II)(II-22-37-10:40A)(12-600)U.S.A.T. REPUBLIC AT PIER NO. 9, HONOLULU, T. H.

Figure 17 - USAT Republic (U.S. Army Transport)
Pier #9, Honolulu, Hawaii, HT
Photo taken at 10:40 AM on 22 Nov 1937. The Aloha Clock Tower is clearly visible near the ship, Honolulu Power plant is in the right center. A 327 foot Coast Guard Cutter (possibly USCG Tancy) is alongside the pier at the far left.
Official U.S. Air Force Photograph Photo #38381 A.C.

We came upon a barbershop that was staffed by about twenty Japanese women, so we decided to get haircuts. After my haircut, the woman gave me a neck, shoulder, and back massage right there in the chair. That was a novelty for a Texan, and it felt really good.

Down the street was the famous Waikiki Beach, which did not meet our expectations. We walked through a couple of the fancy hotels along the beach, including the Royal Hawaiian and the Halekulani. They are really beautiful but so expensive. I noticed they had one suite for $90 per day. One officer complained he couldn't get a $72 check cashed there. I laughingly told him it was undoubtedly too small a check for those hotels.

Steffey and I found a small restaurant on the beach where we had a lovely supper – fish and pineapple. We walked back to town and decided to go see a picture show. As I was waiting in line to buy a ticket, the theater owner called me over to the side. He introduced himself and asked if I was from Texas. I guess he had been listening to me talk, and we were in uniform. He said he had a friend in Texas and proceeded to let us into the show for free. Well, I was grateful for his generosity, and we stayed for the complete double feature. Afterward we walked back to the ship and had a good night's sleep because the boat was tied up to the dock and was not rocking.

2.7.   Sailing from Honolulu – Saturday, 29 Nov 1941

We sailed off into the blue Pacific at 7:30 AM on Saturday, 29 Nov 1941. As we left the commercial harbor, we saw the *USS Pensacola* for the first time. It had been docked inside Pearl Harbor and hidden from our view. Seven other ships joined us to form the *Pensacola Convoy* bound for Manila. We had been expecting a total of nine ships, including two cruisers and four destroyers. It was not to be.

The *USAT Holbrook*, a sister troop ship, had been having mechanical trouble with its rudder and was undergoing repair. We were hoping it would delay our convoy departure so we could have another day of shore leave in Honolulu. No such luck! We

Figure 18 – USS Pensacola, 1937
US Navy Photo #NH97838
Note the mid-ship Float Sea Plane catapult and hoist.

left the *Holbrook* in port. Because the convoy moved with the speed of its slowest ship (*SS Coast Farmer*), the convoy top speed was limited to 9 knots. The *Holbrook* was much faster than that, so even thought it had been left behind, the *Holbrook* was able to catch up with the convoy in only three days. That brought the convoy up to nine ships plus one cruiser and one patrol gunboat.

As we departed Hawaii waters, the Pensacola Convoy included the following ships.[17]

Warships
USS Pensacola, heavy cruiser [CA-24]
USS Niagara, patrol gunboat [AGP-1] [MTB Tender]

Four Troop Transports
USS Republic (U.S. Army Transport) [AP-33]
USAT Willard A Holbrook
USAT Meigs
USS Chaumont (US Navy Transport) [AP-5]

Five Army leased ships
VMS Bloemfontein (Dutch motor vessel)
SS Admiral Halstead (a merchant ship) carrying 18 P-40's, and 11 or more A-24 Bombers, ammunition, artillery cannons, etc.
SS Coast Farmer, a freighter
SS Paul M. Gregg, a tanker
Hallmark, a corvette

Troops on-board all ships included:
2,000 Artillery officers and men
2,600 Air Corps officers and men

The fastest ship in the convoy was the *VMS Bloemfontein*.

The Pensacola carried four Curtiss SOC-1 Seagulls (pontoon seaplanes). SOC stood for "Scout Observation Curtiss." These planes were launched from the cruiser deck by catapult, and were recovered by landing on the sea beside the ship where they could be hoisted back on the deck. The

[17] http://www.ww2pacific.com/notpearl.html -- U.S.N. Pacific Fleet ships not at Pearl Harbor on December 7, 1941, and http://www.ww2pacific.com/ww2.html World War 2 in the Pacific, Menu to the Early Years

planes were used for both reconnaissance and artillery fire control. Ship cannons fire well beyond the deck visibility, so airplanes fly out to observe the impact zone and adjust naval cannon fire.

As we went to sea, we listened to a Honolulu radio broadcast of the Army-Navy football game, followed by the California-Stanford football game. I finished <u>Burma Road</u> and wished I had another book.

After we left Honolulu, the ship had to be totally blacked out every night – no lights. There were no more picture shows on deck. We would have to wait until Manila to see another movie, perhaps a month away. Everyone was speculating on when we would arrive. We started a betting "pool" on the date of arrival. I made a bet of $1 we would be there on or before 25 Dec 1941. I gave 2 to 1 odds on a $1 bet that we would not arrive on any of the three days, 30-31 Dec or 1 Jan.

We played bridge most every night until about 10:30 PM. I won 95 cents one night, and then lost 91 cents the next night – terrible cards.

Photo # NH 97592   SOC "Seagull" is catapulted from a heavy cruiser, circa 1942-43

Figure 19 – SOC-1 Seagull Launch (Scout-Observation-Curtiss) launch from Heavy Cruiser - 1942

The days were clear and beautiful. I went up on the "A" deck without my hat and got a bad sun blister from the tropical sun. Sunscreen was unknown in those days. That evening I took a seawater bath, which I thought made me sick. In hindsight, it was probably too much sun.

That night there was a full moon which was positively beautiful reflecting off the water. It was hot, but the fans helped a lot. In the moonlight one could still make out the *Pensacola* and one or two other ships.

There were two principal ocean routes across the Pacific from Hawaii to the Philippine Islands – the "Great Circle Route" and the "Southern Route." These two routes are illustrated in Figure 20. The Great Circle Route was the shortest and most direct route, passing near Guam and through the Japanese Mandate of the Marianas into Manila. The "Southern Route" went south to Fiji through the Torres Strait, south of New Guinea, then north through the Molucca Channel into Manila. Water stops could be made in Fiji and in Port Moresby. The Southern Route is about 50 percent longer than the Great Circle Route, turning a typically 30-day passage for a freighter into a 45 day passage.

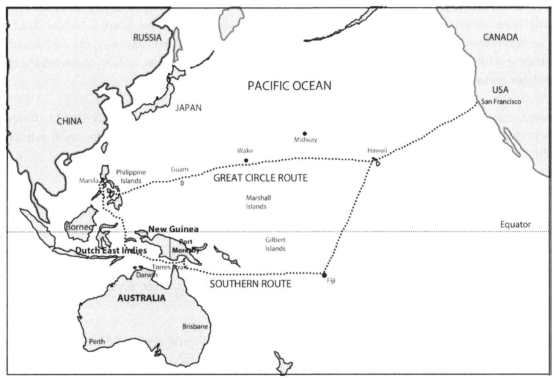

Figure 20 – Two Alternate Pacific Routes from Hawaii to Manila

Before the Pensacola Convoy, the earlier US freighters to the Philippines were using the Great Circle Route. However, in 1941, the Great Circle Route was deemed more vulnerable to a Japanese attack. On 25 Nov 1941 the Navy ordered all escorted convoys to use the Southern Route.

Our ship did not post a route map. Artillery men are mapmakers and surveyors – and there were more than 2,000 artillery men on our ship. We all had compasses and were following the ship's course carefully. The ship was charting a course between 198º and 215º, basically a south by southwest direction. We were finally told we were headed toward the Fiji Islands, and would cross the Equator in a day or two. We knew we were on the Southern Route to Manila, which meant we would have a very long passage. [18] We were hoping we might see Australia, Borneo, or New Guinea.

Every other morning, the *USS Pensacola* made a terrific dash out to either the right or left side of the convoy for some unknown reason. When it returned to its place in the convoy, we concluded that it was nothing we should be alarmed about. We were hoping it was for "pleasure."

News of the diplomatic crisis with Japan arrived on 29 Nov, and we felt it had caught us in an awkward place – in the middle of the Pacific in "good swimming water" if our ship was attacked. Some of the men were feeling homesick and scared all the time. *A Washington D.C. press conference by Secretary of State Cordell Hull following his 26 Nov 1941 meeting with the Japanese Delegation communicated the crisis impasse nature of the trade negotiations between the United States and Japan.*[19]

News came over the radio about the sinking of an Australian cruiser with 645 men on board. There were also reports of a German raider thought to have sunk an Australian ship in Pacific waters not far from our location.

On Wednesday, December 3, General Barnes decided we should have a training exercise on our artillery pieces. On deck we set up four 3-inch guns, one 5-inch gun, and several 30 and 50 caliber machine guns. All the Artillery Officers were assigned to man the guns and stand watch – including me.

December 4 became practice day. The Commander defined three levels of "Alert": "A", "B", and "C" with "A" the highest level.

- In "C" level, the Army manned two of the 3-inch guns and the Navy manned two of the 3-inch guns and the 5-inch guns.
- In "B" level, the Army manned all four of the 3-inch guns and Navy took the 5-inch.
- In "A" level, the guns are manned as in "C" level, however a shell is loaded in the chamber of each gun at all times.

---

[18] The U.S. Army had always intended the convoy to go by way of Port Moresby, New Guinea – per OCMH History of USASOS.

[19] Source: U.S., Department of State, Publication 1983, Peace and War: United States Foreign Policy, 1931-1941 (Washington, D.C.: U.S., Government Printing Office, 1943), pp. 806-09.

We went through all stages in drill in the morning. Then in the afternoon I went out and watched others go through the same drills. We had classroom training that evening with the 2nd Battalion of the 131st Field Artillery, which was on our ship.

The *Pensacola* launched all four of its Seagulls. They flew around for about an hour and then returned. It looked good to see them in the air so far at sea.

It was extremely hot on deck, such that I was taking two baths a day. We had to clean up and be in proper uniform for every dinner.

A Japanese ship was reported in our vicinity. It had lost its supply ship near Australia and was being refueled in the Japanese Mandate Islands. We were going out of our way to avoid those islands.

The ship's Lt. Commander called a general meeting with all the troops regarding blackout rules and watch discipline. Stringent black out rules were imposed with the electricity on the entire ship turned off at 10 PM. With the ship completely closed and the power off, the fans stopped and the ship was terribly hot all night. Watch discipline was also increased. Everyone was instructed to keep better vigilance on lookout. The Naval Officer indicated we were coming into a more dangerous part of the Pacific, but it would be the most dangerous when we reached the Torres Strait between Australia and New Guinea. It was not hard to conclude we were nearing some of the "action."

I played 11 rubbers of bridge during the day and won them all – for a profit of $2.92.

2.8.   Crossing the Equator – 5 Dec 1941

The ship officially crossed the Equator between 10 AM and Noon, but the festivities for *Pollywog Day* began much earlier in the morning. This was initiation day when all *Pollywogs* were initiated into the *Domain of Neptunus Rex*, the "Solemn Mysteries of the Ancient Order of the Deep" and the "Silent Mysteries of the Far East." This was foolery reserved for those who crossed the Equator at sea.

Breakfast, which was normally at 8:15 AM, was moved up to 5:45 AM so there could be an early start on the initiation ceremony. With over 3,000 men crossing the Equator for the first time, the initiation began early and continued until about 3 PM. By then everyone was exhausted.

A pirate's Jolly Roger flag was hoisted up the flagpole, and we were informed that the ship was ruled by King Neptune for the day. Everyone was separated into *Shell Backs* and *Pollywogs*. A *Shell Back* was one who had crossed the Equator before. A *Pollywog* was one who was crossing the Equator for the first time. The previous day the crew had constructed various "instruments of torture." There were several large dunking pools, a tunnel with a fire hose inside, an elaborate "King's Throne" made from a toilet, an "electric chair" with cattle prongs connected to a battery, and even a hangman's scaffold. Early on, a captain and a lieutenant were charged as "mutineers" and had their heads and hands locked in stocks – but that was mild compared to what followed.

After breakfast all *Pollywogs* were summoned to appear before King Neptune to answer a list of charges. Each *Pollywog* went before King Neptune and was sentenced. I don't remember what my sentence was, but it did not matter as everyone was condemned to some kind of punishment. There was variation among the over 3,000 men who went through the initiation, but I was branded with paint – forehead and chest. Then I was literally beaten with long cotton bags about 3-inches in diameter and soaked in slop, paint and mush (which made them terribly hard). My butt was almost paralyzed. Each *Pollywog* was stuffed into the electric chair for a shock from the electrified cattle prod.

There was a "barber" who had hair clippers to cut random pieces of *Pollywog* hair. One *Shell Back* painted mustard all over my face, adding a squirt of castor oil in my mouth before I was dumped backwards from the chair into the pool. In the pool I was forcibly dunked three or four times before I could get my breath. When I climbed out of the pool, I had to pass through a round cloth tunnel that was just big enough to crawl through, while behind me a big water hose squirted in my rear. I was almost drowned before I could crawl through the tunnel. As I came out of the tunnel, there were three or four more *Shell Backs* with clubs to give me hell.

Somehow, someone got General Barnes to sit on the "High Throne" that had been made from a toilet. After he was seated, they turned on a fire hose from

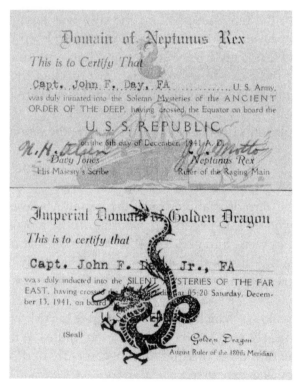

Figure 21 - Domain of Neptunus Rex - Certificate, 13 Dec 1941

under the seat that knocked him off the toilet seat. He was not pleased with the prank, to say the least, but no one got "busted."

I was glad to return to my room, get a bath, and be finished about noon. One of my roommates (Capt. Smith) was a *Shell Back,* which is the reason I was marked for "special treatment." My other roommate, Capt. Steffey, came back to the room with bruises. He had slipped and fallen. It was a wonder someone was not seriously hurt. Next time I will be a *Shell Back*.

Everyone received a special certificate for completing the initiation, which I will long treasure. There were plenty of stories for years to come. I hoped Cile would never have to go through such an initiation.

Played bridge last night and won 8 of 10 rubbers ($1.00).

On Saturday, December 6, we were informed that there was a water shortage on the ship. We had consumed 75 percent of our fresh water supply in only 50 percent of the time before we were scheduled to refill our fresh water tanks. Our next refill was to be in the Fiji Islands. With a water shortage, there was an immediate ban on shaving, and a "Beard Growing Contest" was announced. It was also the end of two showers a day. Fiji was a British Protectorate, so we started dreaming of another shore leave.

Out in the middle of the Pacific, the water was unbelievably smooth. One would never see a lake at home as smooth as that ocean. The only waves were the ones the ship made. Now I know why Magellan named it "pacific" – which means "peaceful."

I played bridge again last night until after 11 PM. I did not realize it was so late, but I had been very lucky. The cards seemed to be falling my way. In the last three days I won $5.38 at 1/40th.

3.   PEARL HARBOR ATTACK – 7 DEC 1941

3.1.   The Seeds of the Pearl Harbor Attack

The seeds of the Japanese attack on Pearl Harbor were planted in 1853 when Commodore Matthew Perry sailed into Edo (Tokyo) Harbor with four steam-powered warships and demanded trade after 250 years of Japanese isolation. The event made Japan realize that they would not be treated as an equal on the world stage without the complete modernization of their military, their industry, their economy, and their society. This reality led to the fall of the Tokugawa Shogunate and the Meiji restoration in 1868.

Japan had observed China's powerful Qin Dynasty buckle under British military power in the Opium Wars of 1843 and of 1860. Fearing that Japan would be next to fall under foreign domination, Japan chose a course of rapid militarism. The Meiji government slogan was **Enrich the country, Strengthen the military.**[20]

To build the military, Japan needed modern industry with a steady supply of oil and steel. Japan is a country with few natural resources[21] and had to trade for a supply of oil and scrap metal, the raw material for its steel industry.

The Meiji government made amazing progress in its first thirty years by importing technology and resources to improve its war machine. By 1894, they were able to win a war with China that gained them control of Formosa (Taiwan). In 1904, Japan won a war with Russia that lead to the annexation of Korea in 1910 and eventually the establishment of a Manchuria puppet regime in 1932.

In 1937, Japan invaded China, ostensibly to secure its borders with Korea and Manchuria. The border had been challenged by China. Japan wanted to establish a new "political order" in Asia to reduce the influence of Great Britain and France and elevate Japanese influence relative to China. The U.S. was concerned about U.S. interests in China, as well as the interests of Britain and France, and discussed economic sanctions against Japan to force Japan to withdraw from China. The U.S. Ambassador to Japan, Joseph Grew, warned the State Department that economic sanctions would drive Japan farther into Southeast Asia and could lead to war. His warnings were not heeded.

---

[20] *The Way to Pearl Harbor: US vs. Japan,* by Yuichi Arima, Inventory of Conflict and Environment (ICE), Trade & Environment Case Studies (TED), ICE Case Study Number 118, December, 2003. http://www1.american.edu/TED/ice/ice.htm

[21] *The Way to Pearl Harbor: US vs. Japan,* by Yuichi Arima.

In 1940 Japan imported 100 percent of its oil[22] and 88 percent of its scrap metal[23] from foreign sources. The United States was a major trading partner with Japan supplying 80 percent of Japan's oil supply and 75 percent of its scrap metal supply.[24] The U.S. produced 22 percent of the world's oil supply in 1940.

A Treaty of Commerce and Navigation, which had been signed in 1911 by the two countries, governed trade between the U.S. and Japan. In 1939 the U.S. unilaterally renounced the 1911 Trade Treaty with Japan. A few months later in July 1940 Roosevelt imposed a partial embargo of oil and scrap metal shipments to Japan. The U.S. embargo led to a dwindling strategic supply of oil in Japan, and caused Japan to feel an increased urgency to act.

Japan countered by invading French Indo-China. Then in September 1940, Japan signed a Tripartite Treaty with Germany and Italy under which any attack by the US upon any of the three countries would be considered an attack on all. As an element of that treaty, Germany and Italy agreed to support the Japanese Empire in Asia.

In July 1941, Roosevelt took the extraordinary step of seizing Japanese money and property in the U.S. and placing a total embargo on exports of oil, steel, and iron to Japan. This embargo was effectively a crippling economic blow to the Japanese wartime economy. The U.S. was pressing three critical issues with Japan: (1) Japan should recognize the Chiang Kai-shek regime and withdraw from China, (2) the Japanese occupation of Indo-China should end, and (3) Japan should withdraw from the Tripartite Treaty with Germany and Italy (The Stimson Doctrine).

The Japanese leaders decided in September 1941 that if they could not obtain oil through negotiations, they had to go to war. There were two war alternatives to get oil and metals. The Japanese Army wanted to attack Russia. The Japanese Navy wanted to attack the Dutch East Indies, Malaysia, and the Philippines. The Navy war plan was favored. The Navy plan required that the U.S. fleet at Pearl Harbor be first neutralized before Japan invaded Southeast Asia.

In 16 Oct 1941, General Hideki Tojo became Prime Minister of Japan and authorized the implementation of the Navy war plan. The Japanese planned virtually <u>simultaneous</u> attacks on Pearl Harbor, the Philippines, and the Malaya Peninsula above British Singapore on 8 Dec 1941. The Philippines and Singapore were stepping stones toward the conquest of the Dutch East Indies including the oil fields of Borneo, Java and Sumatra. The Pearl Harbor attack was intended to

---

[22] Converted into chart form from B.R. Mitchell's <u>International Historical Statistics 1750-1993</u>.

[23] Converted into chart form from New York Times, 4 August, 1940 III-1.

[24] In 1940 an additional 18% of Japan's oil was imported from the Dutch East Indies. The United States was the world's largest exporter of oil, accounting for about 22% of the world supply.

prevent the Americans from intervening in the Philippines, the Singapore/Malaya offensive, or the Dutch East Indies.

As Japan prepared for war, two senior and respected Japanese diplomats, Kichasaburo Nomura (Japanese Ambassador to the U.S.) and Saburo Kurusu (former Japanese Ambassador to Germany, signatory to the Tripartite Treaty, and Special Economic Diplomat to the U.S.) were sent to Washington in a "last-ditch effort" to negotiate an economic agreement with the U.S. over the trade embargo and confiscation of Japanese assets. The Japanese delegation arrived in Washington in September 1941 but reported to Tokyo that they had made no progress. The diplomats were secretly given until 29 Nov to reach an agreement or Japan would declare war.

The U.S. had broken the Japanese diplomatic code and knew that Japan was planning a major military strike; however, the U.S. did not know when or where. U.S. intelligence was predicting the strike would be at the Philippines in April 1942.

On 26 Nov 1941, a Japanese military Task Force departed from the Kurile Islands in northern Japan for Pearl Harbor. The Task Force included an armada of 21 ships, including six aircraft carriers, two battleships, and two heavy cruisers, as well as destroyers, submarines, tankers and support ships. There were over 420 airplanes aboard the ships. The instructions to the Admiral were to return to Japan if diplomacy was successful or if the task force was discovered.

On 6 Dec 1941, Japan sent a 5,000-word message to its Washington diplomats instructing them to break off negotiations with the U.S. The last of the long message[25] did not arrive until early in the morning of Sunday, 7 Dec 1941, Washington time. It was said that the Japanese Embassy staff was not working on Sunday, so Nomura and Kurusu had to decode the message themselves. This message has been described as a Declaration of War; however, others say it neither declared war nor broke diplomatic relations. Decoding the message delayed the delivery of the message to the U.S. Secretary of State, Cordell Hull, until 1 PM Washington time[26] (8 AM Hawaii time). The Japanese attack on Pearl Harbor had begun at 7:55 AM Hawaii time.

The Tokyo evening newspapers of December 8 (December 7 in Pearl Harbor) published a complete Declaration of War on the United States on their front pages.

---

[25] The 5,000 word message was in 14 parts.

[26] *The Way to Pearl Harbor: US vs. Japan,* by Yuichi Arima, Ibid.

3.2.   Pearl Harbor Attack – Sunday, 7 Dec 1941

<u>Sunday, 7 Dec 1941</u>

Breakfast in the Mess was routine at 8:15 AM, but then about 10 AM, the ship address system came on with a Call to General Quarters. We scurried to our assigned positions and learned that an unofficial radio report had been received saying that the Japanese had raided Pearl Harbor. There was a general feeling of disbelief. The report could not be so! We dismissed the report as unconfirmed, unreliable, and nothing to be concerned about.

Then just ten minutes later, all officers were summoned to a special meeting in the Orderly Room. We were informed that the U.S. was in a ***State of War*** with Japan, and the earlier report was correct. Japan really had attacked Pearl Harbor. Our ship was being placed on a higher level of Alert. Everyone had to carry their life belts at all times, regardless of where they were on the ship. Watch discipline was increased again and required everyone to stand a four-hour watch, followed by eight hours off. Everyone would have two watches every 24 hours. I would start my first four-hour watch immediately.

My first reaction was a kind of amazement or disbelief that this was happening. Pearl Harbor was a well-fortified base. How did the Japanese think they could get away with this? As the day progressed, more radio messages began to filter in – some true, some false – but we listened to them all. We were told the battleship *West Virginia* was sunk and the battleship *Oklahoma* was set on fire. We were also told that air attacks had gone on all day in Honolulu. Over 100 soldiers had been killed and 400 to 500 injured.[27] Another report was that the U.S. had sunk four Japanese submarines, six airplanes and a Japanese aircraft carrier [*false*]. It was clear the Japanese had caught us at a bad time – Sunday when the sailors were in port.

There was a short-wave radio on board that picked up Berlin English language news. Berlin radio reported that the *USS Republic* had been sunk. We were very relieved to know that all news reports were not true. It was curious to us that our ship was on the Berlin news.

---

[27] Full Pearl Harbor Casualty List, according to the U.S. Navy, reported actual losses of 2,402 men killed, 1,282 wounded and 188 U.S. aircraft destroyed.

Another report said that two U.S. troop ships about a thousand miles from San Francisco were sunk by torpedo [*false*]. The Army post in Manila had been bombed [*true*], and a U.S. destroyer was sunk in Manila Bay [*true*]. There were attacks on a couple of other Allied military bases in the Far East [*true*].

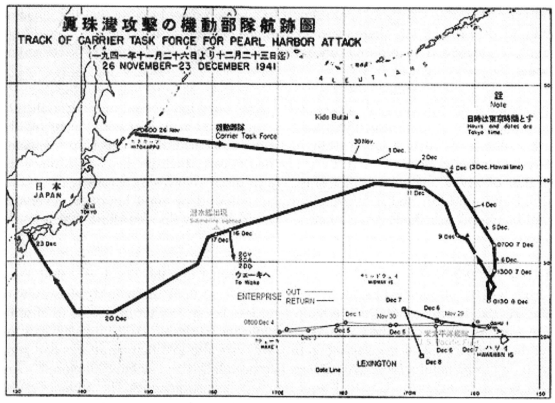

Figure 22 - Route followed by Japanese Carrier Task Force
Pearl Harbor attack –1941

The US Navy historical record[28] of Commander in Chief Asiatic Fleet Adm. Thomas C. Hart show the position of the Pensacola Convoy on 7 Dec 1941 was passing through the Phoenix Islands[29] in the mid-Pacific about half way between Hawaii and the Fiji Islands. This location was consistent with the information in the diary inasmuch as it was slightly south of the Equator and

---

[28] http://www.ww2pacific.com/notpearl.html The US Fleet not at Pearl Harbor on December 7, 1941.

[29] The Phoenix Islands are eight small atolls in the Republic of Kiribati east of the Gilbert Islands. On January 28, 2008, the government of Kiribati formally declared the entire Phoenix group and surrounding waters a protected area, making its 410,500 square kilometers the world's largest marine protected area.

appeared to support the position that the convoy was already moving on a direct line to Fiji Islands. Coincidently, Howland Island is considered a "northern outlier island" of the Phoenix Islands and is the island that Amelia Earhart was trying to locate when she disappeared during her around-the-world flight in 1938.

Messages were passed from our ship to Pearl Harbor and on to Washington. The generals and admirals must have been living on the wireless. Our convoy was awaiting instructions. Our ship was at the bottom of the Chain of Command and would be the last to learn if plans were changed in Washington.

Our ship had been scheduled to separate from the convoy at 10 PM that night and go alone directly to the Fiji Islands to refill our water tanks. The Pensacola Commander, who was in total charge of the convoy, did not want an unescorted troop ship to separate from the main convoy. The decision was made that the entire convoy would go to the Fiji Islands.

The *Pensacola* apparently had extra cargo, including a $30,000 yacht that had been leased to the Navy by the Vanderbilt family for $1 per year. It was resting on the fantail of the cruiser. The Captain was trying to lighten the ship to make it faster, so he decided to jettison the yacht. [30] The cruiser then machine gunned and sank the yacht. The crew also jettisoned anything of weight. We saw extra glassware being thrown overboard. The cruiser began zigzagging back and forth through the middle of the convoy. They launched their four airplanes when we learned of Pearl Harbor. One of the planes did not return, resulting in the loss of three crewmen. We never heard what happened to the plane.

Since we had no official information, rumors were flying around the ship. One rumor was that at Fiji our ship would join another heavy convoy, probably British. Another rumor was that we would not go all the way to the Philippine Islands, but might stop in Australia. We knew Washington was seriously considering several options – continue to the Philippines, stop in Australia to defend Australia, return to Hawaii to defend Pearl Harbor, or return to the States to protect California. My feeling was that we would continue to the Philippines, but I did not know.

---

[30] This story of a yacht being jettisoned from the fantail and sunk is not confirmed by the Deck Log of the Pensacola. The *USS Niagara* was indeed a private yacht purchased by the Navy and converted to become a PT boat tender in the Philippines, however, it was not a WWI $1 per year ease. The *Niagara* did retain the appearance of a yacht to the eyes of an Army soldier.

By evening, the reality of war was beginning to settle in. After hearing the news of the day, I knew my darling wife would be worried to death. My mother would be beside herself. If my folks heard our ship had been sunk, it would be bad. I did not know when Cile or anyone stateside would ever get a letter from me as censorship would be imposed and mail service limited. We had no idea what was going to happen next.

That night I went to bed in my underwear with my pants and life preserver near at hand in case we had to abandon ship.

Monday, 8 Dec 1941

Everyone was awakened at 4 AM for General Quarters and Abandon Ship Drill. We were informed that we would have the same drills every morning from now on. If this crate had sunk, we would have been very lucky to get half the life boats in the water due to the lack of organization and practice. I was assigned to one of the last boats to go off unless I was at a gun station. If you are at a gun station, you leave when the gun was under water and could not fire.

My watch duty continued at 2 PM and 2 AM. I was placed in charge of a brand-new 3-inch gun. A nice piece of artillery!

I was hoping we would join a larger British convoy in Fiji. Our convoy was the first U.S. Registry military convoy ever to cross the Pacific.

The gaiety after initiation of King Neptune died down quickly with all the war news.

Tuesday, 9 Dec 1941

The Convoy continued rocking along at 8 to 9 miles per hour. We were told we were due to arrive in Fiji Islands on Friday, three more days. The Berlin radio news broadcast changed and reported that *USS Republic* had not sunk. We were all glad that we had not sunk, but for our safety, we wished the news had been delayed until we reached land.

We began to speculate on where we might possibly go after Fiji – Philippines? Sydney, Australia? There was much anxiety just waiting to arrive anywhere.

We learned that the Ellice Islands,[31] which were about 300 miles north of us, had been bombed the previous night, so our course was changed to 5 degrees east of south.[32] We

---

[31] Ellice Islands are a mid-Pacific chain of atolls that were formerly associated with the Gilbert Islands. In 1975, Ellice Islands became the separate British colony of Tuvalu.

returned to our course some hours later. Before noon we had changed to 30 degrees east of south.

In the late afternoon a strange airplane appeared and flew above us. The cruiser made a dash and sent up an airplane to investigate. The plane turned out to be a British Scout, which relieved us a little. We must have been in airplane range of either the Fiji Islands or a British ship.

I was placed in charge of Life Boat 8a. I had two lieutenants and about 60 men in my life boat. I wished I had a pistol and canteen for water. We had been in a very dangerous position and felt it is a matter of hours until our worst worry was over. As soon as we made port, the uncertainty of our location would end. We knew we were a real target for the Japanese since we were carrying thousands of men and a $25 million cargo of airplanes and artillery. The Japanese must have been mad that they had not been able to locate us.

The *Chaumont* was having trouble and had to be towed by the *Holbrook*.

The ship address system was busy most of the day. There were many announcements and quite a few meetings. We learned that during the Great War[33], the *Republic* had carried 8,900 men to France with four men assigned to sleep in each bunk. That meant that each soldier had six hours in his bed. We felt we were not as crowded with only 3,160, even though we were carrying double the ship's regular civilian capacity.

I knew the folks at home were alarmed. God only knew when they would hear from me – it may be six months. I was hoping my wife, mother and Dad would not worry because things would probably get a lot worse before the war was over.

I got a haircut today to fix some of the damage done during the Neptune initiation. We had a few civilian personnel aboard the ship, and one of them stood watch with the rest of us. We asked him why he was standing watch, and he said, "If I saw a torpedo coming, I could open a window and let it pass through just like you."

With two more days before we arrived at Suva (Fiji Islands), everyone continued guessing where we would be going next. Rumors grew that we would go to Australia, India,

---

[32]The Japanese task force was reported to consist of one cruiser, two destroyers, and one or two submarines.

[33] World War I

or Burma. Perhaps we were to prepare an Australian camp for other American troops who would follow us.

Our Convoy Commander could take us to any friendly port he wished. His orders had been to deliver us to *PLUM*, but Washington could have changed that order anytime. The Commander was in regular communication with Pearl Harbor, and they in turn were communicating with Washington. We waited anxiously for orders to come down from the High Command.

3.3.　　Washington Decision – 9-10 Dec 1941

On 9 Dec 1941, in Washington, D.C. the U.S. military Joint Board, the planners of the military services, included the Pensacola Convoy on their agenda. In their meeting Brig. Gen. Leonard T. Gerow and Rear Adm. Richmond K. Turner agreed that the convoy should be recalled immediately. Turner wanted the Convoy to reinforce Pearl Harbor. Gerow agreed and added that if the convoy were not sent to Hawaii, it should be recalled to the continental United States. There was fear for the defense of California.

The next day, 10 Dec 1941, at the White House, President Roosevelt suggested that the convoy materiel should be delivered to the Southwest Pacific, and he sent the matter back to the Joint Board. The Joint Board decided that same day to send the convoy to Brisbane, Australia, but the troops were not informed for security reasons.[34]

3.4.　　Back on the USS Republic

Wednesday, 10 Dec 1941
The International Date Line was crossed, so at midnight Tuesday everyone on the convoy skipped Wednesday, December 10th. It was suddenly Thursday, December 11th.

Thursday, 11 Dec 1941
The convoy had begun changing directions more frequently. With so many direction changes, it was hard to tell whether we were heading for Samoa or Fiji Islands. The best guess was still that we would reach land late tomorrow and it would be the Fiji Islands.

I went down into the cargo hold of the ship and located my footlocker. I retrieved my beautiful summer hat (that my wife loved so dearly) to wear if we had to abandon ship.

---

[34] Reference: Louis Morton, III Reinforcement of the Philippines, The Fall of the Philippines (U.S. Army in World War II: The War in the Pacific) United States Army Center of Military History. CMH Pub 5-2, 1953, p.146.

During the past week, I had blistered very badly, so I thought I had better get my hat. During the initiation ceremony we were wearing only our trunks and no shirts. I got terribly sunburned. My skin blistered, and I was peeling large sheets of dead skin.

We were doing a lot of kidding about what would happen to us when the ship was sunk, and we were all dumped into the sea. "They say the sharks run from you at first." It was a kind of nervous humor. There were a few of us who threw in lots of "bull" to try to relieve some of the stress. Worrying would not help the situation, but we still carried our life belts with us at all times. If you had a canteen, you kept it full of water.

The Commander said the Japs were very "chagrined" because they had been unable to find us. Of course we felt he had a questionable telephone line to the Japanese Imperial Command. They would surely know where we were when we arrived in any port. We have been staying out of sight of land so far. The Cruiser kept one airplane and sometimes more in the air practically all the time.

A boxing platform was constructed on the main deck, and a championship boxing tournament was held to entertain everyone – something to take our minds off our precarious situation.

The radio seemed to bring only more bad news. We learned last night that the British had lost two heavy cruisers, the *HMS Prince of Wales* and the *HMS Repulse*, off the Malay Peninsula near Singapore. Allied losses were mounting every day.

At least two men had died on the ship during transit, but I did not learn the circumstances of their deaths. Both bodies were put on ice, as the authorities decided not to bury them at sea. Their deaths were kept quiet, so not everyone knew about the bodies. I am not aware of what happened to the bodies after we reached port.

That evening a rumor was reported that Japs had taken over Fiji Islands, and we were headed for Samoa. We were expected to make a landing at Samoa even though the Japs were there. You never knew what to believe, as there were so many rumors. I could not see how the Japs could have taken over the Fiji Islands, which were so far from their bases. We would find out when we landed.

Friday, 12 Dec 1941
At 4 AM every morning, we were out again to practice General Quarters and Abandon Ship Drills. We were told that daybreak was the most likely time for a submarine attack. The subs would put the sun behind their back as they targeted a ship so the sub could

best see the target ship, while the target ship would have the most difficulty seeing the sub because it would be looking into the sun

The Convoy Commander was continuing to change course at irregular intervals, especially at night. This movement was to prevent any enemy submarine from being able to take aim at us with a torpedo. The Commander was trying to avoid any contact that would reveal our location. After we left Honolulu, we traveled almost two weeks with only three "near" encounters with other vessels. Our first near encounter was with a Japanese aircraft carrier, which was spotted one dawn by our reconnaissance plane about 50 miles away. The carrier fortunately had no planes out at the time. A second near encounter was when we passed two Japanese destroyers, who probably thought we were a naval unit and avoided us. The third near encounter was with a set of submarines and destroyers that we passed in the dark about 15 miles away. In the last 24 hours before we arrived in Figi, we made only 36 miles (compared to over 200 miles per day normally), as we were dodging two Japanese cruisers all day. Some fun! [*Remember, in 1941 there was limited radar and visual sightings were normally the only sightings.*]

The reconnaissance planes off the *Pensacola* were greatly appreciated, as we knew they were our early warning system looking for the enemy. Later, after we arrived in port, we learned from a sailor that another plane had a bad landing at sea that broke the backs of two pilots, who later died.[35]

As a troop ship, we were fairly well armed. There were about twelve 50-caliber machine guns on the "A" Deck, a company of rifleman, four 3-inch guns, and one 5-inch gun. Scattered around the rest of the ship were a few 30-caliber machine guns as well as lots of pistols. Of course we could not even bluff a real fighting ship or an enemy airplane.

"Five of the eight ships in the convoy had no guns and one with two 3-inch guns had no ammunition, leaving only two ships capable of defense. After receipt of information of the outbreak of hostilities, machine guns were mounted on decks and rifles were issued."[36]

On 12 Dec 1941 over the public address system, we received the official announcement that Brig. Gen. Julian F. Barnes, the ranking officer on our convoy, had been designated

---

[35] During this period one of the reconnaissance planes from the Pensacola never returned from a mission, but the Pensacola log has no information about what happened to the crew – the plane simply disappeared.

[36] Military History of the US Army Services of Supply in the Southwest Pacific, Office of the Chief of Military History, 1941-1946, Unpublished Manuscripts, File 8-5.8, Vol. 1 p. 77.

Commander of *Task Force South Pacific*.[37] We were the first U.S. convoy in the Pacific and the first contingent of troops to go through initiation for *Shell Backs*. I wondered if Washington knew about the initiation. I had a feeling that this initiation had been going on for hundreds of years.

About 8 PM that evening, I was up on the top deck and could see a Beacon Light about 15° off the left side of the bow. We were entering a port. It was Fiji, but there still had been no official announcement. We were expecting a brief stop to take on water and would leave before daylight.

We could only speculate on where we would go next. This was all new geography to a Texan. Were we going south to Sydney, Australia?

3.5.   Fiji Islands – Friday-Sunday, 13-15 Dec 1941

With all the excitement of arriving on land, I was up on deck about 4 AM Friday morning to watch our ship enter Suva Bay. Perhaps 30 miles outside the harbor through the early morning light, we began to pass a series of smaller islands. The islands were surrounded by coral reefs that appeared to be only three to four feet below the surface because of the clear water. They must have been much deeper since our ship drew about 33 feet when loaded. The coral extended from half to a full mile out from the beach. We were told that if you were swimming and hit the coral, it would cut you badly. There were several small sharks swimming around the coral, one about 5 feet long, that was chasing a school of substantial-sized fish.

As we approached a larger island, I noticed that our ship was flying a nice new American flag. A British plane appeared overhead to greet us.

---

[37] The following is from the Center for Military History On-Line: On 12 December 1941 American troops aboard the Pensacola convoy were constituted a task force, *Task Force South Pacific*, and placed under the command of General J.F. Barnes, senior officer in the convoy. The convoy was ordered to proceed to Brisbane, Australia, and General Barnes was instructed to assume command of all American troops in Australia and place his forces under CG, U.S. Army Forces Far East (USAFFE) [Gen. Douglas MacArthur]. He was given the primary objective of aiding in the defense of the Philippines. When the convoy docked at Brisbane, Australia, on 22 December 1941, the *Task Force South Pacific* became at that point the U.S. Forces in Australia (referred to as USFA or USFIA) with General Barnes in command.
http://www.history.army.mil/books/wwii/WCP/enchApxB5.html

At dinner the previous night, six of us had created a pool, 25 cents each, as to what time the ship would make port. My guess was 5:17 PM, Friday evening. We actually made port at 4:49 PM, but I won.

The *Holbrook* and *Niagara* had steamed ahead and were first into the dock to begin taking on water and oil. The *Republic* anchored about 200 yards out in the harbor, awaiting its turn. The *Holbrook* and *Niagara* were loading water all day Saturday until 4 PM. We did not pull into the pier until about 5 AM Sunday morning.

The *Pensacola* stayed out beyond the edge of the harbor, perhaps 10 miles back. Since the *Pensacola* had a cruising range of 25,000 miles at 22.5 knots, it did not need to stop for water or oil. They launched their planes and were our sentry outside the harbor. Airplanes remained overhead all the time we were in port. We all felt safe for these few hours. As soon as we picked up water, we knew we would be back in the open sea and vulnerable to Japanese submarines. We expected the Japanese to have spies on Fiji that would inform them where we were. We hoped we could speed away before the Japs had time to intercept us.

No one was allowed off the boat except a few guards, but everyone was on deck taking in all we could see from the ship. This was the town of Suva, the capital of the Fiji Islands. From what we could see, the Fiji Islands were much prettier than Honolulu. There were beautiful coconut trees around the edges of the water, and some beautiful English-style houses. A few New Zealand and Australian troops were on the dock. Only one other ship was in the harbor, a British transport that was much smaller than our ship.

All the people in town had come down to the dock to see us. We must have been the biggest ship they had ever seen. They didn't know ships were made this large. Against the dock our ship was about six or seven stories above the water line, plus the masts. At over 600 feet long, it must have been an unusual sight to the natives, and there were lots of natives. They were all Negroes, black as coal, physically tall with more hair than you could ever imagine worn standing straight out in a big bush like a Derby Hat – very curly. We waved to the few whites and tried to talk to the Negro Fijians, but they spoke a different language. We were in Suva Bay but were tied up to an island with another name that I could not say or spell.

Our radio received the Fiji radio news, but we were unable to understand the language. While in port, we saw three Navy planes that were not from our convoy.

Before arrival, they told us no mail would go out. Then suddenly a special card was distributed. There would be no letters, only the card. On the cards, we were to write our name and the date, but the rest was only to line out certain lines. They only gave us two cards each, so I sent one to Mother and one to Cile. I had several letters that I wanted to mail, but two was the limit. I knew Cile thought I would be in Philippines, and she would be expecting a letter about 1 Jan – certainly not later than 15 Jan. At the rate we were going, we would have been lucky to get to the Philippines by 15 Jan.

Through the few guards that went on shore, we managed a little trade with the natives. I secured a Fiji coin that I hoped to keep as a souvenir. I felt lucky to get it. American cigarettes sold for 35 to 60 cents per pack in Figi and they seldom had them, so I bought a box of English-made tobacco – it did not have as much flavor as ours.

I wanted to buy a pair of short pants but could not. I finally cut off a pair of trousers and a shirt. Now if I could get a pair of long wool socks like the British, I would look like them. The short pants and shirt are nice and cool, but I must be careful not to get more sunburn.

I tried to get some bait to fish from the deck while we were in port but was unsuccessful. Another ship appeared outside the harbor (about 30 miles away), but we could not identify it. We were hoping for three or four battlewagons to escort us, but no such luck. We had heard rumors of such.

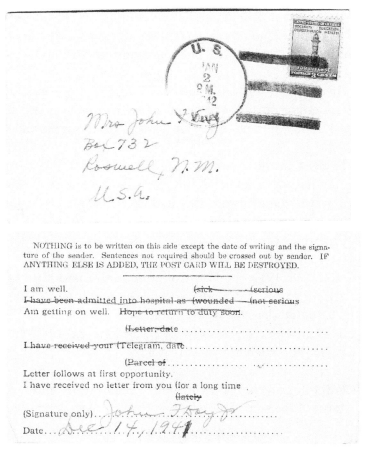

Figure 23 - Post card from Fiji Islands, 14 Dec 1941

One soldier was left on Fiji in the hospital due to sun stroke. He was lucky to be alive as he had been packed in ice but still had a temperature 110°F. The doctors could not understand how he lived.

My skin was still peeling. I had a pain in my right side but was not sick. I was scared I had appendicitis. It must have been from climbing stairs or bending this morning. When we were in port and the ship is not rocking, I seemed to sleep better.

In addition to loading water and oil, the ship took on loads of pineapple, watermelons, sweet corn, pumpkins, lettuce, cucumbers, and several other fruits I didn't recognize. There was also lots of ice loaded. Our diet improved.

3.6.   Passage to Brisbane – 16-22 Dec 1941

Finally about 5:40 PM Sunday evening, 16 Dec 1941, the ship's water tanks were full. Our Captain pulled away from the dock, and we left at full speed. We were the last ship of the convoy to depart, but we caught up with the convoy later that night.

When we left Fiji, our course was almost due south. No one had announced where we were going next. In the open sea with no moon and the ship blacked out, it was really dark. You could not see your hand in front of your face.

The next morning we did not see the *Niagara*. We were wondering if it would follow us a day later as a covering force or wait for another convoy. We later learned that the *Niagara* was the mail ship that had taken all our cards and was returning to the States. We were all counting the "Shopping Days until Christmas" and thinking about our "Christmas cards."

On 12 Dec 1941, the U.S. Congress authorized the U.S. Expeditionary *Task Force South Pacific*. I guess that made our convoy legitimate. General John F. Barnes was appointed its Commander and he was able to select his staff. The Staff had their first meeting on our ship. None of us knew our mission, and only the General and Commander of the Cruiser knew where we were going.

On the top deck, we set up four 75-mm guns and a 37-mm gun which was on the tail (stern) of the ship. This was followed by more artillery drills.

The convoy maintained a due south course for several days. We were guessing that each day we should be covering about 230 miles further south of Fiji Islands. The sea was very choppy some days and better other days.

Personnel (G-1) had me fill out another questionnaire about my past experience. I supposed sooner or later they would assign me to some unit.

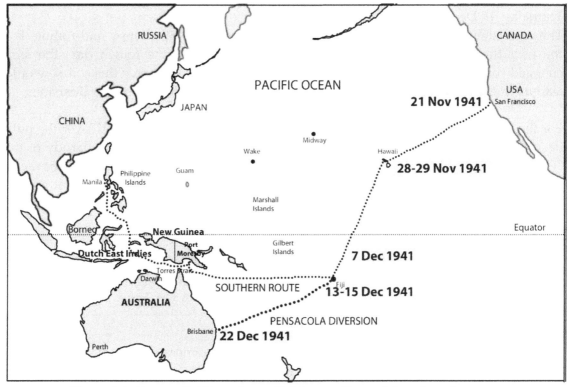

Figure 24 - Pensacola Diversion to Brisbane – Dates & location of convoy

Wednesday, 17 Dec 1941

This morning I went up on the sun deck where I watched the planes practicing dive bombing. They were using two targets and 100-pound practice bombs. I would not want them after me. They all either hit the target or missed it by only a few feet, which would still be effective against a ship.

I was told privately by a friend that the Command was planning to make another "sweep" to collect all diaries. In order to save my diary again, I buried it even deeper in the bottom of my trunk and wrapped it in clothing. I did not take it out again for the next ten days. I developed a technique for making notes of daily events on scraps of paper that I buried in my other papers, until I could find privacy again to enter the notes into the diary[38].

I played bridge a while yesterday and managed to win $4.05. I found that hard to believe.

---

[38] The opportunity to enter the notes in the diary came ten days later on the *Bloemfontein*.

Thursday, 18 Dec 1941

The dark nights were helping the sleep, but the water was still choppy and rolling. For the next three days, we followed a course due south. On the fourth day, the ship changed course to about 250 degrees, a little south of west. We knew this course would lead us to Australia, but we were not sure if we were headed for Sydney or Brisbane.

For the entertainment of the troops, three lads started a radio "broadcast" over the public address system, which they called "Bum Cigarette Hour." This was a parody of the "Chesterfield Cigarette Hour." In civilian life, I believe they were script writers for radio, and they were good. Their main theme song was "The Little Convoy Sailed Round and Round." They had new words and verses every week that made fun of our plight. It became very popular after only two programs.

The weather had turned cooler, as we moved away from the tropics. All life boats on the main deck were swung over the side in constant readiness. Each life boat would carry a 30-caliber machine gun if we abandoned ship.

Friday, 19 Dec 1941

Every morning our routine was to be up at 4 AM for General Quarters and Abandon Ship drills. This continued until 6 AM – all before breakfast.

During the night Thursday, another cruiser appeared to help escort us. It was *HMNZS Achilles* of the New Zealand Navy. The *Achilles* was a famous combat veteran from the Atlantic war with Germany. It had successfully cornered the German battleship *Admiral Graf Spee* off the South American coast at Montevideo, Uruguay, where the damaged battleship capitulated and was scuttled by its Captain rather than sacrificing his crew at sea.

That afternoon two Australian cruisers arrived, bringing our convoy escorts up to four cruisers.[39] The rumors we had heard earlier were true. The Navy was serious about protecting us. We were excited that the *Task Force South Pacific* was about ready to begin operations as soon as we arrived in Australia.

---

[39] The two additional Australian ships were the *H.M.A.S. Canberra* and *H.M.A.S. Perth*. Two days later, two additional Australian corvettes, the *H.M.A.S. Warrego* and *H.M.A.S. Swan*, joined and accompanied the convoy into Brisbane. *Australian Department of Defense Australian War Memorial, Sea Power Centre, AWM78, Folder 292/3 – September 1939 - February 1942, H.M.A.S. Perth War Diary*

Written on Board the U.S.S. Republic Just after War declared

THE LITTLE CONVOY SAILED 'ROUND AND 'ROUND

Oh, the little convoy sailed 'round and 'round
While the soldiers pray'd and pray'd for the sight of ground;
Now beware Jap planes above, For you bastards we've no love,
And the little convoy sailed 'round and 'round.

For days and days we've sailed the briny deep,
Ev'ry night we see those slant-eyes in our sleep
And we hope to get the chance To put some bullets in their pants
While the little convoy sails 'round and 'round.

Now we don't know just how long we have to go,
But we wish to God we'd see a little snow
'Cause we're sleeping 'neath the decks While the sweat runs
          down our necks
And the little convoy sails 'round and 'round.

Now we know you've heard some awf'ly hectic tales,
How we're s'posed to be way down among the whales.
If they sink this old tin can, It sure as HELL won't be Japan,
And the little convoy sailed 'round and 'round.

Now the Emperor ordered out a grand decree,
Sent his bombers out to look for you and me,
If we had him here on deck We would wring his scrawny neck
While the little convoy sails 'round and 'round.

And to all you pilots flying high and low,
Should you meet a guy who hails from Tokyo,
Please don't come a-flying back Without his uh-huhs in a sack,
And the little convoy sailed 'round and 'round.

Now come on boys and wipe away that frown,
For it's true you cannot keep a good man down;
We will all get there some day, If we have to swim part way,
And the little convoy sails 'round and 'round

Figure 25 – Theme Song for "Bum Cigarette Hour" aboard Republic

On Sunday, we went to Church. The sea had calmed down and was beautiful again. There were unfamiliar land-based bombers cruising around above us, so we thought we must be approaching land. I played bridge and listened to "Bum Cigarette Hour" in the afternoon. There was more speculation about what would happen once we arrived in Australia. We thought we would probably unload, and our ships would return to the States.

4.   JAPAN'S MILITARY TSUNAMI – DECEMBER 1941

4.1.   The Philippines Attack – 8 Dec 1941

When the first bomb fell in Pearl Harbor at 7:55 AM, 7 Dec 1941, the time in Manila was 1:55 AM, 8 Dec 1941. Although there is a minus-six-hour time difference between the two cities, the International Date Line adds +24 hours for a total difference of +18 hours.

Japan had intended to strike the Philippines at dawn on 8 Dec 1941. However, fog and bad weather in Formosa delayed the departure of their attack bombers by six hours. Their bombers reached the Philippines at 12:53 PM 8 Dec 1941 roughly eleven hours after the first bombs fell in Pearl Harbor.

The first Japanese targets in the Philippines were Clark Air Field in Luzon, Iba Air Field in Luzon and Cavite Naval Base in Manila Harbor. Clark was the main terminal for the Far East Air Force (FEAF). FEAF lost twelve of seventeen B-17 bombers (plus three additional B-17s were severely damaged), while all were still on the ground. In this 45-minute attack FEAF lost half its total aircraft in the Philippines. On 10 Dec the Pursuit Group lost eleven of forty P-40s that were deployed, and in the next week FEAF lost virtually every remaining pursuit aircraft.

The Cavite Naval Base in Manila Harbor was equally devastated by a 10 Dec attack. After the attack Admiral Thomas C. Hart withdrew all remaining Asiatic Fleet surface ships from the Philippine Islands south to the Netherlands East Indies (NEI), leaving only submarines to meet the arriving Japanese Navy, the largest flotilla in the Pacific.

There has been much controversy over the specific actions taken by MacArthur, Sutherland, and Brereton during those critical eleven hours between Pearl Harbor attack and the Philippine attack.[40] That controversy will not be described here, but for this narrative, it is sufficient to say that the outcome of the Japanese air strikes was devastating to FEAF.

Two days later on 10 Dec, the Japanese landed Army reconnaissance units on the north coast of Luzon. On Dec 12, Japanese landed 2,500 troops in southern Luzon, and later in Mindanao. The main Japanese Army however, struck when the 48th Division came ashore on 22 Dec 1941 with 43,000 troops supported by tanks and artillery in the Lingayen Gulf of Luzon.

Between 17-20 Dec, FEAF withdrew its last fourteen surviving B-17s from the Philippines to Australia. They were later moved to Java.

---

[40] Rogers, Paul P. *MacArthur and Sutherland: The Good Years*, Vol. 1 p 94.

As the Japanese swept down across Luzon, Gen. MacArthur declared Manila an Open City on 26 Dec 1941 to avoid its destruction as a casualty of war. Gen. MacArthur and the remnants of the USAFFE withdrew to the Bataan Peninsula and Corregidor Island.

By the end of December, the Philippines had been neutralized and the remaining American resistance was isolated to the Bataan Peninsula, the Visayan Islands, and Mindanao. The Philippines were surrounded by a Japanese Navy blockade that cut off any further resupply.

Japan had captured Guam and Wake Island. Hong Kong had surrendered, and Borneo had been invaded. Allied Forces were in retreat. Control of South East Asia was within the grasp of Imperial Japan.

4.2. Command Confusion for US Army Forces in Australia (USAFIA)

In the first month after the Pearl Harbor attack, there was great confusion within the U.S. military over who was in charge of American troops in Australia. Gen. John F. Barnes arrived in Brisbane on 22 Dec 1941 with the Pensacola Convoy expecting to take command of U.S. Army Forces in Australia (USAFIA) under the authority of the 12 Dec 1941 Congressional Act that authorized the U.S. Expeditionary Task Force South Pacific. Barnes had organized his command on board the USS Republic before his arrival in Brisbane.

The mission in Australia was to resupply Philippine operations. There was no intention of stationing any substantial number of American troops in Australia. Upon arrival, the mission was expanded to include the supply of the Netherlands East Indies (NEI) using US air units in Northwest Australia.

The War Department approved a plan for Australia to be under the command of Maj. Gen. George H. Brett, an air corps officer, who reported to USAFFE (Gen. MacArthur}. MacArthur was expecting an airlift bridge for supplies from Australia to reinforce his Philippine operations, hence primarily an air corps operation. He was particularly anxious to take delivery of the 55 dive bombers that were contained in the cargo bay of the USAT Meigs. Gen. Brett, an air corps officer, intended to relieve Gen. Barnes, an army officer, of command of USAFIA.

Before Gen Brett could travel to Brisbane to take command, Brig. Gen. Claggett (another air corps officer on Gen. MacArthur's Staff) had flown down to Brisbane from the Philippines and on 24 Dec 1941 took Command of the USAFIA. Gen. Brett arrived one week later on 31 Dec 1941 and on 5 Jan 1942 assumed command of USAFIA from General Claggett. Brett's tenure would be only one week before the Arcadia Conference reorganized again.

4.3.   Arcadia Conference and ABDACOM – 22 Dec 1941

Franklin D. Roosevelt, President of the United States, and Winston Churchill, Prime Minister of Great Britain, met in Washington, DC, for the first meeting of the Joint Chiefs of Staff of the two countries to formulate plans to prosecute the War. The meeting was called the Arcadia Conference (22 Dec 1941 to 14 Jan 1942). Japan had declared war on the United States on 8 Dec 1941. Germany declared war against the United States on 11 Dec 1941. Japan had invaded the Malay Peninsula and was marching toward Singapore. The Philippines were under heavy attack.

Although there was great political pressure in the US after the Pearl Harbor attack for the U.S. to attack Japan, Arcadia made the decision to defeat Nazi Germany first. This was called the "Europe First" doctrine. "Europe First" dictated that the primary thrust of the war was to be in Europe to defend the homeland of the Allied powers – Great Britain and Holland – rather than their colonies in Asia – India, Hong Kong, Singapore, the Dutch East Indies, and the Philippines.

The Arcadia Conference concluded with a decision that military actions in Asia confronting the Japanese Imperial Forces would be limited to a "delaying action." To this end, the Arcadia Conference created the American British Dutch Australia Command (ABDACOM)[41] with responsibilities initially to include land and sea areas of Burma, Malaya, Singapore, Netherlands East Indies (NEI) and the Philippines. A British Officer, Lt. Gen. Sir Archibald Percival Wavell, was appointed supreme commander.

After ratification by the various governments, Wavell assumed command in Batavia, Java, NEI on January 15, 1942. Maj. Gen. Brett was initially placed in charge of U.S. Army Forces in Australia (USAFIA), as an element of ABDACOM. To confuse things further, the War Department (Washington, DC), without coordinating with Gen. Wavell or Gen Brett, instructed Gen. Brereton, Commanding General US Far East Air Forces in the Philippines, to go to Australia and take command of US Air Forces in Australia and NEI. Then in February 1942 Wavell had Brett promoted to Lieutenant General and Deputy Commander of ABDACOM. Brereton was appointed Commanding General (CG) of Air Force in ABDACOM, and Barnes returned to CG of USAFIA (27 Jan 1942). As a practical matter, the Philippines were left to MacArthur alone.

Between 12 Dec 1941 and 25 Feb 1942, there were <u>seven</u> changes in Command for USAFIA.

---

[41] ABDA Com is referred to as "Australia Britain Dutch American" in Australia or "American British Dutch Australia" Command in the United States.

5.   BRISBANE ARRIVAL – 22-29 Dec 1941

5.1.   Brisbane, Queensland

In 1941, Brisbane was the third largest city in Australia, after Sydney and Melbourne. Brisbane population was reported to be 331,000, while all of Australia had a population of 7.1 million people.[42]

Brisbane is located at 27°south latitude, which is roughly the same distance south of the equator as Fort Pierce, Florida is north of the equator (27.4°north latitude). Miami, Florida is 140 miles closer to the equator than Brisbane. As Florida suffers from periodic hurricanes, Queensland also suffers from periodic cyclones, southern hemisphere hurricanes, such as the devastating 2011 cyclone in Queensland.[43] Like Florida, Queensland also is home to crocodiles and swamps.

The Queensland economy is a heavily based upon mining and agriculture, including sugar cane, bananas, and other tropical fruits. Inland beyond a coastal mountain range are sheep and livestock.

Downtown Brisbane is located about 14 miles up the Brisbane River from the ocean. Ocean going ships must navigate the twists and turns of the narrowing river channel to reach the docks. The daily tides and fear of Japanese mines in 1941 demanded special care entering the harbor.

5.2.   The Sand Bar – Monday, 22 Dec 1941

Monday, 22 Dec 1941 – *USS Republic Arrives in Brisbane*
As the *USS Republic* was coming into Brisbane on Monday morning, 22 Dec, we had been told we would dock at 12 noon. From the deck we were enjoying the beautiful shoreline, although land looked very dry. We were still perhaps 10 miles from downtown Brisbane when the *Republic* suddenly struck a sandbar. The *Republic* was drawing about 33-feet, but the river was only 28 feet deep. We were caught by a low tide. After a number of unsuccessful maneuvers by the Captain to dislodge the ship, it was apparent we were seriously stuck. To float the ship off the sandbar, the weight of the ship had to be reduced. A beautiful oil tanker from Oslo, Norway, was located and pulled along the port side of the *Republic*. A line was connected and we began off-loading oil to the tanker.

---

[42] Australian National Census of 1941.

[43] A cyclone is a southern hemisphere tropical storm that circulates in the opposite direction from a northern hemisphere hurricane or typhoon.

The *Chaumont* came along the starboard side of the *Republic* and also started taking oil. Big fenders were lowered to prevent the ships from bumping. We knew we would have to transfer a lot of oil to refloat the ship. The oil transfer started late Monday afternoon, possibly 3 PM, and continued until 9:30 AM the next morning – over 18 hours of pumping.

That night on the sandbar was the first night since San Francisco that the ship was not blacked out. Brisbane was definitely not observing black out rules. The river banks were beautifully lighted, and we were still a number of miles from downtown. We celebrated our arrival in Australia with a picture show on deck.

The ship windows were opened, and the night air was very cool. The Brisbane temperature was a pleasant change from the tropics of Fiji.

We had another late night playing bridge, and I won $1.30.

5.3.   Ascot Race Track – Tuesday, 23 Dec 1941

When they finished pumping oil, our ship cruised up the river. With a high tide, we reached Brett's Wharf in Brisbane at 1:05 PM. The tide was about 7 feet, but we were told it was usually a little higher.

The Brisbane River is lined with buildings. It must have seemed a novelty to have a ship the size of ours going up the river. Our soldiers were all on deck taking in the city. The Australians were all out waving their handkerchiefs and appeared excited to greet the first 3,100 U.S. military soldiers to arrive. They seemed to be saying "The Yanks are here, we are saved." Most of their Australian Imperial Forces were fighting in either the Middle East or in Malaya. There was serious concern in Australia for their security with only a small home guard remaining if Japan should decide to invade. American troops were welcomed with much serious celebration.

When we got to the Brisbane dock, another ship had already arrived. This other ship had been diverted from Singapore because the Japanese were attacking that city. It was unloading a cargo of commercial merchandise – not military goods.

After Fiji, food on the *Republic* had been reduced to two meals a day, as concern for supplies developed. Before disembarking in Brisbane, officers were reimbursed the sum of $14.69 from our total $40 food allowance for the trip for food we had not received. I think all expected the reimbursement. "Someday" I will put in a claim to government for the remaining sum of $25.31.[44] We could have been paid earlier in the voyage and been ready to get off the ship. They must have wanted us to have some money when we left the boat in Brisbane. Anyway we were off the ship about 5 PM after watching our luggage being unloaded. There were no orders to get off the ship, but as everyone was getting off, so did I.[45]

From the dock, we were loaded into trucks (or rather we jumped into the back of a truck) for a ride to the Ascot Race Track, probably 4 miles away.

We were suddenly hit by the novelty of being in Australia. The cars had the steering on the right side and drove on left side of road. We were being instructed on how to speak proper "English," that language we butcher so much in America, they said.

Figure 26 - Ascot Race Track Bleachers – Modern Eagle Farm – ca. 2000
Photo – Peter Dunn

We arrived at this beautiful race track which they said was full the day before with race spectators. When we arrived, we found there were no beds set up. We felt lucky to have a bed, set up or not. We each grabbed a straw mattress, two sheets, pillow, pillow case, and two blankets and carried them ourselves up into the race track stands. The stands were enormous - could possibly hold 10,000 people – so we spread out over the stands. I wanted to be alone, so I picked out the highest spot in the bleachers I could reach. It took me several trips to get my bedding up to the top. I was worn out after making so many trips up the steps.

By this time it was too late for "Tea," as they call our "Supper." I drank a beer with an Aussie lieutenant but decided not to join most of the boys who went into town. I was too tired for a bath, so I went straight to bed. The night was very cool.

---

[44] Army Officers are required to pay for their own meals. They do not eat for free in the Mess. When eating in a Mess, they are expected to reimburse the government for the meals. The Officers had paid $40 in advance for meals for the voyage, therefore they were entitled to a refund for the meals they did not receive.

[45] These were the first U.S. Army troops to arrive in Australia.

Wednesday. 24 Dec 1941

I slept like a log on the straw mattress and a pillow so thick I thought I had two.

Next morning, about 4 AM, we were awakened by a noisy "clop-ity-clop, clop-ity-clop" of horses on the track below us. The jockeys were out for their early morning exercise run for the race horses. This was a working racetrack, and they were making all sorts of noise.

The race track was heaven compared to what we expected, and it did not sway with the waves. We would have thought nothing of having been asked to sleep on the ground. We took showers in the stables where they washed the race horses. The floor was cement and kept very clean. We didn't know race horses had such clean stables. The toilets, however, were a mess, positively a disgrace for any Army to let the latrines get so filthy. My main objection was the toilet paper, which was so slick you could hardly wipe yourself. Hell, it was better than I expected.

Everyone was trying to find out what we were going to do next and when we would sail.[46] We learned that Major Gen. G. H. Brett (Asst. to Gen. MacArthur in the Philippine Islands) had flown down to take charge of U.S. Forces in Australia (USAFIA)."[47] There was no more *Task Force South Pacific*. No one knew anything except we were sure we would be here a matter of days until the ship's cargo was rearranged and all the darn practice bombs and clay pigeons thrown out. We had brought over a million practice bombs. Now we needed real bombs. Hell of a note.

An Aussie lieutenant asked to take three of us into town and show us around. About 10:30 PM, we had a nice walk around part of downtown Brisbane, our first visit. We saw the Eternal Flame, a memorial from the First World War. We went for a ride on the tram. There were quite a number of nice buildings, none over possibly six or eight stories. All streets running one way are named after Kings and other way after Queens. There did not seem to be a lot of other things to see. A few drink joints were open - not like ours at home - not nearly as clean, not as modern (possibly 25 years behind us).

In downtown Brisbane, there was a major bridge across the river with a big sign **PLUME**. Well, we thought that *PLUM* was a secret Code word for our deployment, but there it was, greeting us in Brisbane – not so secret. We were joking saying "We have arrived in *PLUM*"[48] [See Figure 26].

---

[46] As it turned out, the Generals did not know where we were going next either.

[47] Brig. Gen. Claggett came on 24 Dec 1944 and stayed until Maj. Gen. G. H. Brett could arrive.

[48] PLUME was the Australian brand name for a special gasoline from the Mobil Oil Company.

Figure 27 - Northern end of Victoria Bridge, Brisbane, mid 1930's
Showing open air trams and the sign "Plume," a petroleum product

The Aussies were wonderful. They all wanted to do everything possible for us. Officers and enlisted men alike, all who went into town had quite a welcome with plenty of drinks. They wanted us to sign autographs with addresses in the States.

Brisbane reminded me a lot of Fort Worth, Texas. I felt very much at home. Everybody was so friendly, saying "Hello," "Hi," "How are you?" They had never met you before in their life, but they were still very friendly. They wanted you to come out to their house and have dinner.

We wanted something to eat, but Brisbane is not like Dallas, where you have lots of eating places. The only restaurants were at hotels, so we finally found a beer and sandwich in a Pub. There we talked to a few Aussies and had a very enjoyable time. Of course, we had to taste their beer. These damn Aussies were worse than the Germans about beer. Most of all they wanted to hear Yanks talk. Our accent was as interesting to the Aussies as their accent was to us. Their lingo was also fun as they used different words for common objects. We were really enjoying each other's company. Every time you turned around you had to take another drink.

They would ask "Where you Yanks going?"

"We don't know," we would say. And we really did not know.

It was summer in Brisbane, and there were lots of fresh fruits in the markets. Their money had me confused so I would just hold out my hand and let them take what they wanted. I never knew how much I spent without doing a lot of figuring. I wrote down their money - 1/2 penny, 1 penny, 3 pence, 6 pence, 1 shilling, 2 shilling, 5 shillings, 1/2 pound note and pound note. One pound note was worth $3.2687 of our money. Actually a dollar was worth six shillings and a penny.

Finally about 11:30 PM, we got back to the racetrack, and I made my way up to the top of the deck. We were told cigarettes (American) were not to be had in Australia. I had fortunately stocked up with about 20 cartons in the States. When the Aussies did have them to sell, they were about 54 cents per pack. The Navy on the ship was selling cigarettes for 6 cents a pack.

Out in the field near the racetrack, we saw pot after pot of mutton boiling. It looked very greasy. In the field, there were lots of goats and sheep.

The war news from Manila was bad. [49] The situation seemed to be getting worse. It looked like suicide for us to go there now, but I guess someone had to be the goat. If the one above said it's my turn, OK by me.

The planes that we brought as cargo in the *Pensacola Convoy*, of which I think there were about 70,[50] were to be assembled and flown up to the Philippines at once. They were needed badly. A shortage of airfields near Brisbane was forcing the pilots here to land in flat pastures, hayfields, or wherever they could find.

We were allowed to mail another "I am alive" postcard. I hoped it would get home OK.

---

[49] Japan had invaded the Lingayen Gulf of Luzon on December 22, 1941 and was rapidly advancing south toward Manila. Philippine defenses were withdrawing from northern Luzon.

[50] This number is exactly correct. There were 52 A-24 dive-bombers and 18 P-40E fighters.

5.4.   Christmas Day – Thursday, 25 Dec 1941

Christmas was a time of reflection. I thought a lot about my loved ones back home. I would like to see them now and hope they all are happy and remember 21 Nov when I left San Francisco. I guess when I get home Cile and I will have to be remarried, so we can have a second wedding date. We already had one wedding anniversary date to remember, 22 Nov 1934.[51]

I was sitting high in the race track bleachers about 11:30 AM waiting to eat the Christmas turkey we had been promised. I added a few lines to my diary notes since I did not have the real diary. Quite a few of the senior staff were staying downtown at the Lennons Hotel, which was a very nice hotel, similar to our hotels. The hotel was about to go broke till our US Army bunch rented two floors. My place here at the racetrack was OK. I'd rather be here than pay $2.75 a day for a room at the Lennons - like some. They would not stay long at the hotel at that price.

I thought about seeing a show, but all are closed for the Christmas holiday. In fact, EVERYTHING closes on Christmas. If I had my golf clubs, guess I'd play golf. My clubs were somewhere at the dock. The days were hot, especially at noon. The nights were very cool. I liked Brisbane and was so glad Cile and Johnnie were not with me, because I would have left them in Brisbane for the duration of the war. I would have never let them go home.

Surprise! No turkey dinner – just pork. I ate a little. They told us they would cook the goose that night. Well, that way we always had something to look forward to.

We still had received no orders. The war situation seemed to be in a hell of a mess and getting worse. I bought myself a shark knife for Japs. They say they are using knives more than guns in Manila. "Very interesting!"[52] I hope I never have to use the knife on either a shark or a Jap.

The *Republic* was unloaded all over the dock and sailed on Christmas Day back to the States. "Bon Voyage, old gal." There must have been two train loads of junk left on the dock. We gave letters to the sailors on the *Republic*, asking them to mail the letters when they got back to the States. If my friend the sailor does well, Cile should have a long letter about the end of January giving her a bit of news. We had not been allowed to cable.

---

[51] November 22, 1934 was the wedding date for John and Cile.

[52] This is a popular movie line of the day by Peter Loire, a movie actor who was often a detective making discoveries and solving mysteries.

Friday. 26 Dec 1941 – Boxing Day

Today was "Boxing Day" and all stores were still closed. The Adjutant finally came down and told me I would sail on the *Bloemfontein*, the ship they call the *Dutchman*. Everything was done with verbal orders, nothing written. The *Bloemfontein* was the fastest ship in the *Pensacola Convoy* coming across the Pacific. She was a beauty inside - quite a ship, probably 18,000 tons and more. No one of course knew when we would sail. There were meetings twice a day to tell us they knew nothing. They were still unloading and shuffling cargo. That could take another week, but it was OK with me. I was in no hurry to leave Brisbane.

I wanted to have some laundry done, but had a hard time finding a place that could do "one-day" service. The regular laundries kept saying next Tuesday, but we are loading on Sunday. Several of us finally found a nearby tailor shop run by a woman who did a special load of laundry just for us. We were grateful, and I think she was pleased with the money.

Speculation was that we will probably sail to Darwin on the Australian North Coast before bearing north to the Philippine Islands.

5.5.   Royal Queensland Golf Club – Saturday, 27 Dec 1941

One of the Australian lieutenants took me out to a Brisbane country club[53] today and introduced me to quite a few club members, all of whom bought me beer. I drank about five and I still had a game of golf to play. It takes a lot of time here to get anything done because of all the friendly conversations. I played a round of golf and, of course, shot a poor score.[54] Nevertheless, I enjoyed it very much. The course was close to the river. In places you could not see the ball for the mosquitoes. I just fought the mosquitoes away until I came to the ball. I would hit the ball again and start walking to get away from the mosquitoes. I picked up a few souvenir cards for remembrance.

---

[53] Although never named in the diary, the golf course description and location along the Brisbane River (and the proximity of Ascot Race Track) indicate this was probably the Royal Queensland Golf Club.

[54] John F Day Jr. was a passionate golfer during his entire life. A near-scratch player, he was Captain of the Texas A&M golf team in the 1920's. Then in 1948, he was one of four members of the Fourth Army Golf Team that won the All Army Golf Tournament. He was never far from his golf clubs, cigarettes, and scotch whiskey.

These Aussie people did not know what rush was. Everything was low key. Petrol was rationed and very few street lights in town, just a minimum for lighting.

There was a Japanese concentration camp a few miles outside of town.[55]

We were told to board the ship the next day, Sunday, so for our last night in Brisbane we saw a vaudeville show at a local show house. It was presented by house talent and was fair. We seemed to have a different humor than the Aussies. The people here laugh at silly jokes. Sometimes we "Yanks" wonder what they were laughing at. They had been nice to all of us and we were very grateful to them.

---

[55] The Australians, like the Americans, rounded up resident ethnic Japanese when the war started and placed them in internment camps for the duration of the war. After the war most were deported to Japan.

6. PASSAGE TO DARWIN – 28 DEC 41 TO 11 JAN 42

6.1. The *VMS Bloemfontein* – Sunday, 28 Dec 1941

Sunday, 28 Dec 1941

Sunday morning I was still in the top of the bleachers at Ascot Race Track when I was awakened to learn we were supposed to be onboard our assigned ship at 6 AM for a Roll Call. Well, I had not gotten the word. The Adjutant had told me we were supposed to be on board by 3 PM. Hell, some of these birds get so rattled and are scared all the time, they should be in a storm cellar somewhere.

I went down to the pier about 9 AM and got all my stuff on board the *Bloemfontein* and into my cabin. I had my trunk, footlocker, suitcase, bar-bag and golf clubs. My bar-bag still contained three unopened bottles of White Horse Scotch Whiskey I had brought from San Antonio. I wanted to store my luggage, except for the footlocker and suitcase. I would have shipped it all home but could not find a way to do so. We had our first meal on the *Bloemfontein* at lunch at 12:45 PM, and what a lovely meal. What a change traveling on a Dutch luxury cruise ship! Lunch consisted of about five courses, clean table cloths, everything so nice. The food was much better than on the *Republic*. The waiters are Javanese with a few Malayan. They are Hindus, wear their heads wrapped up in a cloth turban, and go bare footed. They speak very little English, but provide marvelous service. I kept my first Menu Card, the top part of which was a post card.

We were supposed to sail about 3 PM, then 4 PM, then 6 PM, but in the meantime the tide went out. We were still at the pier at 11:30 PM. The *Holbrook* sailed at 3 PM – they were out of the harbor and anchored somewhere until we could join them.

The *VMS Bloemfontein* was a "Dutch Motor Ship" (diesel powered) with twin screws and quite fast. The crew said the ship could make 25 knots. The cargo hold was full to the neck in bulk with about 30,000 tons of cargo, but the ship was not loaded in weight. The ship can carry 90,000 tons. The crew expected the ship to still pitch and roll.

We had about 700 men sleeping on the decks and all over the ship. Terribly crowded! They have to put the stoves on deck to cook and have made toilets on the side rails.

Fortunately for me, I was assigned a private cabin (Rank Has Its Privileges). With the privacy of a cabin, I had the opportunity to get my diary out again. I forced myself to transfer all my daily notes from the past ten days into the diary before I lost track of the many scraps of paper. Before going to bed that night, my diary was up-to-date.

My room was air conditioned and the air flow could be directed over my bed. I was not sure how it would be when the port holes were closed, but my back was tired, so I went to bed. The new bunk was good.

> My love to my loved ones: I hope I wake up at sea in daylight.
>
> P.S. I forgot to add that I have Johnnie's and Cile's picture in front of me on my desk. Looks swell to see them. I love them dearly.

Monday. 29 Dec 1941

The ship spent the entire day at the dock in Brisbane – not loading, not unloading. It seemed that the Dutch captain did not want to sail through the Strait of Torres, but wanted to go south around Australia. He was having his way – we were not moving. The general and cruiser commander were unable to make him do anything. The government had a million and a half dollars on the counter for the ship, but until the captain agreed to sail, there was nothing.[56]

This all meant more delay. We would not have been surprised to unload and get on the damn *Meigs,* a cattle boat and slow as the itch. We had to just wait and see. For the moment, the food was great and my room was quiet and comfortable. We had another five-course dinner, a five-course supper, but only four courses for breakfast. Then of course in the afternoon we go to the tea room for our coffee, as coffee was not served with meals in the dining room.

About 6 PM there was a general announcement. We were told that we would all get off ship after breakfast in the morning and go back to Ascot Race Track, that lovely place. We were not pleased to have to leave this lovely hotel. The ship "hotel" was too good to be true. Somebody made a hell of a blunder by loading the ship before finding out whether the captain would sail or not. This is war, and you can't make mistakes like that. I don't know to this day what was going on but I always wondered if the Dutch captain wanted more money to take the risk, or he may have been balking at going to the Philippines. As we were en route to Manila, we might be living a little longer today and our lives may have been saved by our captain not sailing.

---

[56] OCMH History of USASOS Vol.1, p.81-83: Under Maritime Law, the Dutch Master of the *Bloemfontein* had been relieved of his obligation to proceed to the Philippines because of the unloading of his cargo at Brisbane (because of the Australian longshoremen's labor issue). The Master only sailed after consultation with the Commander in Chief of the Dutch East Indies, and then only agreed to sail to Soerabaja, Java, rather than proceeding to the Philippines.

I was really concerned that casual officers were not armed. God be with us, but what in the hell could a bunch of casual officers with no equipment do without at least a gun. We might get there and find no guns available (we could end up with only some clay pigeons or practice bombs from the *Republic*).

Well, I finished packing and was ready to disembark in the morning. At least I had re-packed my two trunks and now had my things in better order. I could now live out of my suitcase for a while. I still had not opened a single bottle of the three bottles of Scotch that I had in my bar bag. So, I bid farewell to the *Bloemfontein*.

6.2.   Sailing From Brisbane – Tuesday, 30 Dec 1941

Tuesday, 30 Dec 1941

I woke up about 6:30 AM and was ready to disembark, then suddenly at 7 AM we pulled away from the pier. We were never told what changed the captain's mind, but at 7:30 AM we had breakfast as the ship was moving down the Brisbane River to sea. At 11:20 AM we dropped off the pilot and headed east southeast. We were not out of the coral reefs yet, so we did not know if we were going north or south. As far as we could see, we were the only ship. The other ships were out of sight.

6 PM - I took a several-hour nap this afternoon and have gotten out my typewriter. It was repaired now, so I can editorialize more. I might say it has been a bloody day, as the English people say. I do not in any way intend to stop writing in my diary, but as long as I have the typewriter, I can expand my diary comments "a little more."[57]

We had stopped believing rumors that circulate around the ship, but we were all frustrated about the lack of real information. The longer we sail, the more we felt we were confined in a "jail" where there is no escape and where we have no influence on the outcome of future events. This can drive some to liquor and some to denial. Some of these crazy people don't realize the war has begun. Quite poetic this afternoon while waiting for "dinner" - "tea" to the English or "supper" to most of us Americans.

"Well, I will cut the bull and write what I intended – a description of my cabin:

---

[57] [*Periodically during the war, Capt. Day typed extra pages on separate paper for the diary. These extra pages have been incorporated into this narrative without differentiation.*]

My Cabin

I have quite a cabin, and this is quite a ship. In peacetime the *VMS Bloemfontein* is a luxury cruise ship that has been leased by the military to transport troops.[58] To describe the ship, the Captain's Bridge is at the top, where the ships officers steer the ship when it is underway. On that top deck there is also a badminton court; however, for our voyage troops are using the badminton court as quarters. Underneath the Captain's Bridge is the "A" deck, which contained the social room, a bar, an indoor tennis court, chairs, and the lounge. The next deck down is "B" deck where the mess hall is located toward the rear or stern of the ship. Just behind the mess hall is a stairwell with stairs going up and down, as well as a hallway to the rear of the ship toward the cabins on "B" deck. The "C" deck was next, possibly 25 feet above water line. My room is on the "C" deck on the starboard or the right side looking in the direction the ship is moving and the first room at the foot of the stairs. I have two port holes in my room, a light at the head of my bed for reading, and an overhead room light. The room light is controlled by a switch at the door. There is also a light over the desk and another over the wash basin. The bed is underneath the port holes with the desk nearby. There is also a lovely chair, closet for shoes and hats, hooks for other things on the wall. There is plenty of drawer space for clothes. The top of the bureau slides out for writing. Several mirrors are around the cabin. On my desk I have Cile and Johnnie's pictures. I could get accustomed to such luxury. Here I am, sitting in my short pants enjoying the cool air.

The Store

On the *Bloemfontein* there is a small store selling a few things made in Java and other Holland possessions. I made several purchases. First, I bought a pair of beads which were made in Java. The natives collect the soil at the bottom of the sea and make something like cement, but much harder. They make the beads by hand. I think they are lovely and very odd. I trust my dear wife will enjoy wearing them. I trust more that I will get home after the war all in one piece and a sane man. I did not forget my Johnnie. For him, I bought a sailor that plays the accordion and has the name of the ship on his hat.

The Engine Room

I went down into the engine room with the Engineer. He is second in command of the ship. They have two diesel motors that can develop 8,500 HP each. The two drive shafts are each over 200 feet long. The ship has twin screws, each propeller is 15.5 feet in diameter, and at the time I was down there, they were making 132 RPM. The Engine Room is a marvel to see and is spotless throughout."

---

[58] The *Bloemfontein, a Dutch ship owned by the Holland African Line,* was originally designed as a passenger liner to serve between Holland and South Africa. The name is a location in South Africa.

Lord only knows whether we will ever get to the Philippines. I bought a hand-made silver cigarette tray for 7½ Guilders (the Dutch dollar worth 53 cents of our money), and I may say it is lovely. I trust that my darling wife will appreciate it. I love her dearly. I also bought a grape server that was rather expensive (ten Guilders), silver and handmade. Gosh, these people do lots of work by hand. I also bought my sweetheart a fish server for quite a few Guilders, and I must say that she will someday have to serve fish in order that she may show the lovely thing. Wish I could send it now. I am sure lonely this evening.

At about 6:30 PM, we still have not seen any of the ships we thought would be with us from the *Pensacola Convoy*. We are wondering when we will pick them up. I suppose we are about two hundred miles at sea. The other ships had a 36-hour head start on us. We are traveling at a pretty good rate of speed, much more than we ever did on the *Republic*. The ship seems to have a list to starboard for some reason and some roll too.

We officers have no deck space, as the decks are filled with enlisted men with canvas over some of their heads. The Officers do have the social hall to roam, which was certainly nice. I walk for my daily exercise.

All six of the life boats look pretty good, but I hope we will not have to use them. The crew loaded a lot of rafts to take care of the six or seven hundred soldiers if we sink. I was assigned to #3 Life Boat. Good day.

Bloemfontein Cargo
In addition to troops, the Bloemfontein carried a cargo that included forty-eight 75 mm field pieces. The field pieces were without sights or other standard supporting equipment.

Wednesday, 31 Dec 1941 – New Year's Eve
This was New Year's Eve, the last day of 1941. I started my 4-hour watch at 12 noon on the aft starboard side. We were inside the Great Barrier Reef which runs along the coast of Australia and would stay inside to the end. This gave us quite a bit of protection for a while against Japanese submarines, or so we thought. The sea was as smooth as a lake this morning, not a break in the waves.

Figure 28 – Voyage of the Bloemfontein - Brisbane, Darwin, Soerabaja
28 Dec 1941 to 11 Jan 1942

I tried to talk to some of the Javanese boys who were on the boat, and they enjoyed trying to talk to me. I used a word translation book that I borrowed from one of the ship's officers, and it was certainly interesting. I wished I knew more about their language.

4:30 PM - I just returned from my watch and found that I had been assigned to 2nd Battalion of 131st Field Artillery while on ship. I was in charge of 3rd Relief on the gun on Port side aft. In addition, I am the Assistant S-2 of the Battalion. Guess "I made good." Well, l do not want to be attached to the National Guard unit (the 131st) after landing, but do not know where I will finally be assigned.

This evening I stumbled in my cabin. My helmet fell and knocked my glasses off. The glasses did not break, so I guessed I have been living OK.

I have had quite a few visitors in my room, and they all told me that my wife was certainly good looking, as if I did not know that. I suppose we will know in a few days if we were going to Darwin.

My daytime watch started at 12 noon. I guess I did a good job watching the sea last night. Our ship passed lots of islands – all on the port side while I am on the starboard side.

I was very restless last night and woke myself twice talking in my sleep. I suppose I ate too much supper. Everything they prepared on the ship was good. I have been trying to learn a few words of the Malay language. *Soernejob* (?).

One of the ships officers told me we are not going to Singapore, at least in this ship, and he thought we would either go to Darwin or Suda Bay (Soerabaja), Java.

New Year's Eve – Knighthood of Torres Strait
Well, there has to be something happening on the ship all the time to entertain troops. Tonight for New Year's Eve, the crew initiated all the officers on board (who had not been through the Torres Strait) into the Royal House of the Torres Strait. This initiation was much more subdued than our initiation crossing the Equator. There was mild water sprinkling compared to the total foolery of the Equator initiation.

From the looks of the map, we know we were approaching the Torres Strait. I understand we have orders not to go through without an escort.

11:30 PM - As the old year ends, we are entering a new time zone. We moved our watches forward one hour, so the first hour of the New Year would be the shortest of the year.[59] Beginning at 12 midnight, I was given a new assignment – I was placed in charge of the 3-inch gun on the fan tail. I hoped the schedule would not be changed again, as I was on a different gun this afternoon from 12 to 4 PM.

New Year's Resolutions

It is hard to make New Year's Resolutions this year.

- First, may the New Year bring greater love and happiness to my loved ones and me, and may God keep eternal watch over us all.
- May success be ours to such greatness that the yellow scum of the earth will be cleaned away forever and finally!
- May yours truly be returned home by the end of the year in as good condition and physically fit, as I was when I left the USA.
- I promise I will do my best for God and our country and my loved ones. Bless my loving wife, Lucille, and son Johnnie, and my mother. Amen.

**Figure 29 - Map of Northern Australia – Darwin and Torres Strait
American Collegiate Atlas 1957**

---

[59] [*This diary entry must be wrong. When traveling west, you normally gain 1 hour or move your clock back one hour.*]

<u>Thursday, 1 Jan 1942</u>

I had trouble going to sleep last night. I tried to sleep a couple of hours before my 12-midnight watch, but had no success. I was on watch until 4:30 AM and had to wake up my relief. About the time I finally fell asleep, General Quarters was sounded and I was up again for another hour. Afterward, I slept a little until 7:30 AM breakfast but then went back to bed for a while.

The *Bloemfontein* is making about 16 knots or better. Last night we went between a series of islands. There seems to be no end to the small islands.

10 PM - I undressed and got a couple of hours rest before going on watch. We are still in and among small islands. I wish I had a movie camera to record the beautiful scenery, but no cameras are allowed.

<u>Friday, 2 Jan 1942 – Catching up with our Convoy</u>

Last night was another beautiful night. At about 7 AM this morning, we spotted three ships ahead of us that were our sister ships. We caught up with the *Holbrook*, the *Chaumont* and the *Pensacola* about mid-day. The convoy had slowed to about 8 knots in order to reach the Strait early the next morning. The passage is too treacherous to navigate at night. The Strait is marked by strong currents due to differing tides between oceans. One side of the Strait is the Coral Sea which opens to the Pacific Ocean. The other side of the Strait is the Arafura Sea which opens to the Indian Ocean. The passage through the Strait is from 1 to 10 miles wide and is a navigation hazard caused by changing currents. Our ship was told to only go through the Strait in daytime.

The scenery was beautiful throughout the day - especially the hundreds of islands we were passing. Most are so small and not on the map – possibly uninhabited. We passed a British ship heading in the opposite direction, perhaps going toward Australia. I was a bit tired this morning after the 12 midnight to 4 AM watch, but will rest during the day.

6.3.   Passing the Torres Strait – Meeting the *USS Houston*

<u>Saturday, 3 Jan 1942</u>

At 7AM, the planes were catapulted from the cruiser. Three ships in front started going in circles, as did we. After about an hour we lined up in single file on our course and started to pick up speed to go through the Strait. We were near *Thursday Island*, when suddenly we saw a different cruiser and a flotilla of about seven destroyers and three or four freighters on the other side of the Strait.

As we passed through the Strait, our convoy was being handed over from the protection of the *USS Pensacola* [*and the Pacific Fleet*] to the protection of the *USS Houston* [*and the Asiatic Fleet*]. We were escorted by a different heavy cruiser, five destroyers and two destroyers of the Corvette class (a total of eight fighting ships for our three troop ships). Some protection – Huh! We understood that Admiral Hart (the Asiatic Fleet Commander) was on board the *Houston*.

The *Pensacola* remained behind the Strait and was off to a new assignment. *She reappeared sixteen days later at Pearl Harbor on January 19, 1942.*

Where were we going? Before we went through the Strait, we were told that the convoy had orders to go to Suda Bay, which was on the east end of Java. After we got through the Strait, and orders were changed to go to Darwin. We really did not know definitely where we were going until we arrived someplace. The two destinations would follow the same route. After all the ships were through the Strait, the convoy moved into the following formation:

Figure 30 - Ship Formation, Diary Entry, diary page 65

Sometimes we would change to a single-file formation where the *Bloemfontein*, *Holbrook*, and *Chaumont* are one behind the other with the Cruiser out in front. It would have made a nice picture, but there were no cameras. This new ocean seemed no different from the Pacific Ocean; however, we were having a few swells.

In the ocean we saw snakes, large turtles, a small whale, flying fish, and sharks. Lord knows what was coming next. Most of the men would have like to stop at the Island of Bali where we were told women are scantily dressed. "Well, it would have been well to see as much as possible while we were in the area."

Saturday, 3 Jan 1942
In the Malay language, it is "hari saptoe" pronounced "h'ari sap'tu" or day Saturday. We seem to be terribly mixed up. We were near Thursday Island on Saturday. It seems that all I do is eat, sleep and stand watch. We are still passing island after island, all are surprisingly small.

Lack of Artillery Training
"Since dealing with the National Guard unit on this ship [*131st Field Artillery*], I have become concerned about a few things, and I want to record a few criticisms. I offer this, and it may be a little harsh. I learned accidently that the artillery unit on this ship only received these guns after getting on the ship. To this day, the enlisted men and officers of the outfit know nothing about the guns. I asked one of them why they were not studying the pieces, and he replied that they would learn after they landed, since surely they would have at least a month to learn. How absurd to think that they have had five weeks on the ship and the guns have been on deck. They could have been learning all the time, and it would have been very efficient. I would hate to think that I was in command of one of the batteries and had neglected to do the all important thing of teaching my men how to use the weapons that my life might depend upon. That was the main reason that I do not care to risk my life in the hands of any officer that fails to be ready (PERIOD).[60]

Sunday. 4 Jan 1942
We turned our clocks back 30 minutes last night. Sure was sleepy this morning. The convoy formation today was like this (Figure 32):

We are still zigzagging all the time using different time intervals for turning.

---

[60] PERIOD was printed in all capital letters in the Diary.

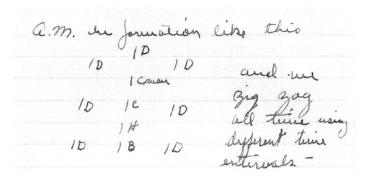

Figure 31 - Single File Ship Formation

I slept all morning and read most of the evening in bed. I tried to snooze a couple of hours before my watch. Due to our zigs and zags, we think it may be Monday night or Tuesday before we get to Darwin, if that's where we are going. About 1 PM, all the convoy stopped in the water for twenty minutes as two destroyers went cutting the water sharply. We did not know why.

We learned today that Manila had fallen to the Japanese.[61] I guess it was good I did not sail sooner or I would have been there.

We all are wondering when we will receive mail from home.

9:30 PM - Like a lot of others on the ship, I have been studying maps. The places we have been on our trip have been an amazing geography lesson – the North Pacific, South Pacific, Suva Bay, Brisbane River, the Coral Sea, the Great Barrier Reef, Torres Strait, Arafura Sea, and soon – the Timor Sea – before getting to Darwin and the Indian Ocean. It is nearly 10 PM so I need to sleep a while before going on watch.

6.4.   Arriving Darwin – 5 Jan 1942

Monday. 5 Jan 1942
We learned today we are definitely going into Darwin. We were ordered to make preparation for disembarkation. I have my things packed and am ready to go. We are expected to arrive about 7 PM, but I doubt the casual officers (to say the least) will get off before tomorrow morning. The ship has been going past quite a few very flat islands.

---

[61] Gen. Douglas MacArthur declared Manila an Open City to the Japanese invading Army to avoid the destruction of the city by war. Japan occupied Manila on 2 Jan 1942. Filipino and American troops continued to fight on the Bataan Peninsula until 8 Apr 1942. Other troops on Corregidor Island did not surrender until 6 May 1942.

The shore seems to have lots of thick brush about four feet tall. The channel is so winding, it is no wonder we need a pilot to take us through. They say Darwin is a hell hole, and we may set up another Headquarters there. That seems to be the only thing the military can do. The military formed another Headquarters for Sydney or Melbourne before we left Brisbane, or at least part of the staff is in both places now. We feel those who are assigned to Headquarters are the lucky ones.

By the news today, we see that Gen. Archibald Wavell (British) is our new Allied Commander. We would rather have had an American.[62]

I hoped I would be able to leave part of my baggage here in Darwin, at least my golf clubs. I hear the courses in Japan are not being used at this time.

About 10 AM, we learned that we are to have things packed and ready to get off the ship. We will stay in Darwin a day and let the troops rest up before we move on. I hoped we would stay longer, but we never have our way here.

A lone British bomber has been flying over this morning which was very comforting to see. I had to put my typewriter back in its case again and in the bottom of my trunk. It might be the last time it sees the portals of life through a port hole.

I must say, the *Bloemfontein* has been a much better cruise than the *Republic* from all points of view. I must have gained five pounds because of the good food and little exercise. My clothes were feeling a little tight.

Tuesday. 6 Jan 1942
The ship anchored about 8 PM last night, and we are still on deck 24 hours later, awaiting instructions. The channel was very crooked coming in, so the ship had quite a bit of maneuvering to get into the Darwin harbor. It took so long that I finally went to sleep.

The Darwin harbor was full of war ships. There must have been at least 40 or 50 ships in or near port. From my cabin I could count at least four heavy cruisers and about fifteen destroyers, as well as 20 to 30 other ships, including a freighter and a troop ship. All ships appear to have just arrived.

The shore line was probably a mile away, but I would say it is hotter than hell. I cannot tell a lot about the scenery; however, there are lots of small bushy trees along the shore. The land is supposed to be sandy and pretty wet, and this is their rainy season. It was

---

[62] Lt. Gen. Archibald Percival Wavell was appointed Commander of ABDACOM.

certainly hot last night. Our ship was blacked out, but the city and surroundings had plenty of lights.

There was one ship [*back in Brisbane*] that had been unloading for 27 days, and they did not know how much longer it would take. No, it was not a large ship. It was a matter of the Australian dock workers. They seem to control everything. They don't seem to know there is a war on. Our commander had been trying to put the Brisbane docks under martial law to get the ship unloaded, but to no avail. Of course if it could be done now in Darwin, it would be much better than waiting till there was an air raid.

I know the bombs will come soon enough, especially because the hospital is being moved here. There are 240 wounded arriving here in Darwin in the next few days, and we have already told Japan that we are moving the hospital here. The wounded will be lucky to get here. The Japs don't fight the kind of war we do. They will strike a hospital. They take very few prisoners. The Filipinos do not bring home prisoners either. Well, you can see I'm thinking about what is coming.

I had two interviews today with colonels on board the *Bloemfontein* about possible assignments after we arrive. The Field Artillery officers will be attached to either 131st Battalion or 26th Brigade Headquarters.[63] I told the officer from the 131st what I thought of his unit, which was not very complimentary. After seeing them operate in the Louisiana maneuvers earlier this year, I was really not very interested in them. Then I told Colonel Searle from the 26th Brigade Headquarters what I had told the other Colonel. He laughed and said "Don't worry, you are coming with me." I care very little for either. It looks to me like we were all a "Shanghai-ed" outfit.[64]

6 PM – We are still sitting at anchor but I feel better as I rested all afternoon. I wished we would do something. It gets tiresome being cooped up without even deck space to walk. The Colonel got an order this evening that we would get off the ship, but before he could finish reading it, the Convoy Commander said we would sail for Java as soon as the convoy was made up. That's the way it has been all the time. We call it "SNAFU",

---

[63] A Brigade is a higher echelon of command in the Field Artillery above a Battalion. Normally a Brigade has several Battalions. The 26th Brigade was most likely intended to take command in the Philippines of multiple Field Artillery Battalions that would have been staffed by Filipino soldiers, in addition to the 131st Field Artillery.

[64] A "Shanghai" outfit is a crew of soldiers who have been "abducted" or "kidnapped" against their will and pressed into involuntary military service. The expression takes root from European sailors in the 18th century who were abducted to serve against their will on sailing ships that were bound for Shanghai.

(Situation Normal, All-F***ed Up). It is about an hour till tea (we eat at 7 PM) and I have to wash my hands and dress.

It rained most of the evening. We were told Darwin gets 60 inches of rain per year.

I would enjoy seeing my family for a while, at least I hope they were doing fine and have received my cables and letters. I know of at least one letter they have not received as yet. That letter should arrive about February 1 with luck - Air Mail Special Delivery.

6.5.   Gen. Brett Flies to Darwin – 7 Jan 1942

<u>Wednesday, 7 Jan 1942</u>
General George H. Brett, Deputy Commander of ABADCOM, flew over from Java to Darwin this morning and is having a conference of some kind. He is probably trying to decide what to do with us. We do not know what will develop.

This morning at 10 AM all but four casual officers left the ship and went ashore.[65] The four who remained onboard include one captain, two lieutenants, and me. It is now rumored we might go to Singapore, but I still think we will go to Java. I bid the other casual officers Bon Voyage and even opened a fifth of Scotch for those that wanted one farewell drink. Of course as it is so hot, I was glad to get rid of some scotch. I still have about half of the fifth I opened, and I am not going to drink it.

Darwin was expecting 241 wounded soldiers to arrive in a couple of days. All doctors, except for one, were taken ashore. I have become acquainted with most of the officers who remain onboard. I hope we will enjoy the rest of the cruise.

We were told we could leave excess baggage on the ship and it would eventually get back to the States. I thought I would send my golf clubs, trunks, and another letter by an officer on the ship. I intend to include this diary and start another.

I hope some of my letters will reach my darling wife. It will give her some information even though I have not had space to describe all my experiences in detail. I thought I can write a book now and could think of several movies to make. In my trunk are several pieces of silver made in Java, as well as a string of beads and the sailor with the name of

---

[65] When the *Holbrook* arrived in Darwin, its troops and cargo were unloaded. The U. S. Army set up a headquarters in Darwin with these troops. Also in Darwin was established a headquarters for the Far East Air Force. Darwin became Australia's Supply Base No. 1 to support the Australian Northwest Territory and the Dutch East Indies.

this ship on his hat. One of the Javanese boys tried to sell me a dagger last night – he wanted 30 pounds, which is close to $100. Well, the dagger was most horrible to look at and when he told me it had poison on the end, I knew I did not want it. In these islands, they fight more with knives than with guns, and there are thousands of islands.

After dinner I got my typewriter out again and started writing another letter. I think of writing letters a lot, but we never know when we can mail a letter. There is always uncertainty whether a letter will ever get home, which makes writing letters hard. I want to know about a lot of things that are happening at home. How are my Johnnie and Cile, Mother and Dad doing? I hope they are not worrying about me.

So far, I have not seen an enemy, but we are now well within Japanese bomber range. If we don't get out of this harbor soon with these 50 ships, I'm afraid the ships will attract the enemy bombers.

5:30 PM - Our ship is still sitting in the harbor. We have no news of when we will sail. I am guessing we might sail in time to get through the mine fields before dark, unless the moon is bright.

6.6.   General Brett's Cable to Washington

General Brett cabled the War Department[66] in Washington, D.C. that:

- *Darwin would be made into a large advanced airdrome suitable for one heavy bombardment group, pursuit planes for local defense, and a long-range reconnaissance squadron. Darwin had problems of little local labor and no railroad connection. Supplies had to come by ship or air which made it unsuitable for a major maintenance base. There was an urgent need for anti-aircraft weapons and ammunition.*
- *Townsville was recommended as the site for a large air maintenance, repair, supply, and erection of aircraft, but Townsville had a shallow harbor that was unsuitable for supply.*
- *Brisbane had two airdromes, one of which was already being used to erect the dive bombers and pursuit planes. Brisbane would become the transshipment point for supplies to Townsville and Darwin.*
- *Brett urgently requested personnel and equipment for air mobile depots, engineers, anti-aircraft weapons, aircraft warning and radio detection equipment with a 300-mile radius.*
- *Brett recommended a large stable American presence in Australia be established before any tactical operations are undertaken.*

---

[66] USAFIA, OCMH USASOS History, p 86, Enclosure 12a

6.7.   Ordered to Java - Leaving Darwin – 8 Jan 1942

<u>Wednesday, 7 Jan 1942.</u>

I now know I will command *Headquarters Battery of the 26th Field Artillery Brigade*. I have been selected to be assigned to that organization along with the three other officers still on board the *Bloemfontein*. The remaining casual officer's got off the ship at 10 AM this morning in Darwin. The officers that stayed in Darwin will probably sail for Java later. I closed my diary note and wrote a letter to my wife that I hope can be mailed. This was letter #6.

[Capt. Day numbered all letters home in chronological order as they were mailed so that Cile would know if there were missing letters. Each letter also carried a single "code" letter. When the "code" letters were arranged in the order of the numbered letters, the letters spelled the geographic location of Capt. Day.]

Letter Home #6 – "Two months of this [*ocean voyage*] is sure getting tiresome and I am very anxious to get somewhere fast. The last orders, if they have not been changed, are that we sail today for the east end of Java, called Suda Bay. From there we may go on to Batavia, Java."

The following is a direct quotation from the diary:

"*JUST FOR FUTURE REFERENCE:* When we left Brisbane for Darwin in December 1941 at Torres Strait, we were met by about seven destroyers and three cruisers. We were at the time headed for the Philippine Islands, as our previous orders stated. When we reached Darwin, a number of cables went back and forth with Headquarters for several days. The delay was due to indecision on whether our convoy should continue to try to reach the Philippines or go to Java instead. Finally it was decided that the convoy should go to Java. The Lord was with us sure as we probably would never have reached the Philippine Islands. I cannot find out who "exactly" was responsible for that decision."

Thursday, 8 Jan 1942

The ship remained at the dock another night. As viewed from the ship, the town of Darwin appeared to be evacuated. Some stores are boarded up, as if they were expecting to be bombed.

6:45 AM - Our ship started to move. We were following five destroyers, one corvette and the *Boise*[67] *(a 10,000-ton Light Cruiser CL-47)*. The *Bloemfontein* pulled in line followed by the *USS Houston*. Our ship was the only ship in the bunch that was not a fighter of some kind. It seemed funny to have so much protection for our one ship – which was OK by me. After a few hours at sea, we were moving fast, I guess as fast as the ship would go. The sea had pretty good swells, but our speed made the ride quite smooth. We saw one water spout and passed through a good rain storm. The farmers would say "crops should be good this fall."

The *Bloemfontein* turned the showers on for a sort time so we could take a bath, something more than a wash basin sponge bath. Today was the last day we can get laundry done.

Australia sure appears as a big empty country. We can look from our port holes at the shore, but there is nothing to see but empty land. There is less there than any place I know.

2 PM – We are all back on watch duty. I was on the bridge from 4 to 8 AM last night. The bridge is where the ships officers are while running the ship. We have a General Quarters drill twice daily, once at daylight and once before dark (by order of the Commanding Officer of *Boise*). The sea is very smooth in the late afternoon. There are good swells, but the top surface is not broken.

We are told we will be in Java in three days – unless we run into an enemy.

> 9:30 PM I am writing a lot for my diary, but I figured you will get to read the diary before I get home. I am trying to add all I can as I know you will enjoy reading it.

I have been playing bridge since supper and won a slam. Unfortunately, we were not playing for money. Another officer had to wake me in the morning for my 4 AM watch. I read another book this evening. Can you imagine me reading so much?

---

[67] The *Boise (CA47) wa*s a US Navy Light Cruiser that was later damaged by an uncharted pinnacle at Sape Strait, NEI when it struck ground 21 Jan 1942 off Java.

Friday. 9 Jan 1942

On my bridge watch from 4 to 8AM this morning, it rained so darn hard we couldn't see the ship 400 yards ahead of us. I have written several letters I hope to mail. I had some candy in my trunk that I doubt I will have room to take with me when we arrive.

5 PM – I have been playing checkers all evening. The sea remains as smooth as glass on top, and we are pushing through as fast as we can. We are likely to be in Suda Bay[68] Sunday morning or perhaps some time during that day as we have to dodge the mine field. There has to be plenty of light to follow the channels. The ship had quite a toss today, bobbing front to rear (bow to stern).

The news we receive is very scant. We know barely that the war is going on, but we know we will be sure before we arrived at Suda Bay. The Japs were bombing islands in the East Indies every day.

The two Allied commanders, Gen. Archibald Wavell and Vice-Admiral Thomas Hart, are both in the East Indies, probably in Java too.

Many times I find I am thinking of my son, John, and sweet wife. Guess it's natural, but I try to keep my mind occupied as best I can to avoid thinking about my family too much. You know, love is a funny thing. It's like everything else, I guess. You never know how [much] you miss it till you can't get it. Guess I had better stop – someone will think I'm homesick.

By the way, keep the liquor that is in the trunk [that I am returning] and we will celebrate when I get home.

Some bunch of firsts we have had on this trip – first troops to cross the Pacific after the War began, first initiated for crossing the Equator, first to arrive in Australia, etc. Well, I can't enumerate them all again as it would take too much paper. Hope you find this diary OK, because I will sure have it hid in the trunk. If you look good, as I told you, you will reap the joy of reading a good book. Love for the day.

---

[68] The diary refers to *Suda Bay*, which has been interpreted as *Soerabaja Bay*, but that is not on modern maps.

6.8.   Passing Islands of Sawu, Sumba, Lombok, and Bali

<u>Saturday, 10 Jan 1942</u>

I saw the islands of Sawu and Sumba from a distance of about 50 miles this morning. We went south of the islands. Sumba was on the south of the West Indies. One of our cruis-

ers, *USS Houston*, and a couple of cans (destroyers) left us at 2 AM – where they went we did not know, but perhaps they were hunting rats. We expected to be among a bunch of islands about 6 PM and into a harbor about 9 AM Sunday.

I have not been feeling too well the last couple of days. I think I needed a good round of medicine, which I will take the first chance I get after we leave the boat. Tomorrow I plan to go to bed and rest as much as possible.

Figure 32 - Route from Darwin to Surabaya

5 PM - Our ship passed between the two islands of Lombok and Bali. The islands were about 10 miles distant. The 12,000-foot mountain-range of Java is easily visible.

6:15 PM - We turned west and are just north and east of Bali, about 10 miles offshore. Looking out the port hole, I see a fleet of sharks and I do mean a fleet, perhaps a hundred, swimming near the surface. It makes one think it would be better to go down with a ship, rather than go swimming. However, if necessary, I'll give swimming a chance. If you can find an atlas, we are going into the east end of Java. That is where I will be stationed. I have to close my trunk and leave it on the ship in the morning when I get off. I hope I will not need the things I am sending back home. There are some things you (Cile) may wonder why I did not keep, but I think I have too many things.

11 PM – "We just received a radio message that a Norwegian boat is being chased by a sub in our vicinity. Our men are on deck sleeping in clothes in case we have to abandon ship. Guess I'll sleep a lot tonight – Ha-Ha – It is so dark outside I doubt any one could see us, but subs could pick us up by sound. Hopefully our cruiser and three destroyers will pick up the Japs first.

In the event I do not get to write in the diary tomorrow and my wife receives this diary, she will know I arrived safely in Java. I kept the diary out to try to add a last word in the morning. Must take a shower now and sleep till my 4 AM watch. Love.

P.S. **If anyone wants to know, I am keeping this diary for my wife and son, mother and father and all other loved ones I know. There is nothing I could write at this time that could express all of my feelings.**

I am putting the whole diary in my footlocker, as I cannot cut the sheets out without ruining the book. I am leaving two letters with the ship's crew to be mailed in the States. I guess that is it for tonight. With a big hug -- John

6.9.   Arrival Soerabaja (Surabaya)[69] Java – 11 Jan 1941

Sunday, 11 Jan 1942

I had a pleasant night last night. This morning the Bay is filled with literally hundreds of native sail and fishing boats. We plan to arrive about noon depending on how long it takes to get through the mine fields. The more I think about it, the more I do not know what to do about sending my trunk home.

We spotted a Japanese submarine at a position 25 miles north of us, and it dived in our direction. Had the sub maintained its same direction, we would have run into it 16 miles from the channel, so we were concerned. In addition, a small Dutch boat had been shelled for three hours by some vessel about 20 miles south of us and was on fire. I suppose the Dutch boat was too small for the Japanese to justify the use of a torpedo.

1:50 PM - We should dock soon. About the middle of the morning we picked up several more destroyers, so we have quite a bunch of ships. We were mostly through the mine field when we picked up our boat pilot to guide us into Suda Bay. The men are getting their equipment ready to get off. As yet, we have no orders as to what we will do or where we will go. I have withheld closing the diary for as long as possible.

---

[69] In 1942 National Geographic maps spelled the port name *Soerabaja*, which is the old Dutch spelling. The U. S. Army in 1942 spelled the name *Soerabaya*. In 1976, Indonesia adopted new spelling *Surabaya*. All three are pronounced the same. This book has adopted the old Dutch spelling of *Soerabaja* to be consistent with the period of the diary. Likewise, Tjilatjap is used instead of Cilachap.

2:45 PM - We are now heading about south. Java is close on our right and Madura Island is close on our left. Along the coast we can see lots of small villages, "Sampans," and native sail boats. It would take a very good map to get the names of all these islands. From the looks of the coast, I think this place looks a lot better than Darwin. I was kind a glad I got to come here instead of being assigned to stay in Australia. Soerabaja is also a naval base. The trees look very thick – more like a jungle. They say there is some jungle in the interior. In the bay, there are a few larger "junks," the ocean going native boats.

All the native Javanese crew members on board the *Bloemfontein* are so excited and glad to get home safely. They say they never make more than one voyage at a time and always stay at home till they spend all their money. Only on very few occasions would a ship owner allow the crew to make only one trip – the ship owners want their crews for a longer period, but after one trip, these boys are rich – when they get home they hire "coolies" to do their work. On the ship they make $14 per month, but get an additional $10 per month hazard pay because of the War. We are now in the harbor and preparing to dock. At least 50 or so ships are in the harbor from all kinds of nations. I must get ready to get off soon, so will close this entry. -- Love

6.10.   The End of Diary Volume I – 11 Jan 1942

6.11.   Japanese Naval Blockade of the Philippines

In Brisbane, the Pensacola Convoy cargo was redistributed among the convoy ships. The crated aircraft were off-loaded from the USAT Meigs to be assembled in Australia, in preparation for being flown to the Philippines. Troops were transferred from the USS Republic to the TMSV Bloemfontein and the USAT Holbrook. The USS Republic returned to the U.S. The unloading and loading of cargo took longer than expected due to a labor dispute with the Australian longshoremen.

On 28 Dec 1941, the USS Pensacola departed Brisbane with the Holbrook and the Chaumont toward Torres Strait. At the time of departure from Brisbane, the convoy destination was still the Philippines. Two days later on 30 Dec 1941, the Dutch Bloemfontein sailed with the destination Soerabaja. On 1 Jan 1942, the Navy changed the destination for the convoy to Darwin.

After passing through the Torres Strait on 3 Jan 1942, escort duty for the convoy passed from the Pacific Fleet (USS Pensacola) to the Asiatic Fleet (USS Houston) with a destination of Darwin. The Houston Convoy consisted of eleven ships, including the USS Houston (a heavy cruiser), seven destroyers, and three troop ships (Bloemfontein, Holbrook and Chaumont). The Houston would later escort only the Bloemfontein to Soerabaja in the Netherlands East Indies (NEI).

The resupply of the Philippines became increasingly difficult with each passing day. As the Japanese Imperial Navy moved south of the Philippines, MacArthur expressed his urgent concerns to Gen. Marshall in Washington for an immediate dispatch of a properly escorted resupply convoy.[70]

Admiral Hart doubted the likelihood of a resupply convoy ever reaching the Philippines. He had withdrawn all his surface ships out of the Philippines to the south. Only submarines were able to reach Corregidor. Submarines were used to deliver medical supplies and ammunition, and to evacuate critical military personnel, especially the intelligence officers and code specialists who had successfully broken the Japanese diplomatic and Imperial Navy codes. All the lithographic plates for maps of the Philippines were evacuated by submarine first to Java and then to Australia.

The importance of air power cannot be overstated in the Pacific conflict. Naval cannon fire and coastal artillery were being replaced by precision dive bombers. Naval blockades of shipping routes could be implemented by land-based aircraft operated from airdromes strategically located near critical waterways.[71] The role of aircraft raised the importance of aircraft carriers in conflicts at sea, at seaports, or at beach landings since carriers effectively moved the airstrip to the targets.

There were three shipping routes from the south to the Philippines: (1) up the Molucca Channel between Celebes and Amboina, (2) up the Makassar Strait between Celebes and Borneo, and (3) around the eastern tip of New Guinea across the Bismarck Sea. The airdrome at Kendari, Celebes and the airdrome on Amboina controlled the Molucca Channel. Kota Balikpapan, Borneo controlled the Makassar Strait. Rabaul and Kavieng on New Ireland controlled the Bismarck Sea. All three channels were under Japanese control by 24 Jan 1942, making resupply virtually impossible.

In a desperation move to penetrate the Japanese blockade and resupply the Philippines, four ships were subsequently outfitted and sailed for the Philippines. The Don Isidro, a small fast interisland passenger liner, sailed on 27 Jan 1942 for the Philippines with a cargo of food and ammunition and a volunteer Army ordinance detachment. The ship was attack by Japanese aircraft for two successive days, such that the Master turned the heavily damaged ship back and beached it on Bathurst Island, north of Darwin. The ship was a total loss with one fatality and many wounded.

---

[70] Rogers, Paul. *MacArthur and Sutherland: The Good Years*, Ibid.

[71] Interestingly, the strategy followed by the Japanese of leapfrogging from one strategic air base to another within range of fighter air cover was the precise strategy adopted by MacArthur in 1943 when the U.S. recaptured the South West Pacific.

The Coast Farmer, a member of the trans-pacific Pensacola Convoy, was one of only three ships to successful penetrate the Japanese blockade. The Coast Farmer sailed on 10 Feb 1942, reaching Mindanao (PI) by sailing south from Brisbane around Australia to Fremantle, then north to Java and on to Mindanao.[72] Subsequently, the vessels Anhui and Dona Nati were loaded and sailed successfully to Cebu on the Island of Cebu. The three ships reached their destination and returned safely, however, these supplies only reached intermediate destinations and never reached Bataan or Corregidor.

Two other supply ships, the Hanyang and Yochow, were loaded in Perth, sailed for the Philippines, but returned after being attack. Both ships unloaded in Darwin after the Japanese attack of 19 Feb 1942.[73]

---

[72] http://www.cnrs-scrn.org/northern_mariner/vol18/tnm_18_3-4_163-172.pdf
[73] OCMH, History of USASOS p 93-94.

7.   JAPANESE CONQUEST OF NEI[74]

7.1.   Colonial History of the Netherlands East Indies (NEI)

The Netherlands East Indies Company, a private chartered stock company, was established in 1602 and by 1619 had established its trading center for Asia in the city of Batavia, Java. The Dutch Company had a monopoly on the Moluccan spice trade for almost 200 years bringing enormous wealth to Holland merchants while paying a 20 percent dividend to its stockholders every year for 200 years. Coffee was introduced into Java by Dutch traders in 1688. With a climate well suited for growing coffee, large coffee plantations flourished.

The Netherlands East Indies Company ships controlled about 80% of all Asian trade (including Japan) until 1796 when the company went bankrupt due to internal corruption. At that time, the company forfeited its holdings of virtually all the Indonesian archipelago to the Dutch government – including Java, Borneo, Celebes, Sumatra, and half of New Guinea. The Dutch government created a colonial empire called the Netherlands East Indies (NEI) that flourished with the trade of spices, coffee, tea, oil, and rubber. The Dutch prevailed over the territory for almost 330 years until the Second World War.

Soerabaja (Surabaya) was the principal seaport and a major trading center in Eastern Java, located on Suda Bay. In 1930, Soerabaja had a population of 366,000 while the island of Java had 41 million people. At that time, the U.S. population was 123 million and the Australian population was 6 million.

7.2.   Japan Accelerates NEI Invasion Timetable – 1 Jan 1942

Oil and rubber remained Japan's primary reasons for war. The rapid success of the Japanese Army in the December offensive in the Philippines and Malaya encouraged the Japanese High Command to accelerate by one month their plans for the conquest of the oil fields of Borneo, Java, and Netherlands East Indies (NEI).

The successful invasion in the Lingayen Gulf in northern Luzon on 22 Dec 1941 by the Japanese 48th Infantry Division pushed the American and Filipino Armies back to the Bataan Peninsula in a matter of weeks. The 48th Infantry was considered the best battle-hardened division in the Japanese Army and was selected to be the Point for the Java offensive in Java. The 48th Infantry was replaced in the battle lines of Bataan on 15 Jan 1942 by the less experienced 56th Infantry Divi-

---

[74] Americans often refer to the Dutch East Indies (DEI) while the Dutch call the region Netherlands East Indies (NEI).

sion, in order that the 48th could be rested and transported down the Makassar Strait in preparation for the invasion of Java, which was targeted for 24 Feb 1942.

The Japanese strategy for the conquest of Java was divided into three phases. The first phase was to control the ocean supply routes to Java. The second phase was to control the flanking islands of Sumatra and Bali. Finally, the third phase was to strike the heart of Java.

Phase I, the control of the ocean routes, began January 9 with the invasion of Celebes. Two days later, northern Borneo was invaded. On January 23, the Japanese invaded Rabaul, New Britain Island (modern Papua New Guinea) which controlled the Bismarck Sea. By January 24, Kendari [Celebes] had fallen, which gave the Japanese airbases within range of East Java, as well as control of the Molucca Sea.

Phase I – Events for the Japanese Conquest of Java Supply Routes

Jan 9   – Celebes invasion
Jan 11 – Menado, Celebes, invasion
Jan 11 – Northern Borneo, invasion
Jan 15 – Bataan – Japan replaces 48th Div. with 56th Div. in Bataan, 48th sent on to Jolo Island & Borneo to prepare for Java invasion
Jan 15 – Wavell takes command of ABDACOM and moved his Headquarters to Bandung, Java
Jan 23 – Rabaul, New Britain Islands, invasion
Jan 20-23 – Bismarck Sea and New Guinea invasion supported by Japanese carrier attack
Jan 23 – Balikpapan, Eastern Borneo won
Jan 24 – Kendari Airfield and Molucca Sea won - key to bombing Eastern Java

Phase II – Events Related to the Conquest of the Java Flanks

Feb 4   – Makassar straits naval battle
Feb 9   – Makassar, Celebes, NEI fall
Feb 14–Mar 28 – Conquest of Sumatra, NEI
Feb 19 – Bali, NEI invasion – Badung Strait Battle
Feb 20 – Dili, Timor and Kupang, Timor fall
Feb 24 – Timor, NEI invaded
Feb 24-25 – Amboina carrier attack

Phase III – Events Striking the Heart of Java

Feb 25 – Java invasion of Java
Feb 27–Mar 1 – Battle of Java Sea – Allies lose Exeter, two cruisers, and five destroyers
Feb 28 – Battle of Sunda Strait – USS Houston & HMAS Perth lost
Mar 9   – NEI Surrendered to Japan

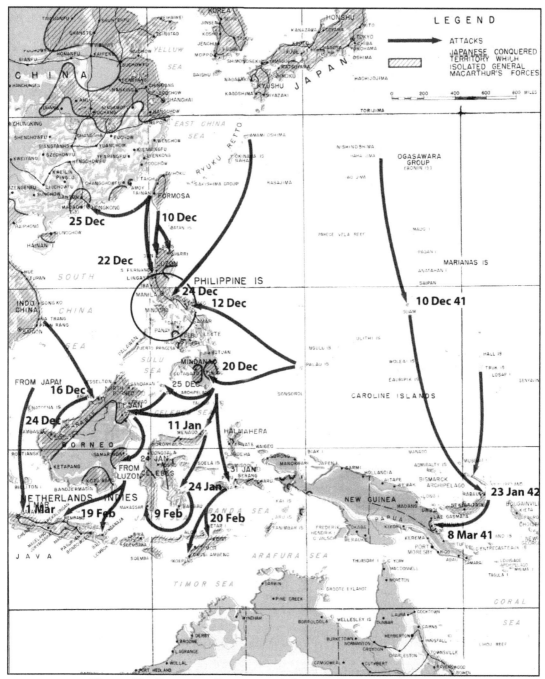

Figure 33 – Japanese Conquest of the Dutch East Indies
Japan Conquest Time Line – 10 Dec 41 to 8 Mar 42

8. FIELD ARTILLERY ARRIVES AT CAMP SINGOSARI – 11 Jan 42

<u>Sunday, 11 Jan 1942</u>

The *Bloemfontein* docked in Soerabaja without delay. A path appeared in the crowded harbor of boats for our ship to pass to the dock. Orders awaited us to disembark at once and load into a waiting local train which carried us to Camp Singosari, about 80 km south from Soerabaja near the Dutch airfield, Singosari, and close to Malang, Java. Our train left Soerabaja about 6:20 PM.

The Javanese had small steam locomotives that were about one-third the size of American trains. They were powered by an "open-hearth" wood-fired steam engine that made a "putty-putt" sound as they moved down the tracks. They reminded me of a scaled-down 19th century European locomotive. Their trains were used for both public transportation and freight hauling – normally coffee and agricultural produce from the plantations to the ports. There was such a small clearance between the train and vegetation next to the tracks that a passenger had the illusion that the train was moving faster than it really was.

Figure 34 – Java Map, Java Assignment: National Geographic, January 1942

We were supposed to arrive in Malang about 8:30 PM but actually did not arrive until about 11 PM. The train and the town were completely blacked out, but we found our way off the train and into trucks for the ride to Camp Singosari. Singosari was about 6 miles north of Malang and would be our home in Java. I had a sandwich and a cup of hot tea for supper and was very glad to get that.

Malang was a city of about 200,000 people, including about 9,000 Dutch whites. Sights along the way revealed a deplorable way of life, as we saw it. There was no hygiene as people defecated everywhere along the road. One cannot drink the water. All food had to be boiled. There were lots of "coolies," rickshaws, and thousands of bicycles - it was a novel world to a bunch of Texans.

11 Jan 1942 – Japanese invaded Dutch Celebes and Dutch Northern Borneo.

Monday, 12 January 1942
I slept like a log last night and am learning to eat anything.

I saw our U.S. Far East Air Force this morning at the airfield for the first time. We have a very small Air Force – much less than anyone knows, in fact, not over 20 bombers in all.[75] I don't know how much the Dutch have in addition. There are a few planes with holes in them from action yesterday. The pilots reported that they sunk two battlewagons yesterday.

I am now assigned to Headquarters Battery, 26th Field Artillery Brigade. I understand I will take command as soon as a dry run inspection can be made. I do not know what I will do in the meantime. It will be a week or so before the ship is unloaded and our equipment is brought out here. I hope to find the rest of my stuff soon.

I cabled Lucille 28 words including my address, "U.S. Forces in Java." The cable cost 19.60 Guilders.[76]

8.1.   Sociëteit Concordia Malang – 13 Jan 1942

Tuesday, 13 Jan 1942
We went into Malang about 4 PM, and it started raining almost immediately. I bought a native rain umbrella, a tropical sun hat, and a new diary. I made my first entry in the new diary by filling in a day or so earlier that I had skipped. I was in town to change money for the entire Battery. We wanted all our Australian money changed from Australian "Pounds" to Dutch "Guilders" – one Australian pound is worth 5.80 Guilder [or US$3.07 per Australian Pound]. I have 3,694.00 Guilders.

9PM – I am sitting in the Sociëteit Concordia Malang, a social club for members of the European community. This Club is a gathering point where locals meet, have a drink, play cards, and dance. There is a Sociëteit in all the major cities in the Dutch Indies. They

---

[75] While the USAFEAF had 20 bombers, the Japanese force that attacked Pearl Harbor had over 400 bombers.

[76] One Guilder (1942) = US$0.53. The cable cost was equal to US$10.39, which was roughly two-days pay for a captain.

welcome American Officers. The Club has parties to celebrate all Dutch holidays, for example, 5 Dec which is Saint Nicolas Day in Holland.

I had just come out of a picture show featuring Jeannette McDonald and Nelson Eddy. The show had a Dutch sound track and Japanese subtitles. I understood nothing. The picture show cost – f1.25 (1 ¼ Guilder). We have to wait until 10:45 PM to catch the bus back to the Camp, which is about 10 km out of town.
(6 1/3 miles).

Figure 35 - Sociëteit Concordia Malang - circa 1935

There are quite a lot of U.S. and English goods available in the shops, but I find things are very expensive. The streets are crowded with lots of natives, and I mean lots of them. The town is blacked out at night, and it is really dark. We have to feel our way around. Very few people understand English so we have to do the best we can with a lot of sign language.

Figure 36 - Sociëteit Concordia Malang - circa 1935

The Air Force received three more bombers yesterday – which seems like very few to fight the Japs. The few airplanes are accounting well for themselves however, when they are up in the air.

Yesterday they sank one battleship and one cruiser on a single flight.
– Love for the day

Wednesday, 14 Jan 1942

Yesterday when I went to town to get a lot of money changed, I got too much silver in exchange. I had to go back today to get more paper notes. The banks only stay open from 9 to 11 AM, which is what I call real "banking hours." I bet our banks at home do not know about that. I bought Cile a lovely bracelet. They had a jade necklace on display, but I could not afford it now, as we have no idea when we will be paid again. I bought a hand-carved head for two Guilders. It would have cost a pretty penny in the U.S. I ran short of food for two meals, so I had bread and coffee for breakfast. I obtained a cot and a mosquito net, so I can sleep a lot better. The flies are terrible. My Pith Helmet is good.

Thursday, 15 Jan 1942

1:30 PM - Today the Cable Office sent me 0.56 Guilder refund as they said I overpaid on my cable. A few others called their wives on the short-wave phone and learned that their wives have not received any cards or letters mailed by us from anywhere, even Honolulu. I feel sure Lucille received the last cable I sent, and if I fail to get a cable soon, I will call her.

It rains almost every day, usually in the evening. We are still unloading equipment. I should be able to get at least a pistol soon. I want to buy a camera of some kind but cannot make up my mind what kind to buy. I am tempted to get a movie, but they are expensive. I saw some furniture in a shop I would like to buy, but cannot afford it either.

Figure 37 - Capt. John F. Day Jr. - Java, 1942
Mustache started after war declared.

We hear very little news, but I think we are likely to stay in this vicinity for some time. Our pictures were taken for identification cards. I wonder how I look with the mustache I started after the Pearl Harbor attack. All the trunks from the *Bloemfontein* that were supposed to have been shipped back to the States have been brought out here. So I now have mine and am able to put all the things I bought in my trunk. I sent out all the laundry I can find.

Friday, 16 Jan 1942
The local newspaper has started printing a column in English so we will have some reason to buy the paper. As usual, rain came again this evening. It continues to rain every evening.

I saw the house where I have been assigned. I am sharing a lovely green and brown stucco house with a tile roof – 6 rooms – toilet, bath and urinal[77]. The toilet has only a commode and a hydrant with a bottle to flush. There is no toilet paper. They do not use paper in the islands because they think it is not sanitary and may carry any number of diseases. We have lots of fun about it. One of the officer's wives had a baby in the States yesterday.

One of my roommates has a radio. We all listen to the Dutch programs. The music sounded like what we would hear in a jungle picture with elephants shrieking. The program included street scenes in China.

8.2.   Taking Command of Hdq. Battery 26th FA Brigade – 17 Jan 1942

Saturday, 17 Jan 1942
Today I took command of Headquarters Battery 26th Field Artillery Brigade. This is going to be a job of organization, as the other officers told me of some discipline difficulties in the Battery.

I went to town at 4 PM as I had made a reservation for a short-wave telephone call to my wife tonight. Thank God. It will be swell hearing her voice and Johnnie's voice again.

As the air corps was so short of men, we are sending men over daily to help load bombs, fill machine gun belts and do maintenance work on the airplanes. We just had a few B-17E's come in and they have twin 50's in the tail. The earlier B-17's had a blind spot in the tail. First day a new one went out, it knocked down thirteen Japanese Zero fighters. The Japs had been riding the blind spot of the tail, but they caught hell this time. One of our subs came in with 9 subs painted on her. One man in my Battery was on the *Liberty*, which was torpedoed recently.

Singosari airbase was the home of the 19th Bombardment Group. The landing strip for Singosari airbase was two grass strips with lengths of 1000 and 2000 meters.

---

[77] The urinal was probably a bidet, which Capt. Day had never seen in Texas.

8.3.   Lt. Gen. Wavell Inspection – 18 Jan 1942

<u>Sunday, 18 Jan 1942</u>
My Battery was inspected by Lt. Gen. Archibald P. Wavell[78] this evening. The old gentleman looks just like his pictures. I'm sure he is a great man, just what you want to see in a General. He was accompanied by Maj. Gen. Gustav A. Ilgen, the 3rd KNIL Infantry Division Commander from the Soerabaja Garrison.[79]

I wear my gun at all times. The town is very dark and guards only yell "Halt" one time before shooting. Most of us are very careful.

Last night I talked to my darling wife for the first time since leaving San Francisco. This was a short-wave radio telephone. The reception was terrible. I could barely tell it was Cile. I never heard an answer to any of my questions. I will try again. It was still swell just to imagine that I knew all was well. I was furious about the quality and went back to see if they will let me speak again.

2:30 PM - Good luck favored me and they told me I can talk to Cile again tonight without charge. I had to do some fast talking. Well, I hope reception is good tonight and I can really talk at least to tell her I love her.

8.4.   Phone Call Home – 19 Jan 1942

<u>Monday, 19 Jan 1942</u>
Dearest Darling wife – I love you. Talked last night to you and I was thrilled to hear your voice. Of course the time seemed to fly as we did talk about 25 minutes. It was certainly worth the money. I'm at a loss to understand why the $135 was not cabled to you from Brisbane. I air mailed a letter to you yesterday including my picture. I later found out we had orders which just arrived from Washington, that say we could only send airmail using U.S. stamps, not foreign postage, but of course we have no U.S. stamps. My wife can air mail to me. I have drawn only $200 since I left San Francisco and cabled $135 to my wife. At the end of this month, I should have $351.20 in pay coming, not counting my allotment to my wife. I will probably draw a hundred dollars.

I have to censor my own letters from now on, so will have to be careful.

---

[78] Lt. Gen. Sir Archibald Percival Wavell, Supreme Commander for ABDACOM, moved his Headquarters from Singapore to Lembang near Bandoeng, Java on January 18, 1942, this date.
[79] KNIL (Koninklijk Nederlandsch Indisch Leger) is the Royal Netherlands East Indies Army.

My housemates and I hired a Javanese houseboy to clean our house. It cost each of us about f1.30 (1.30 Guilders) or about 6 cents per month. So cheap! The culture in Java is such that it is a bad idea to do any work that the natives are supposed to do. It is frowned upon, and just not done. It looks like one is supposed to leave all maintenance and cleaning chores to them. We had to teach the native who cleaned our rooms that it is "bad" to drop his tools on the sidewalk – it looks bad and is not good for the tools.

I fixed up my room a bit. The only decoration is a picture of Lucille and Johnnie.

Tuesday, 20 Jan 1942
Everyone was vaccinated for cholera, typhus and dysentery today. We had a practice air raid alarm.

I wrote my darling another letter. Wonder what she and my boy are doing?

I made a few changes in the Battery today. I went to town a while shopping for a movie camera. They wanted 230 guilders and I didn't want to invest that much.

Six of our bombers sunk a large transport and one of them shot down five Zeros. The rear gunner was shot through the knees with tracer bullets, which made a very ugly wound.

It is now 9 PM and the mosquitoes are trying to eat me like *** so will say good night, get under the net, and give them a run for their money.

Wednesday, 21 Jan 1942
As yet, we have not been able to do any training, as we have so many work details to send out daily. I have no men left in the Battery for drill. In fact I had no one for calisthenics this morning.

I went to town 1:15 PM and carried some laundry.

About seven of us go to a Language School to learn to speak Malay. We attend for one hour most mornings. A couple of Malay businessmen are contributing their time to teach us, so it will cost us nothing. Here Malay is a more common language than Dutch.

After class, I went down in Chinatown and bought a few items. Mostly I wanted to see the place. However, if you visit, you have to also smell it. It has a distinctive odor, so after I returned I put mothballs in my trunk to kill the odor. I hope to ship the trunk soon.

I found a Chinese tailor where I put in an order for a "custom made" uniform - a new shirt, and pants in British or Hong Kong khaki. I must have another light-weight uniform.

   Good night my son and sweet.

Thursday, 22 Jan 1942
Part of my laundry was finally delivered today, so I will have clean clothes tomorrow. They did not put any starch in the clothes, so these uniforms will not be looking good after about 30 minutes.

I heard that we can ship the trunks home in the next few days, so I went down and made more purchases. There were a number of things I wanted to pick up and have shipped home in the trunk. Some are afraid the trunks will be opened for inspection. I was debating on whether to send the trunk or not. Just did not know what to do. I borrowed 10 Guilders from Capt. Parker[80] thinking I would need it if I buy a camera. We still do not know when we will be paid. I sure want a movie camera to get some of these pictures.

8.5.   Buying a Camera – 23 Jan 1942

Friday, 23 Jan 1942
I took the men out to the rifle range today. Gosh, only nine men can fire at one time on the rifle range and only one man on the pistol range. We have had only half a day so far, but we will return next Tuesday.

I seem to go to town every day with my laundry and shopping. I had to try on my new pants and shirts the tailor was making for me. There is always something new to see. We saw another picture show last night, the second one since arriving here. It was an old picture but very good.

I made a complete inventory of the contents of my wardrobe trunk. Do you suppose I will keep it up? I have a slug of bamboo to put in, but there is no room.

The Malay Language School continues. We attend as often as we can. It is a challenge to learn Malay. *Malam yang baik* (Good-night) or *selamat malam*.

---

[80] Capt. William "Ike" Parker, USA, from Alabama, later POW with 131st.

8PM - I returned from town, where I bought a movie camera. I paid 50 Guilders for the movie camera and 10 Guilders for two rolls of unexposed film. I just could not resist buying the camera. It is a Keystone, but I do not know how good it was.

Saturday, 24 Jan 1942
Capt. Bowers has just come over and told me that the S1, S2, and S3 Sections are moving to another place tomorrow about 450 miles distant [Lembang]. Most of the officers are also going. I am hoping my Battery will get to go soon too. At the tailor shop, I tried on my new shirt and pants for the final fitting. The uniforms are supposed to be ready Tuesday.

Sunday, 25 Jan 1942
On Sunday quite a few men went up into the mountains to escape the heat and enjoy the cool mountain air. Singosari is at an elevation of 1,300 feet and has a mild climate in the summer, but nearby Mount Arjuna is almost 11,000 feet high. The high altitude offered significantly cooler temperatures.

Two of my officers, Spinx and Fer***y, were transferred to GHQ-Java. They left this evening. Capt. Sparks has orders to leave tomorrow.

I went into town again this afternoon about 4:30 PM, and returned at 8 PM. I bought a hatchet made in China, a pair of Japanese shoes, and a lovely basket for Cile. A China-man is making a leather case for my camera. After I paid my debts, I was broke. Somehow I managed to get everything in my trunk and still close the lid.

P.S. I missed an opportunity to send a letter as one of our bombers (A-24) left for States and carried mail for those who had something ready to go. I was in town at the time, so I missed the chance. I have still not received a letter or cable from Lucille. Am I mad! I will call home again soon.

8.6.   Fall of Kendari, Celebes – 24 Jan 1942

Kendari Air Base was both a strategic location and perhaps the best air strips in NEI. It was captured by the Japanese almost undamaged and immediately put into service. From this air base, bombers controlled the Molucca Channel. It was a stepping stone to Makassar and guaranteed control of the Makassar Strait. The airstrip was also the Japanese base for bombing eastern Java, particularly Soerabaja and the Singosari Airbase near Malang.

8.7.   Tokyo Rose and Makassar Strait – 26 Jan 1942

Monday, 26 Jan 1942
7:55 PM I was just listening to a radio broadcast of Tokyo Rose, a lot of "horse collar" put out by the Japs. They must think we were as dumb as they are. Well, we had a bunch of their ships bottled up a few hundred miles north of us between Celebes and Borneo and were giving them hell – about 25 or 30 already sunk.[81] Some of my men were working every night loading bombs and cleaning machine guns for the air corps. Some of our planes were returning with holes in them that require a lot of work to get the planes back in the air. The planes of both the Dutch and the US are on the go all the time, especially the last couple of days. This will continue until we clean up the bunch in the bottleneck. Five Dutch planes and three of ours did not return today. We hoped they made it to another field. Our planes here have sunk twelve ships in the last two days, plus one battlewagon.

I have only 68 men left now. The others had been transferred to GHQ Java. I expect the remainder of my Battery to be transferred after payday, which we hope is soon. I have to go to town tomorrow to get my new tailored pants and shirt and see about the case for my camera. We will return to the rifle range in the morning.

9 PM I just got word sixteen more of my men are to be transferred. I will be down to 52.

8.8.   Japanese Bombers Pass Over Singosari – 27 Jan 1942

Tuesday, 27 Jan 1942
There were 27 Jap bombers that made their second attempt to bomb Camp Singosari today but because of bad weather, they could not locate us. A large Jap convoy started toward Soerabaja, which is 50 miles away, but were hemmed in at sea and about all wiped out. We feel lucky.

During the last two days, quite a few men of the air corps have been flown from Borneo and the Philippine Islands to Malang. They are here to help repair the planes. We have seventeen pretty well shot up bombers on the field because Singosari has become the main repair base. We needed more planes. The pursuit aircraft are being kept at Soera-

---

[81] Makassar Strait is off Balikpapan, the channel between Borneo and Celebes. The Battle of Makassar Strait began on 24 Jan 1942 to stop the Japanese Borneo invasion force. This included a naval battle where four Japanese transports were sunk. The USAAF B-17's and Dutch Martin's also attacked shipping sinking two transports.

baja (sixteen P-40's came in since the Jap convoy started down[82]). Most of the men who came in today from Borneo and the Philippines had only the cloths on their backs. One of the pilots told me tonight that the Japs still have at least one aircraft carrier, two cruisers, four or five destroyers, and several other ships left in Molucca Straits. The ships are coming in our direction and will be here soon.

The Guard on Post #4 fired his rifle twice tonight, but I never learned why. This is happening too regularly at night for good sleeping. Everyone is getting more on edge knowing the Japanese are getting closer.

Wednesday, 28 Jan 1942
This evening after dinner I was really mad. I have been mad before, but I can't remember when I was more upset. Since my Brigade Headquarters has moved out to GHQ-Java at Lembang, the 131st National Guard Field Artillery has moved in and taken over my Headquarters building. Here I am with 52 men left out of a Battery and many of my best men gone. They put out orders and amend them about three times. All my men are on guard or other daily duty. I have been complaining to the Commanding Officer about getting duty assignments on a pro rata basis in consideration for the number of men in the other unit. I was able to get our assignments cut down some. They are using three of my field ranges in their Mess. They want to be darned sure I had no men left before they give me any relief. I only have one sedan and four command cars left, and their colonel wanted my sedan. They even want to claim my battery property. I hope to hell my battery gets out of here pronto.

Another of my officers will be leaving Friday. I have only two others remaining plus myself and one of the two is the Provost Martial. Lt. Aaron Gensberg is my other officer, the brother to Frank Gensberg (the one Earl Hunt mentioned in his letter). It just made me mad. Anyway I guess I'm home sick.

I reduced a Private this morning because he did not clean and make his bed for the third time.

> I want to write my wife, but I'm telling you it is a hell of a job to write a letter and say nothing.

---

[82] These planes may have come over aboard the Meigs with the Pensacola Convoy, been assembled in Australia, and flown up to Java.

8.9.   Monkey Island – 29 Jan 1942

<u>Thursday, 29 Jan 1942</u>

I will try to tell you about "Monkey Island." This morning, several of us who were available took a hike and went by what the locals call monkey island. It is not really an island, but a place where the monkeys seem to live in the trees. The natives can call to the monkeys, who come out of the trees to be fed bananas. It is quite some fun to watch the monkeys grab the bananas and eat them. You should see the number of bananas that we buy for a nickel in Dutch! You buy a whole bunch at a time, more than you can eat, so we buy a penny's worth and feed most of them to the monkeys.

There are monkeys all over this place. They love to sit up in the top of the trees and drop things on us. I have made friends with two particular monkeys that come to see me almost every day. We chat and carry on like a couple of fools. I wish Johnnie could see this show.

The monkeys come into my room and make themselves at home. Sometimes they try to take over which is not good. That's not all. They will sleep in my bed, if I don't watch them. That includes pulling the mosquito bar back and crawling into the bed.

We lost our first bomber today. The major was piloting at the time. He had managed to sink two transports before they got him. Several flight crews went out today to try to locate the aircraft carrier. We now have a few pursuit aircraft for protection. The *Meigs* came over with me, but I do not know how many new aircraft it brought. Quite a few more air corps personnel came in today withdrawn from other islands.

Lt. Aaron Gensberg[83] and I have been shooting the bull for a couple of hours. I have been learning to play chess. We are the only officers in the Battery now and are both from Texas A&M. He was in Class of 1933. Voeschesky is leaving in the morning. I will try to write a letter pronto and ask him to carry it to Soerabaja to be mailed.

I asked my Sergeant to bring back my laundry from town tonight. Its 9:30 PM and he is not back yet.

> *Sekarang soedah cape* (For this day enough)
> Darling, I love you very much.

---

[83] Aaron Gensberg, b.31 Dec 1910, d. 13 Apr 1978, Odessa, Ector County, Texas

Friday, 30 Jan 1942

We are still depressed today after losing the major and his bomber crew yesterday. The Japs are making new landings within 30 miles of Singapore, which sounds bad for us. Singapore is 400 to 600 miles from us, and if it fell into Japanese hands, it would bring us into bombing range. No telling what will happen next. Quite a few more P-40's came in which makes everyone feel better. There was a report that five Jap planes were shot down in Singapore today. About six of our aircraft are leaving for Singapore shortly. I can hear them warming up as I write this note in my room.

I have to move my Battery to another building in the morning. There are about 1,000 personnel in total in the camp. We are hoping to move toward Lembang, which is about 50 miles from Batavia, after we get paid. I hope we can get away from the 131st National Guard unit. We take as much razzing as they can give us, but I will not go into that in any detail.

We are told that there are quite a few Allied supply convoys on the way to reinforce us. We are expecting about 500 bombers in the next two months. There are plans for 66 new air fields to be completed by then.

Saturday, 31 Jan 1942

7:15 PM - I seemed to be the only officer in the area this evening. At least I see no others. Lt. Gensberg carried six men to the telephone house, and one of us has to remain in the Orderly Room at all times. When the planes returned this evening, I went down to the airport and took stock. Two men were hurt – one shot in the ankle and the other in leg. Both were hit by explosive bullets - one man will probably lose his leg. Another plane of ours landed in Soerabaja. It was so shot up it could not make it home. We have not received the damage report to learn what this bunch did to the Japanese. Another rear gunner lost his leg.

Today we received some 3,400 rounds of ammo for 75 mm howitzer. That means we can shoot a few days at least, when we have to. Everyone is expecting to be bombed any day now. Luck has been with us more than once so far.

My camera needs to be repaired, so I took it into town. It was supposed to be ready Tuesday. Next week I want to take some pictures. I met a Chinaman in town that went to Wisconsin University for four years studying Chemistry. He spoke good English and has been very nice and helpful to me. He became my personal shopper, finding things I wanted and then getting me good prices. His name was "Nie," and he has a leather shop called "Nie Toko."[84] He wants to take me on Sunday to see the most important places in town. Candy is very expensive in Malang as most comes from America. A 5-cent candy bar sells for 25 to 30 cents Dutch. I was glad I stole some candy in Brisbane.

Until this week, I have had only one roommate, Lt. Birnbalm. I call him the Sheriff since he is the Provost Marshal and spends a lot of time policing the unit. This past week we had a new doctor move in with us. He is very busy tonight taking care of everyone.

8.10.   Entertainment in Malang

Entertainment in Malang is limited. Most of the movies I had seen in the States before we left home. Here with a Dutch sound track and Japanese subtitles, the movies have limited entertainment value, but there is nothing else. The movies change twice a week, and I still go.

It has been rather odd to have free time and always have to find something to do, unless I go to the movies. As yet I have not tried riding a bicycle, which appears to be the usual method of transportation. I am thinking of picking up a bicycle just for fun to tour the town.

I started playing pool several nights a week in town. They play a different style of pool than we have at home. They have a larger table and a little different set of rules; however, it is a good pastime.[85] I go to town and play a game of pool if I can find anyone to play with. That is about the only way I can pass a little time.

One night I was playing pool and accidentally punched a hole in the cloth of the table. That is a real *faux pas* in a pool room. They asked me to pay 25 Guilders for the cloth, which I did pay. About an hour later the manager came up to me and said that "The Committee" had decided to return my money because the table cover was not entirely new. Well, it turned out I was playing with a very important man in Malang, a member of "The Committee." He had sympathy for this lost American GI. He had seen how I ripped the cover, and for reasons I don't know, decided to be generous to keep me playing. The pool hall seemed to be an important meeting place for civic leaders of Malang. I met the local Judge in the Pool Hall.

---

[84] "Toko" in Malay means "Store"

[85] This was probably Snooker.

I am learning to play chess. It is hard to imagine me sitting down for an hour playing a game, but I like it very much. Honey, why don't you try to learn too so we can play when I come home?

8.11.   Swimming at Selecta, Batu, East Java

We discovered a swimming pool about 10 miles from Singosari in the mountains at an elevation of about 3,500 ft. called Selecta, Batu.[86] We had a most enjoyable day at the facility.

Figure 38 - John Day at Selecta, Batu

Figure 39 - Selecta, Batu, East Java Swimming Pool – circa 1935

Sunday, 1 Feb 1942

This morning Capt. Parker and I went to the docks in Soerabaja where they were unloading the *President Polk*. This was the maiden voyage of the Polk, and she really looked nice.

I wanted to take some pictures of the natives, so I borrowed a Kodak to see what I could do. I tried to take one of a native woman taking a bath – well, it sounds funny but they bath in the water on the side of road. It is the same water they wash the animals, wash clothes, and defecate in. At some places they also go swimming in the same water. They let me take some pictures, but the only thing they just don't care to have taken was when they are defecating in the water.

---

[86] Selecta, Batu, East Java continues to thrive in 2011 as a year-round resort with a hotel, restaurant, garden, and play ground. It was built by Reyter Dewild, a Dutchman in 1928. In later years the Bima Saikti Hotel was built and become a popular destination resort for Indonesian government leaders, including the first Indonesian President, Soekarno and Moh Hatta.

**Figure 40 - John Day & unidentified friend at Selecta, Batu
East Java – 1942. Capt. Ike Parker walking in upper left.**

Tonight we went to the "Singapore Restaurant" for dinner.[87] I ordered oysters which were on the menu. After waiting two hours and raising a lot of hell, they informed me that they did not have any oysters – even though they were on the menu. They charged me for the oysters, so I ate some *bommie* (noodles) and *nasi sohrem (fried rice)*. We returned to camp about 3:30 AM.

The tobacco manufacturer that Capt. Parker buys tobacco from asked us to go to the Concordia for Sunday lunch with him and his wife. We joined them and paid the bill as he had asked us to his house once before. We hope to see his movies in the future.

The Sergeant, who was the tail-gunner that was shot in the leg yesterday, died last night after his leg was amputated. Too bad.

8.12.   The Java Countryside and the Dragon Tea Set

Monday, 2 Feb 1942
11:00 AM Seven of our bombers just took off. I am not sure which way they are headed.

Each morning after the Morning Report has been completed, I usually have little to do. It has been rather odd to have to find something to do. On some days, we take a small group on a reconnaissance trip driving around the countryside getting familiar with our surroundings. I am hoping my camera will be ready soon before we drive around so I can take pictures of the countryside. That was not the case today however.

---

[87] Remember in the South one eats breakfast, dinner, and supper. Dinner is the noon meal.

Since I have been here, I have visited Soerabaja and wish I could tell you of the beautiful scenery in the countryside. I have learned where they grow all the expensive coffee. It would take pages to describe everything so I am saving it for my home talk.

I wish you could see the marvelous way that the rice fields are irrigated, channeled, and ditched. They seem to have been this way for centuries. You never see a bunch of weeds anywhere, as the natives seem to keep them all cut away, usually feeding the weeds to the famous bull, the water buffalo.

The roads were built by hand and require a lot longer to build than at home. The ones they build are very nice and very smooth, but they are not generally as wide as ours. Of course they do not drive as fast as we do. About thirty or forty miles an hour is as fast as they will drive.

There are lots of natives on the road at all times carrying bundles of stuff. My camera is still somewhere being repaired and if it does not come back soon, I will have to go after it. I keep hoping to pick it up in the next few days. First I need to get paid, and payday seems to never come. I continue to borrow a little but never have any money.

The most important event of the week – I took three men and a driver on a reconnaissance trip south of Malang about 10 miles. I accidentally came across a lovely tea set for which I made a deal to purchase. This is a lovely **Chinese hand painted china set** (cloisonné?) including a dragon tea pot with gold inlay. There are six cups, saucers, sugar bowl and milk or water pitcher. The set was originally given as a wedding present to a couple that had been married about 50 years ago (*before 1890*). The tea pot pours through the dragon's mouth. I bought the set from the older couple because they needed money and my offer seemed generous to them. I hope I can get it safely home without it getting broken. I will crate the set inside my footlocker for shipment home. I am taking a chance. I know you will enjoy it, as it was positively beautiful. I still have not been paid so again I borrowed more the money.

On Thursday I will again take the men to the rifle range for practice.

8.13.   Army/Native Fraternization

Each unit is assigned a Dutch Liaison Officer who can speak the local language and help us with matters related to the civilian population. Our Liaison Officer (Malang) is: J. W. van Balkum, c/o Jacobson van den Berg and Co., Batavia, Java.

Our Dutch Attaché told us that at least 95% of the native Malay women are infected with venereal disease. He lectured to all the troops and emphasized that you can't fight a war when you're infected with syphilis. During the first weeks after we arrived, matters seem to be under control.

Then one of my men, who I had transferred out, was transferred back. Three days after he returned, he developed a case of syphilis, the first and only case I had had in the battery. I told him that he would not be allowed to go into town until one month after the doctor had pronounced him cured. My guess was that would probably never be. The 131st Field Artillery from Brownwood, which is next door, has about twenty cases already, which is terrible. I would keep the whole outfit on the base before I would let that many get infected.

There are very few Dutch women in Malang considering the number of men. Most of the Dutch women are married with their husbands in the army and stationed nearby. The wives have lots of time alone with the husbands, which is indeed very nice. I might add that there are very few nice looking Dutch women. We had more good-looking girls in Dallas than there are in the entire island of Java. There are many mixed race Indo European and Malay-Dutch women on the street who are very exotic and attractive. Some of our men find them especially appealing.

## 9.	JAPAN ENCIRCLES JAVA

### 9.1.	Air Raids Begin on Singosari Airbase– 3 Feb 1942

Tuesday, 3 Feb 1942

THIS WAS CERTAINLY A DAY TO REMEMBER. About 10:30 AM we received a telephone call from Soerabaja that thirty Jap planes were on their way south toward Malang. Soerabaja was about 10-minutes flight-time from Singosari. I got the battery away from the barracks and into the woods and ditches. The Japs really came in force, bombed and machine gunned us. It was the first real attack on us. One bomb hit a BME [?] and blew it to pieces making a hole about 30 feet wide and 15 feet deep. Two other planes were set on fire. There were quite a number of holes in the buildings, even in my office where I sometimes sit. It had rained last night, but that did not keep us from hugging the ditches and holes. We all were dirty after the "All Clear" was sounded.

I still have not received my camera, or I would have captured some good pictures. I kept hoping the camera would arrive in a few days. We are expecting an air raid again tomorrow, but hope not. Everyone jumps when a plane or gun sound is heard. - *Love*

Wednesday, 4 Feb 1942

The air raid alarm started at 7 AM. It gets monotonous having to hit the ditches and hope to hell that nothing hits you. We decided to carry a chess set into the ditches so we could play chess until the raid was over. So far, we have had about 15 minutes warning to get to hell in a ditch or other protection. We found that we could get out of the buildings in seconds, not minutes.

I try to carry my diary when I hit the ditches. We all have a little junk in our field bag and if we are close enough to reach it, we carry it along to the ditches. I have an extra rifle I carry as well.

No bombs were dropped this morning up to 11 AM; however, some time bombs that were dropped yesterday went off today.

We have only two machine guns and no antiaircraft weapons, which is naturally very little protection. A British antiaircraft unit that had been evacuated from Singapore is supposed to be arriving in a few days. I guess the British can at least show us how to make a tactical withdrawal.

I had all my pretty Chinese dishes crated for shipping and hoped to get them shipped pronto.

The camp got credit for shooting down one Jap pursuit plane today. The plane went down in flames about 10 miles from here. God knows we needed some antiaircraft. We have 50-caliber machine guns but no 50-caliber ammunition. We were trying to get some from other units in the area. That would at least help.

Soerabaja really caught hell today. The Japs bombed the main street, lots of people were killed, and considerable damage was done. Batavia was also bombed.

We had another air raid but no bombs were dropped. It is really a picture when the sirens go off to see how fast we can get to hell and gone. I laughed today till my sides hurt hearing one of my men saying he ran two miles through the heavy undergrowth. He was skinned up so bad I asked him what happened. He said "by God I was scared and kept thinking I would find a better ditch but they were all worse." It takes a change of uniform after you go to the brush or ditches, as it is always muddy. Of course we don't give a damn about our looks at a time like that.

We are at a loss to know why we don't get a lot of pursuit planes to cover us quickly. We lost another bomber at the airport today from a time-bomb. After it went off at 7 AM, all the natives left Singosari and have not come back. We are afraid they will not show up tomorrow either.

When the natives get together, you can't imagine all the jabbering that goes on. You never heard so much noise.

There is usually a lot of fire attached to any raid, but we try to forget that part of the serious side. We are expecting daily raids from now on.

Some of the men are getting rattled by the raids. The second time the gong sounded today it seemed to bother some men fairly badly. A few men went to the woods and did not come back till after dark. Guess they will be better tomorrow. - *Love*

Thursday, 5 Feb 1942
10 AM - I am sitting in a ditch waiting for the SOBs to come over. We just had the alarm but as yet no planes have been seen. We have had so far about 5-minutes notice. It will suit me if they go elsewhere. You know, your heart just naturally beats faster when you know you are waiting. Then when you hear the bombs falling, the heart speeds up more. Funny war!

Yesterday at the airport two more men went up in a bomber on a test flight. A major was piloting and Lt. Smith, who lived next door, was in back. They were shot down in flames and all were killed. So the war is getting pretty hot here. It would be much nicer if we had a bunch of pursuit planes.

Another alarm at 1:30 PM – We are getting better at getting out of the buildings. The planes went to Soerabaja instead of here. There was a hell of a fight there. We shot down a bunch but don't know exact number. Guess tomorrow will be our day as their custom seems to be to alternate between Malang and Soerabaja, dropping bombs on us every other day. Hope not. I have to go to town in the morning so could miss their raid. I want to get out of camp before the Japs arrive. Honey, I sure miss my family. Love

## 9.2.		Bali Cremation Ceremony Movies – 6 Feb 1942

<u>Friday, 6 Feb 1942</u>
The sirens went off at 7:15 AM this morning. Shortly later, there was all clear. I understood they went to Soerabaja again. I went to town at 8:30 AM to see the President of the Bank about one of my men depositing f550 in another name for another man. I had it fixed.

Saturday seven more men and Lt. Gensberg were transferred out. Gensberg was on Special Duty in Soerabaja and was supposed to be back today. I am left with 41 men after these depart.

Out of 60 million people on this island, we understand there are about 30,000 whites (which we doubt). There may be half that many, however, there are quite a few Indo European and Europeans and other half castes. Sure would love to see my family.

This night, Capt. Parker and I were invited to visit the home of Mr. and Mrs. Van Hout. They showed us their home movies and photographs made at a Bali Cremation Ceremony. They called the event a *Bali Nagben Singaraja Cremation Ceremony* or the *Festival of Death*. This is a community funeral celebration in which special Paper Mache temples and animals are built and colorfully decorated for the cremation ceremony. The deceased was put in a specially built temple that was perhaps 100 feet high. The body was probably 25 feet up in the air on a platform that was carried on the shoulders of a large number of natives in a procession to the sound of drums and bells. When they arrived at the cremation site, the special Paper Mache temple, animals, and everything were burned, along with all kinds of foods the natives brought to honor the dead man. Quite a funeral! The Van Houts also showed us pictures of their wedding in Holland only two years earlier with snow on the ground. The evening was most enjoyable.

Back in Camp about 11:10 PM and we were suddenly "called to the woods" by an air raid siren. I saw five planes, but they dropped no bombs. It is now 12:30 AM and the All Clear has not blown, but it is clear enough for us to go back in our rooms and go to bed.

9.3.   Cable from Home Arrives – 7 Feb 1942

Saturday, 7 Feb 1942
By the way, I received your cable this morning, honey. It was received in Batavia on 17 Jan 1942. The message was "received cables well Love" which I was glad to get. It was sent from San Antonio, so I guess you were there. Have a nice visit but be sweet. I love you.

I went to a show at night. We saw Vivian Leigh, I believe in "Come Live with Me." I enjoyed it very much.

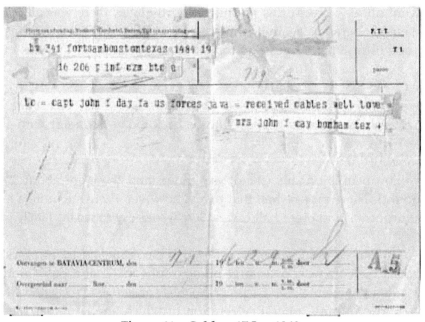

Figure 41 – Cable – 17 Jan 1942
Cile to Capt John F Day in Java, Batavia-Centrum

Sunday, 8 Feb 1942
There was quite a fight in Soerabaja yesterday. Thirteen bombs were dropped on Holland Pier, the pier we use part of the time. Only one of thirteen missed, so I think the Japs did a pretty good job dropping them. They seem to be improving their aim.

This morning we sent nine B-17 bombers on a mission. Three of them were shot down by Jap fighters a short way from the coast. Five men parachuted out of one before the plane exploded. There was a crew of eight or nine men in every airship. We are watching as the 19th Bomber Group is losing a war of attrition – on the ground and in the air.[88] They are losing planes in combat and receiving very few replacements. A few more pursuit aircraft arrived but not enough.

We had our usual air raid alarm this morning. The planes arrived at 11:05 AM.

We are getting ready for the next bunch of Japs to come as we have a new surprise for them. We found some 50-caliber ammunition for our machine guns. If bombers come high, we can't do much about it, but we will give any pursuit planes a hot reception.

We also have four 105mm howitzers scattered around the field. The cannon does not have enough elevation to shoot up in the air, so we dug a trench to lower the carriage so we could point the guns up into the air. We set the shells to burst at 1000 yards so they will burst over the airfield. We have some British 75mm with no ammunition, and twenty-four 105mm's with no ammunition. Finally, we borrowed ammo from the Dutch and spread the pieces around the base.

Some men dug holes near the emplacements. I was about 50 yards away from one gun emplacement with the Sergeant in a ditch, watching the bombs drop from above. The bombs make a whistling noise as they fall.

It was raining, as it does every day. We had to remain in camp until 4 PM with one officer on duty. As I was the only officer in my unit, I could go when I wanted. However, because I was broke, I could not go to the movie show without borrowing money. Everyone else was about broke also, so we don't go to the movies often – especially since the pictures change only twice weekly. Mail goes out once a week, on Wednesdays. I try to write a letter every week even though censorship limits what I can say.

Monday, 9 Feb 1942
At 10:40 AM, we had an air raid alarm, so I casually walked about 300 yards to my ditch. Along with me were the First Sergeant and the Signal Sergeant. After being there 25 minutes we heard a hell of a noise. It sounded like a lot of airships. The first thing we saw was twenty-two Jap bombers, and the SOBs had the nerve to make a practice dry run over us. Well, that's what we get with no air cover.

---

[88] The surviving US bombers were flown out to Australia on February 27th, 1942, the same day the MS Abbekerk sailed from Tjilatjap.

After making the dry run, they circled back and came over to make their first bomb run. I was just about directly under them and could see the bombs falling from 14,000 feet and listened to them whistling all the way as they fell. People were scared. I told them don't worry about it. If you are hit, you will never know it. I told the two Sergeants to say their last words and pray the bombs missed our ditch. Well, they did, and it worked. You can see I am still writing in the diary.

The first bombs burst about five steps from that 105mm and covered up the fellow who was in the hole beside the piece. I was about 30-40 yards away. We had an Oklahoma Indian soldier who came over with us on the *Republic*, who stood up to watch. A fragment caught his cheek, and split it wide open. We yelled at him, "Get down! Get down!" The planes came through dropping bombs. After the first run with all twenty-two planes, eight circled back for a second bomb run.

My house, as well as other quarters, were beside the airstrip and were heavily damaged. My house was the worst of the officer's quarters. My desk had a nice slug through it. All the lights, doors, and windows were blown out. One bomb actually hit about 30 steps from the front door. Needless to say, we were sweating through it all.

When the bombs appeared to pause, I knew we must have had a bunch of casualties. I went back to see what I could find. I looked down the ditch from where I was, and there was a Malay native with a piece of shell through his cheek. He was trying to get up. I looked him over and decided he was not mortally wounded, and I told him to lie down while I summoned the doctor. The planes were still over us, and we were not absolutely sure if they were finished. After a while I could see no more planes, so I went back to our base to assess the damage. In addition to the houses, we had five or six trucks on fire. Several garages and a couple of warehouses were blown up. Sewage and water lines were blown up, and our dining room had been blown out.

It would take several pages to describe in full all the damage so I will just cover a few highlights – four of the 105mm guns that we had hidden to fire on planes were ruined. Four of the twelve pieces that came over from the Second Infantry Division[89] to 131st Field Artillery were ruined. One bomb hit about 10 feet from a Sergeant and the dirt buried him. He was shell shocked, but OK in a few hours. Another Malay native was running in the open when a fragment caught him in the head and killed him. With only one dead and two wounded, we were lucky. The dear Lord was sure good to us.

---

[89] Capt. Day was with the 2nd Infantry Division when he was ordered to the Philippines, so he was well aware of these guns.

Probably an additional ten vehicles needed a lot of work before they could be driven. Tomorrow the Japs will fly over and take pictures. Then the next day they will be back to bomb again and finish their work. We would all enjoy some rest and sleep. I drank a bottle of beer and darned if I didn't fall asleep.

The Japs have an aircraft carrier 50 miles off the coast that our boys were working on today. Hope they had some luck attacking it. The Japs had pursuits to help them. We don't know who else got bombed, but if we had a bunch of P-40's here, it would have at least been better for us.

I have taken all our supplies and stashed them all over the place – away from the buildings and out in the woods to hide them. Very little is left in the camp.

My roommate had his wife's picture on his desk and its frame was broken. I'm still lucky and don't know what my charm is, but my wife's picture is still OK. The natives are working on repairing our house now. My men are helping to clear the streets.

> I guess I will not be buying many more things to send home, as I may not get home with what I have already. I love you so much, Darling.

9.4.　　　Daily Bombing Attacks on Singosari – 10 Feb 1942

Tuesday, 10 Feb 1942
We had our usual air raid alarm at 11:20 AM. We all went to our holes quickly. I went a little further out than before because the bombs yesterday were too close to be comfortable. A bunch of Zero fighters strafed again today, but we were in our holes and ditches so there were no casualties.

We learned today that the Japs made a new landing on Sumatra. I don't know for sure where, but they are moving in our direction. It won't be long before they get to Java.

Capt. Ike Parker and I had a Chinese dinner that was very good. We are learning to eat rice, I especially liked *bommie* (noodles) and *nasi sohrem* (fried rice) which is a funny name for rice, but I think I spelled it correctly. Most of the Chinese food is fair, but some I do not like as much as other things. *Kip* is chicken and *kip safe* is about six pieces of chicken baked on a bamboo stick (chicken or *sate ayan*). *Babi* was pig, and they cook pig the same as chicken.

We had been in Camp Singosari for several weeks when the Japanese began almost daily air raids. The Japanese planes would make two or three bombing passes over the airfield and then follow often with a strafing run at low altitude. We learned what to expect and how to avoid being hurt.

I carried my laundry to town tonight. I also took my rubber air mattress in to get it vulcanized.[90] Pieces of bomb shrapnel had made eight holes in it and I wanted to see if it could be fixed. My camera was still not in. I took my watch in to be fixed, and they said it would be about ten days, which is too long. I was hoping it would be done sooner.

I met another Dutch couple, Mr. and Mrs. Visser. These civilians have been very nice to us, as they like to practice their English. They asked me to go to Concordia Saturday night and dance. He was Manager of a sugar plantation before the war. His father was Director of Indies, and I guess a big shot. I do not know if I will be able to go because I am still "broke."

<u>Wednesday, 11 Feb 1942</u>[91]
As we say – "she <u>ish</u> now" 12:35 PM and I just had lunch. Soerabaja has been under alarm for a couple of hours. We were notified they are under attack and told to be ready. Some soldiers have taken to the woods already, but most of us wait for the siren. So far we had been receiving ample notice.

Figure 42 - Capt. John F. Day Jr., Java - 1942

---

[90] Air mattresses in 1942 were made of rubber, like inner-tubes, and puncture holes had to be patched in the same way we patched bicycle inner-tubes in later years, that is, with a rubber vulcanizing kit.

[91] The 91st Bombardment Squadron was re-manned in Brisbane with pilots from the 27th Bomber Group, and dispatched eleven A-24s to Java on 11 February, but the Japanese threat to Timor prevented the other two squadrons of the 27th from following. Inadequate facilities at its new airfield near Malang delayed maintenance of the dive bombers and prevented their operational use until 19 February.

We are still trying to clean up debris from the last attack. We lost several guns, cars, and houses but were able to repair roofs of most houses by replacing tile. We are living in houses beside the airfield, and the houses all have slate roofs. When one tile at the bottom breaks, the whole roof comes sliding down.

The Japs blew away the whole end of the warehouse and garage where most of my supplies were. I had scattered some of my supplies away from the houses and out in the woods for better hiding but need to move more out. I would hate for my personal trunk to be ruined, especially because of the things I have in it.

> Honey I love you. I love you and wish I could see and talk to you now. I put your and Johnnie's pictures away for present so they would not get broken. Hope all at home are well.

Thursday, 12 Feb 1942
Today was a day of rest so far. No alarm and I can't understand it.

Last night I went in to town to visit Mr. and Mrs. Visser. They have been very nice to me, as they want to practice their English. They gave me a few pictures of themselves and their baby. I wanted you to see them. She is very nice looking, and he is I think very handsome. Their baby was not nearly the child we have of course.

Today was very hot, so I am wearing short pants and a short sleeve shirt. Now I have to fight the flies and mosquitoes.

I had been smoking fully a pack of cigarettes a day. I hoped my cigarette supply lasts a long time.

Since the bombing raid the other day blew all the roofs off the building where my property was, I have a hard time trying to protect my remaining supplies. Because this camp is such a popular hot spot for the Japanese bombers, we had to move more supplies out into the brush with a guard for safe keeping.

Because of the continuing transfers, I am down to only 41 men. We really don't have a lot to do, but I have to be here with the men all day to keep them together and prevent them from running away when the air alarm sounds.

Friday, 13 Feb 1942

3·15 PM - "Friday the Thirteenth" and no bombs have fallen as yet. I could not imagine why the B----- had not been back. We understood that in the past two days 54 Jap bombers have been shot down before they got to Soerabaja. The carrier we sunk prevented their having pursuit protection for the bombers making their bombers more vulnerable. If any more pursuits come over, we are ready for them. We now have seventeen 50-caliber machine guns spotted around the camp.

One Battery of the 131st moved out, but I don't know what my unit will do. I suggested we take over all the Military Police duty in town and possibly manage a warehouse for storage. At least we would have a mission and something to do. As it is, I have a job trying to keep the men busy. We took a hike this morning to get some exercise. There were monkeys all over the place. I am having trouble sleeping in the evenings unless it was very late.

Saturday, 14 Feb 1942

On Saturday there was very little going on. I had a few odd detail jobs to take care of, but generally did very little. I had a ride into town about 9 PM, so I went to the club. After I was there, I was joined by Mr. and Mrs. Visser. We talked and danced some so I did not get home until about 12 midnight. Sure was sleepy the next day.

No air raid alarm today, but it looks like things are about to start happening again. We are hoping lots of help will be coming soon. Everyone is on alert trying to be ready for any eventuality. We know the Japs are coming, but we don't know when.

The chaplain was out to visit us at 4 PM this afternoon, and held a service. Most were busy and very few attended. He could not be here tomorrow, which is Sunday.

Sunday, 15 Feb 1942

The cruisers *Marblehead* and *Houston* were heavily bombed. The *Marblehead* was one of our older cruisers, while the *Houston* one of our newest. The *Marblehead* was hardly able to make port. The *Houston* had a rear gun turret blown off. Both had a number of casualties, so the chaplain had to go there to officiate. The ships were bombed in Makassar Straits up near where we had the slew of Jap ships hemmed in. Two Jap airplane carriers have been sunk of late and that must be the reason we have not been bombed lately. Their bombers are so lightly armed with guns that our P-40's shoot them down like birds. They always send pursuits to accompany the bombers. We are getting in more pursuit aircraft and will be able to give them merry Hell soon. Our bombers are doing nice work too – plenty of damage.

9.5.   Singapore Falls to Japan – 15 Feb 1942

Singapore was one of the Crown Jewels of the British Empire. Strategically located at the tip of the Malay Peninsula, Singapore was a major commercial center for trade between China and India with a population of about 600,000 people in 1941. With water on three sides and an "impenetrable" jungle on the fourth side, Winston Churchill called it the "Gibraltar of the East" or "Fortress Singapore."

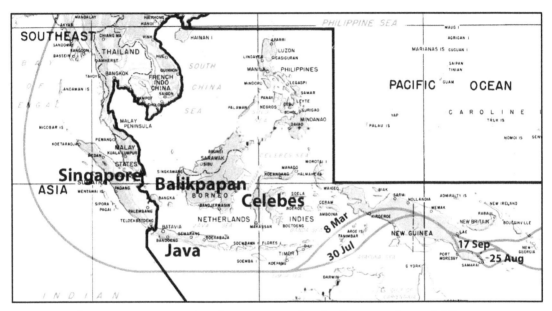

Figure 43 – Greatest Southern Penetration by Japanese Imperial Forces

Singapore depended on the British Empire for its military security on three sides. Because of the war with Germany, Britain had recalled its Pacific fleet to the north Atlantic to protect its supply channels. When the Japanese struck Pearl Harbor, Britain dispatched a Naval task force to Singapore for its protection. Task Force Z consisted of the battleship, HMS Prince of Wales, and the cruiser, HMS Repulse. These two ships were supposed to be accompanied by an aircraft carrier, the HMS Indomitable, however, en route the carrier ran aground and had to return to England for repair. The two remaining ships proceeded without air protection.

On 8 Dec 1941 the Japanese Army invaded the Malay Peninsula north of Singapore. Two days later Japanese bombers attacked and sunk both the unprotected Prince of Wales and Repulse just 50 miles off the Malay coast. By 31 Jan 1942 the Japanese Army had controlled the Malay Peninsula and was knocking on the door of Singapore coming through the "impenetrable" jungle.

The battle for Singapore was fought 8 to 15 Feb 1942. Although the Allies outnumbered the Japanese, they had no air cover. Singapore was subjected to massive bombing attacks that killed many civilians and forced the surrender. A total of 130,000 British and Australian troops became Prisoners of War, the largest surrender of British forces in all history. The POWs became slave laborers for the Japanese in Burma, Korea, Manchuria, and Japan for the duration of the war.

The fall of Singapore forced the British Navy to withdraw to Ceylon, far from the battle zone.

9.6.　　　Japan Invades Sumatra, Bali, & Timor – 14-24 Feb 1942

The fall of Singapore freed up Japanese troops and supplies to proceed into NEI. Sumatra was invaded on 14 Feb. Bali was invaded on 19 Feb. Timor was invaded on 24 Feb. Java was surrounded and the flanks were being secured. The Java invasion was scheduled for 24 Feb 1941.

Monday, 16 Feb 1942

> Yesterday I reserved a time to telephone you this coming Sunday. I am supposed to talk between 9 and 10 AM here. We never know what the atmospheric conditions will be for the short-wave radio or if we will have clear reception. I love you darling.

This morning I went to the laundry to get the bill straight. I had finally secured the "Kimono" which was hand embroidered in Shanghai, China. You will love it. I have quite a few things now and surely hope I will be able to get them home. I would like to send it to you by mail and take my chances on your getting it. If I can catch a plane going, I might be able to get it that way. I will see what I can do.

We got the news that Singapore had fallen. The Japs were also dropping parachutists on Sumatra, so they were getting closer. They are on all the islands but Java now. We will try to hold it. No one knows what will happen next.

> Love you. Sure need a letter.

I had a good sleep this evening. It was raining so hard, we decided the weather was too bad for the Japs to come over.

I had four more men transferred out, leaving me with eighteen. I wish they would transfer the whole darn thing. One would think if a casual officer comes over, he should be put in an outfit. All the other casual officers that have been transferred out have gotten promotions since leaving. I don't like what has happened to me a damn bit.

I did not know many of the other officers in the Camp very well and I cared less to run around with some. They seemed nice enough, but they ran together. I did the best I could.

Palembang [Sumatra] is in Jap hands. Sumatra is west of Java and separated by the Sunda Strait, *a narrow 10 km channel*. The Japs are essentially across the channel from Batavia [Djakarta]. The noose of encirclement around Java is tightening. We are surrounded and feel we will have more Japs than we can deal with very soon. It is apparent we are not getting a hell of a lot of help from outside. I cannot understand why there is no support coming. I have British units on both sides of my unit now in Singosari that have evacuated from Singapore. Our feelings are that the British would fight to the last American, just like they fought to the last Australian in Singapore. I am not exactly in the best of humor at this moment.

9.7.   Shipping the Wardrobe Trunk Home – 17-18 Feb 1942

<u>Tuesday, February 17, 1942</u>
We received word that the *Collingsworth*, an American merchant steam ship, is in Soerabaja harbor and is going back to the States. If anybody had personal property he wants to ship back home, this is his chance. The cargo has to be loaded on the ship tomorrow.[92]

We were in Malang which was about 80 km from Soerabaja so we need to move quickly.

I got all my men together and told them to get rid of everything they did not absolutely need. Soon I had a stack of footlockers, trunks, suitcases, and just plain crates that filled the back of a 2.5-ton truck. Everybody put address labels on his own baggage indicating where it should go in the States.

My big wardrobe trunk would barely close. The first volume of my diary

Figure 44 - Steamer Wardrobe Trunk – Vintage 1940s - Not actual trunk, but identical

[92] Letter #15 dated 15 Feb 1942 stated JFDJr intention to ship the trunk, a foot locker, and his golf clubs. The wardrobe trunk arrived safely. It is assumed that the foot locker also arrived safely containing the Chinese tea set. The golf clubs remained in Java and were never shipped.

was buried inside the second drawer, along with a world atlas on which I had marked all the places my Pacific journey had taken me. We were never allowed to write home exactly where we were, so that was the best I could do. Inside the trunk were all of the gifts I had purchased on the *Bloemfontein* and in Malang – the jewelry, carved wood faces, a small table, a quart of White Horse Scotch whiskey, my books, the silver fish server, silver cigarette case, Chinese tea set, and even six golf balls. Cile would have to break the locks to open the trunk when it arrived since I had the keys. A detailed inventory of the contents was buried in the bottom of the trunk. A copy of the inventory was also mailed to my parents in New Mexico.[93] I also packed my footlocker and expected to ship it as well.

Wednesday, February 18, 1942

Early the next morning my driver and I took off for Soerabaja with the loaded truck. When we arrived at the edge of town, the Japanese were bombing the port, so we pulled off to the side of the road about 10 km outside of town on a hill overlooking the harbor to watch all the fireworks.

About eighteen Jap bombers had come over and dropped bombs. They sunk a Dutch sub that was in the harbor, an old one with about twelve men on board. They also hit an old Dutch light cruiser. About twelve bombs hit the water close to the piers. Between five and thirteen Jap planes were shot down.

We drove by one of the Japanese bombers that crashed and found six dead Japs. On part of the aluminum sheet of the plane, we found the following markings: "Made in U.S.A." Well I guess that's our reward for selling it to them, as well as all our junk iron they use in their bombs.

We drove down to the U.S. Embassy first, and then to the Navy Headquarters trying to locate the *Collingsworth*. The Navy Headquarters told us where to go

Figure 45 - Steamer Trunk

to find the ship. We were still in front of Navy Headquarters when a Navy captain came out to us and asked, "Can I borrow your truck?"

---

[93] A copy of this inventory was discovered in 2001 among the estate papers of Capt. Day's mother and is included in an appendix.

I replied, "What for?"

I learned the captain was named Nathaniel B. Sauve. Captain Sauve said "A submarine just came in from the Philippines with all the master lithographic plates for all the maps of the Philippines, and we need to get them to Australia. We need a truck to haul the plates to the train station so we can get them down to Tjilatjap." Tjilatjap was the main southern port of Java and the main port for ships going to Fremantle, Australia. Tjilatjap was about 300 miles away from Soerabaja. The Captain was literally "hitch-hiking" his way from the Philippines to Australia with the valuable map plates "under his arm" so to speak.

There we were with a 2.5-ton truck, full to the gills with trunks, footlockers and luggage, so what did we do? We unloaded the truck and created a pile of trunks in the vacant lot next to Navy Headquarters. Out of Navy Headquarters came a very heavy crate, about six feet long by perhaps two feet square, containing the lithographic plates. We loaded the box on the truck. Actually the crate was smaller than we expected, but by the time we knew its size, we had already unloaded the truck.

The captain climbed into the truck cab with us, and we drove down to the train station. The lithographic plates were loaded into a boxcar at the train station, and the boxcar was sealed and padlocked so it could not be opened until Tjilatjap. Captain Sauve boarded the train that included the boxcar, and we said goodbye.

We headed back to Navy headquarters, reloaded the truck, and drove down to the dock where the *Collingsworth* was located. On the dock I yelled up at the skipper and told him we had cargo to go back to the States. He swung a big cargo sling down from the deck, and we put everything we had into the net. He hauled it back up and into the ship's hold. After that, we got out of Soerabaja as fast as we could before there was another air raid. Later that afternoon, Soerabaja had another air raid. We were alerted that the planes might be coming on over to Malang. This is a Real War!

When we got back to Malang, I realized I had forgotten to take my golf clubs down to the port to ship home. They never made it.

That night Tokyo Rose announced "US Navy headquarters in Soerabaja has just been bombed." Well, she was correct that they had tried to bomb headquarters, but the bombs missed by about four blocks. She said "They were making arrangements to move." That was true. They were moving as fast as they could to get out of Soerabaja. The Japs had spies everywhere, and someone had told Tokyo Rose.[94]

That was the last I saw of my trunk.[95] Six months later the trunk appeared in Brooklyn, NY and a few weeks after that arrived safely in Bonham, Texas. Cile wired me that it had arrived.

Funny thing, my First Sergeant, Sleber, was a good man, but the boys in the outfit pulled a trick on him. The night before we drove to the port with the trunks, someone put a pair of lady's black panties inside his trunk. He did not open the trunk again before it was shipped out. About six days later somehow it came out what had been put in his trunk. He was panicked. He was trying to call his wife and tell her what they had done to him. Later, we were told the ship had been sunk on the way home. We all felt bad about the ship sinking, but the Sergeant was elated. "Thank God, the ship sunk." I never heard how he came out when the ship actually arrived home safely.

Six months later I was in the Officer's Club in Brisbane talking with some friends when across the room I saw the Navy Captain who had been escorting the map plates. I walked over and introduced myself. In our discussion I learned he had been awarded a "Purple Heart" medal for saving the lithographic plates. I thought that was odd, as I thought you had to be wounded to get a Purple Heart. He said that was what he had been awarded for saving the plates.

> *The following is a direct quotation[96]:*
> *The Commanding General of USAFIA by general order No. 68 made an award of the Purple Heart to Captain Nathaniel B. Sauve. This was awarded for a singularly meritorious act of essential service performed in Soerabaja, Java, on February 18, 1942. While a building housing valuable military documents was being subjected to enemy bombing attack, Captain Sauve without regard to personal risk and danger, proceeded to the building, entered it, rescued the valuable military documents and removed them to a place of*

---

[94] History has shown that there were a large number of the Javanese who opposed Dutch colonial rule and were supporting the Japanese. The Indonesian Declaration of Independence from Holland was issued in August 1945 after the Japanese surrender.

[95] On 19 Feb 1942, the *Collingsworth* barely escaped destruction by the Japanese Navy when she left Soerabaja, Java, clearing the Sunda Strait on 22 Feb 1942, and safely reached Colombo unescorted. The ship eventually reached Brooklyn, NY, and almost a year later on a subsequent voyage off the coast of Trinidad on 9 Jan 1943 the ship was torpedoed and sunk by a German U-boat.

[96] OCMH, Unpublished Manuscript, History of USASOS, Chap V. p.126.

safety, which preserved them and made them available for use in future tactical operations.

Thursday, 19 Feb 1942

About eight Jap fighters came over and strafed. No soldiers were hurt, but of course there were nearly always one or more natives who got killed or hurt. We are getting accustomed to this daily routine, but we will never like it. The British had their anti-aircraft gun set up, but they couldn't hit anything. The official count of yesterday's raid was nine shot down by aerial combat. The Americans sank a cruiser and transport at Bali today.[97] Our bunch of flyers is really doing good work, but if we had had more help and some of the experienced pilots instead of kids just out of school, the war would be a darn sight better.

We feel the next two weeks will tell the tale, and I want to be ready. I expect to move the Battery to the woods in a day or so to get ready for the fight. I wrote a long letter home to send on the freighter and expect to carry it to Soerabaja tomorrow to mail.

Friday, 20 Feb 1942

I had to go to Soerabaja to try to get a truck. They are planning to send twenty trucks to my unit in a few days, but because I had transferred all but 23 men, I don't need the trucks anymore. We had two air raids in Soerabaja while I was there. I saw a beautiful aerial dog fight in which one Jap fighter went down. I returned to Singosari about 1 PM, and we had two more raids. Those B---- slipped in and caught us before the air raid siren sounded. We all thought they were P-40s and watched them till they turned loose their machine guns. They destroyed four bombers on the ground and wounded several men. None of my men were hurt. I missed both dinner and supper at Camp, so a few of us went into town about 6 PM and ate chicken livers and champignon with nasi goring. I really was hungry and ate "till my heart was content."

In town I saw Mr. and Mrs. Visser, the Dutch family I had visited, and had a chat with them. I laughed so much hearing her tale of holding her baby and standing waste deep in water in the air raid shelter during the last attack. It is curious how one can laugh at such tragic events. I think it would be a terrible event if a bomb were dropped in their residential part of town.

---

[97] Battle of Badung Strait, the "cruiser" was a "destroyer." This day was also the Japanese invasion of Bali.

Saturday, 21 Feb 1942

The freighter had sailed, so I was unable to mail my letter. The ship had to leave hurriedly, because the Japs had landed about 300 soldiers in Bali (our neighboring island to the East!) We now have Japs to both our east and west. It is now 11:10 AM and all clear has sounded for the second time.

Colonel Searle gave the order that everyone should stay in camp unless a pass was given by him. He was a little worked up, I guess because of the Japs landing in Bali. I wanted to see a show tonight, but it was not allowed. We had one raid and two alarms this morning. They started shooting first after the first all clear was sounded. We had two more attacks in the afternoon. I think we hit one so badly he will not get home. Our planes got another cruiser and several transports at Bali [not confirmed].

Sunday, 22 Feb 1942

4:10 PM - An alarm was sounded, but then it seemed to stop. I saw the fighters coming and stayed as long as no bombers were over me. It was quite a show watching the aerial dogfights overhead. There were three alarms this morning, and then one this afternoon. All attacks today were strafing attacks. When the strafers start shooting, you just fall in a ditch or behind a wall and pray. Five of our P-40s came over looking for the Japs, but the Japs were gone by the time they arrived. The *All Clear* had not sounded, but all were waiting for a clear shot at the Japs. I had my rifle too if they came low enough. I would take a picture with my movie camera and then shoot him. Later in the evening the strafers came over again.

I understood we might move to another location. Orders had already been changed four times. I had attached the remainder of my Battery to Service Battery 131st to try to find more work to do. I would assist the Supply Officer.

Monday, 23 Feb 1942

This morning about seven of the Jap bombers came over along with several Jap fighter escorts. Our P-40s made contact so we watched the dog fights until we heard the "swish" sound of the falling bombs. When we knew the bombs were on their way, we went for cover. One bomber was leaving a trail of smoke (the work of a P-40). We saw about three or four pursuit aircraft go down and understand a bomber also fell somewhere. Their bombing was terrible this morning, and missed everything. One concussion caused a Britisher to fall on his gun and knock a few teeth out. Of course I found my ditch. When the Jap bombers are overhead, and the bombs are falling, it is really hard to keep the old heart at a normal pace.

It is 11:30 AM and we were in the middle of the second air raid this morning – all clear, no planes. I had all my men moved and could have moved myself, but Captain Pros from GHQ is coming to visit today and I figured he might have more "dope" on our next movement or the transfer of more men.

Tuesday, 24 Feb 1942
I transferred six more men to the 131st, with the balance put on Special Duty with them, including myself and Lt. Birnbalm.

This morning I was talking to Capt. Taylor, the Supply Officer, about our new arrangements when we had our first air raid alarm of the day – 8:30 AM. We just continued on our journey away from camp and returned to Camp Singosari about 11 AM. The alarm was still on so we just went to our own houses. I have been packing things preparing to move this evening. All clear was finally sounded at 11:20 AM. No planes were sighted that I know of. I am going into town this evening to get a haircut.

> I hope to talk to my honey by wireless telephone in the next few days. Cile darling, I love you, I love you. I am so excited to hear your voice. Due to heavy use of cables, telephones, I may not be able to talk home again. Let's hope so. Just can't wait to talk.

9.8.   Japan Attacks Darwin – 19 Feb 1942

On 19 Feb 1942 four Japanese aircraft carriers attack Darwin in the Northern Territory, Australia. The task force was under the command of Vice Adm. Nagumo, the same Admiral who directed the attack on Pearl Harbor. During this attack 242[98] bombers and fighters were launched in the largest single attack on the Australian homeland. [99]

In 1941 Darwin had a population of approximately 5,000, but the city had been evacuated down to 2,000 in expectation of the Japanese attack. The attack destroyed Darwin shore installations, harbor, and airfield making the site unsuitable for Allied ship repair, refueling or aircraft resupply to NEI. The air base of Batchelor Field, about 10 miles outside Darwin, became the airbase for the region.

---

[98] There are two conflicting reports of the number of planes in this attack. One report said 189 aircraft and the second report said 242 aircraft. The author does not know which is correct.

[99] There were six aircraft carriers in the Pearl Harbor attack, compared to four in the Darwin attack.

The USAT Meigs, a member of the Pensacola Convoy was sunk in the Darwin attack. The freighter Admiral Halstead, also a member of the Pensacola Convoy, was in the harbor carrying drummed fuel and sustained damages, but no casualties.[100]

9.9.   Roosevelt Orders MacArthur Out of the Philippines – 22 Feb 1942

The military situation in the Philippines continued to erode. Bataan and Corregidor were surrounded and under siege. Combat was taking a steady toll on the Allied units who were on reduced rations and limited ammunition. Supplies were dwindling, and no resupply appeared feasible. There appeared to be "no light at the end of the tunnel" for the Philippines.

With Singapore having fallen and NEI crumbling, Allied Forces throughout the South Pacific were in shambles. President Franklin D. Roosevelt ordered Gen. Douglas MacArthur to leave the Philippines and go to Australia. Roosevelt wanted MacArthur to regroup Allied Forces in Australia to fight another day.

---

100 The Official Chronology of The U.S. Navy In World War II. by Robert Cressman, p.76.

10.   ESCAPE FROM JAVA – 25 Feb 1942 to 4 Mar 1942

10.1.   Japanese Invasion Force Departs for Java – 25 Feb 1942

On 23 Jan 1942, Japan had invaded Balikpapan, Eastern Borneo, which provided a new airbase, oil complex, and staging area for the attack on Java. Kendari Airfield on Celebes fell on 24 Jan 1942. Makassar had fallen in early February. The Japanese 48th Division departed Lingayen Gulf on 8 Feb 1942. After a week stop on Jolo Island, Sulu Archipelago (PI) the division moved down the Makassar Strait toward Java. The invasion was postponed one day, so the force waited off Balikpapan Harbor on the east coast of Borneo, finally departing south for Java on 25 Feb 1942.

10.2.   ABDACOM Dissolved – 25 Feb 1942

ABDACOM had been activated on 15 Jan 1942 with responsibilities including both Singapore and the Dutch East Indies. The British were concerned about Singapore, and the Dutch were concerned about Sumatra and Java. Australians were worried about their homeland. The Philippines were left to MacArthur. The Alliance partners seemed to have divided priorities.

Following the fall of Singapore and the degenerating military situation in the NEI, the fall of Java seemed eminent. Gen. Wavell and Dr. Hubertus J. van Mook, the Lt. Governor General of the Netherlands East Indies, agreed to dissolve ABDACOM on 25 Feb 1942. Wavell's military command responsibilities were delegated down to his next level subordinates, he got on a plane and flew back to India from where he had come. Dutch Lt. Gen. Hein Ter Poorten was placed in command of the KNIL Army (Royal Dutch Indies Army). ABDACOM Fleet was placed in the hands of Dutch Vice Admiral Karel Doorman.

10.3.   Order to Evacuate Singosari – 25 Feb 1942

Wednesday, 25 Feb 1942

All day there had been one air raid after another. The Japanese were unrelenting in their attacks on the Malang/Singosari Airfield. About 4 PM, I received a letter from Col. Albert C. Searle, my Commanding Officer in Bandoeng. I was just opening the letter when a cable arrived from him. Both letter and cable said the same thing.

I was ordered to take my Battery by train to Tjilatjap, the last open port on the south coast of Java, where we would be evacuated to Australia on Friday evening, 27 Feb 1942. All non-combat units (or those not in a fighting unit) were to be shipped out. Only the 2nd Battalion, 131st Field Artillery would be left behind. All property was to be turned over to 131st Field Artillery. We were to carry only tentage.

Tjilatjap was about 300 miles away. We were ordered to leave Malang in two days. Well, before I could take a deep breath, the phone rang. It was a call from the same Col. Searle. He said, "Have you received my letter."

"Yes, Sir, I just received it," I said.

Col. Searle said, "Well, things have changed. The Japanese are landing more troops in the north, and the evacuation has been moved up one day. I want you to complete the transfer of enough men to the 131st to bring them up to full strength, transfer all the equipment you can't carry to the 131st, and then get your ass on the first train out of Malang to Tjilatjap."

"Yes, Sir," I replied.

Well, the next train departed about 11 PM, only six hours away. There was no way I could get all the men ready, make the equipment transfers, and catch that train. The second train was at 4:37 AM the next morning (*26 Feb 1942*) which was about 12 hours away. We were going to be pushed to even make that.

I met with the lieutenant colonel from the 131st and gave him every man that fit his unit. I ended up with about 30 men left in my Battery.

I sent a Sergeant with our Dutch attaché to the train station to book passage on the train for my unit. Each unit had an assigned Dutch attaché who spoke the language and knew his way around Java. He would lead us to where we caught the train.

10.4.   Trying to Phone Home – Wednesday night, 25 Feb 1942

I wanted to make one last phone call home from Java. If the government was not using the trans-pacific cable[101], the capacity was opened to personal phone calls for a fee. It was expensive, but there was a process to follow to get a chance at a five-minute call home. One had to request a time slot and pay in advance for a connection. During January in Malang I had been successful once in calling Texas. I wanted to try again before we left Java, since I did not know if there would be another opportunity.

I had requested and paid for a connection for the past two nights. Each night, I had stayed up until 1:30 AM and 3:15 AM respectively, but with no success. Each night the

---

[101] The oral history talks of the trans-pacific cable, but the author believes this was a short-wave radio, not a cable.

phone operator would call and report that the cable was too busy with government traffic and there would be no personal calls. For the third straight night, I stayed up until 1:30 AM, but still no connection.

I was packed and ready to go. I left my golf clubs with Capt. Clark Taylor who was from Wichita Falls, Texas and was with 131st Field Artillery. After several rounds of whisky with my friends and bidding Bon Voyage to all I knew, I went to bed only two hours before I had to get up. I fully expected to be back in Java in the near future.

10.5.   The Train to Tjilatjap – Thursday, 26 Feb 1942

The alarm went off at 3:30 AM, and I really had to rush to get the men loaded and ready. We drove our trucks to the train station, where we just abandoned them. The keys were left in the ignition, and we all ran to board the train. There was little time to spare before the 4:37 AM departure. One sergeant missed the train. I think he got drunk, but I considered him transferred to the 131st. I don't know what happened to him.

Figure 46 - The road from Malang (A) to Tjilatjap (B) - 314 miles - Google Map

The Dutch attaché had taken care of me and gotten me a First Class train seat (RHIP – Rank Has Its Privileges). The big advantage in First Class was that the car had a simple air-conditioner – what we called a swamp cooler. In that hot sticky climate, air conditioning was highly valued. In First Class, I was also able to have breakfast in my compartment on the train. Two fried eggs (*spiegel ei*), beefsteak, two slices of bread and two cups *Koffie* for 1.45 guilders. It was the best I had felt in a long time.

Boy! Was it hot! The cooling system for First Class helped some, but the humidity was stifling. The countryside was beautiful with mountains and coconut trees. My new movie camera was out, and I took several pictures, but none survived the war. Time on the train really allowed me to get caught up in my diary. I really missed my typewriter. The train was moving at top speed, some said 60 miles per hour, but I felt it was slower.

The train stopped for about 1½ hours at Djogdja [*Djogdjakarta*[102]] so everyone could get something to eat and stretch their legs. [*There were two provinces in Java in 1941 that were still ruled by Sultans.*] The Sultan of Djogda had a big impressive palace with a military guard. Otherwise, most all towns along the train seemed to be very similar.

10.6.   Arrival in Tjilatjap– Thursday, 26 Feb 1942

As the afternoon passed, the train was running later and later. There was another one of those beautiful tropical sunsets, but darkness closed in before we arrived. The train arrived in Tjilatjap about 10 PM, a full five hours behind schedule.

There was an air raid alarm blasting when we arrived and not a soul at the depot. When we got off the train, we were lost. Our Dutch attaché had stayed in Malang, and we did not know where the docks were. I learned that the train depot was at one end of town, and the docks at the other. We only knew we had to walk downhill to the port. My men walked like a noisy, unruly gang of thugs through the middle of town. Many were still carrying rifles. Some had duffel bags and a few had suitcases. People had been slowly abandoning things rather than carrying extra weight. We had no food, no cigarettes, nothing much extra. As we walked down the street, we passed a few late-night street vendors, and we started buying anything edible. We were sticking everything in our pockets. What you could carry was what you had. By the time we got to the docks everyone had his pockets stuffed. We must have walked a mile-and-a-half to reach the docks.

The streets were filled with cars abandoned by those who had preceded us. Everyone was in a hurry to leave. When we arrived on the quay, there were stacks of crates double-high with perhaps 100 brand-new unassembled British Spitfires[103] waiting to be picked up. They were now abandoned.

---

[102] After 1976, Djogdjakarta became Yogyakarta.

[103] No independent information on the origin of these aircraft has been located by this author. The planes could have been abandoned by either the Dutch or the British, perhaps brought in from Singapore, but there is no record of Spitfires being shipped to Java. The planes could have been a different model of Dutch origin. The author does not know.

At the port, we were directed to a Dutch freighter, the *MS Abbekerk*, which was tied up at the pier. We were told to go on board, so we found the gangway.

By the time we had boarded, it was approaching midnight. We were exhausted after the 20-hour travel day. Everyone spread out looking for open deck space and seemed to collapse quickly into sleep. That was Thursday night, 26 Feb 1942, 24 hours before we sailed.

February 26, 1942 – Earlier that day the first U.S. carrier, the LANGLEY, was sunk by Japanese bombers off the coast of Java.

10.7.   Preparation to Sail – Friday, 27 Feb 1942

We woke up the next morning with the sunrise after about three hours of very tentative sleep. We were hungry. Our last meal had been in Djocka. There was nothing to eat on the boat, so I rounded up my men. We got off the boat, stole a truck and several cars that had been abandoned on the dock, and drove back to town for breakfast. As we left the boat, we were told to be back onboard by 2 PM in preparation for sailing. Breakfast was most welcome.

After seeing what was going on in town, it was easy to understand the chaos of a real evacuation. Vehicles were abandoned everywhere in the streets and on the docks. Soldiers were flooding into the port from different units all over Java. There were soldiers of many nationalities – Indians, British, Dutch, Australians, and Americans. The harbor was full of ships. I saw perhaps 35 ships stacked in the channel, some tied two deep at the pier, since there was no empty dock space. There was a British ship tied up on the outside of the *Abbekerk*, such that troops had to cross over the deck of the *Abbekerk* to get on board the British ship.

A steady flow of humanity was pouring into ships bound in different directions from India and Ceylon to Australia. About five ships were heading for Australia. Our ship ultimately carried 1,500 troops. Considering the number of other ships in the harbor, there must have been more than 20,000 troops passing through the port that day.

I gave away a lot of things. I carried all that I could, but I still had too much. I thought the Dutch would benefit from all the equipment we left behind, but of course the Dutch had left a lot behind for the Japanese when they left Singapore. Surrender to the Japanese had never entered our minds.

When we arrived back at the ship, humanity was still pouring onboard. The wounded were now being loaded onto our ship, and they appeared to be the last evacuees.

The highest ranking military officer among the evacuees was a British Major who had been in charge of the Officer's Club in Singapore. He had received a direct appointment to major and didn't know the first thing about the Army procedures. He was lost. All the high-ranking officers of ABADACOM[104] in Bandoeng had flown directly from Java to Australia or India.

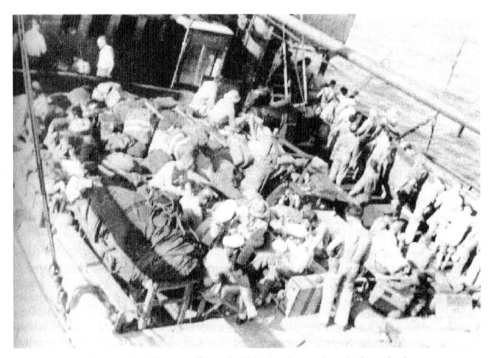

Figure 47 – Troops aboard Abbekerk on the shelter deck

People continued to pour onto the dock and onto the tied-up ships. On our ship, almost everyone remained on the main deck. Only the sick and wounded were below. It was a big boiling pot of humanity. Each person picked out a spot on the deck, usually with a cluster of friends. Nationalities were all mixed up. There was one American lieutenant here, three Australian Navy lieutenants over there, men of all ranks and descriptions scattered around the deck. It was hard to find an open place to sit, much less a comfort-

---

[104] ABDACOM [Australian, British, Dutch, and American Command] was located in Bandoeng and was commanded by the British General, Sir Archibald Wavell. It is significant that this command, which included the U.S. Army Artillery units in Java, did NOT include the Philippine Islands which was under command of Gen. Douglas MacArthur.

able place. Everyone was protecting their gear and their space. One could not leave anything unattended for fear it would be stolen. People were stealing anything and everything. I had never seen anything like it. The ship was so terribly crowded.

I was sleeping on deck and if it had rained, I would have been soaked. Lt. Andrews was with me. He was also on my two earlier boats, the *USS Republic* and the *VMS Bloemfontein*. We were told the *MS Abbekerk* had no cargo and was empty, with exception of troops. I was sure the boat would really toss. We ate hard tack for supper that evening.

10.8.   The Ship – *MS Abbekerk*

Our ship was the *MS Abbekerk*,[105] a Dutch freighter approximately 12.000 tons, called MS for Motor Ship. It had two powerful diesel motors, so it did not leave a coal smoke trail. It was considered very fast for its day, up to 19 knots, but the crew felt it was capable of 21-23 knots. This ship had been sunk in the Thames River in England during the Blitz by German bombs the previous September 1941, but was raised and repaired. Here it was back in full service only five months later.

A water detail was trying to fill every drinking water container they could find on the ship. At the beginning there was no food service, so if you had not picked up something on the street in town before coming to the boat, you didn't eat. Eventually, a mess was organized that served two meals a day, one at 8 AM and one at 3:30 PM.

There were no toilets on deck, so the crew made a crude wooden frame along the rail that allowed people to do their business off the side of the ship.

The ship had insufficient life preservers and few lifeboats for the 1,500 passengers and crew. From looking around, there might be enough life preservers for one-eighth of the passengers. Before we sailed, the crew threw on empty oil drums, bamboo, and rope.

---

[105] *MS Abbekerk* [Motor Ship] – The following information was provided by the website www.msAbbekerk.nl, a website created by Peter Kik and dedicated to his father, Adriaan Willem Kik (1919 – 2000) and the MS Abbekerk (1939 – 1942). The ship was owned by VNS [Verenigde Nederlandse Scheepvaart Mij – Rotterdam] and had been launched in February 1939 at the F. Schichau Shipyard in Danzig [Germany]. Technical specifications include: BRT: 7.906; DWT: 11.604; L x B x H: 150,5 x 19,29 x 9,51/11,70 meters. The two engines 2TE 10 cylinder Sulzer, 2 propellers; Power: 11.000 HP at 125 rpm. The ship was capable of speed up to 17 knots (however, the crew power engineer claimed she did over 20 knots). The crew was 52. The ship was later sunk in August 1942 by three German torpedoes between Spain and England.

We had to take the bamboo and rope to make improvised floats as emergency life rafts. Everyone was busy making life rafts.

10.9.   Departure from Tjilatjap – Friday, 27 Feb 1942

The harbor had 35 ships squeezed into the very narrow river outlet. This was an ideal place for the Jap submarine to attack. Our boat was one of 24 that had been ordered to clear the harbor by sundown. We were the last boat to leave at about 5 PM. Everyone else appeared to have sailed.

Figure 48 - MS Abbekerk, March 1941, at pier in Fremantle, Australia
Photo taken after safe passage from Tjilatjap, Java. Courtesy *Pictures Australia* and www.msAbekerk.nl, Peter Kik

Our Skipper was Capt. C. J. H. Wjkier.[106]   He was a short fat jovial Dutchmen, about 5 feet 4 inches tall. I believe there were two other Dutch officers onboard. The normal crew of the ship was 52 sailors. The crew knew their boat was fast, and their plan was to out run any Japanese submarine.

---

[106] According to Peter Enhanneke of www.msAbbekerk.nl

Our boat was supposed to be part of a small convoy of four or five freighters. As we were pulling out of the harbor, the convoy leader kept radioing to our captain, "Get back in convoy! Get back in convoy!"

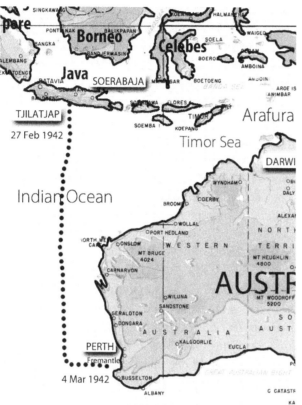

Our captain had his own mind, and replied "There is no convoy here. There is no protection. I am not going out there with a bunch of freighters." So he charted his own course and pulled away from everyone else. By 7 PM, it was getting dark, and we started zigzagging. Shortly, we were all by ourselves – alone in the middle of the big Java Sea.

Now mind you, the top half our propellers were out of the water because our cargo holes were mostly empty. We were told there was not enough weight to keep the propellers down in the water.

As we pulled out of the harbor, I noted in my diary how beautiful the scenery was along the beach. This port was 8 degrees south of the Equator with tall tropical trees and lush green hills in the background – a lot different than Texas.

Figure 49 – Voyage of the Abbekerk - Tjilatjap to Fremantle – 22 Feb to 4 Mar 1942

11.   JAPAN INVADES JAVA

11.1.   USS Langley, First American Carrier was Sunk – 25 Feb 1942

The USS Langley, the first U.S. aircraft carrier, had joined the U.S. fleet in 1923. She had been converted to a Seaplane Tender in 1937 and assigned to the Pacific Fleet. On 8 Dec 1941, she was docked in Manila Bay at Cavite Naval Base. When the Japanese invaded the Philippines, the Langley had been moved south to Balikpapan, Borneo and later to Darwin, where she became part of the ABDACOM Fleet. On 22 Feb 1942, the Langley had been dispatched to Fremantle, Australia where she had loaded forty P-40 aircraft with their pilots for delivery to Tjilatjap, Java. On 26 Feb 1942, seventy-five miles south of Tjilatjap, the Langley was attacked by nine Japanese dive bombers that severely damaged the ship – the deck was on fire, the engine room was flooded, and the ship had a 10 degrees list. One of the accompanying destroyers, the Edsall, took on board all the pilots from the Langley. For fear the disabled ship would fall into enemy hands, the ship was evacuated and its accompanying destroyers sank the ship with canon fire and torpedoes. Subsequently, the Edsall was itself sunk with 31 of 33 pilots from the Langley lost at sea.

11.2.   The Battle of Java Sea – 27 Feb 1942

Dutch Admiral Karel Doorman located the Japanese invasion forces moving down the Makassar Strait heading to Java about 4 PM on 27 Feb 1942. The Japanese forces were protected by a flotilla of four cruisers and fourteen destroyers. Doorman had five cruisers and four destroyers. When the battle ended, the Allies had lost three cruisers and five destroyers. Two cruisers (USS Houston and HMAS Perth) escaped to the west to fight one more day in the Battle of Sunda Bay. Only four old American destroyers managed to escape to Australia. All the rest of the Allied fleet was lost at sea. Adm. Doorman went down with his cruiser.

11.3.   USS Houston & HMAS Perth Lost in Battle of Sunda Bay – 28 Feb 1942

The USS Houston and the HMAS Perth escaped from the disaster of the Battle of the Java Sea to the west under a cover of darkness. They were hoping of escape south to the Java Sea through Sunda Strait (between Java and Sumatra). Unintentionally, they came upon a Japanese invasion force at Banten Bay heading for Java. The Japanese force included four cruisers and nine destroyers. In the darkness of night, the Japanese launched an unprecedented attack of eighty-seven torpedoes toward the two Allied cruisers, quickly dispatching both ships.[107] Ironically, the night time torpedoes also sank two Japanese ships and damage three Japanese transports by "friendly fire."

---

[107] *The Houston had escorted the Republic from Torres Strait to Soerabaja. Sailors who survived the Houston sinking were captured and put in POW camps with the 131st Field Artillery in Burma.*

11.4.   Japanese Landing on Java – 28 Feb 1942 – 1 Mar 1942

After the Battle of the Java Sea, the ABDACOM Navy was literally destroyed. The East Java invasion force proceeded to land essentially unopposed on Kragan, a small village in East Java, approximately 100 miles west of Soerabaja[108] at 00:15 midnight on 1 Mar 1942.[109]

11.5.   Japanese Air Attack on Tjilatjap – 3-5 Mar 1942

On 3 Mar 1942 V Adm. Nagumo, fresh from his Darwin attack only two weeks earlier on 19 Feb 1942, attack the port of Tjilatjap. Between 150 and 180 Japanese planes were launched from four carriers in the Java Sea. Pilots reported sinking 20 ships in the harbor.[110]

On 5 Mar 1942 Japanese pilots reported the sinking of three Allied destroyers and fourteen transports while trying to escape south into the Java Sea. Three additional transports were captured by Japanese surface fire.

During the week of 27 Feb to 4 Mar 1942 Allied Naval losses totaled as follows:
*   Netherlands: CL De Ruyter, Java ; DD Korteaer ; DE Evertsen*
*   Australian: CL Perth ; PG Yarra*
*   English: CA Exeter ; DD Jupiter, Encounter, Stronghold*
*   American: CA Houston; DD Pope, Edsall, Pillsbury, Stewart;*
*   SS Perch; PG Ashville, AO Pecos; AV Langley*

---

[108] The 1942 spelling of *Soerabaja* has been adopted over *the modern spelling of Surabaya.*
[109] Klemen, L (1999-2000) "The conquest of Java Island, March 1942". Dutch East Indies Campaign website. http://www.dutcheastindies.webs.com/java.html.
[110] Mitsuo Fuchida, Captain, & Masatake Okumiya, Commander, *The Battle that Doomed Japan – Midway*, by Two Japanese Officers – published Ballantine Books, 1958, p.49.

12.   AT SEA – ABOARD THE MS ABBEKERK

12.1.   Day #1 - Japanese Recon Airplane – Saturday, 28 Feb 1942

We had breakfast about 8:30 AM, and it was good. If you are hungry enough, anything tastes good. Onboard we all ate in a single chow line, officers and men alike. Afterward, I sat on my "cot" and continued adding to my diary. Sitting on deck, there was plenty of time to write.

That night I had slept on the hatch. When the sun came out, there was no shade and it was extremely hot. Most of us had lost or given away anything we had for shelter as we could only keep what we could carry. I really missed my typewriter. I was hoping my trunk and footlocker would get home safely.

It was not long before the ship started receiving SOS calls from the other ships that had sailed ahead of us. The first call informed us that one of our companion ships had been torpedoed. On the horizon, we could see black smoke. Our captain steered in the opposite direction from the smoke.

About 30 minutes later, we heard from a second ship that needed help. We saw more smoke in a different sector. Again, our captain steered away from the smoke. He was trying to get as far away from the action as he could.

The bad news came in regularly by radio. A convoy 85 miles out was bombed. A ship behind us was under attack. A Dutch ship was attacked by a submarine in our vicinity. We heard the calls for help, but there was never a second call or "all clear." We could only imagine the results. We did not know who was sunk or what happened to any of the passengers.

This news was not encouraging. We were alone in the middle of the sea with damn few life belts. Everyone continued working feverishly making rafts from the oil drums and bamboo. I still doubted there would be enough rafts in the event we had to use them. We were all wishing it would rain like hell so no one could see us.

About 9:30 AM a single bomber was spotted overhead. We were unable to tell whose plane it was, but since there were very few Allied planes anywhere in the theater, we were certain it was Japanese. He circled us for about an hour and then left. We were sure he was radioing our position back to the Japanese submarines.

About mid-day, another Japanese plane came overhead. It was a recon plane and probably didn't have any guns. He started circling overhead and probably radioing our location again. On the ship, there was a 30-caliber Lewis Automatic Machine Gun. A Lewis Gun was a relic of World War I, used by the British and Dutch Armies.[111] It was different from the American Browning automatic 50-caliber machine gun, since it was fed by a round top-loaded drum (or pan) magazine, rather than a belt.

I went back to the sergeant, and said "Let's see if we can find some ammo for that Lewis."

I asked the captain if he had any ammo for the Lewis Gun on the ship.

To my surprise, he said "Yes, but it was down <u>on the bottom deck</u> of the ship on the port side." Well, I didn't know how many decks were on the ship, but the sergeant and I hooked up with one of the Dutch ship officers and we headed below deck looking for ammo.

You can't believe how dark that cargo hole was. It was as dark as pitch and we had a hell of a time climbing over junk to find how to get down to the lower decks. All we had was one dim flashlight. The stairs down into the hole alternate between sides of the ship. One walks down one level on the starboard side, then across the ship to the port side to go down to the next level. Back and forth, back and forth – finally we arrived at the bottom deck – five floors down.

Figure 50 - Lewis Gun with overhead-inserted drum magazine.

We had two surprises. First, the ballast for the ship was one of those Javanese trains, a steam "putty put" locomotive. It was down there as dead weight to stabilize the ship. Second, we found we were traveling on an ammunition supply freighter with several tons of military explosives. There were cases of different kinds of ammunition stacked all over the place. There were some 500-pound bombs rolling back and forth as the ship

---

[111] The Lewis Gun, considered a light machine gun, is a 30-06 caliber air-cooled automatic machine gun that takes a pan or drum magazine mounted on its top. The ammunition is stored perpendicular to the axis of rotation of the magazine. Each drum contains either 47 or 97 rounds.

rolled. As we walked across the floor, we had to be careful where we stepped to dodge the rolling bombs. If your foot was caught between rolling bombs, it could break your ankle. We got past the bombs and finally found a case of Lewis Gun magazines that we managed to open.

Figure 51 - Australian Soldiers firing a Lewis Gun in World War I

A Lewis magazine contained 97 rounds of 30-caliber ammo, which was heavy. We were facing five floors of dark stairs to get back up to the main deck. I picked up one magazine, and the Sergeant took two. The Dutch officer would not carry any. That was as much as we could carry. Then we started back up the stairs. When we came out on top, it was a wonderful relief to breathe fresh air again.

The Japanese plane was still up there circling. Quickly, we located that Lewis Gun, and with a piece of rope, tied the machine gun to the ship rail. There was no real mount. We could get only a little elevation and not much left or right movement from our make-shift mount. We asked the skipper "If the plane comes back over here again, could you turn the ship so we can shoot at him."

Well, the skipper did turn the ship, and we opened fire. Every third shot in the magazine was a tracer, so we could tell our shots were going behind the plane. We were not leading the plane enough. Someone on the boat thought he saw us hitting the tail, but I did not see it.

Shortly, the plane came over us and made three passes finally dropping his extra belly fuel tanks at us. The tank hit about 400 yards behind the boat, so he missed us as we had missed him. He had to have been a reconnaissance plane since he had the extra fuel tanks. By then, we were a day out of port, which meant the pilot was a couple of hundred miles from a land base. Anyway, he finally turned away, and the captain resumed his zigzagging path heading south away from Java.

After the plane left, we sat down and started thinking about what we had done. It never occurred to us that the ship might be bombed while we were down below deck. Had we thought we could be trapped, we might have never gone down. In an emergency, we could have never gotten out. Besides, if one good bomb hit the cargo of this ship, we would all be blown up anyway. The Dutch officer strongly suggested that we not talk about what we had seen down below deck.

12.2.   Day #2 - Moving Away from the Coast – Sunday, 1 Mar 1942

As time passed, we were getting further away from the coast and out of range for the land based Japanese bombers. Our fears moved from airplanes to Japanese submarines. The captain was doing lots of zigzagging, changing directions irregularly to not let a submarine get a torpedo shot at us. The crew was pushing the ship for all it was worth – possibly making 20-21 knots[112]. We had great confidence in the captain. He even got out his rifle and fired at the plane when it made its run at us yesterday.

Periodically more radio reports came in of ships in our vicinity being attacked, and of course they could not say if they were sunk. We would read about the outcome later.

We enjoyed our two meals a day. Lt. Andrews and I keep watch over each other's stuff. Only one of us would eat at a time, while the other guarded our "territory."

Water was rationed to one canteen per man per day. Before leaving Tjilatjap, I paid 10 guilders for a gallon container and was very glad I did. I was able to get it filled twice daily with the help of those around me. They used the water too.

As the ship continued to plow toward Australia and the port of Fremantle, idleness set in. We were all sitting on the hot deck trying to find a sheltered place out of the sun and wind. We were all left with our own thoughts. I filled the time writing in my diary.

[The tone of the diary changed from reporting activities to more talk about feelings and attitudes about my current situation. The diary became a little philosophical.]

> Today is March 1st and I may write quite a bit. It just occurred to me that day after tomorrow is my birthday. I hope I'm still here on my birthday. I feel I will be. As the fortune teller says, "Every day is my lucky day."

> I can say again, it's a dammed helpless feeling to be riding a rough sea, no life belt, maybe half enough life rafts, and too far to swim. Everyone that has a life jacket wears it all the time.

---

[112] The straight-line distance from Tjilatjap to Fremantle is about 1,735 miles. It is not clear how many miles the course of the MS Abbekerk covered; however, passage was done in approximately four and a half days, which implies better than 385 miles per day or an average of over 16 knots every hour they were at sea.

Because there were so many people on the ship[113], there were no safe places if we were attack. It doesn't make a bit of difference where you are. Anywhere was a dangerous place.

Well, we are about ready to get somewhere, I don't care where, but I want to stay there long enough to do some good in this War. If we don't get fighters in Australia, damn if we will not lose Australia too. Seems to most of us, the politicians are fighting the war on paper. How they think so few pilots can win the war for them, I do not know.

I hate it very much that the 131st [Field Artillery] was left behind in Java. I know they do not have sufficient ammunition, and alone there was no hope. Someone was wrong.

It is next to impossible to describe the scene on the ship. With nothing to do, there was so much milling around. Most men have very few clothes. There are a large variety of uniforms and nationalities - Army, Air Force, Navy, British, Dutch, Indian, American, Australian - all are dirty and very few shaved. We keep hoping to see Australia in a couple of days.

I still had my camera ready to take a picture if any more Jap planes came over. I did take a few photos, but none survived the war.

Most say they saw tracers going through the plane yesterday. That may have been the reason the pilot turned off on its last pass. The story gets better the more time passes since the event.

6 PM – The swells had been pretty large and we had been rolling all day. The wind was very strong and it became very cold after dark. We thought we should be a couple of hundred miles off shore now and would probably stay well out to sea until we got near Fremantle.

On March 1, 1942 the Japanese Army landed a massive invasion force on the island of Java.

---

[113] Later reports indicate that there were over 1,500 passengers onboard the *ms Abbekerk* at the time.

12.3.   Day #3 - At Sea – Monday, 2 Mar 1942

The diary went silent today. It was impossible to write all the bad news. Word arrived of the Allied Naval defeat in the Battle of the Java Sea and the sinking of the *USS Houston* and *HMAS Perth*. There was nothing good to write about.

Sleeping was in spells. We can't smoke after dark of course. We take a drink just before trying to go to sleep and it helps. We are expecting to make port late tomorrow evening. So far so good!

Today the Major asked me to organize a Military Police unit for the ship. With so many soldiers and with tensions so high, some fights broke out. To maintain order, we organized an MP unit to keep the peace. I had nothing else to do so it occupied some time.

We had certainly been rolling today with large swells and waves. It was rough walking down the side of the ship. One has to be careful doing your business off the side of the ship.

This evening I purchased a 38 Colt used by the Royal New Zealand Air Force for 15 Guilders. Ten went to the man who owned the pistol, and five went to the lad for getting it for me.

12.4.   Day #4 - My Birthday – Tuesday, 3 Mar 1942

March 3rd was my 33rd birthday and a hell of a day if I may say so. Cold, well, we all nearly froze last night. While we were in Java, I had the good fortune of drawing a leather jacket from the quartermaster which was some comfort from the cold. Most of us have either lost our cloths or were ordered not to bring so much, so last night, we had a lot of cold people.

The first news of the day was that a Japanese raider was shelling a British freighter 600 miles south. There have been subs in the Fremantle area, so it may be very rough getting into the harbor. We learn that we were expected to dock in Fremantle about 8 AM tomorrow morning, Wednesday, 4 Mar 1942.

I had a bottle of White Horse Scotch Whiskey I had brought with me all the way from San Antonio, Texas. It had been stored in the bottom of my footlocker for three months, but I retrieved it when we evacuated Malang. I had been carrying it for the past week, and my birthday seemed like the right time to share it. I was also tired of hauling it.

Lt. Andrews and I opened it, and took a strong drink to celebrate my birthday. Maybe that's why I was able to write so much in the diary so early this morning.

> First of all, to be grateful to my darling wife, I was indeed sorry if not mad at the fact that I had a request in for over two weeks to talk to her and never did get to before leaving. I had paid the deposit and knew that sooner or later it would get through but now I would not be there to talk. I doubted that I would be able to call from Australia but I would try.

These people down here didn't know the score in this war. There are lots of things I'd like to find out about this war.

12:30 PM – A ship was sighted to our starboard but we passed it by. As we are in a Motor Ship and leave no smoke, it was doubtful we were seen. A submarine was reported to our stern this morning but not seen by us, just a radio report. We will make a dive for the Australian coast and go straight in when we turn. That will be another dangerous part. We all will be glad to get there. I would like to go to the hospital for a few days myself to rest up.

1:30 PM – Radio reports raiders and subs in Fremantle. It may be very rough – three ships out of five that departed from Tjilatjap with us have been sunk. We are one of the two lucky ones – imagine how we feel. Sea was still very rough and if the ship was loaded, the water would wash the decks. Thank goodness we only have a freight train and some bombs in the hold.

Years later I learned that of the 24 ships that sailed from Tjilatjap on February 27th, thirteen were sunk before reaching their next port.[114] *Fortunately, our Captain kept us among the eleven lucky ships that survived.*

12.5.   Day #5 - Arriving in Fremantle – Wednesday, 4 Mar 1942

6:25 AM – I woke up at daylight and what did I see – a pilot boat, a light house, and then Rottnest Island[115]. Rottnest Island was about 10 miles out to sea from Fremantle. It was an incredible relief to see land. After a short stop to pick up a pilot, we headed into Fremantle harbor. The sun was trying to pop through the overcast. It looked like rain to me, but they never have a rain in Perth, so it must have been fog. I was dirty like a rat, but put on a clean uniform anyway for the arrival. Most others didn't have clean clothes. We

---

[114] www.msAbbekerk.nl

[115] Rottnest Island is located about 19 km off the coast from Fremantle, Western Australia.

certainly had some rolling yesterday – up, down, and sideways. We had to stop in the harbor to be inspected before going in to dock. That consumed a quarter of the morning. We were so anxious to get off the boat.

As we pulled into the Fremantle Harbor, the first thing we saw were damaged ships along the shore. There was a freighter with the whole front-end blown off – like someone took a hatchet and chopped off the front end. Next thing we saw a ship with a hole clear through it. This was the kind of boat you use to unload cargo, and somehow it was still floating. Then there was a third ship that had been hit. You could tell this was a graveyard for crippled survivors of war which had managed to limp into port.

We came past a U.S. Navy submarine tender. That cheered us to know the good guys were around.

Once in the Harbor, there seemed to be great confusion. All the docks were full, and there was no pier for us to tie up. We dropped anchor in the middle of the harbor while the authorities decided what to do with us.

I had not eaten breakfast, but stole a can of pears. Most of us tried to eat just enough to survive. One of my corporals put several cans of stuff in my bag. It was so heavy, I could hardly carry it. I was longing for a bath and some rest.

Late in the afternoon, we were still sitting on the ship anchored in the harbor. Nerves were frayed and everyone was upset. We could see land and were eager to get off the ship. They fed us the afternoon meal (3:30pm) onboard with the usual corn wooly and dog biscuits. Food seemed terrible, and the coffee undrinkable. The same food that was wonderful four days ago was no good any more now that we could see Australia.

Finally, about 5:30 PM we pulled into a dock. Thank God, we could get off.

By this time, I had no cigarettes. I walked back to the American submarine tender and bought a whole carton. I think they were 6 cents a pack. I took them back to our group, opened them, and told everyone to take what they wanted. I was surprised but couldn't get rid of them all. People had no place to carry them. Duffel bags and pockets were already stuffed. I ended up with five or six packs to leave behind.

13.   JAVA FALLS TO THE JAPANESE

13.1.   Japanese Attack Tjilatjap – 3 to 5 Mar 1942

On <u>3 Mar 1942</u>, *Vice Adm. Nagumo, who led the attacks on Pearl Harbor and Darwin, led his carrier task force against the port of Tjilatjap. A force of between 150 and 180 Japanese planes launched from a Japanese carrier in the Java Sea sank 20 ships in the harbor at Tjilatjap.*[116]

On <u>3 March 1942</u> *the Japanese attacked Broome, Western Australia, from their airbase in Timor. Though Broome was a very small settlement, it was a refueling airbase for evacuees from Java enroute to central Australia. In the 3 March raid, the Allies lost 88 personnel and 22 aircraft, including a number of wounded who were being evacuated from Java.*[117]

On <u>5 Mar 1942</u> *Japanese pilots reported in aggregate the sinking of three Allied destroyers and fourteen transports which were trying to escape south into the Java Sea. Three additional transports were captured by Japanese surface fire. These were perhaps the same ships that departed Tjilatjap with the Abbekerk.*

13.2.   Dutch Surrender Java & NEI – 8 Mar 1942

On <u>8 Mar 1942</u> *the Dutch East Indies, which today is called Indonesia, were unconditionally surrendered to the Japanese.*[118]

At Porong near Soerabaja, Dutch infantry and the American 131st Field Artillery Battalion gave resistance to the incoming Japanese Army. Eventually the Allies withdrew to Madura Island, and

---

[116] Mitsuo Fuchida, Captain, & Masatake Okumiya, Commander, *The Battle that Doomed Japan – Midway*, by Two Japanese Officers – published Ballantine Books, 1958, p.49.

[117] In the Broome attack, the Japanese fighters destroyed at least 22 Allied aircraft, including an airborne United States Army Air Forces (USAAF) B-24A Liberator, full of wounded personnel — more than 30 died when it crashed in the sea, about 16 km off Broome. The Allies also lost 15 Dutch flying boats at anchorage; many Dutch refugees were on board and the exact number and identities of those killed is unknown. At the airfield, the Japanese fighters destroyed two B-17E Flying Fortresses and a B-24 belonging to the USAAF, two Lockheed Hudson's belonging to the RAAF and a Lockheed Lodestar belonging to the Royal Netherlands East Indies Air Force (ML-KNIL). A KLM Douglas DC-3 airliner (PK-AFV carrying refugees from Bandung) was also shot down 80 km north of Broome, with the loss of four lives and diamonds worth US$500,000.

[118] James D. Hornfischer, Ship of Ghosts, Bantam Books, 2006 p. 201 refers to the escape of Americans from Java through Tjilatjap.

on the evening of 9 Mar 1942, Maj. Gen Gustav Ilgen of the KNIL Infantry surrendered at Si-doardjo. Disarming all the troops took until 12 Mar 1942.[119]

On 9 Mar 1942 the 2nd Battalion, 131st Field Artillery, formerly of the 36th Infantry Division Texas National Guard, surrendered to the Japanese Army. The 131st became known as "The Lost Battalion" because the U.S. Army did not know their whereabouts for the duration of the war. A total of 534 members of the unit became Prisoners of War. A total of 86 of these died in captivity (16%), which was actually a high survival rate for Japanese prison camps. Some POWs were transported to Burma and Thailand where they suffered through starvation, brutality, and slave labor working on the construction of the Burma-Thailand railroad. Some were shipped to Japan aboard a Japanese prison ship that was sunk while in route to Japan in June 1944. Those men who survived captivity endured 42 months of misery and deprivation.

As POWs, the 131st was combined with 371 sailors who survived the sinking of the USS Houston. The total 901 POWs were distributed in Burma, Thailand, Japan, and Manchuria. Collectively, 163 died in captivity (18 percent).

On 12 Mar 1942 the Dutch signed the final surrender of the Dutch East Indies.

Capt. William Dwight (Ike) Parker, who had been with Day on the USS Republic and his room-mate in Singosari, was captured with the 131st. He was liberated in Thailand.[120] *[Born: 7 Dec 1908, Died: 7 Sep 1970] He was a resident of Laverne, Alabama. But by the Grace of God, Capt. Day could have been one of the POWs on the Death Railroad.*

Col. Albert Chester Searle, Commander of the 26th Field Artillery Brigade, did not evacuate with his unit from Java. A Regular Army Officer, he requested and was granted permission by Gen. Brett to remain in Java as a representative of the Regular Army during the eventual surrender of the 131st Field Artillery (a National Guard Unit).[121] *He was held as POW by the Japanese from 13 Apr 1942 to Oct 1945 in the Hoten POW Camp (Mukden) Manchuria 42-123. He lived to be liberated from the POW camp, died 15 Dec 1965, and was buried in Arlington National Cemetery, Washington, D.C. [Service Number O7005141, Colonel, Field Artillery].* [122][123] *Col. Searle was born 28 Feb 1892 (Massachusetts).*

---

[119] http://www.dutcheastindies.webs.com/java.html

[120] James D. Hornfischer, *Ship of Ghosts*, Bantam Books, 2006, p. 405-406.

[121] Walter D. Edmonds, *They Also Fought With What They Had: The Story of the Army Air Forces in the Southwest Pacific, 1941-1942:* Boston: Little, Brown and Co., 1951, footnote on p.410 attributed to Lt. Stewart B. Avery.

[122] Source Information: National Archives and Records Administration. *World War II Prisoners of War, 1941-1946* [database on-line]. Provo, UT, USA: Ancestry.com Operations Inc, 2005. Original

In August 1942, the MS Abbekerk was torpedoed by German U-boat-604 and sunk after being hit by three German torpedoes about 500 miles southwest of England during transit between Spain and England.[124]

In just three months following Pearl Harbor, the Imperial Japanese Army had annihilated the Army, Navy, and Air Force of ABDACOM, the combined Asiatic Forces of America, Britain, Holland, and Australia. The remnants of American resistance in the Philippines were under siege - surrounded and cut off from resupply of food or ammunition. The residual Allied forces were in retreat to Australia and the South Seas. Japan controlled the oil and rubber supplies of NEI that it required to sustain its military dominance of Asia.

data: World War II Prisoners of War Data File [Archival Database]; Records of World War II Prisoners of War, 1942-1947; Records of the Office of the Provost Marshal General, Record Group 389; National Archives at College Park, College Park, MD.

[123] Source Information: Ancestry.com. *World War II Prisoners of the Japanese, 1941-1945* [database on-line]. Provo, UT, USA: Ancestry.com operations, Inc., 2010. Resident State: California; Original data: Collection ADBC: Records of the American Defenders of Bataan and Corregidor. World War II Prisoners of the Japanese Data Files, created, 4/2005–10/2007, documenting the period ca. 1941–ca. 1945. Washington, D.C.: National Archives and Records Administration.

[124]; www.msabbekerk.nl by peter@peterenhanneke.nl, 4-04-2011.

14.   AUSTRALIA, AT LAST – 4 MARCH 1942

14.1.   Reflections upon Arrival in Australia - 4 March 1942

After waiting around for a while on the dock, we were ushered to a railroad track where we boarded a local train that left at 9:30 PM. We were being transported to an Australian military base, Northam Army Camp, Western Australia, about 70 miles into the interior.

Low in the east, a new moon is rising. A partial blackout is in effect – the Australians think it is total but it is not. The train, a very old 1900 model, is parked alongside the dock and troops being eager to get to hell off the boat pile into the train, ready to go anywhere. They are told a three-hour ride "at most" was ahead of them and then peace for a while – a nice rest camp. Some picture – a world of freedom and peace – that is hard to believe. At 9 PM the train moved out of Fremantle – a stop every 10 minutes, seemingly a station each time – all so hungry and at each stop all try to pile off and buy anything one can find to eat. Oh, at last, apples and pears – delicious they are – a bellyache follows – the beautiful country can be seen through the moonlight – very rough – lots of pretty flowers – houses are a long way apart, showing the sparsely settled country. The people are wild with joy that the Americans have arrived to save them. What an impression – a bunch of dirty soldiers – partially clothed – some in shorts, almost freezing to death – most have lost their worldly belongings, but are happy to put feet on good old earth once more, knowing well The Lord has granted a stay, so well earned – yet knowing the sorrow to come for the loved ones of the less fortunate left behind. Personally I have some very good friends left in the Java Islands who will suffer at the hands of the Japs."

Guilt was setting in. Why were we the chosen ones to leave Java? Why was our ship not torpedoed? Why did the Jap plane not bomb us? Why were we one of the two boats out of five to get through? Why did the bombers skip us on their way to bomb a town 200 miles from us?

These questions will never be answered.

Back to the train ride – the sky – a beautiful pink – above which I saw some constellations I had not seen in some time. The Southern Cross is a beautiful sight we cannot see at home. I watched carefully the direction the train was traveling. Well, a five-hour ride to a place 65 miles away from the port, followed by a truck and a bus ride to a camp – high on a mountain – very cold – a lunch awaits us at 3:30 AM, followed by choosing a straw mattress, a blanket, and a bed – at last – sleep.

The above was written more as a reminiscent of a trip taken – a book could have been written as a legend or myth that would be hard to believe – even the winds told a hard story – each wind would tell of some sacrifice. The bright and dark skies could have frowned upon us, but the memories will last as everlasting fantasies for a lifetime – good night.

And so concludes an episode of the thoughts of a single man.

Figure 52 –Fremantle to Northam – 72 miles
Rottness Island was shown just to the left of Fremantle - Google Map

14.2.   Northam Army Camp, West Australia – Wednesday, 4 March 1942

Northam Army Camp was an Australian military training center hastily constructed in 1934-5 as part of a general Australian military build-up to train an Australian Citizen Militia. The camp consisted of barracks, mess hall, parade ground, rifle range, and land for military maneuvers. With the outbreak of World War II in 1939, Northam became an important Army Training Center for Western Australia, a role that continues into the 21st Century. Located about five kil-

ometers southwest of Northam, the complex included over 140 "temporary" huts, which have seen use over the subsequent sixty years as Army barracks, Italian POW Camp (WWII), and holding camp for illegal immigrants captured while entering Australia from Asia.

Northam Camp probably had only routine difficulty accommodating the 1,500 military evacuees that arrived in Fremantle aboard the "Abbekerk."

Western Australian Newspaper, Perth, WA – March 1942

*The "**Western Australian,**" a Perth newspaper, was filled with news releases of the "Battle of Java," "Java's Agony," and "Bombs on Broome" in March 1942. After the Japanese attack on Darwin, the Australians were well aware that the war front had moved to their shores. Their towns in the Northwest were within range of Japanese bombers based on Timor and Java, and were under attack. The Japanese aircraft carriers could deliver bombers to the Aussie doorsteps.*

Thursday, 5 March 1942

In Camp Northam, West Australia, after four hours of sleep, I got up. It was very cold, but I shaved, and took a cold shower, which felt wonderful. I had not bathed in about a week. I ate breakfast at 10 AM and received orders to move again. "Move on Soldier, you can't stand here," was the usual thing we heard. We had to move to another camp close by.

Major Mitchell, the Australian Officer, was Commander of an Australian Battalion at the training camp. He held an organization meeting for his new arrivals from 2 to 5 PM. Afterward we cleaned up for supper, and he asked me to have a drink with him before supper. He asked me to give a speech, a little pep talk, to everyone at supper, and boy, did I rock them over. Guess I'm getting good at speaking. I would love for Cile to have seen me. She would not have believed I could do it. I had a lovely meal and drank several drinks of whisky, brandy, wine, and crème de menthe. After supper the Major wanted me to take a walk with him, which I did. He wanted to discuss his thoughts on a role for me in the Camp. Finally, I did my work and went to sleep at 11:45 PM. The Australians treated us very well.

The next morning I was appointed commanding officer of Unit 1 in the camp, which had five officers and 326 men. All were Air Corps men. Some few had already been sent on to other locations. Capt. Suave[125] from Nacona, Texas, was my assistant. He had been in

---

[125] The name "Suave" is spelled three different ways in the diary – Suave, Soeue, and Soule. It is not clear to the author which is correct.

Batavia about 7 years. Nacona was located about 100 miles west of Bonham, and his wife has a friend who lives in Honey Grove [near Bonham where my wife is staying].

I cannot call Cile and am damn certain that she will not get a wire, but will send one as soon as possible.

6 March 1942
It was wonderful to have a night of sleep without thinking about bombers, submarines, or machine guns. It was impossible to imagine we were in Australia, alive and safe. Most men had no more clothes. We knew we were all lucky to be here. I certainly was. We knew three of the five ships that departed from Tjilatjap with us had been sunk.

8 PM - I eat in the Officers Mess with Major Mitchell. He and all his officers have been so nice to us. It would be very hard to say in words just how courteous they have been to all of us.

I spent all day getting orders written for everyone in my group. There were others who had been among the 1,500 onboard the *Abbekerk* now attached to my group.

Capt. Suave and I roomed together. I had brought a radio with me and was sure glad, as it is good entertainment for us. My typewriter was left behind in Java, but I managed to borrow another temporarily. I am trying to get some clothes cleaned. The batman, an Aussie assigned to help us, was doing such a nice job looking after us.

I cabled Cile today the following *"Safe with Love"* Hope she gets it pronto. Bless her heart. I hope she is not worrying but thinking about us. I love her so much.

I have not written a letter home mainly due to my not knowing what P.O. Box to use for a return address. We do not know how long we will be here. We cannot say where we are, as censorship is much more strict here than in Java. I am very frustrated. I love you Darling. Hello to Johnnie.

I also cabled Mr. and Mrs. Visser in Java as a courtesy. I knew they were worried at this stage. I hoped they were OK.

Saturday, 7 March 1942
Up at 6:30 AM with Reveille - Breakfast 7:30 and mostly office work till 10. The Camp Commander, Col. Bilco (Australian), and Maj. Thompson came at 10:45 AM, made inspection of barracks, and joined us for Tea in the Officers Mess. After noon, I cleaned my

guns. Capt. Suave and I went into Northam about 4 PM to see the town. It has a population of about 6,000 and is at an elevation of about 500 feet.

> Darling, I love you so much. Knowing I have such a small chance of getting mail through, I guess I will just write you a love letter here in the diary. I think of you & Johnnie so much and then I think of nothing. My love to all and I love you every day.
>
> I know Cile worries about me, so I must send her a wire. I have tried to send all my letters to Cile so she can forward them to mother, which simplifies things a lot for me. It's so hard to write two letters. It's hard to write even one with all the censor regulations we have.

Sunday, 8 March 1942

Capt. Suave and I went into town last night for dinner. We ate at the hotel, where we had lamb "of course." These people eat lamb or mutton like we eat beef. It was a fair dinner for 3 shillings (which they write 3/). We walked all over the main street, which was a small job, and ran into Padre, our Catholic chaplain. He is in camp here with us and insisted on showing us around. Well, he can sure drink the beer. We made all the places in town, drinking all the beer we wanted.

On the way back to camp, we went with Padre as he made his rounds visiting the hospital. At one point while visiting patients, Padre accidentally led us into a wrong room. The room turned out to be occupied by two girls who had been evacuated from Singapore.

On discovering there were girls, the Padre said "Run for your lives, men." We sure had a good laugh.

Looks like people in Australia will never wake up to the fact that a war is going on. You have to be shot at and bombed to realize what war is. Why the hell they can't keep the place dark at night is beyond me.

I was quite brown, and weighed 170 lbs. yesterday. I am in good physical condition, all considered.

Monday 9 March 1942

I was planning to go into Perth today to see the town, but Maj. Thompson suggested I wait till tomorrow or the next day due to crowed conditions, there and in Fremantle. I guess a lot more evacuees are pouring into Fremantle. So I am waiting.

We were told that all the Air Corps or possibly all the troops here would be shipped out to Melbourne shortly. I will be glad to go somewhere nearer to a larger town to at least see a picture show. This little town, Northam, reminds me so much of a West Texas country town, only about 20 years behind. Most important of all, however, I have some clean clothes. The batman had all our dirty clothes washed. Of course no starch and damn little crease in the clothes, but they are clean.

I sent a short cable to Cile knowing I couldn't call. I hoped she could figure out where I was.

> Still have not had a letter from you, Darling, and have been quite disgusted with everything.

We learned that the Japs went into Broome, Northwest Australia and played hell – about ten B-17E's lost and 15 Dutch flying boats loaded with evacuees – lots killed.

Tuesday, 10 March 1942
I was able to get a Jeep today, so about noon I drove into Perth to see about footlockers, service records, and two men in the hospital. The scenery was beautiful. There were lots of very tall thin trees, not so big around. This was very dry country. I went to Fremantle to the ship docks. There were lots of docks, and they were all very crowded. I saw what they call the beach, and took a few movies. My big thrill was that I drank several milk shakes, and also just plain milk. It sure was good after not having any milk for so long – I even had cereal.

I wrote a short quick letter and hope it will be carried back to States before being mailed.

We learned that the *Langley* (the first U.S aircraft carrier) had been sunk. Its crew was picked up by a tanker, and the tanker was sunk. About 150 of the tanker survivors were rescued by a destroyer that was attacked by three submarines. The destroyer had to drop depth charges at the submarines, and the depth charges naturally killed lots of our own men who were still in the water. About 500 were lost. That was one of our <u>worst</u> losses so far. The *Langley* was transporting quite a few new fighters to Java. The planes were still boxed up.

Wednesday, 11 March 1942
I stayed at Palace Hotel last night in Perth. The rooms in the hotels were all full. My room did not have a bath in the room, so I used the one up the hall. Their hotels are not as nice as ours at home. They appear to be old in their ways. All doors are locked at 7 PM and you press a button when you want in. You must have a room before you can get inside. Some few women on the street were nice looking but mostly walk like farmers. I

went to the ship, *Black Hawk*, a destroyer tender and bought more cigarettes (50 cartons), which I brought back to the men. I found they still had plenty, so I had to sell some as I cannot carry all of them with me. I guess most of the soldiers don't smoke like I do.

We received orders that we would all be moved by rail to Melbourne on the east coast of Australia. We would be on four or five separate trains leaving Friday, Saturday, Sunday, or Monday. I did not get to send any extra baggage ahead, as I was in Perth when they picked up the luggage. I had to carry it all with me. I took a few more shots with my camera.

Wednesday, 11 March 1942 – Gen. MacArthur left Corregidor by PT-boat for Australia. Gen. Jonathan Wainwright became the U.S. commander in the Philippines.

Thursday, 12 March 1942
We returned to Northam Camp today from Perth. There were nine of us in a five-passenger jeep. We must have looked like gypsies packed like sardines in that jeep. I still find the city of Northam, as one fellow expressed it, "About half the size of a New York cemetery and twice as dead."

I do not know which train I will leave on - Friday, Saturday, Sunday or Monday, but I hope it would be tomorrow. I would sure like to be settled for once and get a job. I knew I could get a promotion if I could ever stay in one place. This was the damnedest screwed up outfit I think I had ever seen – another "SNAFU" situation.

Most of the men are over in the mess hall drinking beer. I had drunk my part a few times, but do not feel I need to do it again. I still have not seen a show since leaving Java, and the ones in Java were all old.

The Japs seem to now have control of all Asia, except Australia. We wonder when they would start on Australia. Surely, we will stop them here. We gave them hell in New Guinea that day. There was also a good report from Darwin, however, Darwin had already been blown to hell, so there was not much left there.

I think I like Java better than Australia, taking all into consideration. Java had much more wealth. This country has not been developed. It seems as though everyone lives in town, and no one lives in the country. However, it sure feels swell to not have an air raid every day for a change.

P.S. I love you.

14.3.   Train from Perth to Melbourne

14.3.1.   About Trans-Australian Trains

Australia was settled by six independent colonies.[126] *When railroads were introduced in the 1850's, each colony followed different standards for railroad construction and selected different railroad gauges, that is, the distance separating the two steel rails. Without standardization, six incompatible railroad systems were built. A locomotive from one state could not travel over the rails of a different state. Because a train could not pass from one state to another, each state border crossing required all cargo and passengers to be off-loaded from one train and reloaded on a different train in the new state.*

Australia's first east-west railroad, the Trans-Australian Railway,[127] *began operation in 1917 running from Kalgoorlie to Port Augusta. Because of the lack of rail standardization, passage from Perth to Sydney required six complete train transfers. Among the six states, there were three separate rail standards in use: broad, standard, and narrow gauge. This gauge incompatibility remained until the 1980's when a federal initiative finally forced rail standardization.*

Another problem that plagued Australian railroads was water. The trans-Australian route crosses the Nullarbor Plain, which is a 400-mile stretch of land with no natural water supply. The route does not intersect any year-round river, surface water, or even reliable underground water aquifer. The little natural rainfall drains to the interior where it evaporates. Well water was brackish, unfit for human consumption, and unfit for use in steam locomotives due to high mineral content which corroded the boilers. This meant that the railroad had to set up small remote water storage tanks across the most desolate Outback at 20-mile intervals and deliver water to these tanks by a special water train.

The distance from Perth to Melbourne is over 2,050 miles, about the same distance as from San Francisco to Chicago. In 1942 the passage from Perth to Melbourne required two-and-a-half days, three complete train changes. The route transits the Nullarbor Plain, the waterless region of Australia where the railroad goes over 400 miles in an absolute straight line, the longest straight-line railroad in the world. A map of the Australian rail system in 1942 is shown in Figure 53.

---

[126] Australia's six colonies are analogous to the sixteen British North American colonies, which after the Treaty of Paris (1763) which ended the French and Indian War, included New Brunswick, Nova Scotia, Montreal, and Florida (which was ceded by Spain to Britain with New Orleans going to France.
[127] From Perth to Melbourne to Sydney.

14.3.2.   The Journey to Melbourne

<u>Friday, 13 March 1942</u>

The troops at Camp Northam were divided into four trains for the ride to Melbourne. Two trains would leave Friday, a third train would leave on Sunday, and the fourth train would leave on Monday. I had been designated Camp Commander and would remain behind until the final train departed on Monday. I would be Train Commander of the fourth train. Can you imagine "His Grace, the Camp Commander?" My reign was short, but there was much to do.

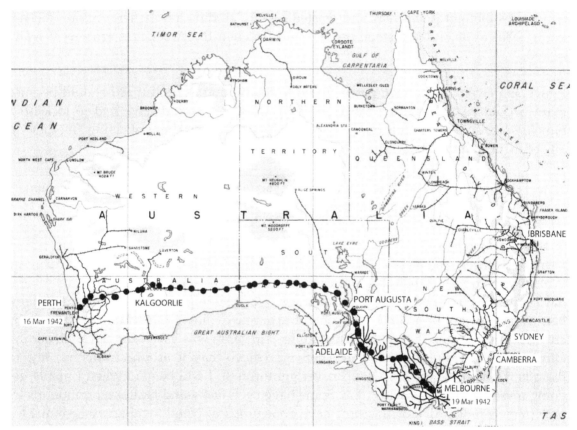

Figure 53 – Rail trip – Perth/Camp Northam to Melbourne
16-19 Mar 1942 - Australian Rail Map – 1941

This train ride was a sardine trip across Australia from Perth to Melbourne in two plus days. I went to the train station to watch the men loaded on the first train. I have never witnessed a more congested and screwed-up mess. Lots of men, Australians and Americans alike, were drunk. Even some of the officers were a poor example of our Army. The Air Corps troops here, and as I had seen in Java, were about the poorest excuse for the

Army as anything I have seen. It is most discouraging to those of us who know something about Army discipline. As the Australians say "I was pissed off." This organization had no discipline and was not like anything I had seen in the States. The trains were loaded to the gills, and I still had 35 men I could not get on board the first train. The stragglers might have to wait till after Monday if we could not squeeze them into a later train. I didn't want any part of the Air Corps.

As to the war situation, I do not know what was going on.

While we were in Northam, we had only one practice air raid. During the alarm the Americans thought it was real, and wasted no time finding a hole. The Aussies did not know what to do, so they stood around and watched the Americans who were really scared.

I gave 35 percent of the men passes to go to town tonight. I felt that I should because many would go anyway. If I started locking up any, I would have had to lock up a bunch. I care so little for this bunch I just don't give a damn. I'm not acting "mother" to any of them, and they know that.

> I will hold on to the letter that I wrote to you the other night and mail it in Melbourne. I think it will get there just as soon.

Sunday, 15 March 1942
I sent two officers and eight enlisted men into town as Military Police to round up every U.S. soldier and send them back to camp at once. Some have been AWOL for several days. All are being reported to Headquarters. We are going to put as many extra members as possible on the second train tonight to get them moving. It will most certainly be crowded, but I cannot help that. The only Jeep in camp was left to me as Commanding Officer, and I am sure glad I have it. There is so much chasing around from one camp to the other. If I had to walk, I would never get through. I will be glad when I finally get going myself. I want a "steady" job. Some have been lucky and had two promotions by now (mostly in the Air Corps). Some have done practically nothing. I know I am due for a raise.

14.3.3.   Train No. 4 Departs from Northam – 16 March 1942

Monday, 16 March 1942
All plans were completed for our final gang to leave tonight at 10:25 PM. Of course sleeping will be out, as I know we will be very crowded. I carried a few cans of fruit to have as we cross the desert. The trip will require a couple of days. I was hoping I would

get all my stuff on board. I have been fairly lucky so far and only lost a little in comparison to others. I had all my junk ready by 2 PM, and I was able to sleep a few hours before supper. They fed us a big final supper which was quite filling.

We left Northam about 7:45 PM. We all got on board the train in a farm outside of camp, and I had a hell of a time finding seats for all the men. The RAF b**** seem to be about the poorest I have ever seen. I tried to write while the train was moving on the narrow-gauge train, but it was impossible. We were bouncing more than on a streetcar. The seats were also very hard to sit on.

Tuesday, 17 March 1942
We had our first train change about 1:30 AM, only six hours down the road. I told my men to get a seat pronto. We all did.

Labor laws seemed to rule Australia. The Australian train conductor and engineer would stop the train twice a day, every morning at 10 AM and every afternoon at 2 PM for their "cup of tea." The train would stop out in the desert where we thought we were "in the middle of no-where" near an isolated water tower to pump up the steam locomotive boiler. They were not worried about another train coming along the single track. They would walk out beside the train and build a small fire, where they could boil water for tea. They carried a small specially-built tin tea set they called a "Billy" that was stored in a special leather pouch that they wore on their belt. They used the "Billy" to make their tea. Nothing else in the world mattered until they had their tea.

When the train stops, the troops get out of the train and stretch their legs. We are an armed train with lots of soldiers still carrying pistols and rifles. One time when the train stopped at a water tank, there were wild kangaroo some distance from the train. Some of the men were trying to shoot kangaroo from the side of the train. I don't think any were good enough shots to hit anything, but it was good entertainment.

Along the way we also saw a few Australian aborigines. These are black men with very long hair who lived in the desert.

During the day we had two meals in the dining car (with milk, which was very special). We crossed over that long stretch of railroad that was a straight line for several hundred miles.

This desert country, Outback as they call it, seems to have considerable vegetation. It appears that much of the terrain is close to sea level and very flat. If they could find water, it could be made into a wealthy country, but the scenery looks very desolate with lots of red dirt.

Wednesday, 18 March 1942

We are still on the train. Last night was terrible as far as rest was concerned. My shoulder gave me trouble. I just cannot lean on it, even sitting up. I need to sleep on my back. It was very cool at night in the desert, and in fact I froze all night.

14.3.4.   Arrival in Melbourne, Camp Royal Park - March 19, 1942

Thursday, 19 March 1942

I could not write on the train, because the train was so packed and bounced too much. Now I am in Melbourne and I want to fill in the diary.

When I got off the train in Melbourne, I was told to report to the Adjutant General the next morning. We were ushered to Camp Royal Park, where all the American troops were assigned. Along with several other officers, I was assigned to a barn that was under construction in which to sleep. At first, we could not unlock the door, but finally we got inside. It was very cold, there was no hot water to wash, and we had not had a bath for several days. I set up my cot, and collapsed in exhausted sleep about midnight.

15.   MACARTHUR DEPARTS THE PHILIPPINES

The military situation in the Philippines continued to deteriorate. On 12 Dec 1941, Japanese landed 2,500 troops in southern Luzon, and later in Mindanao. The main Japanese Army struck when the 48th Division came ashore on 22 Dec 1941 with 43,000 troops supported by tanks and artillery in the Lingayan Gulf of Luzon.

In a few very short days the Japanese swept down across Luzon. Gen. MacArthur declared Manila an Open City on 26 Dec 1941 to avoid its destruction as a casualty of war. Gen. MacArthur and the remnants of the USAFFE withdrew to the Bataan Peninsula and Corregidor Island. Between 17-20 Dec 1941, FEAF withdrew its last fourteen surviving B-17's from the Philippines to Australia. They were later moved up to Java where many were lost.

By the end of December the Philippines were effectively controlled by the Japanese Imperial Forces. The last remaining American resistance was isolated to the Bataan Peninsula, Corregidor Island, the Visayan Islands, and Mindanao. The Philippines were surrounded by a Japanese Navy blockade that cut off any further resupply. All American Naval surface vessels had been withdrawn south from the Philippines to the Netherlands East Indies (NEI).

By 15 Jan 1942 the Japanese High Command was operating one month ahead of their schedule for the conquest of Southeast Asia. They felt so confident about their military situation that they decided to defer the clean-up of the Philippines to secondary military units in favor of moving quickly into their primary target, the Netherlands East Indies (NEI). In the Philippines, they replaced their crack 48th Infantry Division from the front lines of Bataan with the less experienced 56th Division, allowing the 48th Division to rest on Jolo Island, Sulu Archipelago (PI) before the invasion of Borneo and Java in the NEI.

By 23 Jan 1942, Rabaul in the New Britain Islands had fallen. Allied Forces were in retreat in NEI.

On 15 Feb 1942 the British surrendered Singapore with its 130,000 troops and withdrew to India. On 19 Feb 1942 the Japanese unleashed a carrier-based aerial assault on Darwin, the mainland of Australia. Bali was invaded on 19 February 1942. On 17 Feb 1942 the Battle of Java Sea began with the annihilation of the Dutch and American Navy in the Southwest Pacific. ABDA-COM was collapsing, and the Dutch would surrender Java in two more weeks. Control of South East Asia was in the grasp of Imperial Japan.

The first three months of the Pacific War were a clear victory for the Japanese.

15.1.   Roosevelt Ordered MacArthur to Leave – 23 Feb 1942

In Washington, the Pacific War situation was clearly evident. Japan had conquered Southeast Asia. The Allies had suffered defeat after defeat. The only hope for victory was to withdraw, re-group, and fight another day. Gen. MacArthur was viewed as critical leadership for this second phase strategy.

Gen. Marshall and Gen. MacArthur had discussed MacArthur's departure from the Philippines for the preceding month. The following communiqué was sent by Marshall to MacArthur on 4 February 1942:

> *"The most important question concerns your possible movements should your forces be unable longer to sustain themselves in Bataan and there should remain nothing but the fortress defense of Corregidor. Under these conditions the need for your services there will be less pressing than other points in the Far East."[128] [129]*

MacArthur, the dedicated soldier, was prepared to die with his troops in the Philippines. He was reluctant to leave and had declined the offer by Marshall for early evacuation of MacArthur's wife and son.[130]   Finally, Roosevelt issued a direct order that arrived in Corregidor on 23 February 1942 instructing MacArthur to proceed with due haste to Australia and take command of United States forces. Roosevelt's expressed intention was to obtain the approval of Australia and Britain to reconstitute an ABDA[131] alliance in Australia with MacArthur in command. Roosevelt offered submarine or aircraft transportation services, as required, for MacArthur's evacuation. MacArthur replied the next day, requesting a short delay but also indicating his intent to use surface craft and bombers.

15.2.   The MacArthur Evacuation: Corregidor to Melbourne –
11 to 23 Mar 1942

Gen. Sutherland[132] made the arrangements for the evacuation of the MacArthur entourage which included MacArthur's wife (Jean Faircloth), his son (Arthur), nurse for young Arthur (Au

---

[128] Rogers, *MacArthur and Sutherland*, Vol. I. p.183

[129] Beck, John J. *MacArthur and Wainwright*. Albuquerque: University of New Mexico Press, 1974. p. 89-90; Secret File, 2-3-42.

[130] Rogers, *MacArthur and Sutherland*, Vol. I. p.183.

[131] ABDA Alliance stands for American, British, Dutch, and Australian Alliance.

[132] The MacArthur evacuation story has been recorded in at least two first-hand accounts. One account is by Paul P. Rogers, Gen. Sutherland's personal stenographer, a member of the evacuation party, and appeared in his first volume memoir, *The Good Years: MacArthur and Sutherland*,

Cheu), twelve Army officers, two Navy officers, and one enlisted man. The twelve staff officers later became known as the "Bataan Boys." The size of the evacuation party was limited by the maximum capacity of either four PT-boats or three B-17 bombers.

After sunset on 11 March 1942 a squadron of four Navy PT boats[133] loaded the MacArthur party, three loaded at the dock on Corregidor and one loaded from Marivales, and departed for the 500-mile journey to the north coast of Mindanao.

The four PT boats and their passengers were:

- *PT-41 – Gen. Douglas MacArthur, his wife, his son, his son's nurse, Gen. Richard K. Sutherland, Lt. Col. Sidney L. Huff, and Maj. Charles H. Morhouse, MD.*
- *PT-34 – Adm. Francis W. Rockwell, USN Capt. Jimmy Ray, and Gen. Harold H. George, USA Air Corps, Gen. Richard J. Marshall, Col. Charles P. Stivers [134]*
- *PT-35 – Lt. Col. Francis H. Wilson, Col. Charles A. Willoughby, Lt. Col. LeGrande A. Diller, and M/Sgt. Paul Rogers.*
- *PT-32 – Gen. Hugh John (Pat) Casey, Gen. William F. Marquat, Lt. Col. Spencer B. Akin, and Lt. Col. Joe T. Sherr.*

Sea passage was under cover of darkness with all boats under total blackout. The journey required two nights to reach Cagayan de Oro. During the first night, the four boats became scattered. PT-32 had engine trouble and fell behind until they could make repairs. In the early morning light, PT-32 misidentified PT-41 was an approaching Japanese destroyer and was preparing to attack the boat carrying MacArthur. Anticipating a battle, extra fuel, which was on deck, was thrown overboard. Fortunately, the boat realized their misidentification of PT-41 before they attacked, but after they had jettisoned the fuel.[135] The loss of the fuel made it impossible for PT-32 to have suf-

---

published by Praeger in 1990. Master Sergeant Rogers was the only enlisted man included in MacArthur's evacuation entourage from Corregidor and personally typed the orders for the departure of the members. Major Day is referred to in M/Sgt. Rogers memoir, since Rogers was a member of Headquarters Company of GHQ when Day was Headquarters Commandant. A second first-hand account appears in Gen. Hugh J. Casey's *Engineers Memoir*, recorded by Dr. John Greenwood in 1979. There is also an extensive review presented by Peter Dunn in his "Australia @ War" DVD published in 2008 that deals with the MacArthur flight to Australia and the train to Melbourne. This description is based upon these three sources.

[133] The PT boats used were PT-32, PT-34, PT-35, and PT-41. The MacArthur family was on PT-41.

[134] One source also said that Capt. Joseph McMicking (Philippine Army, G-1 USAF) was also on the boat but unconfirmed.

[135] Casey, Hugh J. *Engineer Memoirs*, US Army Corps of Engineers, Office of History, UG128.C37A5, 1993

ficient range to reach Mindanao. When the boats reached the designated rendezvous point, all passengers from PT-32 were transferred to other boats.

A backup plan for MacArthur's escape was to connect with an American submarine at the rendezvous point where only MacArthur and his family would be taken by submarine to Australia. After some discussion, MacArthur decided to proceed by PT boat to Mindanao. Since they were behind schedule, they proceeded in daylight at some risk. The low-fuel PT-32 had orders to wait at the rendezvous to meet the arriving submarine and then proceed to Cebu. When the submarine arrived, the crew reported their PT boat was disabled, scuttled the boat, and boarded the submarine for Australia.

Upon reaching Mindanao the MacArthur entourage was transferred by truck to the Del Monte Plantation[136] in the central Bukidnon Plateau, where the previous year the military had constructed an airfield, Del Monte #2. Of the first four bombers dispatched from southern Australia to retrieve the MacArthur party, only one aircraft arrived safely in Mindanao, and that single aircraft experienced a hydraulic failure that made the brakes and supercharger inoperable. The aircraft was deemed mechanically unsuitable for the return flight. After further delay, two more B-17s were borrowed from the Navy in Darwin and flown up to Del Monte, arriving before midnight on 16 March 1942. The planes were immediately refueled, loaded with the MacArthur party, and departed for the return flight to Batchelor Field at Darwin. The flight from Del Monte to Batchelor is over 1,500 miles which required extra fuel tanks for the B-17. Because of weight limits, some of the party and much of the luggage were left at Del Monte for another plane to recover the next day. The air route was perilous since it had to pass over northern New Guinea, Celebes, and around the island of Timor, all lands which by this time were in Japanese hands. The two planes arrived at Batchelor Field, about 80 miles south of Darwin at approximately 9 AM on the morning of 17 March 1942.

After some discussion in Batchelor, the MacArthur party was transferred to two Australian National Airways DC-3s for the next leg of the journey to Alice Springs, the northern-most station for the Australian railroads. The planes cleared Batchelor field only minutes before a Japanese bomber run struck the field.[137] The travelers arrived in Alice Springs the afternoon of 17 March 1942 and were taken to a local hotel for a nights rest.[138]

The next day (18 March 1942) the group separated into two parties. MacArthur refused to fly the next leg of the journey and insisted on a train. Gen. MacArthur, his family, Sutherland,

---

[136] This plantation was owned by the Del Monte Company, the private American fruit company.

[137] Rogers, Vol. I. p 194.

[138] http://www.ozatwar.com/macarthur.htm, Peter Dunn

Dr. Morhouse, and Col. Huff traveled by train from Alice Springs to Melbourne, while the rest of the staff officers flew directly to Melbourne.

Why did MacArthur insist on a train? All theories appear to surround medical issues raised by Morhouse, the medical Aide to MacArthur and personal MD for the MacArthur family. Was the health of young Arthur or the health of Mrs. MacArthur the issue? Or was MacArthur emotionally exhausted from the ordeal of evacuation? The stated reason was that MacArthur wanted some rest.[139] This author does not know.

MacArthur's party departed Alice Springs on Wednesday morning, 19 March 1942 aboard a special train for the 1,000-mile 70-hour journey over narrow-gauge railroad to Terowie, a small town 137 miles north of Adelaide. Shortly later, they crossed another state boundary where, because of railroad gauge differences, they changed to a second train bound for Adelaide. MacArthur arrived in Adelaide on 21 March where the party transferred to a third train for Melbourne.

The staff officers who flew from Alice Springs departed 19 March 1942 and arrived in Essendon Airport in Melbourne late that evening after an approximately eight-hour flight with refueling in Adelaide.

---

[139] Rogers, Vol. I. p. 194.

15.3.   MacArthur Appointed Commander SWPA - 18 March 1942

Roosevelt, true to his word, appointed Gen. Douglas MacArthur commander of the Southwest Pacific Area (SWPA) Theater after he had received the consent from both Australia and Britain.

The Pacific Theater was divided into four areas:

- North Pacific Area
- Central Pacific Area
- South Pacific Area
- Southwest Pacific Area.

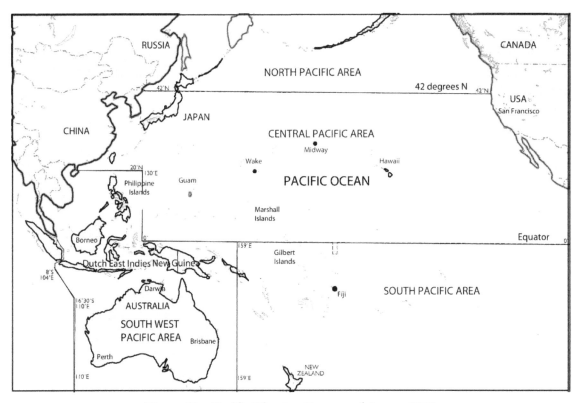

Figure 54 – Pacific Theater Command Areas -1942

15.4.   MacArthur Arrived in Melbourne – 23 March 1942

MacArthur's train arrived in Melbourne's Spencer Street Station at 9:30 AM on Monday, 23 March 1942.[140]

Figure 55 - Gen. Douglas MacArthur and Gen. Richard Sutherland
Australia 1942 – photo autographed by both generals.

Figure 56 - Young Arthur MacArthur, and Au Cheu, his nurse -
Australia 1942, Arthur is the four-year-old son of Gen. Douglas Mac-Arthur.

These U.S. government photographs of MacArthur and Sutherland may have been taken in Brisbane upon arrival in July 1942.

---

[140] http://www.ozatwar.com/macarthur.htm

16.   ARMY ORGANIZATION – JAN 1942

16.1.   USFIA, USAFIA, and USASOS

United States Forces in Australia (USFIA) Command was created on 1 Jan 1942 in Brisbane for the purpose of establishing US Army services of supply (USASOS) to support troops in the Philippine Islands and the Netherlands East Indies (NEI). Four days later, the unit was re-designated United States Army Forces in Australia (USAFIA). The Americans had no vision of stationing large numbers of troops in Australia for any extended period.

On 5 Jan 1942 Maj. Gen Brett transferred his Headquarters[141] from Brisbane to Melbourne where he could better coordinate his supply activities with the Australian Army, Navy, and Air Staffs. In the same General Order No. 1, Brett established five operational supply bases for his American troop activities:

- *Operational Base No. 1 – Soerabaja, Java, Netherlands East Indies (NEI)*
- *Base Section No. 1 – Darwin, Northern Territory*
- *Base Station No. 2 – Townsville, Queensland*
- *Base Station No. 3 – Brisbane, Queensland*
- *Base Station No. 4 – Melbourne, Victoria*

In January and February there were major changes in command when Gen. Brett went to Java to become Deputy Commander of ABDACOM under Gen. Wavell. At that time Gen Brereton in Batavia, Java became commander of US Army Forces in Australia and NEI. Later Brereton became commander of Air Corps in ABADCOM and Maj. Gen. Julian F. Barnes assumed command of USAFIA. When ABADCOM collapsed, Brett returned to Australia and assumed command of USAFIA on 24 Feb 1942. [This was discussed in Chapter 4.1.2 of this book.]

16.2.   United States Army Services of Supply (USASOS) – Feb 1942

In February 1942 Gen. George Marshall became Chief of Staff for the U.S. Army (Washington, DC), and quickly instituted a major reorganization of the Army. He issued an Executive Order that consolidated the Army into three separate, but parallel Commands, as follows:

- *Army Ground Forces*
- *Army Air Forces*
- *Army Services of Supply (USASOS)*

---

[141] USAFIA General Order No. 1 dated 5 Jan 1942.

The USASOS was a consolidation of the technical services and the administrative bureaus of the Army into a single Command. Previously, sixty separate services and bureaus reported to the Army Chief of Staff.

The Technical Services consisted of seven branches:
- The Engineer Corps
- The Signal Corps
- The Ordnance Department
- The Chemical Warfare Services
- The Medical Department – the Surgeon General
- The Quartermaster Crops
- The Transportation Corps

The Administrative Bureaus were defined as:
- Headquarters Commandant
- Adjutant
- Special Services Officer
- Provost Marshal
- Inspector
- Staging Area Officer
- Cargo Movement Officer
- Chaplain
- Army Exchange Officer
- Finance Officer

Civilian organizations call this a matrix organization in which a line commander for combat operations would call upon the specialized staff for technical advice and special services, but retain the responsibility for operational performance. For example, the land forces could call upon the Engineers for assistance with road construction, but the land forces were still responsible for the tactical battlefield. The air forces would call upon the Engineers to build an airdrome or a repair base, but the air forces are still responsible for the combat missions.

A year later in 1943 the name, US Army Services of Supply dropped "of Supply" to become simply Army Service Forces, because the word "Supply" did not adequately describe the full breadth of activities of the organization.

16.3.   MacArthur Takes Command of SWPA – 18 Mar 1942

When MacArthur assumed command of the Southwest Pacific Area (SWPA) (18 Mar 1942), he designated five area commands:

- *Allied Land Forces*
- *Allied Air Forces*
- *Allied Naval Forces*
- *US Forces in the Philippines*
- *US Army Forces in Australia (USAFIA)*

On 20 Mar 1942, USAFIA was formally assigned the mission of administration and supply of all American troops in SWPA. USAFIA was intended to be the conduit of supplies for the Philippines and the Netherlands East Indies (NEI) that were expected to flow from the United States and Australia. To this end, SWPA expanded their "Base Sections" (or supply depots) which were geographically distributed around Australia and NEI to receive and stockpile ammunition and military materiel to support the war effort.

The Base Stations were responsible for the procurement, storage, issue, transportation, construction, hospitalization, evacuation, and signal communications of the United States Army. This included food, ammunition, medical supplies – everything. The Sections were assigned a threefold mission:

1. *To operate a service command for the administration of the base sections, ports, and camps in its area*
2. *To receive and assemble all US troops, supplies and equipment sent to or arriving in Australia*
3. *To perform service of supply and administrative functions for combat troops that would enable them to move freely and with minimum delay (into the combat zones).*

Each Base Section was located near a port with a camp suitable for storage and good access to transportation. Each was organized with a Base Commander, supported by administrative and technical service officers that paralleled the Services of Supply regulations. Three new Base Sections were added bringing the total list to the following:

- *Base Section No. 1 – Darwin (Birdum), Northern Territory*
- *Base Section No. 2 – Townsville, Queensland*
- *Base Section No. 3 – Brisbane, Queensland*
- *Base Section No. 4 – Melbourne, Victoria*
- *Base Section No. 5 – Adelaide, South Australia*

- *Base Section No. 6 – Perth, Western Australia*
- *Base Section No. 7 – Sydney, New South Wales*
- *NEI Base Section No. 1 – Soerabaja, Java, NEI*

USAFIA was in existence for only three months, when on 20 Jul 1942 there was another name change to USASOS-SWPA (Southwest Pacific Area). All personnel and Bases were transferred over to USASOS-SWPA with no change in standing orders.

Initially, the USASOS for SWPA was headed by Maj. Gen. Richard Marshall. When Marshall became the Deputy Chief of Staff to Gen. Sutherland, Brig. Gen. J. L. Frink took command in Sept 1943. Later in July 1944 in preparation for the invasion of the Philippines, Gen. Casey was assigned to head Army Services Command (ASCOM) attached to the Sixth Army and Maj. Gen. J. L. Frink remained in command of USASOS.

16.4.   Troop Strength – 21 Mar 1942

While MacArthur was on his train from Alice Springs to Melbourne, the following incident is reported:

> *Late in the afternoon of 21 March 1942, their [MacArthur's] train reached Kooringa, 80 miles north of Adelaide. One of his staff officers, Col. Dick Marshall, who had flown ahead, boarded the train. He had bad news for MacArthur, who had thought that a huge army awaited him in Australia. He was told that there were fewer than 32,000 Allied troops, including all American, British, and Australian, in the whole country. There were fewer than 100 aircraft, many primitive Australian Gypsy Moths, with fabric-covered wings and propellers that had to be started by spinning them by hand. "God have mercy on us," MacArthur whispered. It was his greatest shock and surprise of the whole war.[142]*

This troop strength should be viewed from the perspective that the British had surrendered 130,000 troops in Singapore, and the Americans were about to surrender over 100,000 in the Philippines. MacArthur knew he was facing a horrific situation.

---

[142] Peter Dunn, *Australia @ War*, http://www.ozatwar.com/macarthur.htm

17. MELBOURNE, USAFIA, AND USAFFE – 19 MARCH 1942

17.1. MacRobertson High School & the Bataan Boys

With no organization and little staff, MacArthur was leading the "ultimate start-up" when he arrived in Melbourne. The Headquarters for United States Army Forces in Australia (HQ USAFIA) had been assigned the use of MacRobertson High School, a small selective-enrollment public girl's school located at 350-370 Kings Way in central Melbourne.

The nucleus of this new headquarters staff was built around the "Bataan Boys," the twelve officers and one enlisted man who had been evacuated from Corregidor with MacArthur. In Australia, they hit the ground running and moved quickly to hire staff to replace the hundreds they had left behind in the Philippines. They had worked together and experienced wartime conditions as a team in the Philippines, commanding over 100,000 troops. Now they had no troops but trusted in each other. After arriving in Australia, many of the colonels were soon promoted to generals.

17.2. Camp Commander of Camp Royal Park – 20 Mar 1942

Friday, 20 March 1942

After pulling into Melbourne yesterday and sleeping last night in the barn at Camp Royal Park, I slept too late for breakfast this morning, but I reported to the Adjutant General, Col. Burdette M. Fitch. He informed me that I would be Camp Commander at Camp Royal Park. I secured some clothes for myself and the men. Cotton was all we could locate. They said there were no more wool uniforms, but I saw a lot of others wearing wool. I kept maneuvering for another couple of days before we got wool, as it was cold and winter was coming.[143]

We finally got paid for February. So welcome!

> I have not had time to send a cable to Cile. Wish I could see her and cry a while. I love her so much. Hello, Johnnie. Daddy loves you so much too.

---

[143] March in the Southern Hemisphere is like September in the Northern Hemisphere. Melbourne is located at 38 degrees South Latitude which is approximately the same distance from the Equator as San Francisco, California. However, Melbourne receives cold winds from Antarctica.

17.3.   401 Collins Street

<u>Friday, 20 March 1942</u>
Col. Fitch told me Gen. MacArthur would be arriving in Melbourne soon. He was coming down from the Philippines, was on his way, and was bringing some people with him, including Mrs. MacArthur, his son, and a bunch of other guys. "You have to get things ready for him."

"Where is the Headquarters to be located?" I asked.

"401 Collins Street," Fitch told me. We are taking over three floors of a 9-story building. You need to set it up."

I figured I had a week to get ready. Little did I know that MacArthur would arrive in three days.

Fitch gave me a drawing of where some things should be in the building, but mostly I was running blind. I went down and toured the building and the specific

Figure 57 - 401 Collins Street, Melbourne - 2007

floors we were to occupy. It was essentially vacant. There was nothing but a bunch of empty rooms, not a damn thing in the building. I had to find desks, typewriters, file cabinets, paper, telephones, and you name it. We needed wall partitions, electrical modifications, and plumbing changes –- everything for the headquarters.

I went back to Fitch. I suggested that the General and his Chief of Staff should be on the top floors and the lesser people on the lower floors. Fitch wanted a drawing, so we drew one up for him. The building had two elevators.

I said "I have to get some supplies. Where am I going to get them?" I did not know where the Quartermaster was, but I learned he was leasing a warehouse, but it was not yet organized and not ready for business. Meantime, I found out where the supply ships were coming into port periodically. I gave Lt. Evans a truck and four or five men, and I sent them down to the dock to see what they could scamper up.

Lt. Evans found out that the crates addressed to the U. S. Army Forces in Australia (USAFIA) were stacked up on the dock with an armed guard walking the perimeter every 45 minutes. After the guard went by, they drove the truck up and started loading boxes. They picked boxes they thought might contain something useful, but they really did not know what was in the boxes.

When the truck was full, the boxes were brought back to Collins Street where they were taken up to the sixth floor to a closed room in the back of the building. That is where the boxes were opened. It was like Christmas. You never knew what you would find when you opened a box.

Every night another load of crates would be brought in from the docks. A single load could be picked up, taken downtown, put on the elevator, taken to the sixth floor, and opened. Desks, typewriters, rugs, paper, and lots of office furniture were found. All the typewriters were put in a separate room behind a locked door for fear someone would steal them. Anything we could use we took into the building. You could never imagine the stuff we pulled in.

In one box I found twelve desktop pen and ink sets. These were the liquid-ink fountain pen type that you would pay $15 for at a store. We gave each general one for his desk.

I did not want anyone to know what I was doing nor what I had in our storage room. I didn't want any of the generals to know, as I didn't want to get caught. A few got wind of our activities and were complaining about me and "my 40 thieves" under their breath, but we were filling up the building, so no one complained too loudly.

About fifty percent of the stuff in the boxes was of no use to us. We didn't want it, but we were left with the problem of how to get rid of the extra. We had no place to put it. We could not take it back and tell them we stole it. We could not give it away or people would ask questions, so we just kept everything extra in one big room and locked it. We were becoming experts in accumulating stuff. This went on for quite a while.

In one crate we found boxes of knitting yarn, every color you could imagine. The Australian gal that ran the elevator was seen knitting one day, so the Sergeant said this was his chance to get himself a sweater. The Sergeant took a couple of boxes of yarn down to her and made a deal with her to knit him a sweater. She said "What size?"

He said "I don't know."

She said "Well, I will guess."

She made a sweater that was big enough for two people. She ended up making three or four more sweaters, smaller and smaller until they finally fit somebody. The Sergeant brought me one, and it was very welcome. I wore it under my blouse.

> The following is a quotation from a Day letter home dated <u>27 Dec 1942</u>:
> *You should see what I received for Xmas. I have never been so surprised in all my life. While in a certain place back in July [Melbourne], I gave a lady, who was operating an elevator in the building, some yarn that we happened to have and had no use for and thought she might like to knit something as she was at the time knitting. Anyway, here at Xmas I received a beautiful white knitted sweater. I mean it really is nice, and I don't even know her name. I know the address and will write and thank her for same. She was about 45 and weighed at least a ton, about 250.*

Finally, the Quartermaster got the warehouse set up, but there was no inventory report available. The only way I could find out what the Quartermaster had in his warehouse was to go in there and look. If I could use it, I requisitioned it. I went to the Adjutant (Fitch) who would write the requisition for the item "by order of General MacArthur." Then we would take it from the warehouse. In the course of going through the warehouse, we also found a way quietly to put the extra stuff from our storage room back into the Quartermaster's warehouse without anyone taking notice. We finally cleaned out our storage room.

I found some more typewriters, about six. Eventually we were putting typewriters in all the general's offices. Although the generals could not type, the generals had stenographers who took shorthand and typed their memos. Although the generals did not use the typewriters, someone in their offices was using them.

Anyway, I set up the Headquarters.

In 1942 shorthand and dictation were very important. There were no computers, no copy machines, and no facsimile machines - not even a "mimeograph machine." There were only manual typewriters. When you wanted multiple copies, you had to type the original with carbon paper, sometimes six carbon copies deep, or type multiple copies of the same document. The manual typewriters had to really be pounded to drive through six carbons in order to make the last carbon legible. Telephones had only one line and were hard to obtain.

17.4.   Assigned to USAFIA – 23 March 1942

<u>Monday, 23 March 1942</u>
Today I was assigned to Headquarters USAFIA and will assist the Headquarters Commandant, who ranks me a couple of months. I was told that my Battery, which had come with me from Northam, would also be assigned to USAFIA and become the basis of the Headquarters Company.

I was moved from Camp Royal Park to the Chevron Hotel for quarters. The Chevron Hotel was an easy tram ride to MacRobertson High School, which had been taken over by USAFIA as temporary office space.

Well, I had been running in circles all day, but finally I had argued them into paying me per diem of $6 from the time I left Java until now that was a lot of money to me.

Tonight was my first night in the Chevron Hotel. I had a bath, unpacked my stuff, and went to sleep about 11 PM.

I will try to stay caught up in the diary for a while. I think Capt. Parker and all my friends still in Java, including all the 131st Field Artillery, have been captured by the Japanese.

On this day, Monday, 23 March 1942, MacArthur's train arrived in Melbourne's Spencer Street Station at 9:30 AM.

<u>Wednesday, 25 March 1942</u>
1:35 AM - I have been smothered with work all day, trying to get my Battery Service Records and Funds straight. I am still Battery Commander for the troops we moved in from Northam, and I have my Morning Report to complete every day. I even received $3.54 of company funds today sent from the States on 11 December 1941. It took more than three months to reach me.

I am in the Headquarters Commandant Office and have lots to do. I will try to write more soon. I need to find some warmer clothes and do some laundry.

I need to send Cile another cable.[144] Love you Darling.

---

[144] Each cable home usually had his extra money attached.

Thursday, 26 March 1942

I am having a devil of a time getting started again keeping my diary. Gosh, this Head-quarters of the Army in Australia takes in a lot, and at present I am trying to establish order so that supplies to HQ can get moving. I have now met all the big Generals of the different Sections and so far so good.

I got back to the hotel about 6 PM, cleaned up, and ate supper. I thought I would go to the show tonight, but when I got down there, I was too late. I came home, took a good drink of scotch, and went to bed. I still have a bad cold, but it seems to be on the mend. I caught the cold while I was at Camp Royal Park. I still have received no mail from home.

Friday, 27 March 1942

Today, I completed the requisition for the supply business and all is going well. I under-stand I will be Company Commander of the Headquarters Company. Don't know what else I am liable to have assigned.

My laundry came back tonight. I suppose it will likely rain if I wear a clean uniform to-morrow. The *Seawitch* should dock tonight, so hopefully my footlocker should be here in a few days from the ship.

Capt Nathaniel B. Sauve and I took a small drink before supper and have looked at three issues of <u>Life Magazine</u>. These were the first issues I had seen since November. Must close and get some sleep. Wish I could see you all. Love Darling.

Saturday, 28 March 1942

8 PM - I just came up from supper. Capt. Sauve and I arranged for a table and ate supper together. We had a good dinner, in fact it seemed like this was the first time I had been able to sit still and take my time eating any meal. I heard a few jokes which I will try to remember, especially the one about the extravagant Americans.

I saw Maj. Gen. Barnes today and had a talk with him. He asked me about the ones we left in Java. He was very friendly. I also met Col. Baird, who was actually our boss. He seems very nice. It seems like everybody wants something. I never saw so many people trying to get things all at one time, and here I am trying to manage it for them. They are all learning my name fast.

Someone said they were having a dance here in the hotel tonight until midnight. As I don't know anyone, I may go down for a while.

17.5.   Queen Mary Arrives in Sydney – 28 March 1942

The Queen Mary arrived in Sydney on 28 March 1942 after a "40-day and 40-night" voyage departing from Brooklyn, New York, on 18 February 1942.[145] *The ship had traveled by way of Florida, Rio de Janeiro, Cape Town, and Fremantle. This was the first time the Queen Mary carried American troops (8,398 troops and a crew of 905). The ship was unescorted during the entire voyage. It was said that the ship was capable of 30-40 knots, which was considered very fast. Among the troops on board the ship were a group of selected US Army officers from Fort Ord, California, who would join Gen. MacArthur's Headquarters.*[146]

17.6.   Sunday Afternoon at St. Kilda Beach – 29 March 1942

Sunday, 29 March 1942

I worked until 1 PM. I can't seem to get rid of this terrible cold. I talked to Sauve after dinner, and we decided about 5 PM we would take a few pictures. I actually talked him into it, so first we went out in front of the hotel and took movies of the Chevron Hotel where we were staying. Then I took a picture of the lovely tennis courts and myself and Sauve.

Then we decided to go to St. Kilda Beach and possibly take some pictures there. At least I had not seen the place and others said it was very pretty. We grabbed a street car in front of the hotel and away we went. As we walked out on the pier, we noticed a couple of girls in front of us and one had on an orange bathing suit. So I got Sauve with the two girls and took their pictures. He wanted to take mine with them, but I told him I was taking the pictures for my wife to see. I was sure that was not the type of picture she wanted to see. Anyway we ate a bag of nuts and came home in time to eat at 6:30 PM. After dinner I had a chance to write a letter home:

Sunday, March 29, 1942
Letter #20
This is an excerpt from the first letter from Australia that arrived safely in Texas. There were seventeen earlier letters, ten of which survived the war. The letter numbers were assigned in numerical sequence by John when writing.

---

[145] S. Harding - Gray Ghost: *The RMS Queen Mary at War*

[146] Among the officers onboard the Queen Mary was William B. Russell, who after the war operated a Men's Clothing Store in Los Altos, California called Russell Huston.

Dearest Cile and Johnnie:

Once more I am able to sit down and write a letter, as I have not received a letter from you or anyone else up to this time. I am about to wonder if you have even written.

Darling, I am still OK and safe again, have had a bad cold but seem to be doing better. Am about stocked up on some clothes again and as soon as the laundry can be returned maybe I can get cleaned up again.

I have seen a big part of Australia now and think it is a wonderful country, but of course not to compare with our country. This place is certainly beautiful. I hope to have sufficient pictures to show you. At this time, I have not been able to get the time to get out and take them. I lost a lot of pictures I took in a previous place [*Java*] and will never see them. They were being developed at the wrong time.

I am living in a large hotel, have a single room and ride the tram to work each morning. I have to work all day and have not even been able to see a show. Can you imagine my being able to see a show after the grind I just finished! I missed several days with my diary but have tried to get caught up. I know I missed several things.

I sure want to know when you receive the trunk and footlocker that I sent home. Be sure and wire me. ....

I was numbering my letters for a long time and got up to about 17 and difficulties arose so I will now start with No. 20 for this one and will number them again from now on. Tell me how many letters you have written too.

Darling, how are you coming with the money situation? I want to know whether you started receiving $200 per month in your February check? Was the added allotment in the March check? I have already written you about the increase in my life insurance and would like to know if you received a notice of the new insurance from the government? Are you saving any money? What about the car and have you paid anymore on it other than the schedule? It seems so long since I left that it really seems that it should be paid off. Really it has been a short time from that point of view.

I am so busy all day and a lot of nights that I am usually ready to go to bed when I get home. Usually when I get thru with supper, it is about 8 o'clock and a bath and it is really bed time. Every day is about the same as we work on Sundays too.

I have hoped that I would get a promotion but at this time I have my doubts. I should ...for more than one reason, so I still have hopes. I will of course let you know should a miracle like that happen.

As I could not bring my typewriter with me, I have had to scamper for a new one. At present I have one borrowed. I will try and keep a copy of all my letters, so if anything is cut, you will know what is after all is over.

Johnnie, how are you doing and what do you do all day. Daddy sure misses you too. Wish I could see you and Mother. You be sure and take good care of her because Daddy depends on you. What are you learning at school? I guess by the time you get this letter, school will be out for the year, at the rate I have been receiving letters. Write Daddy a letter and tell him what you are doing. How about some PX sugar?[147] Is it 5PM yet? [*PX Sugar*] will be one thing we will both always remember.

Your loving husband and dad,

John

Monday, 30 March 1942

I was up and out of bed as usual. My cold is still with me, but I have lots of work to do. I probably should have stayed in bed, but I will fight it out as I always do. I came home about 6 PM, after eating supper, and I decided to go to Camp Royal Park to a program that was being put on by the "Partner Mob." This was an amateur vaudeville-type show similar to those we sometimes saw in San Antonio, but not so good. I enjoyed it more than I expected, and after catching a ride back to the hotel, it was 11:30 PM.

Mr. and Mrs. Newbaker asked me out to their house Wednesday night for dinner, and I accepted. They asked me to bring another officer if I liked.

Tuesday, 31 March 1942

I was sick almost all day with this cold. I took aspirin, whiskey, and cough syrup. I have been waking up every night between 2 or 3 AM with a bad cough. I know I would feel better if that nighttime coughing would stop. I took more aspirin.

It seems the days pass so fast, and yet we feel like we do not get much done. We eat breakfast at 7:30 to 8 AM. By the time we get to work, it is at least 8:30 AM. Lunch is at 1 PM and supper or dinner at 6:30 to 7:30 PM. The late supper seems to drag the day out a bit.

It seems that all the generals are changing quarters. There is considerable shuffling going on. Gen. MacArthur is having his staff move closer to the downtown office.

Most of the men who were in my Battery are in HQ, had been assigned to various departments.[148] It seems funny that my outfit would make history like this. A lot of them have been promoted. A good bunch!

---

[147] "PX sugar" was a strong bear hug kiss that Capt. Day would give young Johnnie every evening when he got home from work. Yes, Johnnie will always remember those bear hugs, and I venture Johnnie's grandchildren also remember the bear hugs and kisses that he dished out to them and that they complain so strongly about. Now they know where the hugs come from.

[148] Headquarters Battery is in many respects the "home room" for all the personnel who support the Headquarters. This includes everyone from the office administrative staff, mess personnel,

March 31, 1942. Tuesday Night about 8PM

Letter No 21

Dearest Cile and Johnnie:

After a very busy day and lots of running around trying to get things that I wanted, I feel pretty tired. I had very good luck in getting the things that I was after. Well, I just do not know what I will start telling you in this letter, only that I love you and that I am still looking for a letter. I had most of my clothes cleaned and can now look a little more respectable.

I have chiseled a typewriter for the present use due to the one I had second being stolen. I took a few pictures the other day but have not had any developed as yet and cannot say as to the quality.

I ride the street car to work each day and back to the hotel for dinner and supper. It cost me one pence for each ride. Johnnie, I wish you were here to make all these trips with me. I know you would enjoy all of them.

I sure want you to save every copy of Life Magazine for me so I can see them at a later date. I want to see all the pictures, etc.

Hope I do not have the trouble that I had the other night. I just do not know much and I feel so bad with my cold that I am going to postpone this letter writing till tomorrow or the next day.

Thursday Night. Darling I am still sick with this cold and just cannot make myself go to bed to get rid of it. I have taken a bottle of cough syrup and several drinks of liquor and several aspirin and still have a terrible cough.

At last we have found a place to get part of the things moved into HQ where I am and should be able to show some better results as we go along.

My footlocker came in the other day, the one that had my blouse. I sent it to the cleaners, and today is the third day that they have been cleaning it. When I do get it back, it should at least be clean.

It is rather cold, especially in the early morning. They say that the cold weather is just starting and will be much colder later in the year. I have been thinking that I would have been better off had I not sent my short coat home. Now I may have to buy a long overcoat but doubt that I can get the material to have it made. The tailor is always so busy and I know that it would take a lot of time to get it.[149] I do not know what I will do. I

---

motor pool, and later, would include the post exchange, liquor store, barber shop, and other supporting personnel.

149 Enlisted men were issued uniforms, however Officers were responsible for supplying their own uniforms. Officers are also charged for their meals.

> have a leather jacket that I wear all the time and usually put a sweater on under my
> shirt so my upper half can keep very warm.

17.7.   First Mail Arrives for Others – 31 March 1942

Today we received about twelve bags of mail for the organization. Of course *[Cile]*, not knowing my outfit, could not have sent me any mail. I was able to watch a lot of the boys read as many as 20 letters. It made me feel bad that I did not receive anything.

The battery received a lot of magazines that were December, January, and few February issues. They are surely relished when we got them here and are passed around. I have not taken the time to see them as yet but will shortly.

I am in practically the same kind of unit that I was in before I left home. Now all the men I brought from Northam have been divided around the various offices and assigned to so many places that it would take more than a bookkeeper to keep up with them. The whole outfit has certainly made history being the first HQ in so many places.

I still have too much baggage in the event that I have to move north, but I will keep it for the present time. I can get most everything in two suitcases and a footlocker   I still carry my bed roll and cot that I have wagged so many miles. Think I will keep them as they have served me well to this date.

I am now working for a kid that ranks me two months. See what it cost me to have to wait the five months for my promotion to Captain! He is the commander and I am next. I still have hopes of getting a promotion anyway. I know I deserve it.

> Darling I love you. I think it is about time I told you again. That seems to be the most im-
> portant thing I am able to tell you in any letter that I write.

Oh, yes, I went out to the beach on Sunday evening about 5PM and looked around. It was so late that I did not get to see it all, but I took a few movies. Guess I will have to have some of them developed to see if any will be good. As yet I have not been able to get any back, as they were in the wrong place at the right time. I do hope they are good even though they are the first I have taken. After all, they do cost some money and are a big part of my expenses.

I guess the reason that I have a time with this typewriter is because I am trying to make a carbon copy of all the letters that I write. This typewriter does not like the extra copies.

I went down in the hotel game room and played three games of ping pong with a friend tonight. I had to quit because I wanted to finish this letter and get it mailed tomorrow. Saw a friend from PI tonight that I knew in Java. It was good to see him again. Guess what I weighed the other day, Honey?

Wednesday, 1 April 1942
Today was April Fool's Day. I could see very little difference from any other day. I never know when the week was over. Every day seems like Monday.

Well, I have been so busy. I still have not taken time to wire Cile. I just must and will in the next day or so. A lot of mail for the Philippine Islands and Java has arrived, but no mail has arrived for me. Guess it will be my luck to sit and never get a word from home. If I could just hear something once in a while, how much better I would feel. Looks like Cile could wire me in care of U.S. Forces in Australia. I love her so much. Wish she were near.

6 PM - Billy Newbaker called and asked if I was coming to dinner tonight. Boy, was I embarrassed. I thought today was Tuesday and told him Sauve and I would be out as soon as I could get dressed. It was 7:30 before we arrived. They had a very nice dinner for us. The Newbaker's have two very cute kids – a girl about five and a boy about two. His wife asked for your address to write to you, Darling. I thought it was very nice of her. I hope she has better luck hearing from you than I have had.

Thursday, 2 April 1942
I have been spending the day getting things for the generals. Guess I make a good "flunky." Don't know what else I'm good for. Col. Fitch, the Adjutant General, told me I was doing a good job, so it must be OK with him.

Today they brought my radio back. The repair cost five pounds 16 shillings, a terrible price. I knew I had been held up.

Today some men in the battery received as many as twenty letters. They sure felt good after getting the news from home. You could imagine how I was feeling not receiving anything.

My cold seems to be worse.

Thursday Night April 2, 1942.

Letter to Mother

Dearest Mother and Dad:

I am fine, have a terrible cold that I have had now for eleven days and you know how they always give me trouble. It has not seemed to improve very much in the last several days. I have taken a lot of stuff and sure hope to see some improvement shortly. I have not been sick other than the cold. I weigh about 170 pounds now (12 stones and 2 as they call it here). That is of course with all my clothes on.

Have a nice room in the hotel now and am at least comfortable at night. I rested well for a change, much different than it has been in the past.

The outfit received some magazines from home today and I have several to read when I get through. It will take me a couple of nights at least to read them all. I have my radio that I sneaked along with me all these months now in playing shape and can listen to something that may come on the air. Don't know when news is broadcast and have not bothered to find out. It seems that I just don't have the time to listen.

I have about secured enough clothes now to look decent and can get them cleaned often enough. It takes several days to get clothes cleaned so naturally have to have more cloths.

I have wanted to go see the zoo, but I have not had the time. I have wondered if it would not be about the same as ours. I did go to the beach the other day late and found that there is very little difference in theirs and ours. Lots of the country is similar to ours and trees are similar as far as looks go, but they are different kinds.

It will be interesting to get some books and read up on Australia. I can tell you lots about it as I have been almost around it and have seen lots of the country. I think most anyone would say that much of it looks like Texas to a certain extent. There is, however, a desert that we do not have, and there are lots of minerals, but the population is so small. They need as many more people as they have already.

There are lots of beautiful things and buildings to see. Many of them are very old and naturally are pretty.

I just do not have the time and space to write all I could in my diary but have recorded a lot that you will enjoy reading. A lot of it I guess no one will like to read.

I think of all of you all the time and wonder what you are doing. Guess I will have lots of vacation coming when I get home. Hope I get to take it at least. Must close and go to bed as it is after ten at this time. I have also written Cile and Johnnie and nothing has been said in either letter of the 26th.

I spent my birthday looking at the sun on my back and had the day to see the sky was very cool. I thought of everyone that certain day and was actually hoping to see another day at the time.

> Write a lot and read the letter out loud to Johnnie if he is there. You may gather from all the letters that I tell about the same thing....put the pieces together and use your imagination and you will know as much and probably more than I do.
>
> Your loving son

## 17.8.	Appointed Headquarters Commandant for GHQ – 3 April 1942

Friday, 3 April 1942

Good Friday, someone said, but it has been a busy day. I was informed verbally today I was to be Headquarters Commandant for Gen. MacArthur's Staff (GHQ-SWPA).[150] Can you imagine how excited I felt! The General's Headquarters was just moving to the tower at 401 Collins St., and I would be moving with them.

I was assigned a desk in Col. Stivers' office. Col Stivers is G-1 (Administration). He was one of the "Bataan Boys" that came from the Philippine Islands with Gen. MacArthur. He is very nice and his wants seem a lot less than most of those who came over from the States. I have so much to do to get started. To begin with, there was no chair at the desk I will occupy.

I understood tonight that my name may be brought up for promotion, but I am not sure. That was on the Q.T. and due to the short time I have been a captain, I have been afraid my promotion would be turned down. However, I am now doing a major's job.

> Love you, Darling.

Saturday, 4 April 1942

I have been busy trying to get all the generals (of which there are plenty) satisfied with their new offices. We have the Construction Engineers doing a complete remodel of our floors in the building. There were lots of alterations, everything from lights and new walls to fixing the toilets. We were looking for furniture, chairs, everything. There was much confusion.

Up on the 8th floor, we set up Gen MacArthur's office. Next door, we set up the office for Lt. Gen. Sutherland, Chief of Staff. The General's Aides Room was close by.

---

[150] General Headquarters – South-West Pacific Area Theater (GHQ-SWPA) was MacArthur's command, which included U.S., Australian, British, and Dutch troops. Headquarters US Army Forces In Australia (HQ-US AFIA) was only the American troops. Day's transfer was to a higher level of command.

I was down on the 6th floor in the middle of the building, centrally located. Col. Charles Stivers (G-1) and Col. Berdette Fitch (Adjutant General) were on my floor, along with Brig. Gen. Marquat (Anti-Aircraft Officer) *[who would later become a two-star general]*. Akin, the Signal Officer, was on one of the floors above me. Brig. Gen. Hugh (Pat) Casey was the Engineering Officer, but I don't remember where his office was at the time.

I had my office mostly set up. There were several more men transferred to me. One, Sgt. Klaibes, I promoted to M/Sergeant from 1st/Sergeant. I promoted Corporal George to S/Sergeant, Corporal Cotner to Sergeant, but S/Sergeant Wade was not promoted.

17.9.   Duties of Headquarters Commandant

The Headquarters Commandant was a different kind of a "flunky." I was like a City Manager in civilian life. I had to manage all the staff and facilities that provide the supporting services for the headquarters. I had to provide the lubrication that enabled the generals to fight the war. I knew everybody and everybody knew me. I was the "go-to" person in the office if you needed something.

The Headquarters started with the twelve colonels and one enlisted man (a stenographer)[151] who came out of the Philippines with General MacArthur. The colonels were soon promoted to generals.[152] I reported to Col. Charles P. Stivers, the Assistant Chief of Staff G-1 [Administration] *[who soon became a general]*.

All the troops directly supporting the Headquarters were under my command. This included two types of soldiers – those attached to the Headquarters Company and those directly assigned to the Headquarters Company. Those attached to the company included office personnel – stenographers, clerks, typists, receptionists, and office administrators who worked for the generals and section heads. Those directly assigned to Headquarters Company included the guards, drivers, and auto mechanics in the motor pool. We had security guards for every door in the building and every gate in the motor pool. After we moved to Brisbane in July 1942, I picked up the mess hall, the PX, and the liquor store. After about four months I had about 900 men and five officers under my command. When we got to Brisbane, the number was over 2,000.

---

[151] The sergeant who came out with MacArthur was Paul P. Rogers, who after the War wrote two volumes of history of the relationship between MacArthur and Sullivan. It has been referred to in many places in this story.

[152] Mercury Newspaper, Hobart, Tasmania, Apr 27, 1942

Dealing with the generals was no small task. Initially, we had the twelve colonels, but quickly we had generals in all shades of stars – one, two, and even three. You don't get to be a general without an ego and an attitude. These were generally very capable men, but very "competitive." Although it was war and the decisions carried life-and-death consequences, each general had his own special whims.

If I got a new fountain pen for one, everyone else wanted a new fountain pen.

"Captain, I notice that General MacNider has a rug on the floor in his office. Where did he get that?"

"I don't know sir," I said.

"Can you get me one?" the general would ask.

"Sir, the Quartermaster told me he was all out."

It was the same story time and time again.

17.10.   My First Letter from Home Arrives – 5 April 1942

Sunday, 5 April 1942
Up at 7 AM. I dressed, ate breakfast fast, and went in the office about 8:30. I made a quick run over to USAFIA HQ in the High School and picked up a Monroe calculator (stole it). I also obtained five men for drivers. After getting them clothed and getting 40 more typewriters, I went back to the office for a second time.

Col. Fitch told me I was doing a jam-up job. Fitch also told Col. MacNider and Col. Whitlock (both G's on MacArthur Staff) that "we have the best Commandant, he is a dandy." Well, I started to ask for a promotion, but knowing it was in the mill, I thought I would hold up.

Anyway after entering the office a second time, I found my first mail from home – a letter from Mother and one from Cile. Oh, yes, a letter from Johnnie, of which I am very proud. I have shown Johnnie's letter to a number of people. Also, I received a Statement of Service. I have never felt better since the war began and was so glad to hear something from home. I almost cried.

I love you all. I will write you tonight.

Monday, 6 April 1942
I was busy all day, finally leaving the office at 6:30 PM. So much managing and running around trying to get things. I still need another officer, which I have been searching for, but I am building my staff up gradually. I hope to be ready to roll very soon.

I mailed a letter to Johnnie and Mother today. Keep thinking I will get another letter soon. I will list in my book very shortly the General Staff, as soon as I know all of them. Most of them are learning I am the guy that sees that they get what they want. I borrowed an issue of "Life Magazine" (February) to look at tonight. I want to move to another hotel downtown as soon as possible where I will be closer to work. Since GHQ has moved to Collins Street *[from the MacRobertson High School]*, the Chevron Hotel is not convenient anymore.

        I love you Darling. Love again.

Tuesday, 7 April 1942
8:55 PM - I just finished my bath and got on my "[pa]jamies."[153] Will write this page and go to bed. I continue to be very busy. It looks *impossible* to get back to my hotel before 6:30 or 6:45 each night. I may get to move nearer to work tomorrow. Today is the 9th day that my blouse has been at the cleaners. I gave them hell again tonight, told them I was moving, and be sure to have it ready in the morning.

The carpenters, painters, and electricians are working tonight trying to get things in order as soon as possible.

I still want to take some pictures around Melbourne, as there are lots of beautiful sights. I have never seen a town with so many pretty parks. I was invited out to play golf but, of course, no time and no clubs. I don't see how I can get away to play.

I have such a conglomeration of jobs. I have to censor letters for the enlisted men in HQ, to pay them, and Lord knows what else. For security reasons, I even have to witness the burning of waste paper. I need another officer but don't know where I can get one who will be OK.

Believe me when I say I'm glad to be where I am. Lots of others would like to be here also.

---

[153] pajamas

Wednesday, 8 April 1942

Tonight, I played a few games of ping pong and am now ready to read the paper and go to bed. My name is on the list to move, and it may come up tomorrow. As usual, very busy day. Someone told me tonight I was a Major, but I think they were kidding me. At least, I know they are kidding until I get orders. I do know at least that I have been recommended.

We have seen quite a number of officers who have come in from the States. None seem to know much about what is going on at home. I don't know much about what goes on here, so I guess we are even. I know very little news to write here.

Today, the 10th day since my blouse was sent off to be cleaned and pressed, I got it back. I'll never send it there again.

> I am thinking of all my loved ones at home and how much I would give to see them tonight. I would sure like to have all the other letters that have been written to me so I could spend the rest of the night reading them. Love.

Thursday, 9 April 1942

I missed writing in my diary this day, and after a day is gone, well, I just cannot remember two days back. So I will fill the space with some of my thoughts and observations.

I want to tell you how pleased I am and how good I feel about being on this GHQ. I come under G-1 (Col. Stivers), who is very nice and has been most congenial as far as I am concerned. I am moving to the Windsor Hotel soon and will get out of this mob here at the Chevron. Of course I will miss seeing a bunch of officers, but I don't care. They are always on the go too so we don't have much chance to make new friends.

At the Windsor Hotel, Col Fitch (the AG), Col. Whitlock (the G-4), Col MacNider (also in G–4) and Capt. Allen (AG Dept.) are the only ones I know from GHQ in residence. I think you have to put up a certain front and blow yourself up a bit at times to get what you want.

On 9 April 1942, the American forces in the Philippines withdrew from Bataan to the island of Corregidor and yielded Bataan to the Japanese.

Friday, 10 April 1942

I worked late tonight. It is now 11:20 PM and I have just come back to the hotel. Had to get Gen. MacArthur and Gen. Sutherland moved to their new offices. Col. Stivers (G-1) was with me all the time. He is responsible for the rooms being ready, and I am responsible for the equipment and furniture. I know some changes will be made after they arrive in the morning. Col. Fitch (AG) was up for a short time looking around. Never saw so many carpenters and workmen in one place in all my life. Think they all like me as they told me I am doing a swell job, but I haven't been made a Major yet. I am afraid all the time they will move a colonel in as HQ Commandant in my place, as the HQ Commandant office is really supposed to be a colonel. All I want is to be a Major.

Saturday, 11 April 1942

I am now making another effort to get the Battery Fund straightened out, so I can turn it over to Lt. Birnbaum. I was supposed to have been relieved from my assignment with the 26th Field Artillery Brigade on my last order, but it was not done. New orders will have to come out on it. Almost every man in the battery has been promoted since I have had the battery. Today they are scattered all over both GHQ-SWPA and HQ-USAFIA. The USAFIA HQ is in charge of the American Troops. GHQ is in charge of US, Australian, Dutch, and British forces in the Theater and is the real brains of the war.

This has about brought things up to date except mentioning that I received two more letters, the second and third since leaving home - one from Cile and one from Gilbert and JoJo. Both letters were swell.

Sunday, 12 April 1942

Actually this night I was asked out to a party at the home of a hosiery manufacturer. I can't remember the name. They have a beautiful home on Melbourne Bay. It was all very lovely inside. Lt. Col. Sharte (the Purchasing Officer for HQ Quartermaster) and the Quartermaster colonel (whose name I forgot) asked me to accompany them with several others. So we went, had a few drinks, danced a couple of dances, and talked to all of them. All think my 2nd Division insignia, which is on my uniform, was big and the prettiest they had seen. Quite a few officers asked me about the unit because they had served in it in the past. Being one of the first Americans shipped over and one of the few Americans who was in Java, I received a lot of questions. I hear some talk that my HQ Battery 26th F.A. Battalion will stay intact until after the war for historical reasons. Got home about 11:30 PM and boy, did I sleep.

17.11.   First Meeting with Gen. MacArthur – 13 April 1942

Monday, 13 April 1942

Finally quit for the day at 7:30 PM. Dead tired and not caught up. Most important thing of the day, of course, I was introduced to Gen. MacArthur in his office. He said, "They are making an old woman out of you, aren't they?"

I said, "Yes sir."

The General Staff is listed below. Most all are the best of gentlemen, and I am proud to be HQ Commandant for the highest headquarters.

	Gen. Macarthur's Staff Melbourne - 1942
Commander in Chief	Gen. Douglas MacArthur
Chief of Staff	Maj. Gen. Richard K. Sutherland*
Deputy Chief of Staff	Brig. Gen. Richard J. Marshall*
G-1 (Administration)	Col. Charles P. Stivers*
G-2 (Intelligence)	Col. Charles A. Willoughby*
G-3 (Operations)	Brig. Gen. Stephen J. Chamberlin (came from Washington)
G-4 (Supply)	Col. Lester J. Whitlock
G-4 department	Col. Hanford MacNider
Anti-Aircraft Officer	Brig. Gen. William F. Marquat
Others mentioned:	
Chief Engineer	Brig. Gen. Hugh (Pat) Casey*
Signal Officer	Brig. Gen. Spencer B. Akin*
	Lt. Col. John C. Grable
AG	Col. Berdette M. Fitch
	Capt. Allen
Chief of Press Relations	Col. LeGrande A. Diller*
Aide to Gen. MacArthur	Col. Charles H. Morhouse* MD – MacArthur's Doctor *Came from the Philippines with Gen. MacArthur

I gave Gen. MacArthur a couple of new heaters for his office. He said I was doing a fine job, which pleased me very much. He is certainly a fine man and looks every bit a soldier. His office is beautifully furnished with dark red carpet, lovely chairs, but not sufficient furniture. A new suite of furniture has been ordered and will be here either this week or the next.

Gen. Sutherland, the Chief of Staff, also has a nice office with furniture. Most of Gen. MacArthur's staff came from the Philippines with him.

Monday Night April 13, 1942. 8:30 PM
Letter Home

Needless to say, I have been feeling good and feeling bad at the same time. I feel good due to the fact that I received another letter from you and a second from Gilbert, on which Jo Ann had added a line for me. I thoroughly enjoyed both letters. At the same time I feel bad, not sick, but frustrated by all the work I have to do, and not enough help to ever get it all done. Maybe I am not supposed to ever get caught up, however.

Well, I am happier than I have been for some time and know you would be too should you know what I know. So we will let it go at that, and I will start writing. As I forgot to start this off properly, I will now start again.

Dearest Darling Cile and Johnnie:

Your loving dad is about to expand on what I do not know but will try to answer your letter and make the necessary remarks. First of all, I was indeed glad to get your second letter which was written Jan 13. You will remember that the first letter I received was written on Feb. 18 so this new one was written a month earlier than the first one I had. As yet I do not know whether you ever received the $135 I sent you back in December. Let me know! The allotment was changed to $200 even before you requested it so I am still ahead of you.

Glad you made the trip fine and everything was OK. Glad to know that you did receive certain cables and at this time I will not expand on it further. Makes me feel good of course that you had a few people that were interested in whether I was safe or not and for you to know that I was OK was sufficient, of course Mother and Dad too. Glad you got the watch and Johnnie received his package.

Know you had a good time in San Antonio and glad to see the kids. Who is Brick? I just can't place who that is now. Glad you did not try to send me a box for Xmas as I probably never would have received it. However, tell me what all you did and do tell all of them thanks a million and I do appreciate their thinking of me, anyway, thanks to Helen as well. Is Harry [Burrow] still at the mill or has he been called up?

Glad you and Johnnie had a big-time Xmas. I thought of you and even though I did not have a good dinner that day, I was satisfied for the time being. I'll bet Daddy Dwight calls Johnnie a WPA worker and would like to see him on his way to school. I met a couple last night that have two children about Johnnie's age and I told them what he said about the start, and they thought he certainly was a smart boy to know so much. Of course I listened to what they claimed too.

Thanks to Joe for the shoes as well and tell him good voyage for me. Give Mac[154] and Brad[155] my regards as well and fill them full of bridge for me. Have played a few times and won most every time. Played for one tenth one time and won three dollars and fifty cents in about two hours. That was on a certain trip and have not had the time lately. Too bad about the gas for the Nunnelee's, tell them I cook with gas and that is a very favorite expression nowadays here. Too bad about my forgetting to send the clubs to you, guess some little man is using them now.

Hope by this time you have the finance end straightened up and are getting the $200 per month and with the $135 you should be in good shape. Might even send you some more soon, what would you think of that? How come that Basil [*Moore*?] was leaving, did he get fired or what. Who is Graham that entertained you and Johnnie at the field and everybody was so nice to you. I cannot place where or who they are. Hope my memory is not leaving me at this stage.

Have my new glasses now and can or should be able to see all the sights. Have two pair, my old ones have new sides and middle and the government was nice enough to replace the old ones that were broken up the road a piece. Your letter was censored, of course, but nothing was cut out. I also censor my own letters as you see, and they are spot checked later on too. Naturally I have to try to be very careful to tell only the truth and nothing but the truth so help me O'Mikuel.

I thoroughly enjoyed the letter from Gilbert which was received the same time as yours and believe me regardless of the length a word is swell anyway. I hope Gilbert is feeling better now as Mother said he had pneumonia and was quite sick for a while. I know the Army will not take Gilbert due to the hip, and I hope Carl will be able to stay with Mother and Dad and I keep writing to find out but no soap as yet. [156]

I feel that Mother and Dad are feeling better by now and do not worry about me. I am such a poor hand at writing but really do try hard. I will close with love to all of you and my Mother and Dad,

Your loving sweetheart and I do mean you.

John

---

[154] Randall McMahon

[155] Brad Nunnelee

[156] Carl and Gilbert are John's brothers. JoAnn is a niece and daughter of Gilbert.

Tuesday, 14 April 1942

I have never mentioned it, but I am on per diem. As long as I stay at the Chevron, I get my room plus $3 per day. I pay $1.30 for meals. When I leave, I may get the full $6 per day and my room, but not sure. Swell, huh. If I can get to be a Major, I can make some money.

At this time I have not been paid for March. I do not need the money so will wait until the end of month and draw for two months. I don't get time to ever go to a show. All I can spend money for is a bottle of whiskey now and then, and I have plenty of that now. I am accumulating money again, as I always do. It looks like I just naturally pick up more clothes all the time. I just must send more junk home and get rid of it. It is impossible to carry it around with me.

> My love to you, Darling. I think of you all the time. Hope you are OK, as well as my "PX Sugar."

17.12.   Paul P. Rogers & the Headquarters Commandant

M/Sgt. Paul P. Rogers[157] was the personal stenographer to Gen. Richard K. Sutherland and served him from 1941 to 1945. Because of his shorthand and typing skills, he was the only enlisted man selected to accompany Gen. Douglas MacArthur and his staff when they escaped Corregidor Island by PT boat on March 11, 1942. Before the war ended, Rogers was promoted to 2nd Lieutenant by Gen. MacArthur.

After World War II, Rogers received a PhD and became a Professor of Economics at Virginia Polytechnic University (now Virginia Tech). In 1990-1991 he published his definitive two volume 700-page memoir entitled "MacArthur and Sutherland" that details his first-hand observations of the people and events of the GHQ in the South-West Pacific Area during the Second World War.

Rogers' books make two references to the Headquarters Commandant. Six weeks after his arrival in Melbourne, Rogers had not been issued a wool uniform. Sutherland's aide, Francis Wilson, "pulled rank" on the Headquarters Commandant (Capt. Day) insisting that something be done about Rogers' uniform:

---

[157] Paul P. Rogers, *1920-1992*

Paul P. Rogers, "The Good Years," pg 291
"I did likewise, although Wilson had to remind the headquarters commandant that I had been in Melbourne six weeks without an issue of appropriate uniform. This was one of the rare situations when Wilson had an opportunity to exercise his rank, and he appeared to enjoy it. I tried to intercede, explaining that I had not asked for uniforms, but Wilson was adamant. The headquarters commandant was required to see to the welfare of the men. He did not know of my efforts in his behalf. He heard only Wilson's hard cold comments. Thereafter, I was a persona non grata in his office."

17.13.   The Windsor Hotel (Melbourne) – 15 Apr 1942[158]

The Hotel Windsor opened in 1883 and predates many of the grand hotels of the Victorian period, including the Savoy in London (1889) and the Plaza in New York City (1894). The hotel was one of the sites of the drafting of the Australian Constitution in 1898. Its Grand Ballroom and Grand Staircase are considered national treasures. In 1976 the hotel was bought by the State Government of Victoria to prevent its demolition. It has since been air conditioned and returned to private hands. In 2005 it was selected by Condé Nast as one of the 18 best hotels in the world for service. In 2011 the Windsor continues to operate as a five-star hotel in the fashionable center of Melbourne.

<u>Wednesday, 15 April 1942</u>
This evening late I moved from the Chevron Hotel to the Windsor Hotel. It is closer to our Collins Street building, and I get a larger room. I am hoping that I will receive my room and $6 per day. I am not sure it will work out, but I can at least hope. Being in HQ, it may be possible. You know we have to think big.

Figure 58 - Windsor Hotel, Melbourne - 2007

I had S/Sgt. George (was Corporal until recently) come to my room, and we worked until 12 midnight on the fund records for the battery, trying to get it straightened up. I will work several more nights before it will be OK. Think I am getting along swell. I put in requests to the Adjutant General (Col. Fitch) today to promote S/Sgt. Weed to M/Sgt

---

[158] The Hotel Windsor was Day's residence from April 15, 1942 until 26 May 1942.

and several others 1st Class etc. If I stand OK with him, he will probably make all of the promotions as I have asked. If not, he may not. Had a busy day and very tired.

Thursday, 16 April 1942
I intended working again tonight but I forgot to tell Sgt. George, so I will have to work tomorrow night.

April 15th 1942 to !

was Hg. Commandant on Gen MacArthur's Staff at time!

Now USaFFE will be GH.Q. S.W.PA.

They have lovely meals here. I think they are much better than at the Chevron.

All my recommendations for promotion went through as written. Sgt. Weed was made M/Sgt. today and did he feel good. He has been doing a swell job so far and I was glad to

Figure 59 - Letterhead Stationery of Hotel Windsor - 1942

help him. I feel very good about them. Now all of my battery with exception of a very few have been promoted since Jan. 17 when I took Command in Java, and I think I should be ready for one myself.

I have not taken time to get my things straightened up in this hotel, as I want to get on the second floor instead of the fourth floor. The elevator is so slow that I loose too much time getting in and out of my room. The sights from my window are beautiful, but I have only seen out my window one time in daylight. I want to

Figure 60 – Grand Ballroom and Main Dining Room - 2007

write a letter tonight to you, Darling, if I can quit here.

Friday, 17 April 1942

I left the office about 10 PM and most everything I could do was done. I am still trying to get offices and floors cleaned up. The engineers have continued making alterations and seem to be getting a lot done, but they sure make a mess. I am getting lots of "wants" satisfied on supplies, but new requests keep coming in.

I will be glad when I can get caught up so I can at least go to a show. I haven't even had a chance to go down and fill in my pay voucher for March so I can be paid. Haven't needed it so have just done without. Don't have time to spend money anyway. I hope you are able to pay and save some money. I would like to be plenty far ahead when I come out of this thing. Will work on the Battery Fund more tonight and try to get it caught up.

Darling, I miss you so. Your loving husband.

**Figure 61 – Grand Stairway
Windsor Hotel - 2007**

Saturday, 18 April 1942

Well, I worked all day today until 10:30 PM. I did go to a store and bought myself a pair of tan slippers. I hope they are not too small. Look pretty good anyway. A friend of mine, Mr. Trumbolt (or something like that), who I knew in Soerabaja and Bandoeng, Java, is sailing for home Tuesday. He has promised that he would write Cile a note when he gets there. He will be there between the 12th and 15th of May. I know it will make her feel good to get the news.

All the Field Officers in GHQ are taken to the best clubs in town. Wish I were a Major and hence a Field Officer. I would get to meet the best bunch of people in town. If I get a promotion, I will probably get in one or two clubs. As it is, I have nothing to do but work, and it sure gets lonesome at times.

17.14.   MacArthur's Special GHQ Train – 19 Apr 1942

<u>Sunday, 19 April 1942</u>
I worked all day today getting so many things for Gen. MacArthur's special train. I didn't expect I would be involved in getting supplies for it. So far, I have been after everything but the train itself. I even had to get pistols and ammunition to equip the officers – about ten Generals in the bunch.

Gen. Sutherland called me up to his office today and wanted me to see his britches. Well, I looked, and there were several dirty places on them. Then, he showed me that the buzzer wire I had put on his desk the night before was black and had rubbed off on his britches. He wanted me to have the wire changed to better wire, at least to where it would not rub off. He laughed, and so did I, but I had that wire changed.

I made several trips to Port Melbourne today. My roommate from the *USS Republic* has been assigned down at the Port and was just promoted to Major. With his help now, I can get hold of anything they have down there. It sure is nice to have a bunch of friends around that you can call upon. It helps a lot.

<u>Monday, 20 April 1942</u>
We are now occupying the 6th, 7th, and 8th floors of a large building on 401 Collins Street. I expect that we are likely to take over the 5th floor pretty soon, as more people will be coming in and different departments will be spreading out. I have just about found enough hotel rooms for all the enlisted men to stay. We are taking over a couple of floors in Victoria Palace Hotel for them. I will be darn glad when all get settled. It seems all I do is have someone moved or get something so they can move. I had my measure taken for a pair of "Pinks."[159] Guess I have to look pretty nice to stay at GHQ. My orders transferring me to GHQ forgot to relieve me from command of the 26th Field Artillery Battalion, but they are coming out now. I was officially relieved on April 3; however, orders will be out Wednesday, April 22nd. Now, I have to get rid of the fund to Birnbaum. Thank God. Never saw a fund that was such a headache before. It will be several more days before I can get rid of it.

> I love you Darling.

<u>Tuesday, 21 April 1942</u>
There was a big press conference today. As usual, about 50 or 60 correspondents came in, as they do daily. Press Relations was on the 6th floor where I was. Col. LeGrande

---

[159] "Pinks" refer to a particular Army uniform.

Diller was the Chief of Press. As usual, I knew quite a lot of things that would be in the papers the next day. They took a lot of pictures today of the generals. I could save a lot of pictures if I had space to put them, but it was too much trouble.

For the past several days I have been securing the equipment for a GHQ Special Train. It will be completed tomorrow. Another headache out of the way! They need an officer in charge of a bunch of stuff for them, but so far no one has been named. I sure do not want it. I have sent in a request for another officer to help me. I have so much I can never get through. I now have a 36-page payroll every payday, letters to censor, and stuff of that kind keeps me going.

Wednesday, 22 April 1942
It is now 11:45 PM, and I have just sent Sgt. George home. After another night of working on the Battery Fund, I hope one or two more nights and I will be done. Thought I would finish tonight, but I didn't. I am getting in bad sorts and need to sleep a few nights.

There is a lot of special stuff to get loaded on the special GHQ train to go to Albury[160] tomorrow, as well as the usual office things. I will also start putting enlisted men in Victoria Palace, and have tons of letters to be censored, as always. Well, I'm going to bed and items will be developed in a day or two more and will try to see them. Love.

Thursday, 23 April 1942
We finished loading the GHQ train supplies about 3 PM. When I returned to the office, I had a dozen phone call messages including several new special jobs. For instance, Col. Morhouse[161] called me up to Gen. MacArthur's office in reference to getting a wall clock for Gen. MacArthur.

The General said to me, "Can you get one?"

I said I was almost sure I could. He said, "It'll certainly be dressed up, won't it."

In addition, I have to get a cigarette box for him, which I ordered yesterday. It should have been in today. The General is very nice and friendly. Seems funny that I am in the real HQ where the war is run. All the news comes from this office.

---

[160] Albury, Victoria, Australia is about 220 miles northwest of Melbourne.
[161] Col. Morhouse was Gen. MacArthur's Aide and doctor.

I have to arrange transportation for Saturday morning for Gen. MacArthur to lay a wreath on the Shrine of Remembrance, an Australian War Memorial.

I went to a show tonight for the first time in Australia.

I obtained a transformer so now I am able to play my radio. It keeps me company in my room. It is now about 7:45 PM and I have more work on the fund. I want to get finished tonight and turn it all over to Birnbaum. I got nearly caught up today.

Love you Darling.

17.15.   Shrine of Remembrance, ANZAC Day – 25 Apr 1942

ANZAC Day (Australia New Zealand Army Corps Day) is a major holiday in both Australia and New Zealand, very similar to Memorial Day in the United States. The "Shrine of Remembrance" is the Victorian War Memorial that honors their war dead. It was built after World War I to honor their troops that died at the Battle of Gallipoli in Turkey. It is similar to the Tomb of the Unknown Soldier in Washington with an eternal flame.

Saturday, 25 April 1942
Everything was closed today. Gen. MacArthur placed the wreath at 11 AM while accompanied by his staff and other big wigs. About seven or eight cars were in the party. I had to order the cars by rank and arrange the route with the locals. Col. Diller (Press Relations) was in the car with the wreath which was just in front of Gen. MacArthur's car. In the newspaper picture

Figure 62 - Shrine of Remembrance and Eternal Flame Melbourne, 2007

I was about two officers down from the last one shown. I was almost behind Gen. MacArthur.

Could you ever imagine that your husband would be accompanying the Commander in Chief of the GHQ SWPA on anything? I wanted to take my movie along, but as I had to be in the party I could not take pictures. It is a beautiful place and as I have previously taken pictures of the Shrine, I can show you easily.

Figure 63 - MacArthur and Sutherland driving to the Shrine of Remembrance.

Figure 64 - MacArthur arrives at the Shrine of Remembrance. 25 Apr 1942.

17.16.   Promoted To Major, Field Artillery – 25 Apr 1942

Saturday, 25 April 1942
Today has been a big day. Gen. MacArthur laid a wreath on the Shrine of Remembrance this morning at 11 AM.

A short time after getting back to the office, I was called on the phone and notified that I had been promoted to Major. I immediately went down and accepted, so I will start being paid as a Major as of today. Naturally I am very happy. Major Thompson, who recommended me for promotion, gave me my first set of leaves and pinned them on me. He was tickled to death to see me get it. Several colonels have also congratulated me.

I wrote you a short note, Darling. I am sleepy tonight so guess I had better get to bed. It is now nearly ten and I have been down in lobby talking to a British Major Lummas.

Figure 65 - Major John F. Day Jr., Melbourne 1942

Sunday, 26 April 1942
Indeed a very quiet day. Worked all morning, partly on the Battery Fund, and now have it ready to take to the I.G.[162] after getting a few signatures. I can possibly get through in a few days. I talked about an hour to the English Major Lummas. I have been sorting junk in my trunk, while listening to the radio. There is not much on the radio, but it is some company. I have to get a roller fixed on the typewriter tomorrow. I got a new pistol the other day, and it is a dandy. I am working now on a submachine gun or a German Lüger which a friend has. It is one like either the Japs or Germans use and is a novelty, but not as good as ours of course.

> Wrote you and mother a letter today and told the same "no news." Darling, Love and kisses.

Monday, 27 April 1942
War developments are looking better, and I think we are getting ready to get things going. I will have another officer, a Lt. Evans, joining me tomorrow. I picked him because he seemed to be a good worker and didn't mind it. I had to rob another unit, but cannot be bothered now.

The censor seems to be holding up all my films for some reason. He may call me tomorrow. I guess he sees ships and airplanes in the movies and here in Australia the censorship regulations are strict. Chances are I will get by due to my position. Hope nothing is cut, as I don't have too many films.[163]

It is nearly ten o'clock and I was going to get to bed early tonight. I have had my bath and am ready for bed, but will take a few more minutes.

Col. Fitch, the AG, thinks I got a quick promotion. Well, six months as a Captain was quick.

Tuesday, 28 April 1942
There is nothing unusual to report. I have a new address book which I intended getting the signature of most of the GHQ staff, as well as others, but I haven't had time as yet to get started.

I wrote a lot of letters to collect money for the Battery Fund. I am still trying to get the books closed out. I want to be through with the whole thing. Hope I never get tangled

---

[162] Inspector General

[163] Movies were taken in Java, and included aerial combat dog fights and ships in the harbor.

with such a mess again. I had one sergeant who was AWOL[164] for 5 days. I busted him and sent him to Birdum, Northern Territory (one of the most northern posts in Australia). It will sure be a lesson to him for the next time he gets a good job.

In 1942 Birdum was between Darwin and Alice Springs. It was the end of the railroad tracks south of Darwin in the Northern Territory of Australia.

> I sent you a wire today, as follows, "Love, pass the cigars", signed Maj. Day. I know you will understand. I think by the end of next month I will be able to cable some money home. I guess all will be surprised to get more money. I am going to bed. Love you, Darling.

Wednesday, 29 April 1942

The censor is holding my films, and I will see him tomorrow at 2 PM to view the pictures. I understand I have a choice: He will hold them "uncut" as they are until the end of the war and give them to me then; or he will cut out certain parts and give them to me now. I may let him keep them until the end of the war. It will give me less to carry around.

This evening I was assigned 22 Filipinos, and tomorrow I will get them started working. At present I have four payrolls monthly, plus two more Per Diem Schedules monthly (the per diem payroll is about $9,000 twice monthly). The four monthly payrolls will be larger than the per diem.

I have written a slew of letters to collect money from old accounts for the Battery fund to try to get it in shape, even though I am transferred out. I have had my typewriter changed from Dutch [characters] to American. That is the machine I have in my room now. It is a dandy.

9 PM - I have been thinking about putting in my application for a permanent commission in the Regular Army and will try to work on it as soon as I can. I have been talking to Lt. Col. John Grable, Signal Corp. Col. Grable is a frequent dinner companion of mine at the Windsor. He has been very nice to me and gave me the suggestion of applying now for a regular commission in the Army. I think I will. I may get the chance to talk to Gen. MacArthur someday about it, and if I get him behind it, I know it will go through. He gets all he wants. Think I can get several to vouch for me. One of the most important is my boss, G-1 Col. Charles Stivers.

---

[164] Absent With Out Leave

> Wonder what you thought, Darling, when you got my cable? Pass the cigars and if you noticed how I signed it – I love you and good night. Hope Mother and Dad are well and not worrying about their son.

Thursday, 30 April 1942

I was so busy all day. Not much to write except I'm dead tired and will let it go at that. I bought myself 6 quarts of liquor for a little over $6. It's Scotch too. A friend of mine, Lt. Germensky, got it tax free and asked me if I wanted it. Well, of course it will likely be sometime before I will have to buy any more, but thought it good for my usual cold.

> Good night, Honey.

17.17.   Kangaroo Hunt – 1 May 1942

Friday, 1 May 1942

So busy I could hardly wiggle, but I managed to steal away from the office at 3:40 PM and went out 35 miles from Melbourne for a kangaroo shoot. Sgt. Say, an Australian, took three of us out. Of course it being so late in the day and taking some time getting to the location, we had little time to hunt. I had an M-1 Garand rifle. Another officer with me had a Tommy gun and another officer had a rifle and pistol, so we were well armed. We saw a few six footers, but we had too short a time period to shoot. We will try to go another time.

Sgt. Say told me he would guide us to get a "Roo" so we can have a hide. We will go again. He wanted us to have a driver along with him, so I got one. Sgt. Say's mother and dad both work. His dad is in the Ministry of Munitions and wants to show me through the munitions factory. I will go, if time permits. His mother is a Red Cross worker, and they have a nice house.

17.18.   Expecting Invasion of Australia – 2 May 1942

Saturday, 2 May 1942

Today was the usual grind. I have not mentioned anything with reference to the Australian situation but will express a few words. I am firmly of the opinion that we will need more than air corps to win the war. We don't have much else here right now. I am expecting air attacks on one of the Northern ports in the next 2 or 3 weeks. I doubt that we can prevent a landing, but can give them a lot of hell when they do land. We sure need a full Army here for any large-scale move, and I cannot see one. I feel that we are getting stronger of course and improving daily, but not to the point where we are sure we could stop them. I wish I knew what plans are at home. As long as I do a good job where I am, I will probably stay. Hope I do. I can make more money here than any other place.[165]

Sunday, 3 May 1942

I thought I would be caught up today and take the evening off, but no such luck. I was lucky to get home at 6:45 PM. By the time I was cleaned up, it was too late to get a hot meal, so I went out for Chinese food. Chinese food in Australia is not up to par with what we had in Java, but nonetheless it was a welcome change.

I visited the censor today and saw my movies for the first time. They are swell. I am having the Kodak Co. keep them in storage until the war is over, so I will not have to fool with them. Swell, huh![166]

I have to take a pill I guess for the first time in many moons. I have a bad taste in my mouth, and I hope it is not related to the Chinese food.

> I want to write two letters home for Mother's Day. I will send Mother a wire, as well as you, Darling, for May 10th.[167] Love and Kisses

Monday, 4 May 1942

This is the week we expect the Japanese attack, but so far nothing has developed. I don't understand the type of war we are fighting. We will have to win it if it is won. The English know how to retreat, and we have to know how to attack. We can never win a war by bombing only. We must have the ground forces. I am sitting here at 11 PM listening to news from London on the radio.

One of my friends, a captain, was killed accidentally near Darwin, along with Gen. [*Harold H.*] George.[168] A pursuit plane ran into him and a bomber on the ground. A news correspondent was also killed in the accident.

---

[165] The extra money resulted from a per diem cost of living allowance that was paid Officers for food and housing as long as they were assigned to GHQ, because the military did not provide them with food and housing. His expenses to live in Melbourne were significantly less than the allowance.

[166] None of the movies from Java ever surfaced after the war.

[167] Mother's Day in the United States was May 9, 1942, however, because of the International Dateline, that was May 10, 1942 in Australia.

[168] Gen. Harold H. George was the FEAF Commander who left the Philippines with Gen. MacArthur. He was killed in a ground accident on 30 April 1942, along with Melville Jacoby, a correspondent for Time Life Magazine, on the taxiway of Twenty-Seven Mile Airstrip southeast of

We have had more planes than usual over Melbourne tonight. The anti-aircraft lights are operating. I hope the bombers don't get here, as too much damage could be done. Most Australians feel safer since the Yanks are here. I wonder why?

Tuesday, 5 May 1942
I went down to get my check for April, but it seems that it has been lost. I guess I will get it soon. I am carrying too much money with me now, so I must send it home in a day or so.[169]

Speculation is still that the Japs will be coming to New Caledonia or New Zealand to cut off our supply lines from the States, possibly before attacking Australia, but no one can tell for sure. They could also hit Townsville and cut off the top of Australia. Of course to take Australia they have only to take four or five big towns. I am more worried about it now than I have been in some time.

Darling, I wrote you last night and sent the letter airmail. Also wrote letters to Mother and Dad and Lee Ray Baxter and the gang.

I took a big drink before supper and still feel it. I should get a good night's sleep tonight. Sure can use it. Good night and all my love and kisses.

17.19.   Fall of Corregidor – 6 May 1942

Wednesday, 6 May 1942
We all knew as soon as Corregidor was invaded by the Jap Army, the island would fall. Well, today, as many as 5,000 Japs struck. I know MacArthur hated to see it go. I knew this morning that he was plenty worried, even before the news arrived. He knew it would fall, and we all expected it, but that didn't make it any easier to take. We had a real blue bunch at HQ today as so many have friends there.

I was as busy as could be, however.

Australia is next and we now know we are overdue for an attack. There is and will be no escape from here. I don't understand why we haven't received more ground troops and

---

Darwin, Australia. The accident occurred when a departing P-40 crashed into a Lockheed C-40 transport that had just landed with the general and others onboard.

[169] By tradition the U.S. Army always paid soldiers in cash, after deducting any regular allotments that were sent home to their families. Payday required a cash payment to each soldier.

mechanized units up to now. That's why we don't understand this war. I know Gen. MacArthur will not gamble at this stage unless we have to. We want to know for sure we can keep going once we start. I still think Townsville may be one of their early places of attack.

Thursday, 7 May 1942

Lots of officers are still blue, but trying to get more going. All realize that we are due an attack shortly. The Japanese are concentrating vessels in New Guinea area, which indicates they are getting ready. I don't see how we can miss.

I will try to send all available money to Cile pronto and guess I should send a lot of other stuff but just don't know what I'll need.

I had to buy a combination overcoat and raincoat – it cost 13 Guineas or £13/13/0 or about $45. It looks very nice. I'll have to look that way as long as I am in GHQ.

Must go to sleep. I love you, Darling.

Friday, 8 May 1942

Today it hit – a big battle near the Solomon Islands. By noon, about eight Jap ships were sunk and later four or five more. This is the beginning of what we have been looking for. It may be a feint as they may go in another place in force. I'm not a prophet by any means, but things just don't look good at all.

I heard in a roundabout way today that I would likely go on Gen. MacArthur's train sometime this month. I had hoped to get along without having to go and still hope I can avoid it. I probably will not know till a day or so before it leaves, as the trip is very secret. MacArthur will probably go to Townsville and stay about 10 days. The whole trip will be about 2 weeks.

A lot more troops are coming into Australia, but not as many as I want. Several more Divisions are coming –- I think three are on their way.

I went to a show tonight and saw "49th Parallel." It was pretty good for a change.

I will send you a wire tomorrow, Darling, and hope it reaches you by the 10th. I love you so much. Goodnight.

18.   MACARTHUR'S WAR RESOURCES – 8 MAY 1942

18.1.   Conflict with Washington over Resources – 8 May 1942

Friday, 8 May 1942

On this date, MacArthur issued a radiogram to President Roosevelt responding to Roosevelt's request for MacArthur's strategic review of the military situation following the fall of Corregidor.[170] MacArthur emphasized that the fall of Corregidor would release many Japanese combat troops from the Philippines, which would enable the Japanese to continue their offensive into the South Pacific. He outlined the impossible situation of a passive defense of Australia, emphasizing the large geographic area to be defended. He included an illustration similar to Figure 66 – USA Superimposed on South West Area – 8 May 1942 which superimposed a map of the United States on the South-West Pacific Theater. He indicated that immediate reinforcements must be received before an enemy strike to avoid "dire consequences" due to a shortage of men and materiel.

His strategy to counter the Japanese numerical superiority was to go on the offensive and attack the Japanese in order to disrupt their plans and force the Battle of New Guinea to become the battle for the defense of Australia. With a smaller war zone and the difficult terrain of New Guinea, MacArthur thought he could better counter the numerical superiority of the Japs. To be effective, however, he needed immediate reinforcements of a balanced ground, sea, and air force which he specifically enumerated to include two aircraft carrier task forces, 500 to 1000 airplanes, and a US Army Corps consisting of three operational combat divisions of troops.

There were also Australian political considerations. Australian Prime Minister John J. Curtin, the Labor Party Leader, was equally concerned about the situation. He had appealed directly to Churchill requesting the return to Australia of three divisions of Australian Imperial Forces (AIF) deployed in the Mid-East and Ceylon, leaving only a shadow military force in the homeland.

Roosevelt and Churchill discussed the matter and reaffirmed their "Europe First" policy. Churchill did not want to release the three Australian Divisions from the Mid-East and Ceylon as the Japanese were moving through Burma toward India. In exchange for leaving the Australian divisions in the Mid-East, Churchill and Roosevelt agreed to send

---

[170]

http://www.history.army.mil/books/wwii/macarthur%20reports/macarthur%20v1/ch02.htm, pg 38.

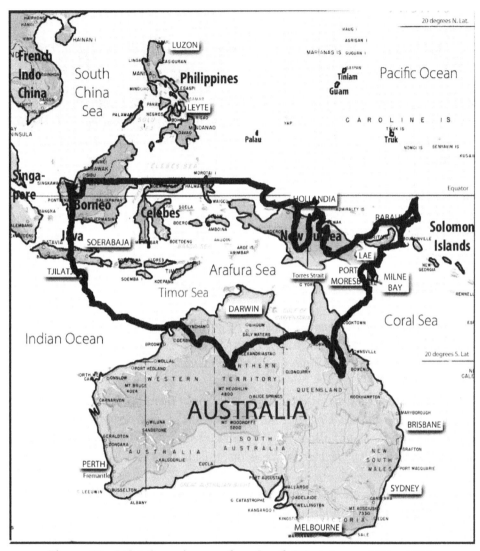

Figure 66 – USA Superimposed on South West Area – 8 May 1942

the US 32nd *Infantry Division (Red Arrow Division)*[171] *to Australia instead of Europe where the division was scheduled to be deployed.*[172]

MacArthur was granted none of his requests. MacArthur was told that what he had plus what was already in route was what he could have. Although originally allotted 530,000 troops, MacArthur would have to do with only 400,000 troops, half of which were garrisoned in Australia in case the Japanese should invade.

In addition to a shortage of men and war matériel, the United States had a shortage of cargo ships and transports to deliver the matériel to Australia. The length of the supply line from the East Coast through the Panama Canal and across the Pacific to Australia was too great and too vulnerable.

18.2.   Battle of the Coral Sea - 7-8 May 1942[173]

Two Japanese invasion forces departed Rabaul, New Britain Island on 4 May 1942. The primary invasion force was intent on the capture of Port Moresby, New Guinea. The secondary invasion force was intent on the capture of Tulagi (and nearby Guadalcanal).

Control of Port Moresby had two strategic purposes. From there the Japanese could launch bombers against Townsville and Cooktown in northern Australia, and perhaps later invade Australia. Control of Port Moresby would also deny the Allies a base from which to bomb Rabaul, the principal Japanese Naval Base for the war in the Solomon Islands.

Tulagi and Guadalcanal were to be sites for a Japanese seaplane base and an airfield to cut off shipping of military supplies from the United States to Australia.

The invasion force for Port Moresby consisted of 12 transport ships containing over 5,000 Japanese Army troops and 500 Navy support units. The plan was to sail around the southeastern tip

---

[171] The unit was originally the Wisconsin and Michigan National Guard, which had been activated in 1940. It was stationed at Fort Devens, Massachusetts in preparation for moving to Northern Ireland.

[172] Samuel Milner, *Victory in Papua*, (The War in the Pacific, US Army in World War II), Office Of The Chief Of Military History, Department Of The Army, Washington, D.C., 1957, CMH Pub 5-2, 1953, p.29-31.

[173] http://www.ww2pacific.com/coralsea.html and
http://www.delsjourney.com/uss_neosho/coral_sea/battle_of_coral_sea/summary.htm

of New Guinea toward Port Moresby through the Jomard Pass and invade from the south. The invasion date was scheduled for 10 May 1942.

Security for these two invasion forces included two Japanese fleet carrier task forces (<u>Shokaku</u> and <u>Zuikaku</u>), one light aircraft carrier (Shoho), nine cruisers, fifteen destroyers, fourteen supporting ships, and 127 carrier-based aircraft.

The US Navy had directed two carrier task forces to the South Pacific. The <u>USS Lexington</u>, under Adm. Aubrey Fitch was sailing south from Pearl Harbor intending to attack Rabaul. The <u>USS Yorktown</u>, under Adm. Frank Fletcher was sailing south to protect the shipping supply routes from the Panama Canal to Australia. Two other carrier task forces (<u>USS Hornet</u> and <u>USS Enterprise</u>) were in the Central Pacific, far to the north and too distant to be able to respond to a threat in the South-West Pacific.

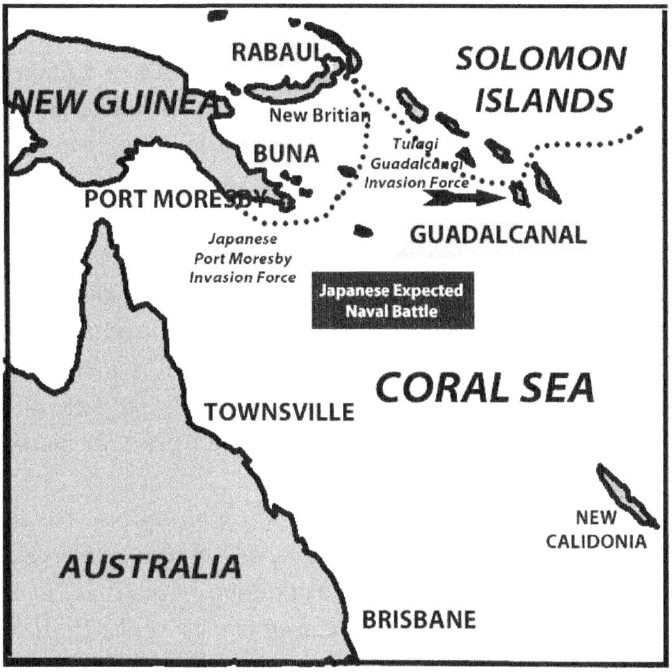

On 1 May, the <u>USS Lexington</u> and the <u>USS Yorktown</u> linked up off

Figure 67 - Japanese Attack Plan - Battle of Coral Sea

New Caledonia and entered the southern Coral Sea, still with incomplete information about the location or intention of the Japanese fleet. Although the Japanese Navy Code had been cracked, the information indicated a major attack was coming in the South Pacific. Although Intelligence had not specifically identified the target, it was strongly believed to be Port Moresby.

On 7 May, an American reconnaissance pilot discovered the Japanese New Guinea invasion convoy of approximately twenty ships and incorrectly believed it to be the main Japanese Navy military force. The Americans immediately launched an all-out attack against the invasion fleet. They sank the escorting smaller aircraft carrier (<u>Shoho</u>), which was to provide air cover for the invading army. With the <u>Shoho</u> sunk and with no air cover for the invading Army, the Japanese suspended the invasion until they knew the disposition of the American carriers.

At dawn 8 May, both fleets discovered the positions of their respective enemy and simultaneously launched attacks. The Japanese hit both the USS Yorktown and the USS Lexington. A secondary gasoline explosion on the Lexington caused the ship to be abandoned and scuttled. The Yorktown retired to Tonga for repairs. The Americans also lost a destroyer and a tanker.

The US pilots put three bombs into the _Shokaku_ deck putting the carrier out of service. The _Zuikaku_, although damaged, evaded detection by hiding in a heavy rain storm, and successfully recovered many of the aircraft from the _Shokaku_. In the combat, the Americans lost more ships than the Japanese, but the Japanese lost more airplanes than the Americans.

The final tally from the Battle of the Coral Sea was a tactical victory for the Japanese, however, it was a strategic victory for the Americans. The Japanese New Guinea invasion force withdrew to Rabaul and never returned. The New Guinea Campaign became a brutal land battle that would continue for the next two years.

The Battle of Coral Sea was the first setback of the war for the Japanese. This was the first time in history that two opposing carrier forces fought using only aircraft without the opposing ships ever sighting each other. In US Navy circles, the Battle of the Coral Sea was overshadowed by the Battle for Midway that followed only one month later. However, the Coral Sea Battle is still celebrated in Australia as the battle that halted the Japanese advance toward the invasion of Australia and marked the major turning point of the war in the South-West Pacific.

A collateral benefit from the Battle of the Coral Sea was that the two damaged Japanese carriers had to return to port in Japan for repairs and were therefore unable to participate in the Battle of Midway one month later. The Yorktown, in contrast, was able to return to Pearl Harbor Shipyard for repairs. Thanks to herculean efforts by the Pearl Shipyard, the Yorktown was able to return to the Navy battle line after only three days in port. When it sailed to join in the Battle of Midway, Pearl shipyard personnel remained on board continuing to make repairs. Although the ship was lost in the Battle of Midway, its presence proved of strategic importance in the eventual outcome of that Battle.

The Battle of the Coral Sea was also the opening round of a conflict within the US Military Chain of Command in the Pacific War between Admiral Ernest King (Commander of the United States Fleet and Chief of Naval Operations) and Gen. Douglas MacArthur (Supreme Commander of the South-West Pacific). Technically, Navy operations in the South-West Pacific were under the command of Gen. MacArthur. However, Adm. King directly instructed Adm. Frank J. Fletcher and Vice Adm. William F. Halsey (Task Force 16 Commander in Hawaii) to report directly to Adm. Chester Nimitz (the newly appointed Commander of Allied Forces in the Pacific) rather than Gen. MacArthur. This command conflict would be magnified and elevated to the President of the United States as the war progressed.

19.   MELBOURNE DEVELOPMENTS – MAY – JUN 1942

19.1.   Murder on the Street – 9 May 1942

Saturday, 9 May 1942

Well, tonight there was another murder on the street. This was the second in a week, both only one block from my hotel. I think I'll move or start carrying a gun with me. Here I have been carrying about $750 in my pocket - $295 belonging to the Battery Fund of 26th F.A. Brigade, which I have not been able to get rid of, and $450 of my own money. My April paycheck of almost £69 will be received Monday. I intend sending quite a bit of money home to you.[174]

> Darling, I wanted to send a thousand dollars to you. Won't you be surprised to get such a large sum? You will know I have been saving then. Really don't have to spend a lot, as I don't have time. If things continue, I will have saved quite a bit in a short period of time. Of course I do not know what is to come next, but it doesn't look too good.
>
> I received three letters today – your Mar 27th letter, one from Dad and Mother and a third from Brad & Joe, all of which I thoroughly enjoyed.

19.2.   Kangaroo Hunt – 10 May 1942

Sunday, 10 May 1942

I went kangaroo shooting today, leaving early in the morning and getting back about 2 PM. I killed the only one I shot at and skinned him. Corporal Say (Australian) says he will have the hide tanned for me to ship home. It sure is a good hide. We must have walked 10 miles during the hunt, so I was really tired when I got back. I did not have my movie camera at the time I killed the kangaroo, but I did take pictures after we got back to the car.

I still have a terrible cold that comes and goes. I worked the remainder of the evening.

Monday, 11 May 1942

Well, it looks like Col. Fitch, the AG, wants to jump on me every chance he gets. It seems jumping on me is just his warm-up for the day. No one else ever gets on me about anything, and I can't see why he should. He has been sore ever since I was promoted, and I didn't have a hand in that. Apparently, he didn't want me promoted because he was a First Lieutenant for 13 years. I sometimes think he would reduce me if he could.

---

[174] To understand the value of $450, in 1941 the MSRP for a new Buick was about $1,000.

<u>Tuesday, 12 May 1942</u>
My cold is worse, and I should go to bed, but I guess I'll live through it. A few more let
ters arrived and naturally I feel better because of the letters. Looks like the Battle in the
Coral Sea has died down somewhat, but there is possibly more to come. Feel so bad I
will write no more today.

<u>Wednesday, 13 May 1942</u>
I received your letter of 18th March today, Honey. You were blue after having received
but two letters from me. I can't understand why so many of my letters have not reached
you.[175]

<u>Thursday, 14 May 1942</u>
I worked until 10:30 PM getting the Filipinos straightened out on the janitor work. Those
outfits are more trouble than they are worth. I reduced two sergeants to privates and
shipped them out today. They raised a lot of hell in the hotel with girls they were not
supposed to take up to their rooms. The Military Police had to be called.

I wanted to write you today, Darling, but have been so busy all day.

19.3.   The Melbourne High Society

I received an invitation from "Lady Knox" for a reception at 9 PM Friday night. Lady
Knox is the wife of the Speaker of the Australian Parliament and a respected politician.
She is a very well-connected member of high society in Melbourne. The society leaders
are going all out to welcome and entertain the officers on MacArthur's staff. I guess I'll
drop by if I'm not sick.

*Lady Knox was the second wife of Sir George Hodges Knox (1885-1960), a highly respected Na-
tionalist politician, who served as the respected Speaker of the Australian Parliament from 1942-
1947. Sir George was appointed an Honorary Brigadier in 1941 and was knighted in 1945. Lady
Knox, the former Ada Victoria Harris, was an active philanthropist, a leader for over 40 years in
the Australian Red Cross Society, a Governor of a major Melbourne hospital, an officer in the
Royal Victorian Institute for the Blind, and served countless other charities. She was a fixture of
Melbourne society.*

*Melbourne society went all out to welcome the newly arrived American officers on MacArthur's
staff with a number of receptions at private homes. At one such reception Gen. Richard K. Suth-*

---

[175] A letter was taking seven weeks from Texas to Australia.

erland, MacArthur's Chief of Staff was introduced to Mrs. Elaine Bessemer-Clarke, the wife of a British officer who was captured by the Japanese on the Malaya Peninsula. Sutherland, 48, had been married for twelve years and had a 10-year-old daughter. Mrs. Bessemer-Clarke, 28, had been married five years and had a two-year-old son. At one of these receptions the two lonely individuals struck up an acquaintance that blossomed in time to become the gossip of the Headquarters.[176]

Thursday, 14 May 1942
First elements of the US 32nd Infantry Division arrived by ship from San Francisco at Port Adelaide, South Australia. Port Adelaide is about 450 miles west of Melbourne.

At present it is Thursday night. I actually lost count of the days and thought it was Friday. I received a letter from Cile today mailed on April 23 with letters from the Nunnellee's, Morgan's, Spivey's, and Massey's. It is sure swell to get them. Mail is now arriving in three weeks.

Friday, 15 May 1942
Such a day – I was so busy. It seemed that I was signing my name all day. I have all of our reports of change in, and we are the only outfit that does have them in. Boy, it makes me feel good that everything is up to snuff.

Cile, I hope you receive the $400 I sent by a Postal Money Order. The next time I will wire the money. I wrote a letter or two tonight. I love you, Darling, and miss you so much.

There is no mention in the diary of the Reception at Lady Knox's residence on Friday night, only the invitation.

Saturday Night May 16, 1942
6 PM – I am still in the office but just about through. It is a very wet Saturday night, and I still have a terrible cold. I have seen most of the shows that are showing and couldn't get a ticket if I wanted too. I will go to bed early after a stiff drink to improve my cold. The other night I took a big drink with lime juice, a couple of aspirin, a cold tablet, and jumped in the bed. The next morning my cold was a lot better, and I have felt much better ever since. I think another night like that, and I will be about well.

---

[176] Rogers: *MacArthur and Sullivan: The Good Years,* Praeger (New York) 1990, p 207.

16 May 1942

Dearest Cile and Johnnie:

I am taking the time to drop you a few lines, even though I have written several other letters to you the past week. Needless to say I have nothing new to tell but just want to write as I always do. I too want to write to Mother and Dad so I am making a copy of this letter and will send it to Mother and Dad. I hope you received the Mother's Day wires on time but as there were so many I have wondered when they would get there. I know you were pleased at least when they came. Cile Honey, you can (had to stop and do some other work and have forgotten what I was going to say) I sent you yesterday $400 by money order and sent the letter air mail. I have the receipt and sure want you to wire me as soon as you get the money. Think you should have it by the middle of June at least. Be sure and wire me. Gosh I know a wire will go thru as others always get them and I never do. You certainly get mine. All you have to put on a wire to address me is the APO 501, and it will reach me. I have just finished spending an hour signing my name on a lot of reports of change. That was writing as fast as I could write too. That doesn't happen every day but sometimes.

"My colored films came out good," the censor officer told me. But, of course, he is going to keep them till after the war is over. You must remember that they are in my name and addressed to Bonham. Another thing, I may send some more money soon and will probably wire it as I have found out that I can wire it for very little. Guess you wonder where I am getting the money. You see I am getting paid per diem as well as my salary and do not get a chance to spend much. I am going to try to get me a cap soon and may wire Joskeys[177] to send one so if you get a bill you will know where it came from. I sure wish I had one now. Of course I had to leave mine in the trunk too. Tell me too when you get the rug. I will probably send the Jade ring soon by mail and now don't expect too much of this as it is not the most expensive but think you will like it anyway. I also have some kind of emerald that will send if possible. It is nice.

I have wanted to get a Koala bear for Johnnie but have not had time to find one. Saw the man about the kangaroo hide, and he said it was coming along fine and would be ready soon he thought. All are gone now and I must go and eat. I will try to write again tomorrow.

Oh yes, I took five pictures to the censor the other day and asked him if I could send them home and he said "No, none could go," but of course they were interesting, but thought maybe they would peep thru So am holding them till the thing is over too. They were made at the former place [*Java*] by Kodak.

Mother, I hope you have a nice Mother's Day too, I sent Lucille and Nannie a wire together, as well as Cile and Mother. I have, as you read before, a terrible cold and have

---

[177] Joskeys was a Department Store in San Antonio, Texas.

done a lot for it. My appetite is not as good as it has been but maybe will be OK soon. You asked what job I was doing etc. I am the Headquarters Commandant of this place.

Love to all,

Handwritten on the copy sent to his Father is the following note:

Dad, I am going to cable you some money which I have mentioned before – Do what you think best – I sure want to save while I can.

Your loving son, John

Saturday, 16 May 1942

Mr. and Mrs. O'Connor asked me to go to the Embassy with them tonight to dance a while. I had a clerk doing some work and finished about 11 PM. I thought I would join them and did about 11:30 PM. Well, we danced a few dances. The place was positively full. You couldn't wiggle. I had a driver and got home at 4 AM. Was I tired and sleepy! I had to get up at 7:15 AM.

The war news is about the same.

Sunday, 17 May 1942

I was asked out to dinner at a very prominent couple's house. They are both 60 years old and most interesting to talk to. They have three sons in the service at present. They also asked me to play bridge sometime, which I will be glad to do. They have a marvelous house and are, I guess, in the high society of the town. I can't recall their name, but will get it soon. I simply must write a thank you letter to them. I got home about 11:30 PM and was I sleepy.

Monday, 18 May 1942

7 PM - I have just come back to the hotel and am now listening to the news. I wrote you tonight, Honey, and told you in the letter for the first time that I was on Gen. MacArthur's staff. I mentioned it in the letter and think it will go through the censor. No other news.

I now have a carbine and a Garand rifle. I don't know what I will do with them. I hope to be able to keep them, as they may come in handy sometime.

As far as news is concerned the consensus of opinion is still that we will be attacked here in Australia unless we receive more men and equipment in the next short while. We are in no way safe, as most people here think. They feel that as the Americans are here, they are saved. May be they are – who knows?

Tuesday, 19 May 1942

I wrote Gilbert a letter this evening and sent a copy to Cile. It was the first time I told them I was in Gen. MacArthur's HQ. Guess it will get thru the censor OK. I received a letter from Gilbert and another from Dad today. Both were good and very much appreciated.

I sent Cile the jade ring, an emerald locket, and another Australian stone.[178] I cannot think of the name at this time. The jade ring came from Java and the others from Australia. I also sent Johnnie a Five Crown piece from Australia.

I bought myself a nice red corduroy bathrobe, a carbine rifle, and numerous other items I hope to keep. How does this pen work? I wanted to get to bed early tonight and here it is 9:30 PM now and I am listening to the news. I am going to call Cile in a few days if I can.

19.4.　　　Australian & American Cooperation – 19 May 1942

19 May 1942

Just a few notes will be recorded at this time. Unknown to the folks at home, here in HQ we especially see plainly that the Australians would like to run the show and let Americans furnish equipment and do the fighting. To me, as you might say "one not in the know," the Australians have promoted a lot of Generals to Major General. All the Area Commanders are Australian. Several other orders noticeably to most of us make it too clear as to their attitude. We are as we have always been. We would rather be under our own commanders and know all will have a better shot all the way around.

I hope I am fortunate enough to remain as I am in this job. However, the time may come when I will have to go to the scrapping end again. Those who have not had the misfortune of hearing the bombs fall and being shot at with machine guns have missed something. Needless to say, your heart will jump in your throat when the bombs fall.

Some of these fellows seem to think it's a cinch to beat the Japs, but they do not know. They have not taken into consideration that the other fellow is just as smart as they are. I have two full-blooded Japs in my company. Both are American citizens, and darned few know they are Japanese. The other soldiers think they are Filipinos. One of them was

---

[178] The family has possession of a lose opal, which is believed to be the unidentified Australian stone. There is confusion, however, because opal was contained in a box from Malang with a second opal.

working on his Ph.D. in Michigan when he was drafted into the service. I will stop for this time, with my love.

19.5.   News of Doolittle Raid – 20 May 1942 (A month after the raid)

Wednesday, 20 May 1942

I was sick at my stomach when I woke up this morning. I wanted to vomit. Ate very little breakfast but went to work. I made it through the morning, but came back to the hotel at 2 PM and went to bed. I have remained in bed all evening. It is now about 8:30 PM and cannot see a lot of improvement. The Doc gave me a few pills to take, possibly they will be of some help. I had supper in my room. I am sure I will be OK to go to work in the morning.

No news. The papers printed the story of Jimmie Doolittle's flight over Japan with the bunch that bombed Tokyo. This is the first time the actual story has come out here in Australia.[179]   Another woman was murdered which is three in last two weeks. There must be a maniac around somewhere. I bet its some soldier who has gone nuts. Good night to you all. I love you.

Thursday, 21 May 1942

I have been a little weak all day with not much appetite, but I have managed. My staying inside so much with so little exercise is making me a poor physical specimen. I sure don't get the walking and running I had in Java. I was in swell shape there. I do walk to work at least once a day, either at noon or in the morning. Of course that's actually very little exercise.

I still have trouble quite often with Col. Fitch, the AG. He sure likes to hop me about anything he can find. I sure get fed up with him sometimes. I got along fine with him till I got my promotion. Apparently he thought I should have waited longer before I got it. Since he had nothing to do with my getting the promotion, he seems to want to take it away from me.
Love & kisses, Darling.

Friday, 22 May 1942

Last night I was all set to go to the dinner at the Chevron for the "6-month-old-ers," all of us who have been overseas for six months. Just before I left the room, there was a call downstairs and who could it be, but the couple that I had dinner with one night, the O'Connors. Well, they came up and stayed till 12 AM. We drank about a quart of liquor.

---

[179] The Doolittle Raid occurred April 18, 1942.

Lt. Evans was in my room waiting to go to the Embassy dance. We finally went over to the Embassy and danced a few dances. I got home at 2:30 AM. Boy, I was dead tired.

Saturday, 23 May 1942
Today I have not had too much pep either. Must stop and get on to the job. I am writing this on Saturday morning, because I just couldn't write last night.

9:15 PM - I thought for a while I would go out to the Chevron Hotel tonight to their weekly dance, but I just couldn't make up my mind. I do want to go some night to see the bunch, if for nothing else. Everyone in the office is busy during the week, so you never get a chance to just talk. The Chevron dance is where you can get caught up with what others are doing.

I was very surprised but very glad to receive a letter from Susie Fletcher today about 4 PM. I answered Susie's letter and wrote you a note, Darling. About 5 PM I received another letter from Hope and Ockie. It made me feel good to hear from them and to know they were thinking of me.

Mr. Hall, an Australian who is in Purchasing for us, told me today he would take me around one day to find a few things to send home. He knows where to go to get the good prices. I will try to go with him one day this week.

Sunday, 24 May 1942
I worked past noon today, so late that I missed my lunch. I ate a couple of sandwiches and had a cup of coffee. About 4 PM I went walking in the park with a Major Lamar (English). We stopped for a cup of tea and then went to the Chevron for dinner with Capt. Sauve. Sauve said his wife was welding now in an airplane factory between Ft. Worth and Dallas.[180] He received his first letter.

I went up and talked to Majors Sparks and Patterson. We have exchanged names and addresses of wives. I will tell you, Darling, so you can write the wives.

---

[180] Consolidated-Vultee Aircraft, later Convair Aircraft and then General Dynamics, Fort Worth, Texas is where John (Johnnie) F Day III would work as an engineer in 1957.

An American soldier has been caught for the murders of the women near our hotel. I think he confessed to two of the three murders. *****his trial will be short. It will probably be in the paper in the morning.[181] It is nearly eleven and I am sleepy.

Monday, 25 May 1942

I returned to the hotel as usual tonight and ate supper. At 10 minutes before 8, I decided I wanted to see a show. I asked Major Lomax to go along and he did. We saw "I'm In the Navy." Enjoyed it very much but was terribly sleepy when we got home.

Tuesday, 26 May 1942

Just after dinner I moved to a new place: 23 Albert St., East Melbourne. This is a small apartment house where quite a number of officers are billeted. I do not know who they are as I seldom see them when I come and go.

I have not felt so good today, but tonight I wanted to get some of my stuff in drawers. I have had a time trying to get things where I can find them. There is no light in one room, and I am sitting on the floor now in front of the heater writing in my diary. There is a little "two by four heater" that does not put out enough heat to warm a duck, much less me.

I have no alarm clock and cannot find one in town. Can you imagine that? I want to have a phone installed in the morning, so I can get woken up the next morning. I am not sure what will happen tomorrow. Love and kisses, Darling.

Figure 68 - 23 Albert Street, East Melbourne, 2007 Photo.
It is unconfirmed that this 2007 building is the same building that was at this address in May 1942.

---

[181] Eddie Leonski, an American soldier, was convicted of three murders in Melbourne and was hanged on 9 Nov 1942 in Pentridge Prison.

Wednesday, 27 May 1942
I stopped at "Russell Collins," the most fashionable place in town to eat.[182] After taking at least an hour to eat with very poor service, I still did not get much to eat. In fact I was still hungry.

I came on home, cleared up a list of things I needed to do, and noticed in the paper that "Hot Spot" [183] was on at the Capital Theater. So I decided I would go. I went down to the theater, bought a ticket for about 3 Shillings, and then noticed that "Hot Spot" would start in a couple of days. "Dive Bomber" was actually on, so I saw it anyway. The shows here are always long and have about a five-minute intermission to smoke or buy a drink.

They were supposed to put in my phone today, but they did not get it hooked up for some reason. I must go to bed as it is almost midnight now.

Thursday, 28 May 1942
No work tonight, so came home and fixed a sandwich in my apartment.

I haven't described my apartment yet. I have a bedroom and sitting room, both carpeted, a kitchen and bath. Can you imagine that? Well, both rooms are so small that they are about the same size as the room I had at the hotel. I bought some cereal. The milkman leaves milk each morning. I bought fruit and a pound of steak. I don't know when I will get time to cook the stuff. I have some bananas, oranges, apples, and a pineapple. I fixed the pineapple like you fix them, Honey, and ate a slice for breakfast.

Tonight I went to St. Moritz ice skating for the first time in my life. I skated, but not for long as I was not so hot. I watched others for a while, drank a milk shake, and here I am back in the apartment again. My big event for today – I found a clock.

Friday, 29 May 1942
I went to the Friday night dance at the Embassy. No date of course, but went with two couples. They wanted to get a date for me, but no, I did not. I had a pretty good time. I had about all I wanted without being drunk. I was about right. I got home about 1 AM, messed around eating a sandwich from the ice box, wrote in the diary, and now it is 1:35 AM. I will close and go to bed. Love and kisses Darling.

---

[182] Russell Collins Restaurant was located in the T&G Building on the southern side of Collins St. between Russell and Swanston.

[183] *I Wake Up Screaming* (aka *Hot Spot)*; 1941, staring Betty Grable, Victor Mature, and Carole Landis, dir. H. Bruce Humberstone; prod. Milton Sperling, Twentieth- Century Fox, classified as Film Noir

<u>Saturday, 30 May 1942</u>
Same old grind. I did not hear the alarm clock this morning but did wake up at 8:15AM. Dressed quickly and went to work. I was "almost" on time. I wanted to go to a show tonight, but every show I called was booked up. Since a show was out, I cleaned up my apartment. I have not had time as yet to find someone to clean it daily, so I do it myself when I can. That seems to be about twice a week.

The best advantage for having an apartment is I can eat a sandwich or whatever I have when I want it without tipping. I eat all my breakfasts in the apartment. The mail for the States is to leave tomorrow, so I will write a letter to get it off. I understand it may be flown at least a part of the way. I wish it was flown all the way, so maybe we would have better service. Goodnight, Honey.

<u>Sunday, 31 May 1942</u>
I worked until 2:10 PM. I went over to eat dinner, but it was too late to get a full meal, so I had a bowl of soup, some ice cream, and cup of coffee. I came back to my room, made my bed, swept the floor, and am ready to go back to town to eat supper. I would cook supper myself, but I have nothing here but meat, and that is not much of a meal.

I wrote you a letter today, and wanted to write again tonight, but there just isn't anything to say. I had a letter from Mc [*McMahon*] today. The letter made it nice. I have not had a letter from Cile now in sometime, can't understand why. I cabled her Saturday, so maybe will hear something soon.

19.6.   Commentary on Australian Unions – 1 Jun 1942

As a new month appears in the diary, I guess I might fill in a little space by cutting loose with some of my feelings. These damned Aussies are so dumb. Talk about labor unions, ours are good compared to these here. The Australians even take time off in the middle of morning and the afternoon for tea. They want to charge you for Tea Money and too charge you taxi fare (mind you) for coming to work. Before 8:30 AM and after 5 PM, they want time and a half for overtime, even though they haven't worked all day. They want us to furnish everything including the men to fight the war, and they would like to run the war. They are making plenty of money out of it, and we are paying it too. Everywhere they can nip you, they do. The taxi fare is so high; it costs about triple what we pay at home. Then if you don't watch the driver, he will add more to the fare.

There have been several times soldiers have been robbed or clubbed after payday, losing all their money. American soldiers spend more on cigarettes than lots of the Aussies get paid. They are jealous of our uniforms and our equipment. There are fights which I guess are to be expected, and brother, don't think the Americans can't take care of themselves. The Aussies will only jump a fight on Americans when they have about a two-to-one advantage. Two of Aussies said "To Hell with MacArthur" in front of the building yesterday to a small sergeant. He jumped all over them both and another American went out and helped cleaned them both. The Aussies left in high gear.

They all want to leave the impression that they are tough as hell and don't give a damn. They are not. The truth of the matter is here in Australia, you have to volunteer for Foreign Military Service. Otherwise, they cannot send you away from home. In our country, if you are fit to be in the Army, they can send you anywhere and you don't grumble. They all get medals every time they turn around. They all have medals for something. This is enough for the present, so will stop. What do you think? "The enemy listens."

Monday, 1 June 1942
A new month and another payday! I am sending $300 to you, Darling. I also sent $100 to Dad to buy a heifer for Johnnie. I have had no letter from you in so long. It seems like an age. That is about the crop at present so I will stop. My kangaroo hide should be ready soon at the tanners.
Love and Kisses, John

Tuesday, 2 June 1942
Nothing new. It seems that another battle is beginning.[184] Wonder when things will start popping. The way this thing is going, the war will never end.

Wednesday, 3 June 1942
No news. I am still plugging along.

Thursday, 4 June 1942
I went to the show tonight and saw "Hot Spot." It was a pretty good show. I have another cold developing. I sure get my share of colds, and they usually get as bad as they can be before I can do anything with them.

Friday, 5 June 1942
I came home after dinner (3:30 PM) and went to bed with my cold. Sure caught one in a hurry this time. Such weather, I have never seen.

---

[184] Preparation was underway in advance of the Battle of Midway, 4-5 June 1942.

I hope I get to stay here on this job till the thing is over but am always afraid I will be sent somewhere else on account of Col. Fitch. The bastard is always after me for anything he can find.

Saturday, 6 June 1942
I stayed in bed all day with a terrible cold. I don't seem to be a lot better. I am guessing it's a light case of flu.

Last night one of our cars was stolen again from the motor pool. This was the same car that was stolen before. I know Col. Fitch will give me hell about it when I get back to the office. He can tell me anything, and of course, I will have to take it. I suggested another guard on the motor pool last time, and he wouldn't allow it. I will go ahead and put the guard on this time anyway.

Sunday, 7 June 1942
I went down to the office and worked today. At 3:30 PM I came home, rested until 6, and then went back and ate supper. I checked the janitors and guards and then returned home at 8 PM. I am undressed and about ready to go to bed.

Turned the radio on and the damn thing went out again. It looks like it doesn't want to run. The naval battle near Midway seems to be turning our way. Hope we get more good news.

Monday, 8 June 1942
Well, I received three letters today. My spirits feel good, but my cold is terrible. I am all but sick, so will not write much tonight. I have felt like hell all day. Love and kisses.

Tuesday, 9 June 1942
My cold is still with me. I get so tired of blowing. Today, I received a letter from Mac that I enjoyed a lot. I was restless all last night, and hope I do better tonight.

19.7.   Visiting Hours for the Victoria Palace Hotel – 10 Jun 1942

Wednesday, 10 June 1942
I have felt much better today, and ate full meals but my nose is still blowing. My nose is so sore. I came home and cooked myself a steak, read the paper, and am going to bed early. If I feel OK, may go to show tomorrow night.

The manager for the enlisted men's hotel, the Victoria Palace, came up to see me today. He wants me to make an order that the men billeted at the hotel cannot carry girls to their rooms. That is some job. It seems to be a bigger job to keep the girls out of the room than it is to tell the men they cannot carry them up. I will try to settle with him, so the men can have one night a week. I hope that settles it. Col. Fitch thinks so. It doesn't make any difference to me. [Copy of the original order that resulted is shown below.]

HEADQUARTERS COMPANY

UNITED STATES ARMY FORCES IN THE FAR EAST

COMPANY ORDER :
NUMBER   2 :   June 20, 1942

    The following regulations are established for the enlisted personnel of this Headquarters now billeted at the Victoria Palace Hotel. All personnel concerned will be required to observe these regulations:

    1. All persons assigned to these billets shall conduct themselves, at all times, in such manner as to bring credit on the United States Army.

    2. No women guests are at any time permitted to enter any part of the building other than those set apart for the use of the public. Saturday nights will be set aside for the entertainment of women guests in the hotel. All women guests must be out of the hotel not later than 12:00 midnight. Arrangements may be made on this night for the use of the hotel ballroom for a social function.

    3. No male visitors, other than members of the Allied Services in uniform, may be brought into the rooms assigned to United States military personnel in these quarters.

    4. No liquor will be consumed in the hallways.

    5. Narcotics or drugs will not be introduced in the hotel.

    6. Food will not be cooked in the hotel rooms.

    7. Gambling is prohibited in any spaces in these government quarters.

    8. All personnel assigned to these quarters shall observe the rule of the hotel management, which are published for the conduct of guests on the premises; boisterous and unseemly conduct in and about the hotel premises is prohibited; loitering in front of the hotel is prohibited; personnel shall enter and leave directly and quietly.

    9. Every care shall be taken to prevent damage to furniture, equipment or fittings in these quarters and other parts of the hotel. Should any damage to this property be caused by United States Army personnel, the person or persons involved shall report the circumstances immediately to the warrant officer or senior noncommissioned officer present.

    10. Smoking in these quarters is permitted. Personnel shall observe necessary precautions to prevent damage to furniture, equipment or fixtures. Care will be taken to prevent fire and to observe fire regulations at all times.

    11. Each individual assigned to these quarters shall keep his space neat and orderly, and shall keep his clothing and equipment arranged neatly in lockers or other spaces assigned for that purpose.

- 1 -

12. Any report concerning the lack of service or unjust treatment will be made to either of the three warrant officers residing in the hotel and not to the hotel management.

13. Uniform of the day will be worn. Personnel must be in full uniform when outside the rooms assigned to them in these quarters, except when actually going to and from the bath, and they must be properly clothed under this latter condition.

14. Any noncommissioned officer may be called upon by the management at any time to assist in enforcing these rules. A written report of such instances will be made to this office by the noncommissioned officer called upon.

15. Water will not be left running in washrooms and baths when those spaces are left unattended; lights will be turned off when leaving rooms; blackout security will be maintained with the means furnished by the management for such purposes, and care will be taken to prevent lights in the rooms from showing outside during blackout hours.

16. Any violation of the above rules shall be reported to the Headquarters Commandant.

JOHN F. DAY, JR.,
Maj. F.A. Hq. Comd't.,
Hq. Co. U.S.A.F.F.E.

Figure 69 - Copy of original order - 20 June 1942

Thursday, 11 June 1942

Today I got my other footlocker all addressed. It looks nice. I can get all my stuff in now and will have it ready to send home on a moments notice. I keep thinking I will stop accumulating things, but I don't. I now have a cadet bag – a new one – nope – I did not buy it but was issued. My cold is getting better, but I now have a deep cough. I have more energy and think in a few more days I will be feeling a lot better. I received a letter from Dwight and enjoyed it a lot. Maybe my mail will start coming in more regularly. I have managed to get a stone bruise on my right foot for some reason and cannot understand it.

Friday, 12 June 1942

I received Cile's telegram of April 26th today. Some speed – 57 days for a telegram from Texas. I cooked myself a steak and couple of eggs tonight. My radio was fixed today, so have been listening to news. I gathered my laundry and messed around. It is now 10:15 PM and I am bed bound.

The murder trial for the American soldier started yesterday. He is being tried for the murder of three women. They are checking him now for insanity. It's a general court martial and will be plenty rough if he is not insane.

Received Cile's letter late and sat down and answered it at the time. It was a swell letter.

19.8.   General MacArthur Day – 13 June 1942

By Congressional Resolution, 13 Jun 1942 was declared "Douglas MacArthur Day." This date was the anniversary of MacArthur entering West Point in 1899. This was an honor that had never been bestowed upon any living man, not even a President. The resolution had been introduced by Senator Robert La Follette Jr.

Saturday, 13 June 1942
Today is *Gen. MacArthur Day*.[185] I went up to his office and went in to pay my respects. I told him for one thing, I was sorry I did not get to the Philippine Islands to help him out.

He said. "My boy, you are living on velvet for the remainder of your life. You should be very proud that you are still here and can do more good than you could have done there." He is certainly a fine fellow.

It seems I write Cile almost every day. I have written a lot of late but saying very little. I sent Cile the Japanese skirt, dress, and hat today. I haven't written her to tell her but will pronto. It is one of the few things I still had left over from Java. I love you so much Darling. Wish I could see you both.

19.9.   "Rat Shoot" at the City Dump – 14 Jun 1942

Sunday, 14 June 1942
What a day! Today is Flag Day, and I have not done much. About 4 PM I had a headache and decided I should get outside for a while, so I left Sgt. George in the office. Lt. Evans and I left for a ride. We went by the house, picked up his 22-cal. rifle and shot gun. He said he knew a fairly close place to go where we could shoot, the "City Dump." We intended shooting some birds, but there were so many rats, we just shot rats. That was a good pastime. The war was on as far as rats were concerned. We killed a bunch and came home at 5:20 PM as it was dark. He burned the office paper trash and I

---

[185] General MacArthur has returned to Melbourne after his secret trip to Queensland.

checked the guard. We came home and both fixed supper, cleaned the dishes, and here I am. It is bed time, so will go to bed.

Monday, 15 June 1942
I had just finished supper and emptied part of my garbage when Lt. McGruder and another Lt. whose name I cannot remember came by and asked me if I wanted to go with them to the "Tivoli." I had not heard of "Tivoli" but decided to go with them. It was a stage show and was pretty rough at times. Most of the Australian jokes are terrible; they seem to be crude compared to our jokes. They had some scenes where the girls were about nude. They had a G-strap with their apples hanging down. It looked to me like they all drooped. I had a lot of fun laughing anyway. We had seats on the second row, which was all that was left when we arrived.

My cold is some better. I duly used twelve handkerchiefs today.

19.10.   More Attacks on Darwin – 16 Jun 1942

Tuesday, 16 June 1942
It seems that pressure is being put on Darwin once more. Heavier air raids are coming daily now. We figured something will pop soon.

Well, today I received a cable from Cile and two letters dated first part of April (two months for delivery). I cannot tell when the cable was sent. By the way, these are the last two letters I guess that you used the wrong address – the one that was given to you by Betty Songuinate. Hope you don't use it anymore. I will wire you, Honey, in a day or so.

I went to a picture show tonight and saw "Bad Man of Dakota." I enjoyed it very much.

I took one pair of pants back to tailor, and told him I would not be seen in them. He is making a new pair for me. Guess I'm getting fat, since my blouse is getting tight. I have ordered another so I can have one to wear each day. It takes about a week to get one cleaned and pressed. This is the worst I have ever seen.

Wednesday, 17 June 1942
No mail today.

I have found a good spot to take some moving pictures. From on top of this building we are in, I can see almost the whole town. On the first clear day I will take the rest of my present roll of film. There are now six rolls in the storage house, which is not as many as I would like, but I just haven't been taking any pictures lately.

I came home tonight, cooked myself a steak, two eggs, lettuce and tomato salad, peaches in the can, coffee, and cheese. Am I full!

I cleaned my house a little tonight. My bed had not been made up for a couple of days, but that is OK. I haven't tried to get anyone to clean the house, and now I am not going to as it gives me something to do at night. There has been some improvement in my cold. I am down to six handkerchiefs per day.

Thursday, 18 June 1942

I had nothing to do at home and I didn't want to stay home, so I went to see "Hot Spot" again. It was OK for a while, but I must have gone to sleep at about the middle. When I woke up, the people were leaving, so I did too. Of course I was mad at myself because I didn't go to bed as I should have.

I bought a couple of pounds of candy for myself to take home and eat when I want it. In the office, candy is gone in only a matter of minutes.

One of my Filipinos had been going with a Chinese girl and told her his name was "Johnnie Howard." The girl's mother came in and wanted to have a very confidential talk with me. She was afraid her daughter was going to marry him and wanted me to talk to him. I did. Well, I found out first his name was "Costaloma." He had been giving the girl £8 because she said she needed some clothes and also she was going to his room. I asked him why he gave her so much. He said "it not much – she needs 'um." I never laughed so much in all my life. Anyway the girl's mother has made two trips into the office about the matter.

20.   WAR MOMENTUM SHIFTING – Jun 1942

20.1.   MacArthur's Supply Lines

A war cannot be won without timely supplies, including food, ammunition, and matériel. Napoleon said "An army marches on its stomach." As this Pacific war proved, supply lines would become a significant determining factor for victory. Both the Japanese and the Allies paid special attention to their supply lines.

To begin, the Japanese wanted to cut the supply lines from the United States to Australia. This caused their interest in the Solomon Islands and Tulagi.

The Allied counterattack was to begin in New Guinea and the Solomon Islands, so the question of Allied supply lines to these islands was extremely important. To supply Port Moresby, New Guinea, there were two options: by sea and by air. The resupply of Port Moresby by sea required ships to cross the Gulf of Papua, which were vulnerable to the Japanese Navy. If you crossed the Gulf successfully, the port facilities were inadequate to handle the volume of supplies needed.

To resupply Port Moresby by air, Allies had to control the sky, airports were required in both the Australian Cape York Peninsula and in Port Moresby, and cargo aircraft were required in abundance. Further, the range for 1942 military cargo aircraft was such that to reach Port Moresby the aircraft could be no farther away than Townsville, Queensland. Brisbane was beyond the range of a loaded cargo plane. Therefore, cargo flights had to refuel in Townsville before departing for Port Moresby. Unfortunately, the air fields in Townsville were inadequate to handle the loaded aircraft or the heavy traffic.

To describe New Guinea infrastructure as primitive in 1942 would be a compliment. Port Moresby had only two short and poorly constructed air fields, neither of which could handle a loaded transport plane. Air fields in the Cape York Peninsula were limited, poorly constructed, and unable to support both military and cargo aircraft. The C-47 cargo transport, the work horse that would ferry supplies from Australia, had a door that was not large enough to accept a military truck. Further, C-47's were in very short supply.

Townsville is 850 miles north of Brisbane. The distance from Melbourne to Townsville, Queensland was approximately 2,000 miles, the same distance as from Melbourne to Perth, and a distance far too great for a useful supply line. MacArthur needed a military supply center in Queensland before he could embark on any offensive counterattack. This supply center needed access to good transportation and communications including:

- *a major seaport for cargo ships*
- *a railroad network for the movement of materiel*
- *air bases for heavy cargo aircraft support*
- *a network of highways for the movement of people and materiel*
- *training facilities to prepare troops for jungle warfare*
- *a location for the General Headquarters close to the combat zone*
- *a network for communications with all combat zones, as well as Washington, DC*

20.2.   MacArthur's Secret Inspection Trip to Queensland – May-June 1942

MacArthur's secret inspection trip was a reconnaissance trip to gain a first-hand impression of the facilities and infrastructure of northeastern Queensland prior to selecting a location for his supply base and for his headquarters. He wanted to see if the facilities north of Brisbane, including Townsville, Cloncurry, Cooktown, and Horn Island, could be used to support his Theater of Operations. To supply New Guinea by air, new airfields were required in the Cape York Peninsula. On the other hand the Great Barrier Reef presented a natural hazard to shipping going into Townsville, but not into Brisbane.

MacArthur's reconnaissance trip was made by train. In 1941, runways for aircraft in northeastern Australia were limited and primitive at best. MacArthur was from an era where train travel could be comfortable, so the train was preferred over air, hence the secret GHQ Train. Time on the train would not be lost but would be effective planning time for the staff.

The reconnaissance team was to include all of MacArthur's staff, but especially Gen. Casey, MacArthur's Chief Engineer, who would be responsible for the construction of the necessary infrastructure.

Gen. Hugh (Pat) Casey (1898-1981) was possibly the most underappreciated soldier in the Pacific War. A 1918 graduate of West Point, Casey served in Germany after World War I where he became fluent in German. After the war, he held various civil engineering positions before he returned to Germany on an ASME Fellowship to the Technische Hochschule Berlin (TU-Berlin) where he earned a Doctorate of Engineering in 1935. After graduation, he served on a number of flood control and hydroelectric projects in the Pittsburg District and on the Ohio River. In 1937 he was assigned to the Philippines to advise the Philippine government on various flood control and hydroelectric dam projects. While in the Philippines, he came into contact with Gen. Douglas MacArthur and his Chief of Staff, Lt. Col. Dwight D. Eisenhower. Casey returned to Washington, D.C. in October 1940 where he became Chief of Design and Engineering in the Construction

Division of the Quartermaster Corps. In July 1940, Casey, George Bergstrom[186], and their staff were given the task to design the world's largest office building for the military, which was to be built in Washington, D.C. The building, which later became known as The Pentagon, was essentially designed over <u>one</u> "very busy weekend."[187] Casey was truly an engineer's engineer.

In September 1941, MacArthur requested that Casey be assigned to the Philippines as Chief Engineer, where he was promoted to Brigadier General in January 1942. At the time of MacArthur's evacuation from the Philippines (March 1942), MacArthur specifically ordered Casey to accompany him to Australia, as his skills were considered critical to the success of the war effort.

In the Census of 1933, Brisbane was the third largest city in Australia with a population of 300,000. North of Brisbane the railroad ran to Townsville, which had a population of 25,000.[188] Townsville had been the gateway to the inland gold mines at Charters Towers. Although it had a port facility, Townsville was considered inadequate to handle the heavy supply requirements for the war effort, cially because of the hazard to shipping created by the Great Barrier Reef, loed just off the coast. All available port facilities would be employed (including Townsville), but Brisbane was selected as the primary port facility to support MacArthur's military operations for several reasons, one of which was its location south of the Great Barrier Reef. New air bases would be scattered around Queensland, and a training facility could be constructed in Rockhampton area. The main logistical center would be located in the Brisbane area, and MacArthur's GHQ was to be relocated there as well.

Figure 70 – Coral Sea Islands Map

The exact dates of MacArthur's secret train trip to Queensland and the passengers aboard the train are unknown to this writer; however Maj. Day's diary has no mention of direct contact

---

[186] George Bergstrom was a former President of the American Institute of Architects.

[187] http://en.wikipedia.org/wiki/Hugh_John_Casey

[188] Cairns is about 200 miles north of Townsville and in 20111 was better known as a resort than Townsville. However, in 1933 Cairns had a population of only 11,000 with no real port.

with Gen. MacArthur from 8 May 1942 until 13 Jun 1942. It is presumed that the reconnaissance trip occurred during this time interval. [189]

While on the train, Casey prepared recommendations regarding the need for facilities in Queensland and New Guinea. He would lead a monumental program of construction with the support of Col. Leif Sverdrup, Chief of US Construction Section, Australian Gen. Clive Steele, and the Australian Allied Works Council. The Australian Air Force also organized an Engineer Construction Battalion that worked mostly independently. During the course of the Pacific War, Casey and Sverdrup were directly or indirectly responsible for the construction of over 800 airfields, roads, bridges, buildings, and port facilities scattered along the island path between Australia, New Guinea, the Philippines and Japan.

Immediately, Gen. Casey and Col. Leif Sverdrup, Chief of Construction Engineers, embarked on a major program to build airbases in both Port Moresby and northern Queensland. Gen. Casey began a monumental civil works project that became the foundation of modern Papua New Guinea (PNG).

20.3.   Battle of Midway – 4 to 5 Jun 1942

The Battle of Midway was the first decisive victory for the US in the central Pacific against the Japanese Navy, and it proved to be pivotal in the outcome of the war. It was a triumph directly attributable to the success of US code-breaking skills that allowed the US to have advanced warning of the Japanese intentions and time schedule.[190] This advance knowledge allowed the Americans to develop their own trap for the Japanese that proved very successful.

The Japanese plan was to lure the US Navy out from Pearl Harbor to defend Midway and then destroy them with an attack by overwhelmingly superior forces. Adm. Yamamoto was under the impression that the US Navy had only two aircraft carriers available to fight: the USS Hornet and the USS Enterprise. He had been informed that BOTH the USS Lexington AND the USS Yorktown had been sunk in the Battle of the Coral Sea. Indeed the Lexington had been sunk, however the USS Yorktown had only been severely damaged. As was stated earlier, the Yorktown was able to limp back to Pearl Harbor where in 72 hours the Pearl Harbor shipyard repaired the major

---

[189] The author was unable to confirm this train trip from Gen. MacArthur's personal desk calendar in the possession of the MacArthur Memorial Museum Brisbane. However, the preparation for the trip is clearly detailed in the diary of Major Day.

[190] http://en.wikipedia.org/wiki/Battle_of_Midway,

http://www.ww2pacific.com/midway.html;

http://militaryhistory.about.com/od/worldwarii1/p/Midway.htm;

http://www.history.navy.mil/photos/events/wwii-pac/midway/midway.htm

damage to the <u>Yorktown</u> and declared it ready to rejoin the Battle Line. The repair crews were still working on board as the carrier moved out to sea steaming toward Midway Island.

In addition to three carrier fleets, the US had land-based B-17 bombers operating from Midway Island. What Yamamoto thought was a four to two carrier advantage was reduced to a four to three carrier advantage plus nineteen US B-17 bombers based on Midway – a very rough parity between the two sides.

Further, Yamamoto chose to spread his fleet over several hundred miles of sea in order to disguise the number of ships under his command. This spread fleet in the end denied his carriers adequate anti-aircraft and scouting protection.

During the battle that followed, the Japanese Navy lost four aircraft carriers (<u>Kaga</u>, <u>Akagi</u>, <u>Hiryu</u>, and <u>Soryu</u>), a heavy cruiser, other ships, and 250 aircraft, while the US Navy lost one aircraft carrier (<u>Yorktown</u>), a destroyer, and 150 aircraft.

This battle was the beginning of a war of attrition for Japan, especially the Japanese Navy. The Japanese industrial complex was not able to produce enough new ships and planes to replace the carrier and military aircraft losses. Most damaging to the Japanese war machine was the loss of trained pilots. The Japanese pilot training program was accelerated in order to produce the quantity of pilots needed to replace their battle losses. As a consequence, new Japanese pilots did not have the flight experience and training of early Japanese pilots and proved less effective in combat. The losses of trained pilots and aircraft proved a strategic loss for Japanese military power.

Another critical loss to the Japanese Navy was the loss of one of their best carrier commanders, Rear Adm. Yamaguchi of the <u>Hiryu</u>. Late in the Battle of Midway, Yamaguchi chose to go down with his sinking carrier, denying Japan one of its most effective leaders.

As Japan could not meet its replacement requirements, the United States was just beginning to organize its industrial strength and pilot training programs. In the time Japan took to replace four carriers, the US built 24 new carriers plus support ships. The US was able to produce a steady supply of men and machines to replace their war losses.

20.4.   Marshall's Counterattack Directive – 2 July 1942

The victory at Midway created the first opportunity for the Allies to counterattack. MacArthur had assumed he would be in charge since the operation was to be in his South-West Pacific Theater. He recommended to the Joint Chiefs a plan to immediately attack the Japanese stronghold for the South-West Pacific in Rabaul, New Britain Island. This would require a series of offensive amphibious landings in New Guinea and in the Solomon Islands.

For reasons that have led to much speculation, Adm. Ernest King was strongly opposed to Mac-Arthur being in charge of these amphibious operations. King wanted the Navy to be in charge and basically opposed any role for MacArthur's Army, essentially refusing to support them.

General Marshall, who was Chairman of the Joint Chiefs, was unable to obtain the agreement of Adm. King who was organizing an amphibious landing force of his own within the Marine Corps. Finally, Marshall obtained agreement by re-dividing Area responsibilities in the South Pacific between the Army and the Navy and issuing a Directive dividing the operations into three tasks:

- *Task One – Seizure and occupation of the Santa Cruz Islands, Tulagi, and adjacent positions (Guadalcanal).*
- *Task Two – Seizure and occupation of the remainder of the Solomon Islands, of Lae, Salamaua, and the northeast coast of New Guinea.*
- *Task Three – Seizure and occupation of Rabaul and adjacent positions in the New Guinea-New Britain-New Ireland area.*

Task One was assigned to Adm. King, who designated Adm. Ghormley to oversee operations. Tasks Two and Three were assigned to Gen. MacArthur.

Amphibious landings require close cooperation between Army and Navy. Not only does the Navy have to deliver the troops safely to shore, they also must provide ship-based artillery support and carrier-based aerial cover for landing forces. This would become a contentious issue between Adm. King and Gen. MacArthur for the duration of the war.

20.5.   MacArthur's Move into New Guinea – July 1942

20.5.1.   The Engineers

Gen. Casey was dispatched to begin the first of many major construction projects of the war to support the resupply of Port Moresby. In New Guinea, Casey had to build a first-class seaport facility, lengthen and strengthen two airfields to accept larger aircraft, AND build three new airfields in the Port Moresby area. In addition, the Cape York Peninsula required five new airfields including Townsville, Mareeba, Cairns, Cooktown, and Coen between Brisbane and Horn Island. All of this construction was to be well on its way in ten weeks. The first US Engineer unit moved to Port Moresby in late April 1942 to support the Australians, but the movement in force began in June.

20.5.2.   The Air Corps

MacArthur wasted no time preparing his organization for attack. On 13 Jul 1942 Maj. Gen. Kenney was assigned to MacArthur to take command of the Far East Air Corps. Gen. Brett would remain until Kenney could reach the South Pacific 28 Jul 1942.

Gen. Kenney is credited with the proposal to cut the military trucks in half in order to fit them in the availableC-47 aircraft doors and then re-welding them in New Guinea.

20.5.3.   The Infantry

By agreement with Churchill and the Australian government, the Allied Army was to be under the command of an Australian, Gen. Sir Thomas Blamey, who had recently returned to Australia from the Mid-East. However, by agreement the Australian and US forces would maintain their own separate and independent supply lines. Brig. Gen. Richard J. Marshall (Deputy Chief of Staff to MacArthur) was initially placed in charge of US Army Services Of Supply (USASOS).

MacArthur's Army consisted of two US Infantry Divisions and two Australian Divisions that were finally returned to Australia from the Mid-East. The two US Infantry Divisions were consolidated into I Corps. The 41st Infantry Division (primarily National Guard units from Washington, Oregon, Idaho, and Montana) was the first US unit assigned to Australia arriving in Melbourne on 9 April 1942 after a voyage from Brooklyn, New York through the Panama Canal. The second Army unit assigned to Mac Arthur was the 32nd Infantry Division (Wisconsin and Michigan National Guard, also known as the Red Arrow Division) which arrived 14 May 1942 at Port Adelaide. Both US Infantry Divisions were moved to Rockhampton, Queensland in July where they began training for jungle warfare.

21.   THE HOME FRONT – TEXAS - 1942

21.1.   Bonham, Texas

In 1940 Bonham was a small sleepy southern town, like many villages "on a side-track" frozen in time. With a population of 6,349, the town was located in the northeast part of Texas, about 60 miles from Dallas and 17 miles from the Oklahoma border. The center of commerce for Bonham was the downtown city square, built around the 1888 Court House with its Civil War Monument and a statue of the city namesake, James Bonham, a hero of the Alamo. The climate was hot and humid with plenty of mosquitoes in an era before air conditioning and DDT. To cool off at night, one would go to bed with wet sheets that would cool the sleeper as the water evaporated during the night. A "refrigerated room" was found only in the bank president's family room and was considered the ultimate of luxury. There were two "picture shows" in town, one of which showed a western movie and a weekly serial every Saturday afternoon for a child's admission of nine cents. An ice cream cone was five cents. An RC Cola came in a 12-ounce glass bottle for five cents. Outside the city limits were two lakes for recreational swimming, but one always kept an eye out for water moccasins. The Great Depression and the Dust Bowl had taken their toll on the social fabric of the region, as hobos still passed through town "riding the rails" on trains heading west seeking work. Transients would often stop to find a meal, always knowing the marked houses that would provide a handout.

Bonham's most famous son was Samuel T. Rayburn. "Mr. Sam," as he was affectionately called, served in the U.S. Congress for 47-years, beginning in 1913 and as Speaker of the House of Representatives for 17 years, the longest serving Speaker in U.S. history.

Figure 71 - Cile Hackley, 1934

21.2.   Cornelia Lucille (Cile) Hackley

Cornelia Lucille (Cile) Hackley was born in Bonham on August 5, 1915. She was the fifth generation of Hackleys to live in Bonham. About 1856, Richard and Nannie Hackley moved to Texas from Lincoln County, Kentucky. Two years later, Sarah Hackley, Nannie's mother and a widow, rode the Butterfield Stage to Texas to join her children and grandchildren. To get money for her relocation, Sarah sold the bounty land grant that her late husband, Jimmie Hackley, earned for his service with Andrew Jackson at the Battle of New Orleans in the War of 1812.

The Hackleys were Bonham grocers for two generations. Hackley & Edwards Grocery and Produce was located downtown on the west side of the Bonham Square. Cile's parents, Dwight and

Lucille Hackley, were merchants. Her mother had a dress shop, her father sold men's clothing, and her grandmother was a master milliner making women's fine hats.

A petite woman about 5 feet 2inches, Cile attended Bonham schools and graduated valedictorian of her high school class of 1933. She was artistically talented - an oil painter, a performing dancer, and a maker of handicrafts. She loved music, particularly Hoagy Carmichael's "Stardust." Her parents wanted her to be the first person from the family to go to college. In spite of pressure from her mother, Cile had her blue eyes set on a young textile engineer who was working at the Bonham Cotton Mill. On November 22, 1934, at the age of 19, Cile married John F. Day Jr., age 25, at the First Baptist Church of Bonham carrying the same lace handkerchief her mother had carried in her wedding.

A labor strike shut the Bonham Cotton Mill in 1935 and forced John to leave town to find work. During the next five years John and Cile lived in three different Texas mill towns. Johnnie arrived the next year in New Braunfels. They were living in Brenham in 1940 when John was called to active duty. By that time Cile was 25 years old with a 4 year old son, Johnnie.

After Capt. John Day sailed from San Francisco for Manila on November 21, 1941, Cile and Johnnie returned to Bonham where they moved in with Cile's parents. The Hackleys converted the upstairs attic of their two-bedroom 1926 house to a bedroom and bath, where Cile and Johnnie lived for the duration of the war.

Figure 72 - Cile & Johnnie Day, 1937

Figure 73 - Hackley Home - 611 Chestnut Street, Bonham - after 1943 Ice Storm

21.3.   Jones Field, the Bonham Airport - 1941

**Figure 74 - Cile & Johnnie in the Upstairs Bedroom
Bonham, Texas - Christmas 1943**

Bonham had a city airport beginning in 1929. Ten years later Bonham Aviation Company started giving flying lessons at Jones Field. When war approached in June 1941, the Secretary of War authorized the construction of a Primary Training Base for the Army Air Corps at Jones Field. The expanded facility was leased to Bonham Aviation Company, which continued to train pilots until five months after V-E Day. During the course of World War II, over 5,000

pilots received their primary flight training at Jones Field.

Figure 75 - Jones Field Air Cadet Graduation Ceremony

As the war effort intensified, the number of cadets at Jones Field increased. Bonham found itself with a serious housing shortage, as the Base did not have sufficient barracks to house all the cadets. The town was without adequate apartments or rental housing, so the Base solicited private homeowners in town to rent spare bedrooms to accommodate the cadet officer overflow during their training period. The Hackleys opened their house and rented a bedroom to a series of officer cadets.

21.4.   The Bonham USO

Entertainment and recreational opportunities were in short supply for the cadets at Jones Field.
Bonham was a "dry" county, that is, there was no legal beer or alcohol sold. With gasoline rationed, it was not easy to drive to Oklahoma and the nearest Roadhouse.

The community service clubs organized a local USO Chapter for cadet entertainment in 1942. The USO mission was "to raise the spirits of the armed services." A building located at the corner of 5th and Willow, only one block from the Bonham Square, was remodeled and became the USO. It was furnished with newspapers, magazines, a pool table, ping pong table, and a radio – even stationery to write letters home. There were colas, candy, and friendly conversation.

Figure 76 - Cile with two Cadets
In front of the Bonham USO

Figure 77 - Watermelon Social - Jones Field Cadets
Hackley backyard – 1942

Cile became a leader and a driving force in the management of the Bonham USO. The women's social clubs of Bonham worked to staff the club with hostesses to make the temporary visitors as welcome as possible. Regular events were organized at the USO, including weekend hot dog roasts, watermelon socials, hand-cranked ice cream socials, magic shows, fortune telling, and other activities.
Private homes in Bonham were opened for some of the USO events. This photo was taken in the Hackley backyard.

Figure 78 – 1943 USO Party, Hackley back-
yard
Cile in the middle, Johnnie on right, car is
Day's 1941 Buick

Illusionary Amputation At USO

—Photo by L. R. Ill.

WITH A FIENDISH GLEAM IN HIS EYE, WALLACE WOMACI
magician, severs John P. Liebel's arm off at the wrist during a
gun presented at the local USO Club last Sunday afternoon.
'cint Cadet Liebel is receiving flight training at Jones Field, Bi
lis home is Blue Ash Hills, Van Meter Pike, Lexington, Ky., a
the son of Col. Willard K. Liebel

Figure 79 - Wallace Womack
Magic Show, Bonham USO

21.5. Letters from the Southwest Pacific - 1942

During the 40 months of his wartime service in the Southwest Pacific, Major Day maintained an active correspondence with his wife (Cile), his parents (John and Flora Day), and his siblings and their families (Gilbert Day, niece Jo Ann Day, Carl and Hazel Dawn Day, and Alta Pearl Day). Major Day frequently made carbon copies of his letters in order to send the original to his wife and a copy to his parents. Cile liked to read and reread John's letters and wanted to keep his letters for herself. In a day before the invention of photocopy machines, Cile would retype John's letters and mail the retyped copy to John's parents or another relative. Some of the surviving letters in the possession of John's mother were the copies that had been retyped by Cile.

MY TIME IS DAY TIME

(Or Why Didn't the Older Generation Do This More Often?

——

War brings havoc to womankind;
It scars her beauty, warps her mind.
Is it any wonder men rebel
At the calloused paws of Welder Nell?

Delicate? Sweet? Lovely? Demure?
Hell no! These adjectives fit no more.
They're no longer ladies; tough as men,
With few exceptions -- God bless them!

Lucille Day is one such name;
It should go down in the Hall of Fame.
Her factory is Bonham's U.S.O.
Where Herr Schoat's cadets love to go.

Her tools are laughter, smiles, finesse,
Instead of a jackhammer or a drill press.
She remains a lady, bless her soul --
A ray of hope, a major role.

When "Pappy" returns from Aussie's shore
He won't grasp a hand that's blistered and sore.
Instead he'll return to the genuine 'Cille
Instead of a muscled, masculine "heel".

Jim Morgan, Jr.

THE YOUNG MEN'S CHRISTIAN ASSOCIATIONS • THE NATIONAL CATHOLIC COMMUNITY SERVICE
THE SALVATION ARMY • THE YOUNG WOMEN'S CHRISTIAN ASSOCIATIONS
THE JEWISH WELFARE BOARD • THE NATIONAL TRAVELERS AID ASSOCIATION

Figure 80 – USO Citation for Lucille Day

Major Day's mother (Flora Gray Day) retained the letters and copies that she received. About thirty years after Flora's death in 1968, about 70 letters were discovered among old family papers by Hazel Dawn Day, who sent the letters to "Johnnie" (John Day III). In 2011 John III begun transcribing the letters.

All the letters written to Major Day by Cile or by his parents have been lost in the attic of time. Insight into the content of those letters can only by inferred from Major Day's responses in his own letters.

Major Day said in his letters that he was retaining a copy of all his letters. None of these copies have survived. Because Major Day numbered his letters, we know that there are missing letters.

The earliest surviving letter was written to his Mother on November 20, 1941 prior to boarding the ship for the Philippine Islands. The last surviving letter was written January 27, 1945 from Leyte, Philippine Islands. The letters are distributed in time as follows:

> *Year – Number – Location*
> *1941 – 8 – San Francisco, Brisbane, and Singosari, Java NEI*
> *1942 – 37 – Java, NEI, Melbourne, and Brisbane, Australia*
> *1943 – 14 – Brisbane, Oro Bay and Lae NG*
> *1944 – 10 – Lae, NG, Leyte, PI*
> *1945 – 1 – Leyte, PI*

While Day was in Australia at GHQ, he had access to a typewriter and typed his letters. After Day was assigned to New Guinea and moved into the combat zone, many letters were handwritten on small pieces of stationery and the frequency of letters declined. When he arrived in the Philippines, he again had access to a typewriter but letters were less frequent.

There are large gaps in the dates of letters, especially during the preparation for and invasion of Lae, NG and Leyte, PI when Day was busy with war activities.

There are a number of threads that are woven through these letters. A few of these threads are followed below.

21.5.1.   Letters about Johnnie - 1942

The following are excerpts from letters by Major Day from Melbourne:

March 29, 1942 – Letter #20

> Johnnie, how are you doing and what do you do all day? Daddy sure misses you too. Wish I could see you and Mother. You be sure and take good care of her because Daddy depends on you. What are you learning at school? I guess by the time you get this let-ter, school will be out for the year - at least at the rate it has taken letters to reach me.
>
> Johnnie, write Daddy a letter and tell him what you are doing. How about some PX sug-ar? Is it 5 PM yet? That will be one thing we will both always remember.

March 31, 1942. Letter #21

> I ride the streetcar to work each day and back to the hotel for both dinner and supper. It costs one pence for each ride. Johnnie, I wish you were here to make all these trips with me. I know you would enjoy all of them.

April 2, 1942

> Cile, Please read my letters out loud to Johnnie if he is there.

April 4, 1942 Letter #22

> I enjoyed Johnnie's letter as well, and have enjoyed showing it to quite a few others. They thought it was so smart for a boy at his age to be writing letters. Of course I wholly agreed.

April 13, 1942

> I'll bet Daddy Dwight[191] calls Johnnie a WPA worker and would like to see him on his way to school soon.

---

[191] Daddy Dwight was Johnnie's nickname for Dwight Hackley, Cile's father and Johnnie's grandfather. The WPA, Works Progress Administration, was a 1935 federal government Depres-sion Era program that offered work to the unemployed on civil construction projects across the country during the Great Depression. Workers on WPA projects were sometimes viewed as "on the dole" or "taking a hand out," perhaps in the same way workers on welfare are sometimes viewed today.

> I met a couple last night who have two children about Johnnie's age and I told them what Johnnie said about the stars, and they thought he certainly was a smart boy to know so much.[192] Of course I listened to what they claimed about their children too.

May 19, 1942 –

> I sent Johnnie a One-Crown Piece today. [*One Crown = Five shillings*]

May 31, 1942 – Baby Sister

> Cile, in Mc's letter[193] to me dated April 14, he told me that Johnnie said he thought it would be nice to surprise Daddy with a baby sister when he comes home. I thought that was something. I told several about it, and all thought it very amusing. Of course they had not seen Johnnie, or it would have been even better. Tell Mc thanks for his offer, but I cannot accept it this time.

July 3, 1942 - War Bonds

This news article appeared on the front page of the Dallas Morning News on July 3, 1942. Johnnie had set up a small table downtown on the Bonham Square in front of the Smart Shoppe, his grandmother's ladies ready-to-wear store. Johnnie was 5-years-old, rather than the 3-years reported in the newspaper. He was selling war savings bonds and stamps to everyone who walked by.

In the vocabulary of 2012, the newspaper article went viral and was picked up by other newspapers across the state. The telephone started ringing, as people started calling Johnnie wanting to buy war bonds from him.

In the beginning, it was local people, many who knew Major Day, but as the article was picked up by other newspapers, checks came in from all over Texas.

Youngster Fights On Home Front, Daddy Over There

BONHAM, Texas, July 3.—Like his daddy on Gen. Douglas MacArthur's staff in far-off Australia, 3-year-old Johnnie Day is fighting the war.

Dressed in his soldier uniform and cap, the son of Major John Day is holding the street sector in front of his home, and doing right well, too.

Tackling every passer-by, Soldier Johnny up to Friday afternoon had sold $42.50 worth of war bonds and stamps.

Figure 81 - Dallas Morning News, July 3, 1942, Front Page

---

[192] Johnnie's great-grandfather, Homer Thompson (Dad Homer), was an amateur astronomer, who spent hours with Johnnie under the night sky teaching him the names of planets, major stars, and constellations. Dad Homer endowed Johnnie with a lifelong interest in science and engineering.

[193] Mc is Randall McMahon, John's best friend, golfing partner, and regular Saturday bridge player.

**Figure 82 -
Johnnie Day,
July 1942**

Mr. Neil from El Paso sent in a check for $5,000. He had known Major Day from his childhood in Eden, Texas. He continued to send checks to Johnnie for the duration of the war.

In 1942, the average American home sold for $6,900, and the average new car sold for $925. $5,000 was a substantial amount of money. Major Day with special overseas allowances was earning $8,000 per year, which was also considered a large salary in 1942.

August 25, 1942 - Summer on the New Mexico Ranch

Glad you had a nice trip to New Mexico to visit Mother and Dad and the ranch. I know you enjoyed it, and I am sure Mother enjoyed your visit even more.

I am so glad that Johnnie is learning geography. I guess he will derive something from the war anyway. That is swell, Johnnie, and when I come home I want you to know all the capitols of the different countries.

An article appeared in the Dallas newspaper about Major Day, describing his experiences in the Southwest Pacific and his recent promotion to Major.

Well, I have never been as embarrassed in all my life as I was when I saw the pictures of me in the paper and all the bush wah. You would have thought I had just died and someone felt that a good word should have been said. I never did like a lot of stuff like that. After all having a few shots and bombs thrown your way doesn't warrant so much praise.[194]

I am tickled to death at what Johnnie is doing [selling war bonds], and I want to follow it. Keep me informed and if other clippings come out, send them to me for sure. Definitely.

News Story Assists Young Bonham War Bond Seller on Job

BONHAM, Texas, July 4.—Reading on the front page of The Dallas News that 3-year-old Johnnie Day, son of Major John Day, with Gen. Douglas MacArthur in Australia, was conducting a personal campaign here for the sale of war bonds, H. R. Van Zandt telephoned Johnnie's home bright and early Saturday morning, requesting that the lad bring him a $100 bond at once.

"Well, Johnnie is asleep right now," Van Zandt was informed.

"Wake him up and send him over," was the reply.

In a twinkling, Johnnie was at the Van Zandt home to conclude the transaction.

"Yep, we soldiers are on twenty-four-hour call these days," the lad commented.

**Figure 83 - Bonham Daily Favorite,
July 1942**

---

[194] This newspaper article did not survive the war.

September 8, 1942 - Malaria

Johnnie, I have been worried about your being sick and with malaria too. I am going to wire tomorrow and hope to hear that you are OK.

Honey, see that he gets the best care. I know you will.

Did Johnnie sell some more bonds?

September 22, 1942 - Malaria

I would be sure and have Dr. Woodard look at Johnnie after he has finished the medicine. Malaria seems to come back quite often. I have had some men who were well and then a couple or three weeks later they would have to return to the hospital.

You have not mentioned any more about Johnnie selling bonds. How many did he sell in all? How many did you buy?

September 24, 1942 - Java Trunk Arrives

Glad you liked my taste on all the things I sent home. Most of all, I am very glad that the trunks got home. From all reports that I was able to obtain, I thought that the first trunks would never get there, but one good surprise in a lifetime is OK. Some trip too – from Java through the Panama Canal to Brooklyn Navy Yard, and then to Texas in seven months.

I know that Christmas is coming and that I will have to send something home about a month or more before Christmas. Now remember this trunk, Cile. If you don't get anything more, you have already received the trunk.

Shrine of Remembrance Photo Album

I am having some of my pictures put in albums, and they will sure look nice. Some pictures I could send home provided they are not lost in the mail. If I mailed them individually, that would break up the story, so I will keep most of them. I am sending a few that you will like and one is autographed and you will see me in the picture if you look closely. My glasses can be seen but I did not know I was in it at the time. It is the General and the Chief of Staff. It is for Johnnie.

September 1942 - Johnnie Starts School

Johnnie celebrated his sixth birthday in August 1942 and entered Bailey Inglish Public Elementary School in Bonham. The photo shows Johnnie on the first day of school on the front porch of the Hackley home. Prince, a German shepherd, was six-months younger than Johnnie and his constant companion and protector.

Figure 84 - Johnnie Day and Prince on the first day of school. September 1942

October 1, 1942 – School Problems

Cile, I notice that Johnnie is disgusted about school. What grade is he in or is he still in the kindergarten? Maybe he should be advanced a grade? He surely must have something that will hold his interest or else he will not like it. I think he has had sufficient elementary training and possibly should be in the first grade or whatever his next step is? Maybe you should go to see the superintendent and have a talk with him. Ask him what he thinks is best. I think he will advise you properly.

I know Johnnie does get tired going over things that he has learned long before. You know we spent many nights with him teaching him things that other kids might not learn for several years. All that of course will be of value to him at some later date but at the present he should be learning something like reading and writing. I want to impress one thing that he surely wants to learn and learn as a habit or routine, not being made to learn as a "have to do job," like brushing his teeth.

Within a week Johnnie was advanced to the Second Grade.

Brushing his Teeth

Cile, be sure and brush his teeth yourself if necessary till he does it properly. He should be taught to brush his top teeth down and his bottom teeth up. Be sure and brush his gums each time. The latter is most important, and it seems that most kids never learn it till they are grown or not at all. Also brush the inside of his teeth and gums as well. You may wonder why I mention this but, after being in the army as long as I have and seeing the amount of ignorance as to the proper method of cleaning the teeth that I have seen, you would wonder too. Many times the gums will bleed when brushed properly, at least until they have been toughened up. Pardon all the explanation, Honey, as I know you know all the above but just wanted to remind you again.

Sportsmanship

Johnnie, I am quite surprised to learn that you are such a poor loser. Now remember that you cannot always win on everything, and Daddy sure wants you to be as good a loser as you are a winner. Always congratulate the man that beats you in any game and not run off the place. The first thing you know, you will not have any friends that will come to see you. Remember that I sure want you to do better than that. It's too bad I wasn't there or the dirt would have flown. I am quite surprised at you for your action and if this recurs, I am sure you mother will prevent your having access to the croquet set at all!

October 7, 1942 - General MacArthur

I have enjoyed the pictures you sent me a lot and have showed them to all I have seen. I took one of you and Johnnie to the General [MacArthur] and showed him one of the clippings in the paper about Johnnie selling the war bonds. He autographed a picture for Johnnie. I have it now and am sending it to him. I have already sent one but this is another, the same picture as was on the *Life Magazine* cover some time back.[195] I think you will like it. Johnnie, it is for the good work and the good boy that you have been and I am glad to be able to give it to you. I know you will be proud of it.

Dec 7, 1942

Dear Mom & Dad

Johnnie will be so big when I get back I guess I will have a time recognizing him. Cile says he now sleeps with the stuffed koala bear I sent him.

---

[195] This is the autographed photograph of MacArthur and Sutherland taken in the train station, I believe in Brisbane [shown in Figure 56].

22.   USAFFE GHQ MOVES TO BRISBANE – JULY 1942

22.1.   Plans Begin for the Move to Brisbane– 19 June 1942

Friday, 19 June 1942

Today I was informed on the QT[196] that the HQ will move to Brisbane between July 8 and July 15. As HQ Commandant, I have the responsibility of getting things moved. This will be some job, as we will take everything – even the rugs on the floors.

Non-essentials have to go home. I will send the Mulga wood table[197] home about Tuesday or Wednesday. Boy, it's swell. The table will have to be put together after it arrives. The other things are lovely. Honey, you will be proud of your old man when you get this table. Hope the ship doesn't sink. I must close and go to bed as have no new news to tell, except for a new joke or so and don't have the space here to record it. Love & kisses.

Saturday, 20 June 1942

I recommended Lt. Evans for promotion to First Lieutenant today. He has eight-and-a-half-months service as a Second Lieutenant and does a good job. Work for the move has begun. We are trying to get everything ready.

Sunday, 21 June 1942

Today is Sunday, so I couldn't do much. Trams run about one per hour on Sunday. It seems like everything is rationed – even tram rides. Sometimes I wonder what they will ration next – haircuts and shoe shines?

I looked at all the Mulga wood stuff I bought. Cile will sure be glad to see it. I hope to get it shipped home soon. With my movie camera, I took a few more shots but did not finish the roll.

Col. Stivers and I will fly to Brisbane to look the situation over. Hope to go about Friday. I will enjoy **my first plane ride,** even though it may be a hassle.

---

[196] "On the QT" is a slang expression for "on the quiet." H. L. Mencken, in The American Language, 1921, comments on the American fondness for abbreviations like OK, PDQ, COD, as well as QT. The expression describes something that had been communicated in a confidential or nonpublic way.

[197] Mulga wood is from a tree in the central plain of Australia. It is a strong hardwood used by the aborigines for digging sticks and boomerangs. It has a dark heartwood with a light sapwood that produces two beautiful colors in the grain. The wood is so dense that it will not float in water.

In Brisbane, I have to set up a mess hall. I am hiring cooks and a mess staff so that all the men will be able to eat together. I hate to start running a mess hall too.

Evans was promoted today. Some service – recommended on Saturday and promoted on Sunday.

Monday, 22 June 1942
Well, today has been one of the busiest days I have had. I have been getting a memorandum fixed up for the AG to sign so that I can get the necessary information about packing and crating for the move. In addition, I have been getting material for crating everything. I am wondering how in the hell I can get all of my stuff together. What a bunch of stuff I have.

I stopped the tailor today from making me another blouse. It is no use, as I don't think I will need it since I am going north. I went by and tried on my pants, the second pair this tailor has made for me. First ones I would not be seen wearing on the street. This pair is better but needs an alter job so I can wear them. A sorry tailor!

Tomorrow night is the big "6-months docking-party" for us *Republicanites*.[198] They say it will be a blow-out, and all will get drunk. Stags will be at the Chevron Hotel.

I received a letter from you, Darling. Also I received a letter from Mc and Ruth [McMahon], and another from Mother.

22.2.   Shipping Non-Essentials Home – 23 Jun 1942

Tuesday, 23 June 1942
I went out yesterday and paid the £13 for all the Mulga wood stuff. Actually it would have cost $100 in the States, but I only paid the equivalent of about $43. My kangaroo hide is not ready, but I should get it soon. I hope you will make a rug out of the hide. I also have four wool rugs to send home this week for Mother, Lucille, Nannie, and you, Darling – one per family. The rugs cost over £2 each, or about $8. I handpicked them, but still could not get the mohair I wanted, which is lovely but costs a fortune.

11:25 PM - I have just returned home from our "6-months docking-party." It was sure good. We had frog legs and then steak with all the trimmings. I have a copy of the invitation, the menu, and the convoy song which I will send to you. The song is the one we

---

[198] Republicanites were troops who were aboard the *USAT Republic* crossing the Pacific on the Pensacola Convoy.

made up on *Republic*. At the dinner I read the names of all those we left in Java as a remembrance. We all know war is serious business.

Wednesday, 24 June 1942

I went over to the Chevron tonight and saw the picture show staring Spencer Tracy and I can't remember her name. The weather was so foggy I had a time getting there, and on the way home it was worse. I got back about 11 PM.

Thursday, 25 June 1942

I got home about 7 PM. I started packing and trying to get my junk into my footlocker. I guess when the time comes, I will do it fast. I am having some job getting the headquarters ready to move.

I am supposed to fly to Brisbane Monday, but I may not have to go. It depends on what information I can obtain from Col. Stivers when he comes back.

I went to the dentist late yesterday evening and had my teeth cleaned. Today they are a little sore, but I feel better.

Oh, yes, Honey, I shaved off my mustache today, so you can win your bet with Mc. Don't know what you bet, but you won. That's the fourth time in seven months now I have shaved it off. It is now reaching 11 PM, and I still have to read the paper.

Friday, 26 June 1942

This evening I went to the "Australia Hotel" with Capt. Farnham for drinks and dinner. It was the first time I've been there for dinner. I had a dozen oysters on the half shell and fried chicken that tasted like fish. I drank four "Brandy Crusts." They were not bad. The place was usually very crowded. They say everyone meets there. The dinner cost me a pound and a half. I was full but sleepy. I came in at 10:30 PM and after a little messing around, I'll write in the diary and go to bed.

Col. Stivers (G-1) was just promoted to general. Also Col Willoughby (G-2) and Col Whitlock (G-4) are now generals.

It seems like my phone has rung every five minutes all day with questions about getting ready for the move. Gen. Stivers says I need a couple more officers so I am getting one. I think one will be enough so will start there.

Figure 85 - Maj. John Day, Melbourne, June 1942

Saturday, 27 June 1942

I received a cable from you, Darling, telling me you received the $700 and jewelry. Good. Hope you like it. The four sheepskin rugs are on their way along with the mulga wood and the stuffed koala bears. You should be getting something now. I am again about broke but will be paid in a few days. I have most of my bags labeled now.

I am supposed to get my picture finished tomorrow. There is one more one-hour sitting and I will be finished. My typewriter will be in my footlocker when I send my stuff to you. I must send some things soon.

Love and kisses, Darling.

Sunday, 28 June 1942

I worked until noon, as usual for Sunday, when the phone rang. I was invited out for dinner and another kangaroo shoot. Well, off I went. We made the usual circuit, saw some kangaroos, but didn't get a shot. Corporal Say is from Camberwell, a suburb of Melbourne. He went with me, had his driver's Tommy gun, and scared the kangaroo away as before. I would have killed several had he not been along. They say the hunting at Brisbane is swell. By the way, the Aussies say "I didn't get a roo today," which is what they call kangaroo. I told Evans he could go hunting tomorrow.

Brisbane is the place in Australia where I started, so I guess I will start over again when I get there. Our new APO No. 500 will follow us as we move around.

I had two interviews today with men who might become Mess Officer for the Company. Either would do but am asking for a Lt. Gardney. He is a navigator who recently had some bad luck on a trip to the Philippines. The Japs had taken the field where he was supposed to land, so the plane ran out of gas and was forced to land in the water off an island. His hand and fingers were injured in the crash and now he can't operate the sextant. The Air Corp will let him go. If I don't take him, I will have to find him another job. I have not received my cooks yet either, and I am supposed to get six.

I will fly to Brisbane probably Thursday and come back Sunday night – a short trip. Honey, you would raise the devil if you knew I was flying, wouldn't you.[199] I love you so.

Tuesday, 30 June 1942
Today was payday. I cashed my check too. It was confirmed that I leave for Brisbane by plane Thursday to get the ground work laid for the movement. There is a lot to do in a short time. Equipment will mostly go on the 7th or 8th with Lt. Evans and about 20 men. Most of the first echelon of men leaves on the 15th. The second echelon leaves on 21st and the balance will leave only a very few days later.

Lt. Evans killed a wallaby, which is a small 'roo [kangaroo]. So tonight we had Roo Tail Soup. He had it cooking all day, as it had to cook about six hours. Boy, it was good.

I am trying to figure out what to send home. I know if anything happens to me, you would probably not get all of my things, probably only half.

I made final plans for my trip to Brisbane. I tried to get things in order so Lt. Evans could take care of everything. Evans emptied the trash and papers from the office. I will take my camera on the trip and will take some pictures from the plane. I have colored film too.

Wednesday, 1 July 1942
Sgt. Cottner got my plane ticket, which of course cost me nothing. I had to pick up my orders.

Everyone in the office had a special task for me to investigate in Brisbane. General Marshall, the Deputy Chief of Staff, wanted me to see about having the Lennons Hotel roof repaired. Gen. Stivers wanted something else. Col. Fitch wanted to find out about the supply of whiskey and some other things. Of course I drink so little the supply of whiskey doesn't worry me, especially because I have about six quarts left in my closet. I need to figure out how to get the whiskey to Brisbane.

Last night I had Lt. Evans down to my apartment to eat supper with me. We had chicken soup, chili-toast, boiled ham, fruit, and coffee. It was quite a meal, and we could not eat it all. I had to clean out my ice box because some things would spoil before I get back to town. I packed my suitcase, laid out my clothes to wear, and went to bed early (12:30 AM).

_____

[199] This was Maj. Day's first airplane flight, and Cile was worried about any airplane flight.

22.3.   Advance Party Flight to Brisbane – 2 Jul 1942

Thursday, 2 July 1942

I woke up at 5:45 AM, dressed, and went into the kitchen. For breakfast, I had one small piece of toast, a cup of coffee, and a bowl of Post Toasties. I think the Aussies call them "Corn Flakes." My driver called for me at 6:15 AM. I had him come in and have a piece of toast and a cup of coffee. His name is Pat Belt, and he is about 6 foot 2 inches or maybe 6 foot 3 inches. He is tough looking and enjoys driving, as most of our drivers do. We left the house at 6:30 and started to Essendon Airport. After driving about eight blocks, I suddenly noticed that I had left my ticket at the house. We went back, and there it was, sitting on the table. We arrived at the airport at 7 AM. I checked in and who should I find also on the plane but my friend, Col. John Grable of the Signal Corps.[200] Grable and I ate together almost every day while I was at the Windsor Hotel. We have known each other for some time and have had several nice talks. In addition, we had an Air Corps Major (can't think of his name now) who at one time lived in Honey Grove, Texas.[201] He worked for the Texas Highway Department and claimed he built the only good roads ever built in Fannin County.

We boarded the plane and, well, I was off on my first airplane ride. We were each assigned seats. Mine was No. 5. There were 21 passengers plus the stewardess and two "flight officers," as they are called here in Australia. The plane was an American-made Douglas DC-3 transport, owned and operated by Australian National Airways.

First, we fastened our safety belts for the takeoff. The engines were started, and I watched the hangars go by. I could see the beautiful layout of the town as we circled the field and departed along our course. We were headed first to Sydney. We climbed through the clouds and were in a fog – I could see only the wings. Soon we were above the clouds. What a beautiful sight – white as snow with beautiful high banks of clouds. I saw myself looking down at the clouds and nothing above – just the beautiful blue sky – a lovely hazy blue color of grandeur and bewilderment. The streets below appeared between clouds and had a reddish tinge caused by reflections. (How am I doing with this description?) The stewardess passed out newspapers and maps of the route to be taken. I read the papers, both the "Sun" and "Argus," the two best papers printed in Mel-

---

[200] Col. Grable was involved in the construction of the first secure telephone link between Brisbane and Washington, D.C. which employed PCM technology implemented with vacuum tubes.
[201] Honey Grove is only 15 miles from Bonham, Texas, where Cile and Johnnie are living.

bourne. Fortunately, I was carrying my briefcase with my diary and other junk. My valet pack[202] is in the baggage compartment, so I was in good shape for the flight.

I got my briefcase, took out my diary, and found my fountain pen had leaked ink all over the place – altitude does that to most pens. Knowing that Col. Grable had a fancy $25 fountain pen especially designed for altitude, I borrowed his fountain pen and start writing. I needed something to write on, so when the stewardess brought me a cup of coffee, I placed the tray upside down in my lap and used it to write on. Looking out of the window, I saw marvelous peaks and valleys of clouds, just like you could see in the Grand Canyon, only white. We were so low on the clouds that at times we ran through the peaks of some. Now and then through the clouds, we could see the ground, the creeks, and some lakes. The winding roads, pastures, and fields make a lovely sight. We hit a big air bump that bounced us up and down, making the ride very rough for a short time.

9:35 AM - We passed over Sugarloaf Reservoir, a large lake 70 miles out of Melbourne. I could see Alexandria some distance away. We passed over Mt. Buffalo where they have the Victorian Winter Sports. It was snow covered and beautiful.[203] We could see Mt. Butler from a distance, also snow covered. We crossed the Ovens River which starts at Mt. Hotham and runs into the Border River, a large river. We passed over Canberra, the capital of Australia. I could not tell much about it as we could see it only in spots through the clouds. We passed over Lake George which was usually dry but now is full of water.

9:50 AM - We are running into some rough weather. A strong air pocket! We just hit a nice bump. All passengers were tossed from their seats. We are climbing in altitude, and it is getting colder. I've had to write in spells as at times I almost lost everything in my lap. The clouds are so thick I cannot see past the wing tips. It is raining like hell.

11:45 AM - We arrived in Sydney at 10:40 AM.[204] We made good time, I guess, for traveling about 450 or 475 miles from Melbourne. While landing at Sydney airport, I saw a beautiful chain of mountains and then a lot of lakes, the ocean, and the Parramatta River. The river runs into the harbor, which is very beautiful. I think Sydney is one of the prettiest harbors I have ever seen. I saw the famous Sydney Harbor Bridge close to where the Jap submarines came in to attack the city. The harbor, or rather the bays, are

---

[202] Garment bag

[203] July in the Southern Hemisphere is winter, like December in the Northern Hemisphere.

[204] Approximately three-hour flight time for 450 miles.

Figure 86 - Australia: Melbourne to Sydney, about
924 air miles, Atlas 1955

large and actually separate the city into two parts. North Sydney has about half a million people and south Sydney has about three-quarters of a million. Sydney is in New South Wales (NSW), which we entered when we crossed the Murray River.

I stayed on the airplane about 15 minutes while we were on the ground as some passengers left and new passengers boarded.

Before arriving in Sydney, I was sitting next to a jockey by the name Percival. When we left Sydney, I was in the same seat, but I had a new neighbor, Mr. Bruce Small, a bicycle manufacturer located on Spencer Street in Melbourne.[205] After we left Sydney, he became my guide telling me about everything we saw out the window as we flew along.

About 33 miles out of Sydney, we crossed the Hawkesbury River, which is one of the larger rivers in Australia. The river is probably a half-mile wide and naturally salty at the sea. The beauty of it was the number of bays that end at a mountain and the size of the bays – said to be very deep. We passed lakes like I had never seen; most of them are about a mile from the sea, but everywhere.

After passing over Newcastle, we started leaving the plantation area and gradually we came to high mountains and valleys. All seem very thick with brush and trees. I had seen no farms as yet, but we were flying at about 6,000 feet altitude. It was now 12:15 PM and we see nothing but hilly country. The valleys seem to have sandy soil in the bottoms. The stewardess is bringing salad of some kind so I'll stop and eat. I had had a glass of beer with the jockey. The sun is out and very bright. Lots of this country seems good for nothing - shrubs, bushes, and practically no grass.

The plane landed in Brisbane about 2:40 PM.[206] I rode to town and reported to Col. Donaldson (Base Sec. 3 CO). After spending time with him until about 5 PM, I was driven to the Engineers HQ where I contacted Lt. Parker. He took me downtown and showed me the AMP Building that HQ will occupy. Finally, we went to supper about 7:30 PM. After supper we worked on plans until about 10 PM. I was so sleepy I could hardly stay awake. I told Parker I just had to go to sleep. I did not sleep well at all. I woke up about three times to see what the commode was like – it came in very handy.

---

[205] After the war, Bruce Small became Mayor of the Gold Coast south of Brisbane.

[206] Another estimated three hours flight time for 475 miles.

Friday, July 3, 1942

I woke up at 7:15 AM, bathed, shaved and dressed. I discovered that they had put me up in a suite at the Lennons Hotel. I have a bedroom, sitting room, bathroom, ice box, stove – it's quite a place. The colonel had told me he would get me fixed up.

Lt. Parker came down to my suite, and we had breakfast in the room. Then we went down the private elevator to the place where the enlisted men are to stay. I stayed there till noon figuring out the changes that will be necessary in the building. We went to eat in the Mess that the Base Sec. HQ Detachment runs. The food was very good. I had a driver assigned to me.

After dinner we went back to HQ for more discussions and to the Engineers Office for specific plans. Here it was 10:45 PM, the evening was through, and I still had lots more to do tomorrow. I closed and got ready for bed. Love

Saturday, 4 July 1942

Today is another big day. It is now 11 AM and I have not left the room at the Lennons Hotel. Lt. Parker came down at 9 AM. We had breakfast in the room again and have been making notes together ever since. I am about caught up.

My plane for Melbourne will leave tomorrow at 2:30 PM and arrive about 9 PM. I have plenty to do back in Melbourne to get ready for the move.

I want to go to the races this evening if I can get away. Think I'll bet on the jockey Percival, who traveled with me on the plane up to Sydney. They say Percival is one of the best jockeys in Australia.

Well, I went to the races this evening and bet on all the races but one. I was buying a ticket for that last race when the bell rang to close the bets, so they gave me my money back. I would have won 38 shillings on that last race. Anyway I came out for the day £1/11/0 ahead of all my expenses. That is about $5. I came back into town with the race crowd, shaved and cleaned up. I had a talk with Lt. Col. Smith, the Commandant here at Base Sec. 3.

Gen. Stivers will be in Brisbane tomorrow about the time I leave. I am enjoying this lovely suite in the Lennons Hotel, but some general will have it by the time I get back to Melbourne. I have to see Col. Donaldson in the morning and complete my notes before I catch the plane at 2:30PM. I have to go eat now. I lost my good pencil at the races.

22.4.   Return Flight to Melbourne – 5 Jul 1942

<u>Sunday, 5 July 1942</u>
I had a breakfast meeting with Col. Donaldson, Base Commander, and Lt. Parker in the Engineer Office. I reviewed with them all my notes on building modifications and other information that I had developed. I thanked them for all their courtesies. They were certainly nice to me.

Lt. Parker carried me out to the airport about 1 PM. At the airport, I met Gen. [Spencer B.] Akin[207], MacArthur's Chief Signal Officer, who gave me some inside information about communication facility requirements for Brisbane that he had overlooked, but I need to deal with. It meant more work for me.[208]

Well, the plane left at 2:30 PM. I had a rear seat on the return flight, which meant a little more vibration than the seats near the front. All in all, it was a nice ride to Sydney. We flew over the ocean part of the way, and again saw the beauty of Sydney Harbor from the air. Everything was lovely.

There were three war correspondents on the same plane, and they shot dice all the time we were flying. One owed the other about $250 when we got to Melbourne.

The plane arrived in Sydney about 5:30 PM. I stepped outside the plane for a nice cool breath of air, then back into the plane for Melbourne. The continuing flight was nice and smooth all the way. We arrived in Melbourne 9:10 PM, but my driver was not at the airport to meet me. I had to call him. Later I found out he had taken the wrong road to the

---

[207] Brig. Gen. Spencer B. Akin and Lt. Col. John Grable, both Signal Corps officers, were responsible in 1942 for setting up the secret secure voice and data communications link between Brisbane and Washington, DC called "Sigsaly" or "Green Hornet." This was one terminal of a worldwide network for Roosevelt, Churchill, and their field commanders. The terminal, located in the basement of the AMP building, was a digital frequency-hopping system using pulse code modulation (PCM) implemented with vacuum-tubes. This single-side band system used a precursor of what forty-years later would be PCM technology for commercial cell phones.

[208] Maj. Day said nothing further in the diary about this special assignment for Gen. Akin. Speculation is that the U.S. Army Signal Intelligence Service (SIS) needed to locate a secret office for the Central Bureau in the Brisbane area. The Headquarters Commandant was responsible for all office leases. The Central Bureau, the technical office that deciphered intercepted Japanese messages, was later located in a private residential neighborhood at 21 Henry Street, Brisbane. The building was marked by an historical plaque in 1988.

airport. I was back at the apartment about 10:30 PM. I went to bed after taking a bath and slept like a log.

Monday, 6 July 1942
A very busy day – terribly busy all the time. All plans are about complete for the men. Lt. Evans will leave Wednesday at 8 AM. We have about eleven railway cars loaded with equipment and supplies and another seven or eight more with cars and trucks. About twice that many railway cars will go on a later train. I guess I will be in the last echelon to get away from Melbourne. All details will have to be wound up. I may get to fly up to Brisbane again, which would be nice if I could. Of course it is now about 11 PM and I have just come from the office after checking the guards and seeing how the crating of the typewriters is coming. Things look fine, and I am now about to type a letter to be photographed or radioed over to you, Honey. It may not get sent as quickly as I want because the forms were passed out to everyone while I was in Brisbane. My letter will be late.

22.5.   First Headquarters Train Departs for Brisbane – 8 July 1942

Tuesday, 7 July 1942
We wound up with eleven rail cars of equipment and seven rail cars loaded with autos. I have 20 men and six Filipinos to leave at 8:35 AM tomorrow morning to accompany the eighteen rail cars. I will be at the office with them at 7 AM to check them out. So must get to sleep, good tonight. 7AM seems awful early now since I have been fighting the battle of Melbourne.

Wednesday, 8 July 1942
Up and at the office at 7 AM. All men present, and all left on the train at 8:35 AM. Hope things are ready for them when they arrive. I have my doubts. I still have a lot of the kitchen staff to hire now so must start doing some figuring fast.

Thursday, 9 July 1942
I had a time getting steel cots for the men. The quartermaster didn't want to let us take them to Brisbane, so I had to go to the G-4 (Gen. Whitlock) and have him "speak" to the quartermaster. Boy and how he did! It was a very few hours before they called me to come and get the cots. I bet the whole bunch will be glad to see us go. It will sure suit me also. I don't think Brisbane is quite as nice as Melbourne, but OK. We want to win this damn war and go home. I get so damned mad at these Australians at times. They like to get all the money they can from us and give us as little as they can.

Friday, 10 July 1942

Crating and packing is mostly done. There are a few odds and ends left, but we have another load ready to go. We will probably send it Monday with Lt. Worthington and a couple of men. Next week will be another busy one. Guess I will have lots to do and a short time to do it. Hell, who cares, I'm sleepy now.

Saturday, 11 July 1942

Nothing new. Worked all day. Most of today was busy winding up details on the last three or four railcars of stuff. They will leave Monday. I will have most of the stuff to finish for the last morning on July 20th or 21st. Guess I will have Lt. Evans come back to Melbourne and help wind up the balance.

Sunday, 12 July 1942

I worked till 3 PM. Due to the fact that Lt. Worthington is leaving tomorrow, I thought this was my last chance to go hunting. Thought I would take off the balance of the day and maybe go shoot another kangaroo. Well, I didn't get away until about 4:30, so I knew I would have a very short time to hunt. I made a quick "rekkie."[209] It was so dark I couldn't see the end of my gun, but I still got six shots. I hit one, but only turned him in the air. He will probably die, but he didn't fall and got away. I got back about 8 PM. I cooked myself a steak and some spuds. I went down and checked the guards and returned to shine my ornaments. I gathered my laundry, and now I am about ready to go to bed.

13-16 July 1942

The last week in Melbourne before departing for Brisbane is missing from the Diary. It appears Maj. Day was too busy on those days to write in his diary.

Friday, 17 July 1942

I have not written for several days in this book, so will have to drop back and fill in later. A letter arrived from Cile today. It is sure swell to hear from her. We did not need to work as long tonight as I thought we would have to.

I took my footlocker with radio, typewriter, and movie projector to the station to be shipped home. I do hope this trunk gets there.

It is 10 PM and we are still packing and crating. I have never been so busy in all my life. I am going to bed and try to get caught up with sleep.

_____

[209] A "rekkie" is a slang expression for a reconnaissance or quick "look around."

Saturday, 18 July 1942
I bought myself a couple of cases of Black Label Scotch. It's tough to get in Brisbane. Honey, I always get too much, but if so, I can sell it. The big job will be getting it there without getting it broken.

I managed to go to a show. Thought I would probably get a ticket in one of the suburban theaters, but all were full. Finally, I gave two shillings to get in and stand up in back. After getting in I noticed I had seen both shows. I saw them again anyway, but left just before it was over as I was dead tired and sleepy.

I miss my Honey and Johnnie. I enjoyed your letter again. It was swell. I wish you knew how much I enjoy hearing what you have to say, Darling. I love you most of all – 'night.

Monday, 20 July 1942
This is our last night, and I have 40 odd men reporting back after supper to finish up. It looks like a late night is ahead of us. All the boys are doing fine.

22.6.   Aboard MacArthur's Train to Brisbane – 21 Jul 1942

Tuesday, 21 July 1942
I worked till 4 AM Monday night getting things wound up at the office. Then I had to finish packing my own things before going to sleep. Then it was up at 6:45 AM. You can see how much sleep I really got.

Then in the morning there was the loading of the special stuff, secret files, the General's personal baggage, and many other details that had to be attended to. I was very busy.

We left Melbourne at 2:25 PM today. Hope all goes well. Feel good about getting everything so complete, as we had so short a time after the stuff was released.
Love N Kisses, Honey & Johnnie

Wednesday, 22 July 1942 – On the Train
We are on the train now, and I wrote a little on the typewriter, as it would be next to impossible to write while the train moves. There is too much shaking. This is a "fast special train" that takes 42 hours to go about 1,400 miles. In the States, a special would go in less than half that time.

Gen. MacArthur is on this train, and his car has no heat. This is winter, so it was cold. He has to eat with his coat on. He is certainly a hero. People love to see him.

The train now is just out of Sydney, and it is rolling quite a bit. I have been watching for things to take a picture of and hope to see some things soon. Therefore this letter will be in jumps.

First of all, I have been so busy for the past week that I have not had time to make entries in my diary. This note will take the place of the days I skipped and have not written in the book.

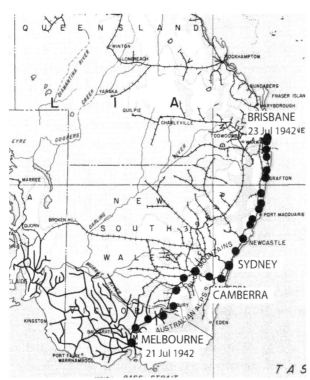

Figure 87 - MacArthur Train Route from Melbourne to Brisbane - 21-23 Jul 1942

Well, I think I did a good job as we actually have practically everything on the train. We left a few things that I had planned to leave. The cars are plenty loaded. Actually I have shipped about twenty-five railcar loads of things, all included.

We are now on *Gen. MacArthur's Special*. We have thirteen cars, 37 officers, 120 enlisted men, six MPs, three special train "Dicks," Gen. Pat Hurley and his aide. The only person we left in Sydney was Admiral Leary.

Since we left Sydney, I have had the conductor tell me when we were coming to places that would make a good picture, and I have taken a lot so far. I could kick myself for missing a good picture of the General and Mr. Curtin, the Big Man of Australia, a couple of admirals, and several big wigs.

I have had so much stuff to keep up with. I have to look after all the enlisted men and see that they are fed. There is no food on the train, so when the train stops, all get off and eat. I have to have the necessary men available to do the special running around for the General. I have had several nice compliments from them so far, that I had certainly done a jam up job. That sounded nice to me and my ears, and even the AG, Col. Fitch, told me that I had done a good job.

The train is shaking so that you will have to excuse my hitting so many wrong keys on the typewriter.

The train stopped in Sydney, and Gen. MacArthur went to Admiralty House to have breakfast with the Prime Minister.[210] I had to get the MPs to accompany the General as the colonel that was in charge of the six MPs accompanying the General was standing around with his finger in his "****". Anyway, I told him that he had better send his MPs in the second car following the General. We had to remove a couple of officers from a car so the MPs would have a car. It worked out OK.

While we were stopped in Sydney, we grabbed an unused Army car that had been set aside for us, to do some sightseeing. First, we ate breakfast at the Australia Hotel, one of the best and largest in Sydney. It was a lovely breakfast with orange juice, cereal, a couple of eggs, toast, ham, and of course coffee. Some meal! After breakfast the driver, a WAAAF, showed us what she thought we would like to see with only one hour in Sydney. I took a picture of the famous bridge in Sydney Harbor, as well as ships passing under it. She drove us around part of the port and up to some of the beautiful homes. I must say that many of the homes are very beautiful and are set on high places with lovely views out over the sea. We saw a destroyer in the port, as well as a hospital ship and several other smaller ships. On arriving back at the train station, we walked around for a while waiting for the General to return from his breakfast with the prime minister.

From Sydney the train headed for Newcastle where we would stop 45 minutes for a meal before going on to Brisbane. The train will arrive in Brisbane at 8 AM tomorrow and then I will have one hell of a time getting things straightened out.

I sent Lt. Evans ahead a couple of weeks ago to do as much as could be done toward getting things ready. That was after I made my plane trip to lay the ground work. I had him fly back Sunday, rather than Monday, to take over the rear echelon and bring the balance of the things up. It also gave Lt. Evans a plane ride, which is very special. He has done a good job so far, and I will make him the Company Commander, Headquarters Company.

I have a new officer, Lt. Laughlin, a Second Lieutenant, who I will break in as the Mess Officer probably. That way Evans can help him get started. I will take Lt. Worthington and show him how to run the supply end. I will do the HQ Commandant's job with three officers under my wing. I have to direct the company supplies and transportation,

---

[210] The Admiralty House is the residence of the Governor General and is next door to the Prime Minister's residence, Kirribilli House. The Diary said MacArthur went to Admiralty House, however, it may have been Kirribilli House.

as well as all the other jobs that come into the thing. Now I understand in Brisbane I may have the PX also. STOP.

The train is now passing through a lot of orange groves, and I will try to catch one of them in a picture. I am trying to save some film to catch the General at least once before the trip is over. We are going along the coast, and this country is very beautiful. We have passed through a number of tunnels, one in fact is the longest in Australia. The Hawkesbury River, I think is among the largest rivers in the country, but not the largest.

You see, my writing has roamed from before we left to after we left and back again. This thing I am writing is all about the trip before and after we left Melbourne so don't mind my way of slaughtering the trip.

Last night at supper, tea to the Australians, I stole a pocket full of almonds from the table. The lady that waited on our table saw that I was eating lots of almonds, but I don't think she knew I was putting them in my pocket. After we left the table, she gave a sack full of almonds to one of the Dicks (*detectives*) and told him that I liked them so well that she thought I should have some more to take with me on the train. Here, 12 hours later, I am still eating almonds, and thanks to her, I have plenty for the rest of the trip.

It is now 12:30 PM and I guess we will soon get into Newcastle. I have the schedule in my pocket but will not take time to get it out as we will be there in due time anyway.

I bought four books for you, Darling, and will send them to you one of these days. Maybe I will read them, but I doubt that. I have not had time to read anything. I bought me a pair of slippers for £3/5/- before leaving Melbourne. I have not worn them but they are the crepe-sole type, so if I ever get the time to play golf again, I will at least have the shoes to play in. I can also wear them daily so that is much better.

I had one of the clerks bring this typewriter on the train for me so that I would have something to write on as I knew there would be too much shaking to write on paper. Fine business too!

Last night we crossed a border and had to change trains. They took my baggage and moved it to my compartment and all I had to do was to see about the transfer of property, eat, and get in the coach. Now I have my mouth full of almonds.

The new state has put three detectives on the train instead of the two we had from Sydney, so now I have to get up and find a place for another Dick. Guess it is a good thing I saved several extra places on the train. They have all come in handy so far. Well, it's all in life.

I bought a paper and a *MAN Magazine* to look at, and I am wondering when I will get the chance to read them.

I have just pulled out my diary and note that I have things pretty well screwed up for the last several days so will start off brand new on the 20th and see if I can keep it OK from now on. [*Editor's note: Is this ever true!*] I know that this diary will be worth its weight in gold for the days to come, so I take the best of care. This page that I am now writing will be glued into the diary at one of the pages so it can be certified by me that I am so and so and sooo.

At present we are passing some very tall slender trees, some kind of gum tree.[211] In my rush of taking pictures on the train, I might say that I know some of the films will not have the proper exposure, but maybe they will be OK. The train was moving and I was shaking and due to the light being on the wrong side part of the time. Well, that should cover the excuses so will stop with that.

I might add that I had a lot of help from Major Kerfees. He was the officer I had a lot of dealings with getting all the railcars spotted and on time. I think he did a fine job. In civilian life he is a railroader of some kind. Col. Johnson, who is his superior, was president of a railroad and made the remark that he would give me a job after the war, if I didn't have one. He is certainly a prince of a fellow. Kerfees' address is in my book.

I met the *Life Magazine* photographer and correspondent, who are traveling with us. They have been shooting the bull and asked me to have drinks with them, which I did.

I wanted to write a letter today so that it could be mailed as soon as we get to Brisbane. You, Darling, will not know that I have moved, but in the future it may be in the newspaper. As yet, the movement of the headquarters has been withheld from the newspapers. This (typed) page is full now and we should be ready to eat shortly, so I will stop here.

> All my love for you, Darling. I miss you more than ever and love you with all.

---

[211] Eucalyptus trees

Thursday, 23 July 1942

We arrived in Brisbane on time at 8 AM today. Worthington had plenty of men and transportation available so all went off fine. Everyone, but me, came to the hotel and is already cleaned up. Poor me, I had to see that men and stuff go up first. I have a good bunch of officers, I think. They all seem to work fine. There were plenty of people at the station to meet the General in Brisbane. All seem to love him.

Saturday, 25 July 1942

What a story as will be told. Most of the bunch seems to have had supper at the hotel tonight. The dining room was certainly full with plenty of drinks going around at dinner.

All my men have put out swell, and we are getting things in fine shape. I got everybody quiet, drank a good drink of the Black Label, and hit the hay at this late hour.

   Love & kisses, Darling. I miss you so much.

23.   JAPANESE NEW GUINEA OFFENSIVE – JAN 1942

23.1.   New Guinea - 1942

New Guinea is the second largest island in the world[212] spread between 1° and 12° south latitude stretching 1,600 miles from east to west. The island has an area about 9% the size of Australia. The land is divided by several major mountain ranges that have peaks reaching 16,000 feet. In 1942, the maps of New Guinea remained largely incomplete with large segments of the interior uncharted.

The mountain ranges played an important role in the colonial partition of the island between the early Dutch, German, and English explorers. The colonial powers divided the island into three segments according to the ease of accessibility from the coastline. The western half of the island was controlled by the Dutch and called Dutch New Guinea. The eastern half of the island was divided between the northeast and southwest by a formidable mountain range called the Owen Stanley Range. The northeast partition was controlled by Germany and called Kaiser-

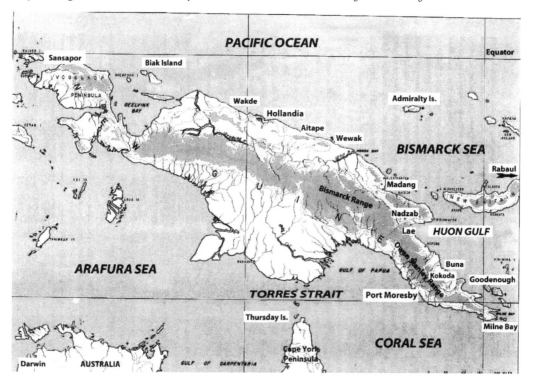

Figure 88 - New Guinea 1943

---

[212] The island of New Guinea is only surpassed in area by Greenland.

Wilhelmsland. The southwest partition was controlled by Great Britain and called Papua. As part of war reparations following World War I, Germany forfeited their claim to the northeast partition to Great Britain. The British then placed the entire northeast and southwest territory under Australian administration as the Territory of New Guinea.

The native population had occupied the island for over 50,000 years. They speak over 1,000 different languages – 10% of the world's languages. Adjacent villages sometimes cannot communicate due to different languages. The tribes were in a constant state of war with each other for land, pigs, and brides. Bow and arrow, spears, stone axes, and wood shields were standard weapons of war. Headhunters and cannibals were common among the natives into the twentieth century. A strict eye-for-an-eye code of justice prevailed.

Missionaries usually settled near the coastlines, leaving the interior to the natives. Only when gold was discovered in the mid 1930's did white men venture into the interior. When early miners entered the "uninhabited" interior, they discovered rich agricultural valleys with established self-sufficient farming communities with a population of many hundreds of thousands of natives. The soil is volcanic and very rich with nutrients for agriculture. The native population had well-tended gardens where they raised an abundance of fresh fruit and vegetables including staples of sweet potatoes, papaya, bananas, broccoli, and fresh green beans. The diet was supplemented by pig, fish, and birds.

The mountains create distinctively different rain patterns in the north and in the south of the island. Port Moresby in the south has a monsoon rain pattern with heavy seasonal rain between December and March, while Lae in the northeast has rain literally year around. Lae has the nickname "Rainy Lae," and has average annual rainfall of 184 inches per year (15 feet per year). Cloud bursts can drop 12 inches in 12 hours. The north coast, where most of World War II was fought, is typically hot and muggy with year-around rain punctuated by large swampy regions filled with heavy tropical vegetation – jungle. The jungle includes thick kunai grass which grows taller than a man and can limit visibility to a few feet.

The island is infested with every major tropical disease imaginable – malaria, dengue fever, elephantiasis, typhoid fever, and hepatitis. In addition to the mosquitoes, the jungle is populated with poisonous spiders, pythons, rats, lizards, flying kangaroos, and some of the most rare and beautiful birds in the world.

23.2. Beginning Japanese New Guinea Invasion – Jan 1942

In <u>January 1942</u>, the Japanese first invaded New Guinea and the Solomon Islands when Maj. Gen. Tomitaro Horii, Commander of the South Sea Forces of the Imperial Japanese Army, attacked Rabaul, New Britain. Rabaul was to become the second major military base for Japan in the South Pacific, along with Truk Island which was already in Japanese hands.

On <u>8 March 1942</u>, the Japanese expanded their footprint in New Guinea by moving into Lae and Salamaua on the Huon Gulf. This invasion was at virtually the same time as the Japanese Army was overrunning Java and the Netherlands East Indies. Lae was developed by the Japanese to become a major port to receive supplies for the region.

Horii's assignment was to capture Port Moresby. The Battle of the Coral Sea (<u>7-8 May 1942</u>), blunted Horii's plan for an amphibious landing from the south, but did not deter his ambition. Horii proceeded with his alternative plan, a land campaign from Buna across the Owen Stanley Range to Port Moresby.

Figure 89 - Japanese Invasion of New Guinea

23.3. Buna-Gona and the Kokoda Trail - 21-22 July 1942

Buna is on the northeast coast of New Guinea on the Solomon Sea. Port Moresby is on the south-eastern coast of New Guinea on the Coral Sea. The two towns are separated by the 10,000-foot peaks of the Owen Stanley Range. There are no roads for vehicles across the Owen Stanley Range. The land connection between the two ports is a treacherous 60-mile (96 km) footpath that is characterized as muddy, single-file, and filled with many switchbacks.

At lower altitudes, the trail passes through the heat, humidity, and malaria near the coasts. At higher elevations as the Kokoda Trail traverses a 7,000-foot pass, the hazard becomes the precipitous drops along the razor-edge peaks. The footpath passes through an isolated village called Kokoda. A small grass airstrip in Kokoda Village in 1942 was the only intermediate supply point, but for all practical purposes, supplies, food, and ammunition along the trail had to be carried in by either soldier or native porter.

On 21-22 July 1942, Gen. Horii opened his campaign by seizing the Buna-Gona beachhead with 8,500 troops in a night assault, which was accomplished before the Allies could fortify the beach. The island of New Guinea was defended by about 400 Papuan Island Militia led by an Australian officer. In the next few weeks the Japanese landed a total of 20,000 troops. The Militia fought a delaying battle until reinforcements could arrive but was slowly pushed back toward Port Moresby.

For the next six weeks the Australians and Japanese fought a brutal battle with tactics that were described by Major Day as "similar to cowboys and Indians." The thickness of the jungle meant that adjacent soldiers could not communicate with each other. Each soldier was essentially fighting his own individual war. There were many ambushes and surprise attacks with a lot of hand-to-hand combat. There were stories of brutality in the treatment of prisoners, the beheading of prisoners, and cannibalism during this combat. Malaria and dengue fever struck both sides.

Two weeks after the Japanese landing at Buna, the Americans landed in Guadalcanal on 7 Aug 1942 opening a second front in the Solomon Islands. The battle of Guadalcanal and the Battle along the Kokoda Trail were fought simultaneously. It is most significant that the attack on Guadalcanal was supported by two aircraft carriers and an armada of 75 ships used to support 60,000 ground troops. MacArthur and the Allies in New Guinea had no Navy ships for artillery support, due primarily to the personal conflict between Adm. King and Gen. MacArthur. Adm. Carpender told MacArthur he would not allow one destroyer into the area of Buna "because they lacked maps of the coral reefs." MacArthur was without Navy support, hence no heavy artillery. His war would be fought with small landing craft. It would be 18 months before the US Navy would allow an aircraft carrier near New Guinea.

24.　　BRISBANE & GHQ – 23 JULY 1942

24.1.　　The City

Brisbane is an incredibly beautiful city situated on a double bend of the meandering Brisbane River, or oxbow.[213]　Brisbane is the capital of Queensland. At 27 degrees south latitude, Brisbane is the same distance from the equator as Tampa, Florida, and enjoys a Florida-type climate, complete with seasonal tropical storms such as the 2011 cyclone. Brisbane grew on the basis of an agricultural economy. In 1941, the city was the third largest city in Australia with a population of 331,000 people.[214]

Major Day always compared Brisbane to Fort Worth, Texas, which he loved, for its informality and friendly people who are known for their attitudes of independence and self-reliance. In Texas, Fort Worth is called a "cow town" because of its very large stock yards and slaughter houses. Brisbane was also a portal for the Australian livestock trade with heavy cattle country just beyond the Australian coastal range.

Figure 90 - Aerial photo of Brisbane, 2010

---

[213] An "oxbow" in a river is a 14th century English expression for a *double bend in a river that resembles the wooden stock used in the 19th century to hitch two oxen to a heavy wagon.*
[214] *By 2010, the population of Brisbane was over 2 million people.*

24.2.   The AMP Building

The AMP Society was an Australian mutual insurance company that had been in business since the 1890's. The company built their 10-story headquarters building between 1930-1934 at the corner of Queen Street and Edward Street in the center of the downtown Brisbane's commercial district.

When wartime came, the Australian government, by military order, evicted every tenant from the second to the ninth floors and took over the building for its own purposes. The building, which was built with reinforced concrete, was considered reasonably bomb proof, and was offered to Gen. MacArthur for the SWPA headquarters.

Figure 91 - AMP Building, Queen and Edward Street, 2010

GHQ occupied the building from July 1942 until November 1944. Gen. MacArthur located his office in the Board Room on the eighth floor. The main entrance to the building is through a lobby on Queen Street, but there was a private entrance on Edward Street with access to a private elevator that became Gen. MacArthur's private entrance. The private entrance allowed MacArthur to avoid the main lobby with its three elevators and the Reception Area and reach his chambers on the eighth floor.

Figure 92 - MacArthur Entrance - Edward Street 2010

Figure 93 - MacArthur Chambers
on Edward Street, Brisbane - 2010

Figure 94 - MacArthur Office, 8th Floor,
AMP Building - 2010

Figure 95 – Johnnie at MacArthur's Desk -
2010

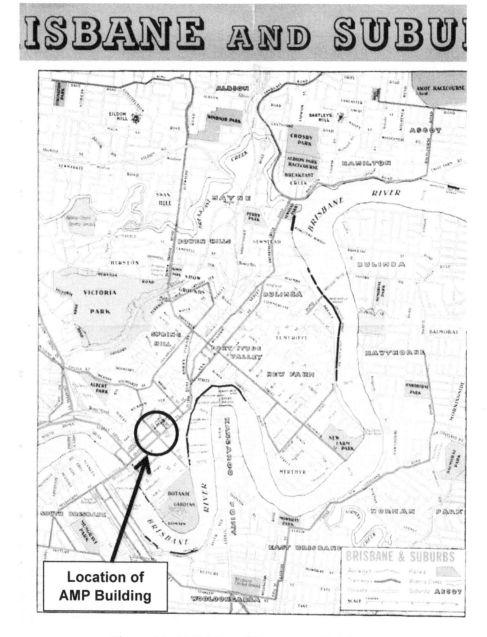

Location of AMP Building

Figure 96 - 1942 Map of Downtown Brisbane

Office assignments in the <u>AMP Building</u> were similar to the 401 Collins Street building in Melbourne.

The <u>eighth floor</u> was set up for Gen. MacArthur and Gen. Sutherland (Chief of Staff), and their aides. Also on the eighth floor were Brig. Gen. Willoughby (G-2) (Intelligence), Gen. Chamberlin (G-3) (Operations), and Gen. Marshall (Deputy Chief of Staff). Also on the Eighth Floor was Lt. Col. Morhouse, Gen. MacArthur's aide and personal physician.

The <u>seventh floor</u> was Gen Akin (Signal) with his communication center, including his staff, the telephone switchboard, teletype, and the code room.

The <u>sixth floor</u> was Gen. Stivers (G-1) (Administration), Gen. Whitlock (G-4) (Supply), Gen. Marquat (Anti-Aircraft), Col. Fitch (AG), and Maj. Day (Headquarters Commandant).

The <u>fourth floor</u> was Lt. Gen. Kenney (Air Force Commanding General) with all the Fifth Air Force and Air Service Command officers.

The <u>Commercial Bank Building</u> on Queen Street was adjacent to the AMP Building, where GHQ occupied the <u>seventh</u>, <u>eighth</u>, and <u>ninth</u> floors. To avoid having to go down eight floors and back up eight floors for a meeting, the Engineers punched a hole in the wall of the eighth floor to connect the two buildings. The Engineer Office with Gen Hugh Casey occupied the <u>eighth</u> and <u>ninth</u> <u>floors</u> in the Commercial Bank Building.

Col. Diller (Public Relations) was also in the Commercial Bank Building on the <u>eighth floor</u>.

24.3.   The Lennons Hotel – Officers Quarters

When we arrived in Brisbane, GHQ took a number of rooms in the Lennons Hotel. It was the only air conditioned hotel in Brisbane at the time. We had about six floors for MacArthur's principal officers. Fortunately, I happened to be included. I was on the fourth floor.

Figure 97 - Lennons Hotel, undated photo from MacArthur Museum Brisbane

Gen. MacArthur was down the hall from me on the fourth floor. Mrs. MacArthur was also on the fourth floor with young Arthur and his nurse [Au Cheu]. MacArthur had two aides, one was a captain in the Navy[215] and the other was Col. Sidney L. Huff. Col. Huff was actually Mrs. MacArthur's aide and worked out of the Lennons Hotel.

Johnnie was nineteen-months older than General MacArthur's young son, Arthur Mac-Arthur IV. Every time I saw young Arthur, I would think about Johnnie, trying to imagine how big Johnnie had grown since I last saw him. Johnnie actually wrote a letter to young Arthur at Christmas, but it is hard to be pen pals when you are five and six years old.

Sunday, 26 July 1942
Well, as you would expect, everybody wanted something – this, that, or the other. All were wondering when everything would all be set. If they would just sit tight for a short time, all would be set.

I worked pretty late and am dead tired. I will have to take time soon to catch up on my diary or else it will be a flop around these pages. After the nice trip up from Melbourne when all went well, I thought soon I would be caught up once more. Needless to say, there are still things I have yet to do, but time and paper do not permit a list.

24.4.   Expanded Duties for Headquarters Commandant

Monday, 27 July 1942
Lt. Evans came in from Melbourne today, so I am turning HQ Company over to him. I am making Lt. Worthington the Supply Officer, and Lt. Laughlin the Mess Officer. I think this will relieve me of a lot. My office now is not permanent, but I will have one as soon as all the shifting is over. I have most everything spotted outside of a few things. Since we arrived, I have heard no comments as yet with reference to the move. However, it appears that all have been well pleased.

We worked last night until about midnight. The night before, we worked until 1:30 AM. We had to move the safes and some really heavy stuff. During the day we could use only one elevator, but at night we could use the three front elevators. With all the help we had, it made it much nicer and faster.

---

[215] The Navy Aide is thought to be Capt. H. J. (Jimmy) Ray USN.

GHQ – South West Pacific Area
Telephone Directory[216]
December, 1942, Page 7

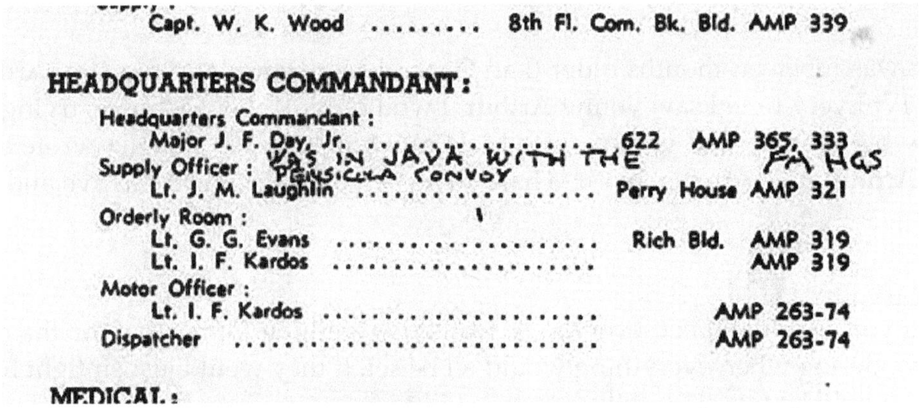

Capt. W. K. Wood .... 8th Fl. Com. Bk. Bld. AMP 339

HEADQUARTERS COMMANDANT:

Headquarters Commandant :
   Major J. F. Day, Jr. 622   AMP 365, 333
Supply Officer : *WAS IN JAVA WITH THE PENSICOLA CONVOY FA HGS*
   Lt. J. M. Laughlin .... Perry House AMP 321
Orderly Room :
   Lt. G. G. Evans .... Rich Bld. AMP 319
   Lt. I. F. Kardos .... AMP 319
Motor Officer :
   Lt. I. F. Kardos .... AMP 263-74
Dispatcher .... AMP 263-74

MEDICAL :

Figure 98 - GHQ-SWPA Restricted Telephone Book Page 7 of December 1942
Classified as a Restricted Document, this book is in the possession of the
MacArthur Museum Brisbane, Australia.

I received an excellent letter from Alta Pearl today, which I enjoyed very much. I just must take time to write. We have had so damn much to do. Only part of the office is set up, and everything is temporary. Maybe in a day or so we will get settled.

24.4.1. Leasing Office Space

Arranging office space was more than signing a lease. In time there were several buildings to deal with. In addition to the AMP Building and three floors next door in the Commercial Bank building, we had five floors in another building, and a couple of smaller buildings as well.

We needed to line up the furniture, typewriters, and office supplies. Carbon paper was always in demand – used and reused. There were always building modifications, carpentry, electrical modifications, and plumbing problems that required our Construction Engineers or a civilian contractor.

---

[216] The General Douglas MacArthur Brisbane Memorial Foundation, Level Eight MacArthur Chambers, 201 Edward Street, PO Box 1247, Brisbane Queensland 4001, Australia , *U.S. Army Signal Corps Telephone Directory, December 1942,*. Original Copy in the possession of Major William A. Bentson, Army of the U.S. Ret., 15 Kapunda Street Toowong, Brisbane, Queensland, Australia.

24.4.2.   The Mess Hall – Perry House

When we arrived in Brisbane, Lt. Laughlin became the Mess Officer. We set up the Headquarters Mess Hall to feed everyone in Perry House which is located on Elizabeth and Albert Streets. This was a big job and took several weeks to get organized. It was mid-August before the Mess opened, but we quickly built up mess service to about 900 people who were in our direct command. Over the next few months we had to house and feed all the men passing through the Replacement Center en route to New Guinea and the front lines. By September [1942] when Gen. Eichelberger and the 32nd Division passed through Australia, his troops were attached to me for food and housing until they moved into the combat zone in New Guinea. That was perhaps another 1,500

Figure 99 - GHQ Shoulder Patch

troops. We were feeding a total of perhaps 2,500 men every day.

The Mess Sergeant was a Master Sergeant I picked up from the Replacement Center. He was supported by an array of cooks and stewards. He had to plan the meals, buy the food, and prepare everything – he had a big job.

I taught him to go out along the coast and buy local products – fresh fish, turkey, chickens, vegetables, anything you could eat. We paid cash out of the mess fund for everything. We learned that Mrs. MacArthur liked raw oysters on the half-shell, so the Sergeant had standing orders to buy fresh oysters if he saw them in the market.

We still served a lot of boiled lamb or mutton that was awfully greasy and no one wanted. Once in a while we went hunting on weekends and brought back a couple of kangaroo that we gave to the Mess Sergeant. One day we invited Gen. Stivers over to have a bite of kangaroo steak. Everybody got a bite, including the enlisted men.

24.4.3.   The Motor Pool

Lt. Kardos became the Motor Officer and took over the Motor Pool. The Motor Pool had about 85 to 90 trucks and vehicles plus 24 staff cars for the generals. We had mechanics, drivers, and everything. All the general's drivers were in Headquarters Company. After the incident of the stolen car in Melbourne, guards were doubled on the motor pool.[217]

24.4.4.   The PX (Canteen) and Barber Shop

In Brisbane I was assigned the Post Exchange (PX) or Canteen, as it was called. We were running a general store that sold everything – cigarettes, underwear, aspirin, and condoms. We had a grocery store, a barbershop for officers, and barbershop for the enlisted men.

24.4.5.   The Liquor Business

The liquor business was my responsibility and was always a problem. Whiskey was rationed, but I had two whiskey stores – one for the officers and one for the enlisted men. The enlisted men got their allotment, same as the officers. I was the only person who could buy liquor for the entire Headquarters – including the generals. Other units could buy their own allotment, but I bought for the Headquarters.

Liquor was strictly regulated and rationed. Only so much liquor was allocated for each person, officer or enlisted man. Everyone wanted scotch, but there was never enough scotch, so we bundled several bottles of wine for every bottle of scotch. We had plenty of wine. If you wanted scotch, you had to buy some wine. The Aussie's make a distilled wine that is a lot like vodka; it must be 135 proof. They pour about an inch in a glass and fill up the rest with milk. Then down the hatch! It will curl your hair.

The problem with the liquor was always the General's Aides – they were always trying to get around the ration limit. I was often caught in the middle between the generals and their booze. I set up a small annex to the liquor store in my hotel room, where I always had a few bottles for "emergency calls" from the generals. I guess word got around about my small stash.

---

[217] See 5 Jun 1942, Section 13.6 of this report.

New people were coming into GHQ from the States all the time. One of the new people that came in was Philip La Follette, a former Governor of Wisconsin.[218] He had been called to active duty, made a colonel, sent overseas, and assigned to G-4 [Supply].[219] I had met him but did not really know him. About 3 AM one morning there was a ring on my phone. The call was La Follette. He said, "Hey, I got a friend down here, and we want a drink."

I said, "It's 3 AM. I am asleep. I don't have anything to drink, only some wine,"

"That's OK, we will take it. We are coming up," said La Follette.

I proceeded to hide everything I had except for one bottle of that 135 proof Australian wine that I set on the table. They came up. I pointed to the table with the single bottle and said "That's all I have."

"That's fine," said La Follette.

I retrieved three glasses, and poured out a big slug in each – no milk, nothing else. "Do you want some water?" I asked.

"Oh, no, this is fine," said La Follette.

I quietly poured my glass into a plant, and headed back to my bedroom.

La Follette said "OK, down the hatch." He and his friend proceeded to guzzle down the contents.

There was the biggest howl you have ever heard. They couldn't get to the bathroom fast enough. They were hollering about throats burning while tears were coming out their eyes. I started laughing. Anyone that comes in my room at that hour – that is the type of drink they get. He never came back at 3 AM.. La Follette would later become Chief of Staff for Gen. Sutherland.

---

[218] Philip La Follette served three terms as Governor of Wisconsin and was the brother of Robert La Follette Jr., the Senator who had introduced the Congressional Resolution designating 13 June as "Douglas MacArthur Day." He later supported the "MacArthur for President" movement in 1948.

[219] His activation may possibly have been in association with the activation of the Wisconsin National Guard – 32nd Inf. Division (Red Arrow Division) – that later fought in Buna & Gona, NG.

One day I found out our liquor supplier was giving whiskey directly to Col. Huff. Whatever Huff wanted, he got, and it was taken off my allotment. I cut that off quick. I told our supplier if you are going to give anybody anything, it is going to come through me or you lose all the business for the Headquarters.

So Col Huff was cut off, and he came to me. I said "Colonel, last time you pulled the wool over my eyes. You got what you wanted, and they charged it to my list. Remember there are only so many bottles to go around. You got your allotment last time, so this time you don't get anything. Next time we get our allotment, we will put you back on the list, and you will get your fair share.

"I don't like that very much," said Col. Huff.

"I don't care if you like that or not. We have to make the liquor go around." To me an aide doesn't command any one. He is a "flunky" for the general.

24.4.6.   Security for the Headquarters

Security was on everyone's mind. There were armed guards at every entrance to the AMP Building, the Commercial Bank Building, the Motor Pool, Perry House, and most other facilities. When you entered the AMP Lobby, you were greeted by a burly M/Sergeant, flanked by guards, who would confirm your identity, issue a written pass, and call your host to come meet you in the lobby. All guards were drawn from HQ Company.

24.4.7.   The Filipino Janitors

And then there was office maintenance. Some of my worst problems were with janitors. I inherited about 100 Filipinos for the janitorial staff, and they were always in trouble. They rented a house and turned it into a brothel, including some Aussie aborigines. Venereal disease was a big problem. One of the Filipinos got one of the ladies pregnant, and the woman's father came down to Headquarters demanding a marriage. There were strict rules against marriage, so the Filipino was shipped off to New Guinea.

24.4.8.   Japanese Nisei Interpreters

One group attached to my unit consisted of 167 Nisei interpreters. These were all first-generation Japanese – born in America and all volunteers. They were assigned individually or in pairs to join combat units as interpreters. We lost some in combat too. I had one Nisei officer and one Nisei sergeant who ran the show. We never had a discipline problem with the unit. Those boys would get their paychecks every month, take out £5 for their pocket money, and mail everything else back home to their parents – all their parents were locked up in those special internment camps in Arizona, Utah, and across the western states.

The problems I had with the Nisei were the Australians. The Aussies went mad when they saw a Jap. They were always trying to kill them. They hated Japanese and couldn't see any difference between these Nisei and any other Jap. There were a couple of fights where we had to call in the MPs.

We were acquiring more people for the Headquarters all the time. The Replacement Center was only about 8-10 miles away. I had first choice on the replacements coming in from the States. We would go out there, look through the papers of the people coming in, and pick the people we wanted. We would go to the AG, and he would issue orders - "By order of Gen. MacArthur." That was it. I picked the best I could find before anyone else could see the list. We were always short of people. I had sergeants performing many officer jobs.

Tuesday, 28 July 1942
This was a lousy day. Supplies are short. I think we are doing OK, but then the AG always wants to find out something else.

Well, here I am as usual, dead tired. I will be glad when I can get about three good night's sleep and then go to a show. I know if I ever get to a show, I will go to sleep. I haven't seen all they have on. I have not seen "Claudia," a stage play.

Looks like the fireworks [*the war*] will start pretty soon. Much is in the works.

Soon it will be payday again so think I will send more money home. Times may be hard one of these days. Wish I had a letter or so to stem the tide.

Wednesday, 29 July 1942
10:45 PM – I have just come in from checking the guards, the janitors, and the men hanging the General's curtains. The floor has been terrible as they tore out a wall in a dozen places – plaster is everywhere and naturally the floor is in very bad shape. They are beginning to make some improvements. I think the Filipinos will be doing better as we go along.

24.5.   Maj. Gen. George C. Kenney Arrives – 29 Jul 1942

A new Maj. General of Air Corps came in today, Gen. George C. Kenney. He is taking command of the Air Corps. I'm afraid Lt. Gen. Brett has been relieved and may go home. You never can tell. Gen. Barnes went home a short time ago. In this wartime environment "You must produce!"

Maj. Gen. George C. Kenney was born in 1889. After finishing high school in Brookline, Massachusetts, Kenney attended the Massachusetts Institute of Technology for three years before dropping out to go to work as an industrial technician. In 1917 he volunteered for the Air Cadets of the Army Signal Corps. During World War I, he flew 75 combat missions where he received two confirmed aerial "kills." One of his confirmed "kills" was reputed to have been Hermann Göring, who later became head of the German Luftwaffe in World War II. After World War I, Kenney became Commander of the 91st Aero Squadron. He remained in the Air Corps between wars with a series of assignments, one of which was to Command the Air Force Experimental Division at Wright Patterson Air Base. During his experimental career, he was involved in the development of the first US "wing-mounted machine gun." He had been promoted to brigadier general, had been to France to observe German air warfare tactics, and was in command of the Fourth Air Corps in California when he was summoned to join MacArthur.

MacArthur was extremely disappointed with the performance of his Air Corps and particularly Gen. Brett. Since the difficulty Brett had in providing planes to fly MacArthur from the Philippines, MacArthur apparently had grave doubts about Gen. Brett's abilities. MacArthur desperately needed a "can-do" commander for his Air Corps. To move forward, he knew he needed a big change. Kenney became his "can-do" man. Kenney shared MacArthur's aggressive disposition toward the enemy – he wanted always to be on the attack.

Thursday, 30 July 1942

Lt. Worthington, Lt. Laughlin, and I ate a long dinner. We started at 8:35 PM and drank a bottle of sparkling burgundy which I guess was the reason we ate so long. I have a sore throat, and I am always afraid of getting trench mouth eating at cafes all the time. There is a lot of it, and it is easy to see why after seeing how dirty lots of the kitchens are where the food is prepared.

I received your letter #17 today. Swell to get one. I was afraid I would not get one for some time due to our moving. Maybe the mail situation is being straightened out.

I am going to send some more film to be developed very soon. I guess I will not get to see them, but maybe they will be OK. I love you all and will be glad when things start popping. I think soon. Love

<u>Friday, 31 July 1942</u>
On the QT I heard Gen. Brett is being released shortly. That will be unpublished news. One thing about a general getting screwed up, they send him home. If less than a general, they transfer them to the firing lines – as far north as possible. Sometimes I wonder what kind of bunch we do have up front. All joking aside, I know the bunch now scraping is OK.

I am very anxious to see the fireworks really start before Russia is gone, and then we will have hell. We are sure losing the hell out of this war up to now.

I am working on Air Raid plans now. I am to be Chief Air Raid Warden for the entire HQ, Navy, Air Corps and Australians. Some fun, eh? Well, every job where there is a lot of work and no honor, I always know who will get it. It could be that I am the right guy? Love.

24.6.   Lennon Hotel Guests

Well, it wasn't long before the generals started bringing a few female friends around the hotel. There was one floozy who appeared with a different hair color every day - red hair today, yellow tomorrow, green the next – she ran a beauty parlor.

The first general I was aware of that had a serious girlfriend was the Air Corps General, Gen. Kenney. His friend was an Australian girl, I think one of the secretaries. I don't know where he got with her, but he was with her every night.[220]

Figure 100 - Beryl Spiers Stevenson, 1943

Seventy years after the fact, Gen. Kenney's affair with Beryl Stevenson has become legend. Beryl Stevenson[221] was one of two shorthand stenographers who were evacuated from Java when the Japanese invaded. An Australian by birth, she had worked for two British generals in Singapore and Java. In Melbourne she was working with Gen. George Brett who

---

[220] Nothing in the diary specifically names Gen. Kenny's friend. There is only hearsay that his friend was Maj. Stevenson.

[221] Beryl Spiers Stevenson Daley, 1916-2007, Sydney Morning Herald, March 21, 2007.

was dismissed. In Brisbane, she was working for Brett's replacement, Gen. Kenney.[222] *On at least one critical mission to New Guinea in 1942, Stevenson escorted Gen. MacArthur as his personal stenographer.*[223]

The second relationship within the General Staff developed between Major General Richard Marshall (Deputy Chief of Staff to Gen. Sutherland) and Mrs. Louise Mouatt. Mrs. Mouatt, an English subject, was also a skilled stenographer who had been evacuated from Java with Beryl Stevenson. Her husband was a Japanese Prisoner of War. Both Mrs. Mouatt and Mrs. Stevenson were viewed as highly skilled stenographers by their respective bosses.[224]

24.7. Monthly Reflections on Australia – 31 Jul 1942

"Another day, another dollar. Lots of days, and lots of dollars." Here I am back in Brisbane once more, and due to the fact that I have now been completely around Australia, maybe I should write a book. I could tell some real stories! However, even though I have been all around the damned place, I haven't seen a lot of the wild country. I've been to the bush, as they call it, seen wild animals on the loose, seen land that is not worth a damn, and seen land that is fine. There is a beautiful sea coast in numerous places. The highest mountains (as they call them) are about 6,000 feet – just a good hill where we come from. The most interesting thing of all I guess is the people. They are fine people, but so far behind us they may as well start over. They need leaders and laws most of all. Some principles could be changed.

---

[222] Dunn. Ibid.

[223] Tunny, Noel. *Winning from Downunder*. Boolarong Press, Moorooka OLD 4105 Australia. Tunny indicates that she was made a Lieutenant before she accompanied Gen. MacArthur to New Guinea in 1942.

[223] Rodgers, Paul P. Green Library, Stanford University Praeger Publishers, One Madison Ave., New York, NY 10010, Greenwood Publishing Group, Copyright 1990, published 1991, p66-67,

[224] Tunny, Noel. Ibid.

25.   THE FEMALE RECEPTIONIST – 1 AUG 1942

25.1.   Mrs. Clarke is Coming

<u>Saturday, 1 August 1942</u>

GHQ had been in Brisbane about three weeks, when Gen Akin called me up to his office. He said "Major, do you know Mrs. Clarke is going to be our new receptionist?"

"General, we don't need a female receptionist. We have enough trouble as it is," I said.

"Well, whether you want it or not, we are going to have one. I want you to find a place to put her, get her a desk, and get her set up," said Akin.

"General, I have a Sergeant down there that does reception all the time. I have enlisted men who do other things down there. Only place I can put her is down there on the main floor where the Sergeant sits now," I said.

"Well, think it over," he said.

Gen Akin is in charge of the Signal Corps, and he doesn't have a damn thing to do with me or the Receptionist's job, which is a part of the Headquarters Commandant's responsibility. So I went back to my office and picked up the phone to call Gen. Stivers. Gen Stivers was G-1 (Personnel) and my boss. "General Stivers, I want to come down and talk to you for a minute."

"Come on down," said Gen. Stivers.

When I walked in, he was sitting behind his desk with his head down. He pulled off his reading glasses and looked up at me across his desk. "What's on your mind, Major?" he said. He always called me Major, never John.

"Sir, Gen Akin just called me up to his office and told me we are going to have a civilian receptionist, Mrs. Clarke. He told me to find a place to put her and get things ready for her," I said.

Stivers immediately jumped to his feet. With a shocked voice of great surprise shouted "What?" He paused a moment, and then immediately started bouncing toward the door. "Well, Well, Well. Come with me!" he said.

Stivers was immediately out the door and down the hall in a flash. As we passed Col. Fitch's office, he stuck his head in the door and without skipping a step shouted "Fitch, come with me." Stivers had one star and Fitch had none. So here we go down the hall, like a camel caravan with an oasis in sight, straight into the open elevator on the sixth floor and headed up to the eighth floor. The only offices on the eighth floor were Gen MacArthur, Maj. Gen. Sutherland, MacArthur's Chief of Staff, plus their aides and stenographers.[225]

Gen Stivers walked directly into the office of the Chief of Staff. Fitch followed him. I peeled off and went to the office of the aides. I figured I had no business in there with all the Generals, and besides, I could hear all that was going on from the aides' office.

Gen Stivers addressed Gen Sutherland, "General, Major Day tells me we are about to have a female receptionist."

Maj. Gen. Richard K. Sutherland was Gen. MacArthur's trusted right hand. He had been Mac-Arthur's Chief of Staff in the Philippines since 1938 and had his supreme confidence. Sutherland was the only person in GHQ who could speak for Gen. MacArthur in his absence. Sutherland was 48 years old (14 years younger than MacArthur), a Yale graduate, known for a brilliant mind with incredible powers of concentration. He spoke fluent French and had been sent by the U.S. Army to the French École Militaries in Paris.[226] Gen. Sutherland was the son of Howard Sutherland, a U.S. Senator from West Virginia, was married for about 12 years, and had a 10-year-old daughter.

Sutherland replied, "Oh, Charlie, didn't I tell you about that. I guess I forgot about it. I mentioned it to Akin the other day. Yea, I thought we should dress up Headquarters just a little bit, and Mrs. Clarke will be here in Brisbane before long. So take care of it for me, will you? Do what you got to do."

"OK, General," said Stivers.

Out the office marched Stivers leading the caravan back to the sixth floor. Fitch was right behind him. I fell in behind Fitch and pulled up the tail as we marched down the stairs. We passed Fitch's office, and Fitch fell out. "OK General, I will see you later," Fitch said.

---

[225] M/Sgt. Paul P. Rodgers, stenographer to Gen. Sutherland, was on the 8th floor.

[226] Sutherland appears twice in the U.S. Federal Census for 1930: first, with his wife and parents in West Virginia, and second, in the U.S. Embassy, Paris, France.

I followed Stivers back to his office. As we entered his office, he didn't say a word. He walked around behind his desk and sat down. He reached on the desk, picked up his reading glasses where he had set them, and put them back on his nose. He raised his head, looked across the desk at me and said "Yes, Major, we are going to have a female receptionist." We both started laughing and couldn't stop.

That was it. Stivers said "Work up a plan, tell me what you want to do. Thank you very much."

Stivers was always the same way. He was a wonderful man. I believe he was truly surprised by the events of the day. Neither of us had any idea where this was going to lead. That night the diary read:

Saturday, 1 Aug 1942
Gen. Akin called me in and advised me that Mrs. Clarke was going to be the Receptionist. Well, a damn w**** in my estimation. They say she has plenty of money and her husband is in Egypt.[227] Well, it's damn funny she wants to hang around with a few of the generals. I have fought against having a receptionist in the form of a woman of any kind. I went down and talked to Gen. Stivers about it and he is on my side. Thank goodness. So in the fuss – well, you see I have one of my men doing the job now and a good one too. Anyway, I had to go with G-1 (Gen. Stivers) and AG (Col. Fitch) to the Chief of Staff (Gen. Sutherland). I am in the clear and they told me I did the right thing by coming to them. Anyway, I don't know what the hell is going to happen to the b**** as yet. In the meantime I guess she is getting the works regularly from Sutherland.[228]
Good night darling and Johnnie.

Sunday, 2 August 1942
Today is your birthday, darling, so I sent you and Johnnie a cable. Hope you enjoy it. Only wish I could be with you to help you celebrate.[229]

Lt. Gen. Brett was relieved of command today. That makes about five generals relieved and sent home. They sure have to cut the ice here or get going.

More dealings today with this damn Receptionist. Boy, am I sick of that! Well, there was no place to put a Receptionist but down on the first floor at the AMP building entrance.

---

[227] He was actually a Japanese Prisoner of War in Malaya.

[228] Mrs. Clarke is sleeping with Gen. Sutherland on a regular basis. Manchester, p. 349.

[229] This actually was Johnnie's birthday, but Maj. Day always switched the date with his wife's birthday, August 5, and Johnnie's birthday, August 2.

Everyone came into the building through the main door, although General MacArthur had his own private entrance. I had guards on all the doors and the elevator, even without her. Every visitor had to verify the purpose of his visit, show his ID papers, and obtain a pass. The visitor's host was called and came down to Reception to accompany the visitor into the building. Every visitor was logged in and logged out.

I told Gen. Stivers what I wanted to do, and he said go ahead. Akin said nothing further.

I got a desk set up near the front door equipped with some of the things I thought the Receptionist would need – phone book, notepad, passes, and pencils. We put in a telephone order, but the phone installation would take several days. I thought we would be ready before she arrived.

I worked until seven tonight. Worthington and Evans came up, so we drank a bottle of champagne before supper and then took about an hour and a half eating, followed by a bull session. Capt. Hoay, who was on the *Republic* with me coming over, came by and added to the discussion. He is leaving Wednesday for Townsville to check finances there. Here it is 10 PM now, and I am about ready to read and go to sleep.

Monday, 3 August 1942
I have never sat down and cussed an SOB any more than I have one man here, Col. Fitch, the Adjutant General, I have never said much about the b****** as I have always tried to get along with him. I get along with everybody but him. He is trying so hard to be a brigadier general that it hurts. All the heads of Sections are brigadier generals now, except him. He is unbearable at times. I personally don't give a damn what he is or how he gets it. I have always tried to run my job the best possible, but he tries to run everything and get his say on everything. Somebody is going to scratch him one of these days. Everybody who knows him would be glad to see him as a private in the rear rank. Personally I have tried the best I possibly can to get along with him and do what he wants done. I have even overdone things to please him, but he is never satisfied with anything.

I have said not once but numerous times that I got off per diem. I am ready to go to the field with pleasure. Actually, I think I would get a promotion sooner if I were to go now. I have expected several times that I would be sent to the north for some damned reason. Lord knows when. Stop. Stop. Stop.

<u>Wednesday, 5 August 1942</u>

Johnnie. Today is your birthday[230] and you are 6 years of age. You weigh about 57 pounds and must be about 40 inches tall. I've been gone almost nine months. A lot of time has passed and so much has happened. No one has any idea when I will get home either. The war is still beginning and lots of people will go under the axe before anyone says stop. I hope I can make the grade.

I received several letters of late. Most of them are older than usual, so I guess I am getting caught up on old mail. I have been surprised to get so many since arriving in Brisbane.

Best Wishes for the day and the years to come. I love you both. You are my love and only wish I could see you even for a very short time.

<u>Thursday, 6 August 1942</u>

I have to go to the dentist soon. My gums seem to bleed when I wash my teeth. I don't know but it may be the "No Tooth Brush" I use.

Evans and Worthington came up and we drank a bottle of champagne. It is like drinking water. You can't even say you get sleepy from it, as I am always that way.

One of my men turned a jeep over today after taking the car without permission. It will cost him plenty. I am going to court martial him.
Love and kisses for the Day

25.2.   My First Meeting with Mrs. Clarke

<u>Friday, 7 August 1942</u>

A week later, a young woman walked into my office. She was well dressed, wearing a hat, gloves, and a tailored suit, certainly dressed a cut above a typical Aussie on the street. I know now she was 28. My desk had a big sign across the front that read Headquarters Commandant so anyone walking in the office knew who I was.

"Hello, Major. How are you?" said Mrs. Clarke. Now recognize I had never laid eyes on this woman before in my life. She walked over to me and put her hand on the shoulder of my uniform. This was not what I considered normal military decorum.

---

[230] Actually, August 5 was Cile's birthday, not Johnnie's. All his life Maj. Day had trouble mixing these two birthdays.

**Figure 101 - Elaine
Brookes, Engagement
Photo**
28 Oct 1935 - Sydney
(N.S.W.) Morning Herald,
p.4

"How you doing?" she said with that melodic Australian accent. She was the kind of woman who would catch your eye clear across any room. "I am the new Receptionist."

"I heard you were coming," I said. "Do you have a place to stay?"

"No, not yet," she replied.

"Well, why don't you take some time and find a place," I said. When you get fixed up, let me know, and we will put you to work."

Before she left, I asked my Desk Sergeant to take her down to the Base Personnel Office and get her added to the Base Payroll that covered civilians. "We don't have any females on the military payroll," I explained.

The diary entry at night read:

Friday, 7 August 1942
The Receptionist came and they turned her over to me. I sure was sweating that deal out. One general said do one thing and another said do something else. Boy, I didn't know what to do, but try to do the right thing. Thank God.

GHQ is taking over three more floors in another building. That will make three in one building and five in another for GHQ alone, and that does not count the Air Corp, Navy, etc.

**Figure 102 - Elaine Brookes in
wedding cake photo**
10 Jan 1936 - Courier-Mail
(Brisbane, Queensland), p18

I mentioned I am the Chief Air Raid Warden now by order from the General for the entire AMP building. They can give me more damn jobs.

Today I ate dinner at the "Shingle Inn," as I do most of the time. My meals now cost me almost a pound a day. That's about $90 per month to eat. That's rough, isn't it?

25.3.   Elaine Gertrude Brookes Bessemer-Clarke (1914 – 1986)

Elaine Bessemer-Clarke (aka Mrs. Clarke) was born Elaine Gertrude Brookes on January 2, 1914. She was the second daughter of Sir Norman and Lady Brookes of Cliff House, Frankston, Melbourne. Sir Norman was a major shareholder and served on the Board of Directors of the Australian Paper Company Ltd., a company his father had founded and been Managing Director. In the first decade of the twentieth century, Sir Norman (1877-1968) was the dominant world tennis champion who in 1907 won the Wimbledon Championship in singles, doubles, and mixed doubles and won the first Davis Cup ever for Australia by defeating England for the first time. He was credited with establishing the Australian tennis dynasty. He was associated with the Australian Davis Cup team until 1924. He became President of the Lawn Tennis Association of Australia in 1926, where he remained for 28 years until 1954. In 1977, he was inducted into the Australian Tennis Hall of Fame.

As second generation wealth, Sir Norman was an established member of the Australian aristocracy. His wife, Dame Mabel Brookes [nee Balcombe], was Melbourne's leading society hostess for many years. Their three daughters were raised with servants, private education, and training in the social graces, including proper etiquette of the gentry. They traveled extensively.

Reginald Bessemer-Clarke was a world ranked English tennis player who appeared twice at Wimbledon, last in 1938. He was the great-grandson of Sir William Bessemer, the steel pioneer

Figure 103 - Norman Brooks, Miss Elaine Brooks, and Reginald Bessemer-Clarke
Hyde Park, London, August 22, 1935

and inventor of the Bessemer furnace. Andrew Carnegie made his fortune when he brought the Bessemer furnace technology to the United States. Reginald and Elaine had been introduced to each other as chance tennis partners at Lady Crosfield's Melbourne tennis party while Reginald was on the World Amateur Tennis tour.[231]

On January 7, 1936, Elaine married Reginald Bessemer-Clarke at St. Paul's Cathedral (Melbourne) before 500 guests with eleven maids of honor and two train carriers. The wedding, which approached the scale of "Australian royalty," was attended by the Australian Governor-General and Lady Isaacs. After the wedding, the couple had a honeymoon trip back to their future home in London by way of Honolulu, America, Japan, and China.[232] Elaine and Reginald Bessemer-Clarke established residence in England. Their son, Anthony Bessemer-Clarke, was born in Fakenham, Norfolk, England on 2 Feb 1940.

There was no shortage of newspaper photographs of Elaine (Brookes) Bessemer-Clarke, as she regularly appeared in the social columns of The Argos (Melbourne), the Courier-Mail (Brisbane), The Morning Herald (Sydney), and other Australian papers. She was extremely well connected in the highest Australian social and political circles.[233]

Sometime between 1939 and 1941, Reginald became an Officer in the British Army. He was serving on the Malay Peninsula, when Singapore fell on 15 Feb 1942. Reginald became a Japanese Prisoner of War, and remained incarcerated until liberated in 1945.

In February 1940 with the German Blitz in London and with Reginald off at war, Elaine returned by ship to Melbourne with her infant son to live in the comparative safety and comfort of her parents' home in an exclusive suburb of Melbourne: 56 Walsh St, South Yarra, Fawkner District.[234]

Sometime between March 1942 and July 1942 at a Melbourne society party to welcome the newly arrived American officers, Elaine Bessemer-Clarke (age 28) met Gen. Richard K. Sutherland (age 49) and began a liaison that would last for over three years. The relationship would eventually lead to MacArthur dismissing and replacing Sutherland.[235]

---

[231] The Adelaide SA, 26 Oct 1935.

[232] The Courier Mail (Brisbane, Old Queensland: 1933-1954) 7 January 1936, p. 17.

[233] The Argus, Melbourne Newspaper, (Melbourne, Victoria:1848-1954), 27 March 1944, pg.6.

[234] Australian Electoral Rolls 1903-1954; Elaine Gertrude Bessemer-Clarke; 1943 Victoria, District: Fawkner, SubDist: South Yarra, 56 Walsh St., Defense Worker, Registration #1192.

[235] In Paul P. Rogers definitive two volume history, "MacArthur and Sutherland," there are more than eighteen references to "X." Rogers consistently refrained from naming Elaine Bessemer-Clarke by name, probably because at the time he was writing Mrs. Clarke was still living. Suther-

Friday, August 7, 1942
GUADALCANAL INVADED BY U.S. MARINES
The first U.S. amphibious landing of the Pacific War occurs as 1st Marine Division invades Tulagi and Guadalcanal in the Solomon Islands.

Saturday, 8 August 1942

To start with, I never write any real news in my diary, but there are lots of things the papers don't know. But today is different. We took another island. We will be in a better position to drive the Japs back. I will not name the island for reasons of security. *[Maj. Day is probably referring to Guadalcanal.]*

I finished Court Martial charges on four men today. One is to be a Special Court and three are to be for Summary Court.

I will have the Mess operating about Thursday next. I went to the "Cremone," a Vaudeville show. The show was very poor, but there were some good jokes. The best joke was this:

> Question: "What is the similarity between a "Zero" and a pair of "scanties"?
> Answer: "A good Yank can bring them both down."

They are having a dance in the hotel tonight. There seems to be quite a crowd, but I don't care to go. I must go to bed.

Sunday, 9 August 1942

I worked until about 1 PM. I went to the hotel and ate lunch (it took me one-and-a-half hours to be served and eat). Lt. Evans wanted me to go to Southport with him, which was about 53 miles south along the coast, so I went along. We left about 2:45 PM. Southport is a summer resort under ordinary conditions, but this is winter, so the average temperature is about 60° F. At present due to gasoline rationing, very few can go to the beach so it was extremely quiet. We took some pictures, went through the zoo, and then drove to another town about 20 miles farther south. Some dumps. The place smelled like fish. We left about 6 PM and came back to Brisbane. On our way we ran over a small kangaroo and killed him. We matched for the 'roo [*kangaroo*] and I won. Well, he hasn't been skinned as yet, but if possible I would like to have him stuffed. Some fun, eh? We

---

land died in 1966. Elaine Bessemer-Clarke Roe died in 1986. Rogers' volumes were published in 1990 and 1991 before his death in 1992.

started eating supper about 8 pm. Now it is 9:45 pm and I am through so am going to bed.

Monday, 10 August 1942

What a day. Busy all day. I feel in a bad humor tonight, drugged, blue, or just anything you would want to call it. I was for once going to come home early and get a good night's sleep. Well, I did get home early, maybe about 10 PM. Lt. Worthington wanted me to come by his room so I did. He, Lt. Strait, and some lieutenant I didn't know were drinking sparkling Burgundy. I drank about three glasses and didn't notice the time. It was 11:45 PM when I came back to my room and went to bed.

I never get to see all of a paper, just a headline. Of course now and then I find out a few things about what's going on, but naturally I have to keep it quiet. That must be the crop of news for tonight, but I'm still in a bad humor.

Tuesday, 11 August 1942

So many things in one day! To hell with Fitch, the SOB! He would like to see me depart from this station and if he gets half a chance, he will send me. Being the AG, he might have some influence but I get along swell with everybody else. Well, the truth is no one gets along with Fitch. I do believe he has fewer friends than anyone I know. I have done everything I know to please him. Nothing good is ever mentioned. Sometimes, I think I would rather be up where the fighting is going on, but then I see the money I make and the nice place I have to stay in, and I decide to keep my mouth shut and keep going. **I disapprove very much of some things that are going on, but well, maybe all will work out for the best.** Who knows? Love & kisses, darling.

25.4.   The Receptionist's First Day at GHQ

The new Receptionist took a week to 10 days to find a place to live. I did not realize she was locating an upscale apartment for herself, her two-year-old son, the child's Nanny (who she had brought up from Melbourne), and a Cocker Spaniel dog." She located in Lagshaw Flats in New Farm, a nice suburb of Brisbane.

I should have known immediately I was in BIG trouble when for her first day of work she arrived in a car chauffeured by Gen. Sutherland's personal driver. Mrs. Clarke came up to my office on the sixth floor and asked. "Where is my office?"

"Well, a Receptionist doesn't have an office," I said. "Follow me." We walked back into the elevator and proceeded down to the main floor to the building entrance where the Sergeant at the Reception Desk was sitting.

"Sergeant, this is the new Receptionist. You are to hang around and get her trained," I said. Security for the General Staff was always a concern and the Receptionist was part of that security. "See that she does it correctly. Get another chair, stay here for a while, and get her started."

Mrs. Clarke sat down in the desk, and immediately squealed, "This chair is too hard. I want a softer chair than this." The chair was like every other chair in the building. There was no choice.

"OK, we will get you a different chair," I said.

"Where is the telephone?" said Mrs. Clarke.

"It will be here tomorrow," I said.

"What about paper and pencils," she asked.

"Look in the drawers," I said. And so it began.

25.5.   The Glass Partition

A few days later she called me to come down to Reception for a minute. She said, "You know, if I am a receptionist, my desk is out here in the open and anyone can just walk around me. I need a glass around my desk with a hole where I can shove a telephone through, pass a note, or talk with the visitor."

"Well, I will see what I can do to arrange it." I said. The Master Sergeant had never had a problem with no glass, I thought.

"Also my feet get cold here with the doors always opening and closing," she said.

"I will get you an electric heater that you can put under the desk," I said.

The woman was never satisfied. I wasn't sure who was working for whom.

Now glass cutting is not a skill the Army maintains in its Construction Engineers Battalion, so we had to find an Aussie glass cutter. I called up a local glass cutter, and I told him I was calling from Gen. MacArthur's Headquarters. We had a job that needed to be done. We would appreciate it if he could take care of it.

The glass cutter replied in a typical laid back Aussie way, "Well, you know I do jobs when I get to them. I do them as they come to me. You don't come ahead of anybody else."

"Don't you give Gen MacArthur any privilege?" I asked.

"Not at all," he said. "It will be a couple of weeks before I can get to it."

I told Mrs. Clarke, "He will do the best he can."

The glass cutter had to order the glass, so after a couple of weeks he came over to the office to measure what he needed. There was much discussion about what the glass would rest upon, the desk or the floor. Finally it was decided it would go straight to the floor, and wrap all around the desk. It had to have a hole in the front. The cutter did a good job and had fixed it up pretty well. We even found an electric heater that would fit under the desk.

25.6.   Mrs. Clarke's Nickname – "Bessie-Marie"

The relationship between Gen. Sutherland and Mrs. Clarke was common knowledge within GHQ. Rumors circulated about Gen. Sutherland's male prowess and his sleeping with Mrs. Clarke on a regular basis. Col. Egeberg, MacArthur's doctor and aide, was quoted as saying "Sutherland was screwing the socks off her every night."[236]

Major Day in his diary referred to the Receptionist as "Mrs. Clarke," but in his oral history, she was always "Bessie-Marie." Bessie-Marie may be a slang variation on the name "Bessemer." It is unknown if this was a name used "to her face" or in slang "behind her back." It could be either. The author has never located any written document where the name, Bessie-Marie, appeared in print.

25.7.   The AMP Lobby Remodel

Well, it wasn't much longer before I got another call. "The glass wasn't quite enough," she said. Bessie thought the desk was too low for her to greet visitors – she wanted to look the visitor in the eye from her desk. She wanted a small platform to elevate the desk about six inches off the floor, and the platform really needed to be carpeted. "I like that good thick carpet," she instructed holding up her hand to show a distance of about three

---

[236] William Manchester, *American Caesar*, Little Brown and Company, 1978, p. 349.

or four inches between her thumb and forefinger. That would elevate the platform about ten inches off the floor.

So I called up the Base Engineer. He was a full Colonel. I guess I had been using him a lot lately for other jobs around the office, so much so I had pretty much burned out my welcome.

"Colonel, this is Major Day," I said. *Colonel Sverdrup was Chief of Construction, which included air fields, hospitals, barracks, roads, everything. He was consumed with construction in New Guinea and Australia. The AMP building was a long way down his priority list.*

"OK, what's up now?" he replied with a note of sarcasm.

"Well, we need to have a platform built in the lobby. We want to raise the Reception Desk about six to eight inches, plus carpet on the floor. It may take about a 15 or 16 yards of carpet?"   Carpet in Brisbane was VERY expensive, perhaps £15 a yard (£1=about $3 in 1942).

"Major, do you know I have to take a carpenter off building the hospital to do this?" said the Colonel with a tone of anger in his voice.

"Colonel, I don't know about your problems, I just have to get the job done. Now if you want to complain about it, you can call Col. Fitch, Gen Casey, the Chief of Staff or anybody you want to, but I have to get the job done," I said.

"I ain't calling nobody. I'll get the job done," said the Colonel.

So in a few days the carpenter came over, brought the lumber, and built a platform that was about so high. The carpet was put on top, and the carpet did cost £15 a yard. I saw the bill. We put the desk on top of the new carpeted platform.

25.8.   A Second Receptionist's Desk

Well, guess what, Bessie-Marie thought the old desk did not look right on the new platform. "I need a little bigger desk," she said.

"Let me see what I can do," I said. By this time the woman was really getting on my nerves.

I had a meeting with the Base Engineer and the carpenter to discuss the desk. We showed him about how big the desk needed to be. The carpenter actually built a new larger desk for her that I thought was very nice, but of course the glass now did not fit the new larger desk. We had to go through the whole glass procurement cycle again.

Glass cutter took a little longer this time to do the new glass shelter, but I thought we were finally in business.

Wednesday, 12 August to 22 August 1942
There is a lapse in the diary entries. A separate typed page was inserted into the diary.

The following is to be placed in my diary as of the above date and up and until about the 26th or 27th:

Due to my feelings and several other things during and about this time I have intentionally neglected writing daily in this book.[237] Firstly, because I know so little and secondly because what I had to say was of very little interest. In order to try to get back in the harness and write daily, I must make a clear start.

Needless to say, the war in the Solomon Islands has been in high gear and things are really on the go. With fresh landings and fights that are at present in progress, we cannot say just what the score really is.

I have had a terrible sore throat and my gums have been sore. The doctor says I do not have trench mouth, but something is wrong. I am still waiting to see what will develop. It has now been about three weeks of it all and I am plenty sore. It even hurts to eat a piece of toast, so I think I will let the doctor go to hell for a few days. I will try to let things rest, and see if they will get better by themselves.

I received a mass of letters on about 18 Aug 1942 and then a few more a few days later. All in all, I have had about thirty letters in the past several days and have answered several of them and have done quite well by the long ones I have written. I have taken a lot of pictures that I will have some day. The pictures should be very interesting to see. I am still anxiously waiting to hear that all my things that I sent home have arrived safely in good shape.

---

[237] It appears that the arrival of the female Receptionist has so completely disturbed Maj. Day that he has temporarily stopped writing his diary.

We have had two air raid alarms in the past week and of course there was nothing to either. It is a lot of fun to see these people take cover. They are really scared. When the alarm sounded yesterday, I was in a store in the process of picking up some pictures I had made. The clerk told me to come back later, because he was closing up. All my talking didn't make any difference to him. In only a very few minutes the streets were cleared with exception of some of the soldiers. Those who had been in air raids pay little attention to them at first. Only when the planes are above is it time to move. I doubt that we will have a raid here in Brisbane until the situation changes in the Solomon Islands. Things look pretty tough at the present time most everywhere, and that's no bull. Love and kisses. John

Sunday, 23 August 1942

I received nine letters this morning from everyone including even Merle and EP [Bennett]. Sure makes you feel swell to get them and better to read them. Lt. Evans and I went to the prize fights again Friday night, as we have done every Friday night for last four weeks. Gen. Marquat was there too. It was the first time I had seen him at the fights, but there have been other officers there. My gums started bleeding the other day, so I went back to the dentist. He said it was like trench mouth, but not trench mouth. He made a slide to see. Anyway, he has treated them for several days and now they are sore. I have cut down on my smoking. Gosh, I was smoking too much.

August 24-25, 1942 – Battle of the Eastern Solomon Islands
*Two U.S. carriers (*USS Saratoga *and* USS Enterprise*) engaged two Japanese carriers (Shkaku and Zuikaku) in the third naval carrier engagement of the war after the Battle of the Coral Sea and the Battle of Midway. The Japanese were attempting to reinforce their troops on Guadalcanal while the U.S. carriers were providing air cover for the American invasion force. During the resulting naval battle, the USS Enterprise was badly damaged. The Japanese lost significantly more aircraft than the Americans and the Japanese troop reinforcements were delayed in reaching Guadalcanal. Neither side could claim a clear victory; however, the delay of Japanese troop reinforcements to Guadalcanal was considered a strategic victory for the Americans.*

Thursday, 27 August 1942

My throat is a little sore, and my gums are still sore. I feel bad. I'm tired, and I don't give a damn. I'm getting along fine with all as far as I know. I have been busy as a cat on a tin roof all day. I ate very little dinner, but think I'll eat some supper. Had telegram from Jim Daye in Melbourne telling me my kangaroo hides had been shipped, so I should have them soon.

I have been so full of nervous energy that I can't seem to sit still long enough to write. I brought my diary to the office so I could be sure and write. It seems that when I get home at night, I just won't sit down and write. After reading the paper and eating dinner, it is usually 9 or 9:30 PM if I eat at the hotel. If I am going back to the office, I usually eat at "Shingle Inn" which is fair. Nothing new so will close. All my love.

Friday, 28 August 1942

I went to the dispensary to see the dentist again. My gums on one side are sore, so by golly I knew something was wrong. Finally, after a thorough exam he said he thought I had a touch of trench mouth in one place, so I am on the ball to get rid of it. Don't know where I got it, but guess in one of these filthy cafes or drug stores. It is positively ridiculous. Well from now on I am using straws.

I have a few more pictures, and I am getting them put in a book. Last night, Lt. Van Akin from Melbourne was up visiting on a 10-day leave, so he and I went to a show and saw James Cagney in "Captains of the Clouds"[238] along with a lot of other stuff. It passed the time and that's about all I could say. He also stayed in my room and was sleeping when I left in the morning.

Saturday, 29 August 1942

Well, Worthington wants tomorrow off to go to Southport and go swimming. Evans wants to go hunting ducks. So I guess Laughlin and I will work in the morning. Laughlin wants to play tennis tomorrow evening. I presume I will work. There shouldn't be a lot to do, however. I started to write a letter but know very little to say so will wait until tomorrow. My clothes are shrinking fast. It seems every time they are laundered, they get smaller. Well, of course I do weigh more than I did. I am still sitting most of the day, so you know how it is.

The Japs made a landing on the tip of New Guinea[239] where we have a bunch of Aussies, and certainly they should be able to take care of the situation. The headlines say they are having a hard time, so guess that means in tomorrow's paper they were pushed back by superior forces. These damn people are crazy as hell, I think and at other times crazier. It all seems a joke, I think not to all.

I have been invited out to some doctor's house for Tea tonight at 7 PM. I may go.

25.9.   The Great Deer Hunt Adventure – 5 - 6 Sep 1942

The Diary is missing a week of entries at the time of the deer hunt, but a letter describes the hunt:

---

[238] "Captains of the Clouds," 1942 Warner Brothers, James Cagney's first Technicolor movie.
[239] Milne Bay, Oro, New Guinea 27-29 Aug 1942.

Tuesday, 8 Sep 1942

Letter

Dearest Cile and Johnnie, Mother and Dad:

Needless to say that I have not written in several days but you absolutely cannot write a blank all the time. I guess I would fuss a lot more than you would when I fail to get letters, honey, you are always better than I am when it comes to things of that kind. I was going to write yesterday and was busy all the day and finally got to bed about 11PM and certainly did not feel like writing then.

As I have some news to tell you this time, I will start now and tell you of my hunting trip. On Saturday morning, I received permission from my boss [*Gen. Stivers*], in other words a VOCO,[240] that I could have Saturday evening and Sunday off to go hunting, and did I go!

With two Australians in the office, we drove inland about 100 miles near where one of them comes from.[241] We left Brisbane about 1 PM Saturday and arrived at the destination about 8 PM.

Actually we stopped on the road and shot some ducks, which we cleaned and fixed two of them into a duck stew for breakfast Sunday morning. We shot six ducks, three of which I shot and two of them were out of the air. I was using that famous 12-gauge automatic which I love to shoot. I was using number three shot. I killed one wood duck and two black ducks. They were the first wood ducks I had ever seen. They were very good for morning stew too.

Before going to bed Saturday night, we went out with a flashlight (torch to the Australians), and I shot a flying fox, the first of those I had ever seen too. I have seen flying squirrels before, but never a flying fox. Well, this bloke had a wing spread of about three feet. The animal is really a fox too with a head, a body, gives birth to babies, suckles its young, and flies in the air. He gets around like a bat but is not one. You can see its eyes at night when they sparkle.[242]

---

[240] VOCO is a military term that stands for a Verbal Order of the Commanding Officer.

[241] The deer hunting most likely took place about 50 - 80 miles west northwest of Brisbane near the towns of Toogoolawah and Esk where the English settlers had introduced deer for meat and sport. This is a very mountainous region where the deer acclimated very well and multiplied. Some of the old families who lived in this area must have extended their hospitality to the Yanks for the hunting expedition.

[242] Actually, the flying fox is the largest "bat" in the world, *Genus Pteropses*. They use eyesight rather than echo location as they fly at night.

We finally went to sleep about 11 PM or maybe midnight. They said I snored. Can you imagine that? I told them I never did that before [a complete lie]. The snoring was probably caused from my walking about three miles that evening, which I was not accustomed to.

We waked up about 5 AM Sunday, and they said it was very late. We started eating stew, which was very good. I really filled up knowing that we were to walk a lot in the mountains. We drove out a ways and finally left the car about 8AM. We were off for a walk over the roughest ground that white man ever trod. My poor feet were catching merry hell, up one hill and down another.

It was about 11 AM and we had not seen any water to drink. In fact, the Aussies could not find water to boil their "Billy tea." My two Australian companions had to have their tea. They carry a "billycan" around their belt to boil their tea even out in the outback. It is just a damn nuisance to me, but I was their guest, so of course we took the time. Then all was OK.

Well about noon we found a stream with water that "almost ran," which was their measure of freshness, but they decided to pass. There was another stream a little further along where the water looked OK. Did I take a big drink! We boiled the Billy tea, ate a baloney sandwich, and enjoyed a piece of cake. By golly, anything would have tasted good at that time.

Soon thereafter, I saw a couple of deer on the opposite hill and took a shot. They were so far I couldn't get the deer in the site of the gun (or whatever excuse I could tell). Anyway they were too far to hit I guess.

I shot a 'roo, as I wanted to see if I could hit one. I actually shot him through the neck and he dropped stone dead. Some shot if you ask me. Well, I could have shot several of them but was always afraid that I would scare the deer should they be in the vicinity. We were on a very steep hill and probably five miles from the car when we jumped up several deer. I cut down one and rolled him. He rolled

Figure 104 - Dead kangaroo

about 350 feet down a hill before he stopped rolling near the bottom. I also took a shot at another deer and thought I hit him, but he did not fall.

Then on the other hill about three hundred yards away, I saw one was running, so I shot and knocked him down. He must have rolled about fifty yards. Was I a happy lad! Boy, shooting two in almost one moment. Well, one Aussie had a sitting shot and his gun jammed, so you see he undoubtedly would have had something. The second Aussie was to the rear and missed out. Otherwise we would have certainly had more.

We went down the steep hill to where the first deer rested. I shot him through the head, and he died instantly. We decided that we would go up the other hill and drag the second deer down in the shade where the first one was lying. We would then skin them both.

When we got to the place where the second deer lay, I was worn out from climbing the hill. We decided that we would skin that deer on the spot, which we did. The two deer were so big that I knew we could not carry them all back to the car. It was about five miles to walk back, and there was not a chance to get the car closer as the terrain was too rough. After cutting off all quarters, I decided that that was all I could lift, much less carry. I decided that I was going to carry all that I could with me and give it to the men.

We then skinned the other deer and also cut off the legs. I am sure we had 150 pounds of meat and the two hides. We cut a pole that we could put through the legs and with the two hind quarters on the back and the two front ones in the front and the hide around the pole, I began the walk. One of the other fellows carried the guns and the billy cans. The other Aussie carried the same as I carried. At first I could walk about a hundred yards before I would give out.

Page 2

We were on the side of a rocky hill and I knew I had a couple of blisters on each foot by that time but was afraid to look. We would sit every time I thought we had walked a couple of miles. Anyway we arrived at the car about three hours later. I have never been so hot and so tired.

Figure 105 - Aussie with Roo

I took a movie of the hides, and boy they were both perfect as both were shot through the head. That will happen once in a lifetime probably. I also took a picture of one of the men holding the hams the way we carried them.

It was just starting to rain. We knew if we did not get to hell out of there quick, we would have to stay for the duration of the rain. We started walking as it rained. After we got to the car, we drove about ten miles down the road when my Aussie friends said we had to stop. My companions had to stop for a beer. I slipped to a store next door and ate a couple of ice creams. We arrived back to their place about 10 PM that night. We were still about 100 miles away from Brisbane.

To top off the trip, on the way home the muffler came loose and had to be fixed. I fixed it by lying down in the mud, crawling under the car, and tying it up. I did not care about dirt by then, as we were already filthy. Well, the damn thing came loose a second time, but it was a wonder it did not break. Once more I tied it up, and maybe did a little better job than the first time. It lasted the remainder of the trip.

I forgot to say, I brought home the Roo Tail to make soup for a few that have never tasted it.

When we got back to town, I had the mess hall cooks clean the meat. I ended up with between 125 and maybe 150 pounds of meat. When carrying it, I thought it was 200 pounds. I have the meat on ice, and in about a week, we will serve some of John Day's venison to all the men. This pleases me very much.

I told Gen. Stivers all about the trip and am going to take him over to the mess hall for lunch on the day we serve it. All have asked me about the trip, and none seem to think that deer get as big as they do here in Australia. I would not hesitate in saying that some possibly weighed 300 pounds.

My trip was entirely a success, and I certainly enjoyed it. It will be some day before I forget the trip. I am only sorry that I could not have had some of you along to be with me and do some shooting too. There is plenty to shoot. My marksmanship was what you call "superb," heh?

Love, John

Thursday, 1 Oct 1942

> Letter to Cile
> Dear Cile and Johnnie:
>
> By the way, I see Mc is wondering about the deer I killed. There were two, and yesterday I went out to see how the tanning was coming. They will be finished Monday or Tuesday. They are tanned in a brown color like the leather jackets here. They sure look nice. I am sending them and the snake hide to you. I guess you will have to keep them till we find something we want to make out of them. The roo hide is being tanned with the hair on it and will be ready in another week probably. Be sure and show Mc what kind of a deer and (not a dear) that I killed. I tell you when you get to a good spot, there are so many wallaby and roo to shoot, that it is a real sport.
>
> As to the other kind of "dear," I could say that there are nothing here like the pretty girls that are at home. I guess the censor will pass that anyway. It may be that the mixture we have at home makes the difference. Most everyone here works at something. Some drive for other outfits, not this one.
>
> I am a little afraid Mc and Ruth are trying to kid me or are you darling? If I wrote anything at all about anything of that nature, I am sure someone would try to make fun, kid or at least have something to say.
>
> Tell Mc I am spending all the money I make on Aussie women so that I don't even seem to have enough to pay for my clothes. You can tell that is true by the approximately $2,400 that I sent to you in the past four months that I have not spent here.

8 Sep 1942 – Malaria - Letter to Cile

> Johnnie, I have been worried about your being sick and with malaria too. I am going to wire tomorrow and hope to hear that you are OK. Honey, See that he gets the best care. I know you will. Did Johnnie sell some more bonds?

Tuesday, 8 Sep 1942, - diary

No news. I wrote two long pages to Cile. She is better than I am about writing, but I have had so little to write. I really did my stuff on this one and will save it for the mail plane in the next couple of days. We all try to catch the planes when we can. I have not received many letters of late. Guess the things will come in spells as usual. I am worried about Johnnie being sick. I will call tomorrow to find out. Good night and all my love. John

Wednesday, 9 September 1942

Today has been a fast one. No news. Things in general in New Guinea don't look too good. The Aussies seem to be getting pushed back just as the papers had boosted them up. I can't understand it. They should cover the holes, you know. I just wrote a long letter to Cile. Also I sent a copy of the letter to Mother and Dad, another letter to Pete Daniels, and answer to his letter. It is 7:25 PM and I have to eat. Boy, can I eat tonight. I tried on my new shirts today, and they fit like I thought they would. I will not get them for a few more days, I guess. Love and kisses. Hope Johnnie is better now.

Thursday, 10 September 1942

It seems odd that I have not been keeping this diary daily, as I did in the past, however, I must say that the daily happenings here are normal and practically all alike. Normal routine and writing the same thing all the time certainly gets monotonous and probably worse to read. I have taken spells and tried to write a typewritten sheet and place it in the book. Have added quite a collection of pictures to my list since starting, and with lots of luck, I will bring them home.

I know the fight in New Guinea at the present is going badly for us. Quite a lot of people fail to understand what we are fighting and the details about our equipment etc. Really it is a tough fight. It's bad that all cannot realize how hard a fight we have. Lots of tactics used today are the same as the Indians used many years ago and people seem to never learn. Have just seen one of the complete sets of jungle equipment and from what I gather, it is the only set in Australia. Too bad we need lots of it. I like the carbine rifle fine. Wish I had one.

September 22, 1942 - Malaria

> I would be sure and have Dr. Woodard look at Johnnie after he has finished the medicine. Malaria seems to come back quite often. I have had some men who were well and then a couple or three weeks later, they would have to return to the hospital.
>
> You have not mentioned any more about Johnnie selling bonds. How many did he sell in all? How many have you bought?

September 24, 1942 - Java Trunk Arrives

> Glad you liked my taste on all the things I sent home. Most of all, I am very glad that the trunks got home. From all reports that I was able to obtain, I thought that the first trunks would never get there, but one good surprise in a lifetime is OK. Some trip too – from Java through the Panama Canal to Brooklyn Navy Yard, and then to Texas in seven months.

26.   FIRST SIGN OF CILE'S MEDICAL PROBLEM – SEP 1942

Beginning in late 1942 Maj. Day began to receive letters making him aware that Cile was having medical problems. His requests for information directly to Cile went unanswered. The following are excerpts from his early letters to both Cile and his parents:

Sept 25, 1942 (Brisbane)- Cile Sees Doctor

Dear Cile and Johnnie
Well, I see you have been to see the doctor. I wonder what's the trouble? I would sure like to know and wonder if it is something that we had before. From the way you mentioned it, I couldn't tell?

January 17, 1943 (Brisbane) – Are you feeling better?

Dear Cile and Johnnie
I hope the doctor is doing you some good after all you have been trying to get done. Are you feeling better or not?

Feb 16, 1943 (Brisbane) – Tuesday night

Dear Mom and Dad:
I think Cile is getting very tired of my being gone and seems to be showing it in her letters. I think she is probably a little dissatisfied in some way.

Really I think she would have been better off to have a house of her own and probably would have been just as cheap. I think she would have been better about it that way. However, I think her being near the rest of the family has certain advantages for her. It makes very little difference to me, however, I have felt at times that she has spent lots of money some way but I would not dare tell her any more than I have as I really do not know all the circumstances. I feel sure she is doing the best she can under condi-tions. I suppose you have read some of the things I

Figure 106 - Cile Day, Bonham, 1943

have told her what I thought about the funds. Well you need not mention it further to her as I still feel she will do better this year than in the past year. She has experienced many things she has not had to deal with before.

Major Day was never aware of the extent of medical expenses that Cile was paying.

27.   NEW GUINEA CAMPAIGN GOES BADLY – SEPT 1942

27.1.   Kokoda Trail War (Continued) – 13 Sep 1942

On the night of 13/14 Sep 1942, both the Australian and the Japanese troops along the Kokoda Trail were on the verge of exhaustion. The Australians had been pushed back across mountains toward Port Moresby. Horii's troops were dug in along Imita Ridge near Ioribaiwa, about 12 km (7 miles) from Port Moresby. The Japanese soldiers could see the lights of the Port Moresby and the Coral Sea beyond. They could taste victory. Although victory was within their grasp, the Japanese were exhausted and had been without food for some time. Horii was questioning whether his troops would be physically able to hold the positions they occupied. He had over-extended his supply line that chained across the mountains over the Kokoda Trail back to Buna. His supplies of food and ammunition were breaking down.

On this day the Australian battle-hardened reinforcements from the Mid-East finally arrived to support the exhausted and battle-weary Australians along the Kokoda Trail, but other war developments caused the new Australians to never be tested by the Japanese.

27.2.   Japanese Guadalcanal Loss – 14 Sep 1942

On 14 Sept 1942 on Guadalcanal, the Japanese experienced a major defeat when their counterattack failed to recapture Henderson Field. In this Guadalcanal battle over 800 Japanese died while only 100 Americans died. Following the Guadalcanal loss, the Imperial High Command in Tokyo decided that Japan did not have enough men and supplies to support campaigns in both New Guinea and Guadalcanal. Tokyo decided that their remaining supplies and reinforcements should be sent to Guadalcanal rather than New Guinea.

Horii was informed that there would be no more reinforcements and no more supplies for him in New Guinea. He was ordered to withdraw back to the Buna-Gona beachhead until the Guadalcanal situation became resolved. The Japanese language has no word for "retreat," so Horii ordered his troops "to advance back down the mountain" to the Buna beachhead. His troops continued to fight a strong delaying battle with the Aussies. It would be almost three weeks before the Australians would realize the Japanese were withdrawing.

Horii dispatched his engineers back to the Buna beachhead to construct military fortifications for the defense of Buna. He had no intention of surrendering control of Buna. These fortifications included a series of interconnected bunkers built from coconut trees providing well-camouflaged machine gun emplacements.

27.3.   American Flanking Attack on Kokoda Trail – October 1942

On <u>4 Oct 1942,</u> Gen. MacArthur personally visited New Guinea to meet with Gen. Blamey. MacArthur and Blamey had no knowledge of the Japanese decision to withdraw, but were concerned about how to quickly remove the Japanese from the mountains in order to capture Buna. Allied supplies were a focus of discussion, which led to a reorganization of supply channels that consolidated the Australian and American supply under a single command. Most supplies were being airdropped. Success had been notoriously poor. In 1942, the technology of air drops was primitive in both navigation and bundle preparation. Many drops were lost in the jungle and upon impact many packages simply burst. Further, there was a shortage of C-47 aircraft to execute the necessary air drops.

MacArthur's solution to clear the Japanese was to attack them from their flank in the mountains. His plan was to deploy the untested US 32nd Infantry Division to attack the Japanese from the east. For this, he needed to identify another trail through the mountains. Military maps of New Guinea in 1942 were poor. A trail recommended by GHQ in Australia was found to be totally impractical.

Secretly, Gen. Casey and Col. Sverdrup, the two top military engineers, were called upon <u>personally</u> to undertake three covert survey treks across the Owen Stanley Range behind Japanese lines to map trails and find an alternative to the Kokoda Trail. They also measured the water depth in harbors in the Buna-Gona area for a possible amphibious attack as an alternative to the mountain trail. Gen. Casey and Col. Sverdrup were later awarded the Silver Star for their efforts. They identified a 130-mile-alternative trail, called the Kappa Kappa Trail, which would by-pass the 69-mile Kokoda Trail through the mountains. The strategy was that the alternate trail should allow the 32nd Division to strike the Japanese from the side.

27.4.   Advanced Echelon of GHQ Moves to Port Moresby – 6 Nov 42

Brisbane remained MacArthur's GHQ, but as the combat activities grew in New Guinea, the generals began to travel often to the front to confer with the combat commanders and to inspect the battle situation. To support the general's visits to the combat zone, GHQ established an Advanced Echelon to provide food, housing, and administrative support for the generals while they were in the combat zone.

The Advanced Echelon was the responsibility of the GHQ Headquarters Commandant and was an extension of Headquarters Company. The Advanced Echelon started as a small detail in Port Moresby, but rapidly grew to a Company of men. In time it represented about 10% of the GHQ Headquarters Company.

Government House

The Advanced Echelon was set up in Government House, the former residence of the Australian-appointed Governor-General of Papua New Guinea, which at that time was a Protectorate under Australia. Government House was a complex of three buildings around an outdoor covered court yard. The facility provided reception space, office space, bedrooms, kitchen and an open veranda for dining and conversation. M/Sgt. Paul Rogers, Sutherland's stenographer, in his memoir describes the facility as covered with "tropical vines and bushes clustered around and festooned over the building. Blazes of red and fuchsia flowers filled the air with fragrance. Palm trees and bushes surround the building."[243] According to Rogers, the House had a well-furnished library of English classics that provided Rogers with hours of leisure entertainment.

A resident staff of native housekeepers, cooks, gardeners, and servants supported the maintenance of the facility. When the Americans moved in, a supporting staff of security guards, drivers and vehicles were added.

Maj. Day said "Most of my men were in Brisbane, but I always had a smaller operation in the forward headquarters. As the battle front moved up along the north coast, more of GHQ shifted forward."

After I left GHQ, many of the "behind-the-scene shenanigans of Bessie-Marie" dealt with activities at these advanced headquarters with Sutherland in either Port Moresby or Hollandia, but we will come to that.

As the combat zone moved up the north coast of New Guinea, the Advanced Echelon of GHQ also move forward, eventually reaching Hollandia in Dutch New Guinea in Sept 1944. [244] Before the Leyte invasion in October 1944, the MacArthur Command was divided –when MacArthur moved into the Philippines with the combat forces, first to Tolosa (south of Tacloban, Leyte, PI), and eventually Manila (PI), Sutherland remained in Hollandia and took command of the rear echelon American forces.

---

[243] Rogers, *The Good Years*, pg. 326-327.

[244] Although Indonesia won independence from Holland in 1949, Dutch New Guinea was not transferred to Indonesia until 1961. The name, Hollandia, Dutch New Guinea, existed from 1910 to 1962. It was then briefly known as Kota Baru and Sukarnopura before becoming Jayapura City, capital of Papua, Indonesia, in 1968.

27.5.   U.S. 32nd Infantry Division Is Deployed New Guinea – 15 Sep 42

Churchill agreed to allow the diversion of a second US Division to Australia in exchange for leaving Australian (AIF) troops in the Middle East. The 32nd Infantry Division (the Wisconsin and Michigan National Guard), known as the Red Arrow Division, was at Ft. Devens, Massachusetts beginning to ship out to Northern Ireland.[245] At the last moment the unit was redirected to Australia, arriving at Port Adelaide on 14 May 1942.[246] The 32nd would join the 41st (Washington State and Montana National Guard) which was already assigned to Australia. Both units expected to be employed in the defense of Australia.

The 32nd Division had been activated on 15 October 1940, and had participated in the Louisiana maneuvers in the summer of 1941. Although the unit was authorized 11,600 soldiers, it had about 10,000 including 3,000 new troops that had just completed basic training. The unit had no combat experience, was poorly equipped, and was trained for European warfare. Military equipment for jungle warfare was still in the United States. The new light-weight M-2 Carbine was not yet in Australia, so the 32nd was equipped with the heavier M-1 Garand rifle. They were sent to Queensland to Camp Tamborine, about 30 miles south of Brisbane in July 1942 to begin training for jungle warfare. One month later, the camp was renamed Camp Cable, in honor of a GI who died in a torpedo attack on the way to Australia, becoming the first war casualty in the 32nd Division. Two months later they were deployed to New Guinea.

On 15 Sept 1942, the 128th Infantry Regiment of the 32nd Infantry Division was flown to Port Moresby, New Guinea in the first mass troop movement by air in World War II. . The 126th Infantry Regiment traveled to New Guinea from Australia by ship.

On 14 Oct 1942, two battalions of the 128th Infantry Regiment left Port Moresby on a 130-mile movement across the Owen Stanley Range on foot to flank and surprise the Japanese from the east. This was the first American troop engagement in New Guinea and proved to be the only American troops to cross the mountains by foot.

After a 42-day trek across the mountains, the 128th Infantry Regiment made first contact with the Japanese on 16 Nov 1942[247] and joined the Australians who had been engaged for so many months.

---

[245] In fact, the Engineer unit of the 32nd Infantry Division had already shipped out to Europe when the order to Australia arrived. A substitute Engineer Unit had to be located to accompany the 32nd Division to Australia.

[246] See Section 13.1, p.164 of this book.

[247] Samuel Milner, U.S. Army History of World War II in the Pacific, OCMH *Victory in Papua* said combat began 16 Nov 1942.

Seven days later on 23 Nov 1942, *Japanese Maj. Gen Tomitaro Horii drowned in an accident while crossing the Kumusi River (near Kokoda Trail) when the raft he occupied overturned. He would be replaced by Gen. Hatazo Adachi.*

27.5.1.   The Battle of Buna, Gona, & Sanananda – 16 Nov 42 – 2 Jan 43

The next six weeks proved to be one of the bloodiest periods in the New Guinea campaign, and one that has sparked more controversy than many other battles during the war. The combat at Buna was vicious. The Japanese Engineers had constructed heavy reinforced bunkers made from coconut trees. These bunkers were interconnected by a catacomb of passages that allowed safe movement of ammunition. Further, the Japanese were fighting to their death.

Buna was captured 2 Jan 1942 and Sanananda captured 22 Jan 1942.

The following is a quotation taken from Samuel Milner in the identified source:[248]

> *Australian losses had been so heavy that brigade after brigade had seen its battalions reduced to company strength and less before it was relieved. But if the Australian units had suffered severe attrition, so had the 32d Division. General Eichelberger put the situation to General MacArthur in a sentence. "Regiments here," he wrote in mid-January, "soon have the strength of battalions and a little later are not much more than companies." The casualty reports bear out General Eichelberger's observation. Out of their total strength in the combat zone of 10,825, the three combat teams of the 32d Division had suffered 9,688 casualties, including 7,125 sick, **a casualty rate of almost 90 percent.** The 126th Infantry, hardest-hit of the three, had 131 officers and 3,040 enlisted men when it entered the combat zone in mid-November. When it was evacuated to Port Moresby on 22 January, 32 officers and 579 enlisted men were left--less than a full battalion. The regiment as such had ceased to exist.*

> *All together 3,095 Australians and Americans lost their lives in the campaign, and 5,451 were wounded. Total battle casualties were 8,546.[g] These statistics are before malaria, dysentery, dengue fever, and other diseases took another 2,000 casualties.*

> *The figures given are for the entire Papuan Campaign, including the period 22 July through 16 November, in which the Australians lost 2,127 killed, wounded, and missing. Combined Australian-American casualties for the fighting at the beachhead, the last*

---

[248] Samuel Milner, U.S. Army in World War II, OCMH, *The War in the Pacific, Victory in Papua, New Guinea.* Chapter XIX, The Victory, pages 369-378.

phase of operations, were 6,419 killed, wounded, and missing. **There were 2,701 more casualties in the Papuan Campaign than on Guadalcanal,** *where 1,600 were killed, and 4,245 were wounded, but there, during much of the fighting, the positions were reversed: the Japanese were attacking, and the Americans were holding a fortified position.*

The following is a quotation from: Australia Commonwealth Military Force Report, **Battles of WWII, The Buna, Gona & Sanananda Campaigns,**

> *The Allied forces were to take heavily fortified Japanese positions at Buna, on New Guinea's southeast coast. It proved to be one of the most difficult campaigns of the war. Fighting in the hot, steamy jungles, the 32d was desperately short of basic equipment, weapons, medicine and even food. In the terrible heat and drenching rain the men of the 32d, many of them burning with fever, had to reduce Japanese positions one at a time, usually by rushing them with grenades. Most of the Japanese fought to the death, but finally, on 2 January 1943, Buna fell.*

> *It was the Japanese Army's first defeat in modern history, but for the 32d Division the cost was high: 1,954 were either killed or wounded, with 2,952 hospitalized due to disease. After Buna, the 32nd participated in the long campaign to drive the Japanese from the rest of New Guinea, and went on to see heavy fighting in the Philippines.*

TIMELINE

July 21-22, 1942 – Japanese seized Buna-Gona beachhead.

Nov 6, 1942 – Advanced Echelon of GHQ moves to Port Moresby, New Guinea.
Nov 16, 1942 – U.S. 32nd Red Arrow Division enters combat at Buna, New Guinea.

Jan. 2, 1943 - Allies take Buna in New Guinea.
Jan. 22, 1943 - Allies defeat Japanese at Sanananda on New Guinea.

2 Mar 1943 – Battle of Bismarck Sea.

4 Sep 1943 – Allies recapture Lae-Salamauna, New Guinea.

Sunday, February 7, 1943:

> Letter to Cile
> Even though it is true, it is hard to explain, but I believe there isn't any Individual sacri-
> fice to compare to a man that has to fight in the jungle. The conditions in which he has
> to fight are indescribable. When a man is in a hole and cannot see more than a few feet
> in any direction, expecting to shoot or be shot at any minute. Needless to say, it is a ter-
> rific strain on his nerves. I do not think it could be brought before the people [general
> public] strong enough to make them have any concept of the actual fact. I have been in
> there but much luckier than many others.

27.5.2.   MacArthur's Press Release

*In this press release, General MacArthur's headquarters announced that the losses had been low,
less than half those of the enemy, battle casualties and sick included. It gave as the reason for this
favorable result that there had been no need to hurry the attack because "the time element was in
this case of little importance." [249]*

*General Eichelberger[250] has written: "The statement to the correspondents in Brisbane after Buna
that 'losses were small because there was no hurry' was one of the great surprises of my life. As
you know, our Allied losses were heavy and as commander in the field, I had been told many
times of the necessity for speed."[251]*

*Buna damaged the relationship between Gen. MacArthur and Lt. Gen. Eichelberger, the field
commander of I Corps, which included the U.S. 32nd Red Arrow Division in New Guinea. In
Maj. Day's oral history, Day mentioned Gen. Eichelberger with respect and his strained relationship MacArthur.*

27.5.3.   Malaria, Dysentery, Dengue Fever, and Scrub Typhus

*In addition to jungle combat, the hot temperatures, the flooding rain, and the rough terrain, New
Guinea hosted an abundance of tropical diseases that were perhaps the greatest hazard to soldiers.
Malaria, dysentery, dengue fever, and scrub typhus were widespread and took more casualties
than combat. In 1942, medical knowledge of tropical diseases was primitive.*

---

249 Communiqué United Nations Headquarters, Australia, 28 Jan 43, in *The New York Times*, 29
Jan 1943.

250 Robert L. Eichelberger Lt. Gen. and Milton MacKaye, *Our Jungle Road to Tokyo*, Viking Press,
1950.

251 Lt., Gen Eichelberger to Paul Rogers, 8 Mar 54, OCMH files.

Malaria was the greatest health problem of all. Medical knowledge of malaria had been gained during the construction of the Panama Canal, but knowledge of how to prevent it or treat it had not spread widely. Most Army doctors had never come in contact with the disease nor been trained to deal with it. The disease is caused by a parasite that is spread by a mosquito bite. Before the War, quinine was the principal medicine used to treat the disease; and Java was the major producer of quinine for the world. With Java under Japanese control, the US and Australia had no supply of quinine. The Allies initiated a medical task force that focused American and British drug companies on a major program to produce two synthetic drugs, Atabrine and Plasmoquine, which were alternatives to quinine. However, this program did not begin producing drugs for SWPA until December 1942. Prior to the arrival of the synthetic drugs, there was an epidemic of malaria in New Guinea. Before the drug began to arrive, the Australian troops reported 4,000 battle casualties, 12,000 malaria casualties, and 2,000 additional casualties from other tropical diseases.[252]

Bacterial dysentery was perhaps the second greatest medical threat in New Guinea. It was caused by a breakdown in hygiene in the disposal of human waste and refuse. Flies were the usual sign of sanitation problems.

Dengue fever was another tropical disease caused by a virus that was transmitted by mosquitoes. Many issues for control of dengue fever were the same as for malaria.

Scrub typhus was spread by small mites that were found in the grass. If a soldier sat or lay down in mite-infested grass, the mites could attach themselves to the soldier and infect him. The incidence of scrub typhus was much less frequent than malaria and dysentery; however, typhus was much more lethal. Medical reports indicate that in 1942 in SWPA, 9% of the soldiers that contracted typhus died.

27.6.   No Entry in the Diary for Ten Weeks – 10 Sept 1942 to 26 Nov 1942

From September 10, 1942 until November 26, 1942 there are no entries in the diary. This is the period when American troops were being deployed in New Guinea and the Advanced Echelon of GHQ was being set up in Port Moresby (See Sec. 22.5.1. Battle of Buna). The war was keeping GHQ very busy. The next diary entry (26 Nov 1942) is made when he gets four days leave and goes to the beach at Southport.

---

[252] CEW Bean, *The Australian Army*, Sydney: Angus & Roberton, and unpublished thesis of University of New South Wales, *Australian Organisation, Logistics and Doctrine*, 23 Mar 2011.

The following V-mail letter was damaged when opened by the Censor, so there are many words missing. The "---" indicates the location where letters are missing. The letter is shown on the following page.

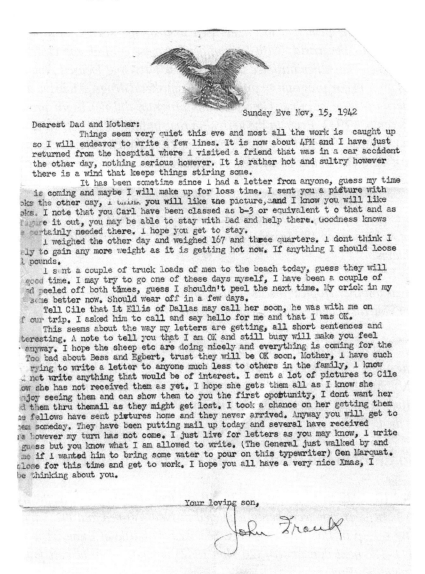

Sunday Eve Nov, 15, 1942

Dearest Dad and Mother:

Things seem very quiet this eve and most all the work is caught up so I will endeavor to write a few lines. It is now about 4PM and I have just returned from the hospital where I visited a friend that was in a car accident the other day, nothing serious however. It is rather hot and sultry however there is a wind that keeps things stiring some.

It has been sometime since I had a letter from anyone, guess my time is coming and maybe I will make up for loss time. I sent you a picture with ---oks the other day, I think you will like the picture, and I know you will like ---oks. I note that you Carl have been classed as b-3 or equivalent t o that and as --- figure it out, you may be able to stay with Dad and help there. Goodness knows --- certainly needed there. I hope you get to stay.

I weighed the other day and weighed 167 and three quarters. I dont think I ---ly to gain any more weight as it is getting hot now. If anything I should loose --- pounds.

I sent a couple of truck loads of men to the beach today, guess they will --- good time. I may try to go one of these days myself, I have been a couple of --- peeled off both times, guess I shouldn't peel the next time. My crick in my --- some better now. Should wear off in a few days.

Tell Cile that Lt Ellis of Dallas may call her soon, he was with me on --- f our trip. I asked him to call and say hello for me and that I was OK.

This seems about the way my letters are getting, all short sentences and ---teresting. A note to tell you that I am OK and still busy will make you feel --- anyway. I hope the sheep etc are doing nicely and everything is coming for the --- Too bad about Bess and Egbert, trust they will be OK soon. Mother, I have such --- rying to write a letter to anyone much less to others in the family, I know --- not write anything that would be of interest. I sent a lot of pictures to Cile ---ow she has not received them as yet. I hope she gets them all as I know she ---njoy seeing them and can show them to you the first opportunity, I dont want her --- d them thru themail as they might get lost. I took a chance on her getting them ---e fellows have sent pictures home and they never arrived. Anyway you will get to ---em someday. They have been putting mail up today, and several have received ---s however my turn has not come. I just live for letters as you may know, I write ---guess but you know what I am allowed to write. (The General just walked by and ---me if I wanted him to bring some water to pour on this typewriter) Gen Marquat. ---lose for this time and get to work. I hope you all have a very nice Xmas, I --- be thinking about you.

Your loving son,

John Frank

Figure 107 - Censored Letter (November 15, 1942)

Figure 108 - Example of Censored Envelope

November 23-24, 1942 – Japanese air raid on Darwin, Australia

Thursday, 26 Nov 1942

I am in Southport tonight to begin four days leave. I had one of the drivers bring me down. By a phone call from Brisbane, I learned they had another big "gang" fight between the Aussies and U.S. Don't know all the damage, but guess the Aussies will eventually learn to respect our MPs as several got shot.

Friday, 27 Nov 1942

About 20 Aussies were wounded, one killed, and a few not expected to live. One of our captains was dragged out of a cafe and beat to death. Thank God, I am gone. Quite a few officers were beat up. As the Aussies have a few thousand more in town than ourselves, all we can do is shoot. Those bastards are crazy with jealousy of the U.S. troops.

*26-27 Nov 1942 – **Battle of Brisbane** was a physical brawl that lapsed over two nights between the service men of the US Army and the Australian military. Although the two Armies were close allies in the battle with Japan, certain jealousies developed between the Aussie and Americans over pay, privileges, and particularly the attention of the Australian women. The Aussie soldiers felt they were being treated as "second class" compared to the visiting Americans. These jealousies lead to open hostilities, including a two-night physical brawl, that included the death of one Australian soldier.*

Saturday, 28 Nov 1942

Slept till about 9:30. Got up, ate breakfast, slipped into bathing pants and headed to the beach, which is about a block away. Rode the waves a while. Lay down on beach and slept a while longer. Boy, was I hot. Hope I don't get sick. Ate again about 2 PM and read papers. Ate again at 7 PM and went to a show. Came back. Had a few drinks, saw some kids I knew and went to bed.

Sunday, 29 Nov 1942
Found some crazy post cards to send to someone. Don't know who.

DAY WITH NO ENTRY

Tuesday, 1 Dec 1942
Reported to work today from 4 days leave in Southport. I surfed once daily and slept about an hour in the sun. Boy, am I brown. Once more I look natural. Sure would have been swell to have had my family along. That is one thing I am likely to do when I get home.

Wednesday, 2 Dec 1942
What a day. Was busy all day and am about caught up with work. As per usual, when you leave, someone messes something up. These three lieutenants I have, well sometimes I wonder how I made so many busts. I guess I did.

Thursday, 3 Dec 1942
My tummy ached today. They gave me salts. I have been on the run since and should waltz (to rhyme). Feeling better. Saw show last night, "The Great Storm." After seeing part of it, I realized I had seen it with Cile I think in San Antonio. Well, was good so I saw it over. Also they showed "Murder in the Navy" or some such name. It was OK too.

Friday, 4 Dec 1942
Well, the salts I took yesterday is beginning to die down a bit. Boy, I would say it was some blow out. Even today I have been doing OK. At least my tummy doesn't hurt.

I sent Cile a cable yesterday requesting letters. Getting letters from Cile of late has been like Xmas presents.

Capt. Wood asked me to go to the fights tonight. I may go. Have nothing else to do. Think I have seen all the shows.

Things have been quiet of late with reference to the fights last weekend. Very little publicity in papers was given to last episode. The Aussies had nothing to say.

I have been invited to dinner at 1 PM on Christmas Day at the home Mr. Claude Watson, 14 Enderley Ave., Clayfield, Queensland.

27.7.   Christmas Day with the Watsons – 25 Dec 1942

Clayfield was an upscale suburb of Brisbane, about four miles from the downtown business district. In 1942, the community consisted of large homes on generous lots with many large mature trees and established landscapes. The Watson home was on a hill that overlooked the city.[253]

Claude Watson was a middle-aged merchant with a successful import-export business. In addition to his wife, he had two daughters, Evelyn, 20, and Mona, 18. Claude was a very keen card player and a follower of cricket. He built the house in 1919 after he returned to Australia following his military service with the 1st A.I.F. (Australian Imperial Force). He had served in northern France and Belgium as a gunner with the 5th Howitzer Battery during the First World War.

Figure 109- Claude Watson Residence of 1942
2010 Photograph

While he was in Europe, he was billeted for a period with a family in the village of Thuin, Belgium. According to Claude's grandson, John Galwey, Claude's letters expressed his great appreciation for the hospitality shown to him by his Belgian hosts, who had suffered so much under German occupation. Because of the kindness shown to him as a serviceman in a foreign country, Claude went out of his way to extend his hospitality to American servicemen serving in Australia. His custom was to invite a number of Yanks to his home on every holiday.

Despite the mid-December summer heat of Brisbane, where the temperature averages 87°F, Christmas was a time of special celebration. Many customs of Merry Ole England had found their way to Australia with little modification. A Christmas tree was very important. The Watsons usually cut a fresh pine tree for the house. Decorations adorned the tree, some of which were homemade family treasures.

---

[253] The property was subdivided in 1970, and a second large house was built on the land down the hill from the Watson home. Several of the large old trees were lost in the subdivision. The house was acquired by Bernard and Mary-Anne O'Neill in 1997.

According to Claude's grandson, who had lived in the house as a child, Christmas Day was al-
ways celebrated at mid-day in the formal dining room with a traditional English hot meal that
consisted of roast chicken, ham, and vegetables. The table was adorned with grapes, almonds, and
ginger. Dessert consisted of an English plum pudding that was served with custard and brandy
sauce. Following tradition, "lucky" Australian silver coins were baked into the pudding.

In those days wine was not imbibed, but the gentlemen would partake of the great Australian beer
or scotch whiskey. After dinner, cigars and port were served to the men.

The dinner table was always alive with conversation that included the Yank's memories of past
Christmases in the northern hemisphere and Claude's daughter's memories of past Christmases
in Australia. Privately, Claude feared that a young Yank might take one of his lovely daughters
back to America. He was greatly relieved two years later when a young Australian officer by the
name of Galwey appeared on the scene and married Evelyn. Mona married an Australian Air
Force Officer a few years later.

27.8.   The Last Diary Entry – 4 Dec 1942

The last entry in the Diary of John Day was 4 Dec 1942. His memoir continues, however, on the
basis of eight-hours of video-recorded oral history that Day gave in 1988.

27.8.1.   USAFFE Name Officially Changed to GHQ SWPA - 1 January 1943

January 17, 1943

> Dear Cile and Johnnie
> I note from your letter all the Christmas presents Johnnie had, and it seems that he did
> pretty good, considering. Should I have been there, I feel sure he would have broken the
> record.

Part II - ORAL HISTORY & LETTERS – Jan 1943

The remainder of this book is based upon this oral history, the letters, and research from US Army official military records, particularly those in possession of the Office of the Center of Military History, Ft. McNair, DC. Footnotes and references are throughout this document.

28.   BATTLE OF BISMARCK SEA – 2-4 Mar 1943

The Battle of the Bismarck Sea was a strategic turning point in the battle for New Guinea and the Solomon Islands. The Battle demonstrated the power of the Signal Intelligence of the U.S. Army Signal Corps and the success of land-based American air power against Japanese shipping by denying the Japanese the opportunity to reinforce their troops in New Guinea by sea. It was possibly the finest hour for the Army Air Corps in the South Pacific and certainly a decisive influence on the Allies success in Operation Cartwheel, the neutralization of the Japanese military complex at Rabaul.

28.1.   Japanese Reinforcements for the South Pacific

After Maj. Gen. Horii's death in Nov 42, Lt. Gen. Hatazo Adachi was appointed Commander of 18th Japanese Army for the South Pacific. In Dec 1942, the Japanese Imperial Headquarters decided to reinforce the South Pacific and transferred two Army Divisions to the South West Area, one from Korea and one from China. The 20th Division was transferred from Korea to Guadalcanal and the 41st Division was transferred from China to Rabaul however, neither had arrived when the Japanese evacuated Guadalcanal on 4 Jan 1943. The Japanese redirected both divisions to Wewak, New Guinea where they arrived between 19 Jan and 19 Feb 1943. A convoy of five transports and five destroyers delivered 10,000 troops to Wewak without incident. Wewak was safe from Allied air attacks, although the Japanese 20th Division still had to be moved down the coast to Madang, and the 41st still had to be moved across the Bismarck Sea to Rabaul. There were no roads in the region, and water remained the only mode of transportation.

Gen. Adachi was assigned responsibility for the northeast coast of New Guinea, including Wewak, Madang, and Tuluva (New Britain Island). He was planning to move his headquarters from Rabaul to Lae, along with the remainder of the 51st Division that was already in Rabaul. He had successfully shipped one Regiment of the 51st Division from Rabaul to Lae which arrived on 7 Jan 1943.

Adachi was planning an even larger supply convoy of eight ships and eight destroyers to Lae, but thanks to information in an ULTRA intercepted Japanese-coded message, the Americans received a one-month advance notice of the coming second New Guinea supply convoy.

28.2.   Poor US Air Force Performance

American air attacks on shipping between Rabaul and Lae had been very poor. Even with ad-vanced intelligence from ULTRA on the sailing of the convoy, the US Fifth Air Force was unable to do serious damage to the convoy. A Japanese convoy of five transports and five destroyers suc-cessfully reached Lae on 7 Jan 1943 to deliver troops and supplies. Of five transports and five de-stroyers in the convoy, only one ship was struck and its troops were rescued by the destroyer es-corts. One transport was beached at Lae, but its cargo was recovered.[254] All the other ships safely delivered their cargo to Lae.

During the three days the Japanese convoy transited the Bismarck Sea approaching Lae, the Air Force flew a total of 37 sorties of one to twenty aircraft attacking the ships. There was limited co-ordination between aircraft. Many of the sorties were only single individual planes. There was no truly coordinated or systematic attack. The only direct hit on a ship was from an Australian Catalina at night. This poor performance was a great embarrassment to Gen. Kenney.

Immediately, Gen. Kenney made major changes to improve the bombing accuracy against ship-ping. First, he de-emphasized high and medium-altitude bombing (B-17s) in favor low-altitude bombing (B-25s). The low-altitude approach required his planes to fly between 50 and 100 feet. Second, to protect the low-altitude bombers from ground fire, he had 50-caliber machine guns mounted in the noses of B-25s.

The legendary "Pappy" Gunn[255] was in charge of Maintenance in Townsville, Australia, when he demonstrated that two machine guns could be retrofitted into Douglas A-20 Havocs. After-ward, at Gen. Kenney's request, he added ten machine guns to the Martin B-25 Mitchell. The B-25 had a longer range, a larger bomb load, a co-pilot, and instruments for all-weather and night operations. It was however, slower and less maneuverable. This aircraft modification had to be done very quickly.

---

[254] This ship remained beached in the harbor until after the war and became an identifying land-mark for Lae harbor. The hull appears in Figure 137 in this book.

[255] Col. Paul "Pappy" Gunn (1899-1957) retired as a pilot from the U.S. Navy in 1939. He then founded both Philippine Air Lines and Hawaiian Air Lines. When war broke out he was commis-sioned a Captain in the US Army Air Corps and served in the Philippines and in Australia. He became an assistant to Gen. Tunney for special projects and is best remembered for his machine gun modifications to the A-20 and B-25. After the war he rebuilt the Philippine Airlines. He died in an airplane crash in 1957.

Air tactics were developed for two B-25s flying at low altitude to work together to attack a ship. One would strafe the deck to suppress anti-aircraft fire, while second plane would "skip" the bomb into the side of the ship. "Skip bombing" required the bomb fuse to be modified to not explode upon first impact when it hit the water a low angle. The bomb bounced or "skipped" off the water into the side of a ship before detonating. This technique was tricky since the plane had no bombardier and the pilot had to release the bombs.

All the pilots had to be retrained. The Air Force had three weeks to modify the airplanes, retrain the pilots, and practice. This technique proved very successful against shipping.

28.3.   The Battle – 2–4 Mar 1943

When the Japanese convoy departed Rabaul on 28 Feb 1943, the US was ready – but the weather was not cooperating. The Japanese convoy was able to hide under a weather front. On 2 Mar, the convoy was still out of range for the B-25s, but 29 B-17s attacked. Fighter protection was a problem such that nine of the 29 B-17s were damaged by Japanese fighters, but the planes did sink one ship carrying aviation fuel.

The next morning (3 Mar 43) the convoy entered striking range for the B-25s. The storm had cleared as the ships passed through the Vitiaz Strait. During two twenty-minute attacks, one in the morning and one in the afternoon, the Japanese convoy lost eight transports and three destroyers. Another destroyer would sink the next day from its wounds. Four Japanese destroyers escaped. US losses were three P-38s and one B-17.

Japanese sources reported their troop losses as between 3,000 and 7,000 men. In addition, their artillery, food, and medical supplies were lost. The 115th Infantry Regiment of the 51st Japanese Division was wiped out. Only 820 Japanese soldiers reached Lae, and they were without their equipment. The loss of aviation fuel stopped Japan from transferring 400 aircraft to Lae for combat support. This substantially weakened the Lae garrison.

One of the most important outcomes of the Battle of Bismarck Sea was that that the Japanese learned they could no longer resupply their troops by sea freighters if there were Allied ground-based aircraft within range. After this battle the Japanese were forced to use submarines and small coastal barges for supply missions which substantially limited their military supply capacity. This radically changed the nature of the war in New Guinea.

The Japanese intentions toward Port Moresby had been thwarted first by the Battle of the Coral Sea and second by the Battle of the Kokoda Trail and the loss of Buna. Guadalcanal fell on 7 Feb 43. On 2-4 Mar 43, the Battle of Bismarck Sea laid the foundation for the Allied invasion of Lae. Operation Cartwheel was working.

28.4.   Signal Intelligence and Gen. Spencer B. Akin

The battlefield success of the U.S. military in the Pacific was in a large part a result of the superior signal intelligence and code-breaking skills of the U.S. Army Signal Intelligence Service (SIS), the U.S. Navy Decryption Center (CAST), and later, the Central Bureau in Brisbane. A great measure of credit for this intelligence success was due to Gen. Spencer B. Akin, Chief Signal Officer for SWPA.

The great distances across the Pacific Ocean necessitated the use of radio communications by both warring powers. While the European Theater made extensive use of landline communications and existing telephone infrastructure, the Pacific had only the radio, and all radio communications were subject to interception. Encryption was paramount.

*At the end of the First World War, the War Department and the State Department had jointly funded a clandestine bureau called the **Black Chamber**, whose purpose was to decipher foreign diplomatic codes. This was the 1920s version of the National Security Agency (NSA). The organization had successfully broken the Japanese diplomatic and Imperial Army codes. Then in 1929, a major government budget cut back resulted in the State Department withdrawing all funding for the **Black Chamber.** Herbert O. Yardley, manager of **Black Chamber**[256], found himself unemployed and in need of money, so he decided to write a book about the exploits of his secret department. **The American Black Chamber** was his best-selling book in 1931. The book blew the cover on the American program to crack the codes of foreign governments. In many respects, the incident bears a striking parallel to the 2013 exposé of Edward Snowden, Bradley Manning, and WikiLeaks. The revelations of the book caused all foreign governments to change their encryption systems and set the United States signal intelligence program back by ten years.*

*Then in 1934, the U.S. Congress passed a Federal Communications Act that prohibited U.S. government agencies from intercepting radio messages between foreign governments and the United States. Gen. George Marshall, Chairman of the Joint Chiefs of Staff, appears to have turned his back on the Act and insisted that his SIS maintain its war readiness by "practicing" their code skills on Japanese communications. The U.S. Navy had previously organized a special department in 1920, independent of **Black Chamber**, to address the Japanese Imperial Navy code (JN-25). The Navy was not impacted directly by the exposé of **Black Chamber**.*

In 1938, the U.S. government established a network of secret signal intercept sites to collect foreign government communications. These sites were scattered across the Pacific from Petaluma,

---

[256] Edward J. Drea, *MacArthur's Ultra, Codebreaking and the War against Japan, 1942-1945*, University Press of Kansas, 1991, p.8 – Herbert O. Yardley was the author of the book.

*California, to Panama to Corregidor. During the 1930s, the United States did a fair job of deciphering the Japanese diplomatic code called **Red**, but in 1939, the Japanese introduced a new code called **Purple**. The Americans were again completely lost.*

*In August 1939, Lt. Col. Spencer B. Akin, a Signal Officer, was recalled to Washington, D.C. from an intercept station in Panama. Akin was promoted to Colonel and placed in charge of the U.S. Army Signal Intelligence Service (SIS), the U.S. techno-analytic code-breaking service. He was charged with cracking **Purple**.*

Akin[257] was born in 1889 in Greenville, Mississippi, the son of a career military officer. He graduated from the Virginia Military Institute in 1910 and immediately entered the Army. After serving in the Philippines and in Texas before the war, he rose to the rank of Major in the Signal Corps during World War I. He was a trained crypto-analyst.

*As a first step, the SIS identified 33 different Japanese codes that needed to be deciphered. Budget cutbacks during the Depression reduced the staff for the SIS to only six employees, so with such limited resources, the organization focused all its efforts on only one code - **Purple**. This code was used by the Japanese Diplomatic Corps and the Japanese Military Attaches. With the Japanese aligned with Germany, the United States hoped to learn of Japan's intentions through their diplomatic cables to Washington.*

*After 21 months under Col. Akin, the Army SIS cracked **Purple.** By early 1941, SIS had developed and built eight analog machines to decode **Purple**. Four machines were in Washington, three were in London, and one was on Corregidor. Two of the eight machines were transferred to the U.S. Navy. The very existence of the **Purple** translation machine was considered Top Secret.*

When MacArthur took Command in the Philippines in the summer of 1941, he made the specific request to Washington for the services of Col. Spencer Akin to become Chief of Signal Intelligence for the Far East. Akin assumed a dual responsibility in the Pacific: first to establish a reliable communications network throughout the Pacific, and second to manage the military encryption operations against the Japanese, both offensively and defensively.

*At the time of Pearl Harbor, the State Department and the U.S. military services could read wireless communications of the Japanese Foreign Service and the Japanese Imperial Navy. However, the Japanese Imperial Army (JIA) used a totally different code system. The early work on **Purple***

---

[257] Akin served as Chief Signal Officer for SWPA and U.S. Army Forces Pacific until after the war. In 1947, he was promoted to Major General and became Chief Signal Officer for the U.S. Army. He retired in 1951, and died in 1973. He is buried at Arlington National Cemetery.

gave the U.S. Army code team skills, but it would not breach the Japanese Imperial Army code for another two years (June 1943[258]).

*On Corregidor, U.S. Navy Lt. Rudolph J. Fabian (CAST) had charge of the **Purple** machine on Monkey Island, Ft. Mills. Maj. Joe T. Sherr of the U.S. Army was in command of SIS (Intercept) Station 6, also on Corregidor. Secrecy and "need to know" maintain security but at the expense of timeliness for new information. Although Maj. Sherr was located only 30 miles from Gen. MacArthur, he reported directly to SIS in Washington, D.C. If Station 6 intercepted a Japanese communication, the message was first relayed to SIS-Washington before it was hand-carried to Lt. Fabian to be decoded and translated. Any message deciphered from a **Purple** machine was classified code name **MAGIC**. After translation by Fabian, the message was returned to Sherr before being hand-delivered by courier to Gen. MacArthur. **MAGIC** communications were classified for the Eyes-Only of Gen. Douglas MacArthur, bypassing Gen. Willoughby, MacArthur's G-2 Intelligence Chief, although first passing through the hands of Gen. Sutherland, MacArthur's Chief of Staff.*

Usually it took three days from the time an intercept was made until the decoded and translated message could be delivered to Gen. MacArthur. This time delay created some interesting situations. For example, the translation of the intercepted coded message from Japan ordering Japanese diplomats to break off negotiations with Washington was delivered to Gen. Sutherland five hours after he heard the news over the public Manila radio station.[259]

*When the Japanese invaded the Philippines, the Army intelligence staff, the Station 6 staff, the Nisei language translators, and the **Purple** machine itself were evacuated by submarine from Corregidor to Australia. These men were considered too knowledgeable of U.S. code activities to allow them to fall into Japanese hands. Of the six men from Station 6 who were not evacuated, five died in captivity. Those who were evacuated became the nucleus of the Central Bureau in Australia, the Allies technical code-breaking activity. Akin[260] and Sherr were among the last twelve people to be evacuated from Corregidor with Gen. MacArthur aboard his PT boat flotilla. In Australia, the Central Bureau was under the command of the promoted Gen. Akin.*

Signal intelligence flowed to GHQ throughout the war. It assisted the planning for operations in New Guinea, the invasions of Leyte and Luzon, and the anticipated invasion of Japan. The reputation of the SIS crossed service boundaries, such that Adm. Halsey and Adm. Sprague both

---

[258] Drea, Ibid. p.2.

[259] Drea Ibid. p.12.

[260] Maj. Gen. Akin was awarded the Distinguished Service Cross and the Silver Star for gallantry in action in 1942, and the Air Medal and the Legion of Merit in 1946.

asked for and received detachments of Army Signal Corps to be stationed aboard their command ships before the Leyte and Luzon invasions.

The signal intelligence successes in the Pacific were many. The primary benefit of signal intelligence was knowledge of the deployment of the Japanese troops and aircraft that enabled timely offensive or defensive action. Among many major military successes attributed to special intelligence was the Battle of Bismarck Sea, which stopped the Japanese reinforcements from reaching Lae, New Guinea. Signal intelligence was critical to the timing of the American surprise air raids on Wewak, New Guinea, which virtually ended the Japanese air presence in New Guinea. Another signal intelligence success led to the brilliant leap-frog by MacArthur over the main Japanese forces at Hansa Bay to invade Hollandia almost unopposed. Finally, the dramatic interception and destruction of the aircraft carrying Adm. Yamamoto to the Solomon Islands was another major success that had a dramatic impact on the course of the war.

29.   THE THIRD DESK FOR THE RECEPTIONIST – Mar 1943

29.1.   Design of the Third Lobby Desk

<u>January 1943</u>

About a month after she received the second desk, there appeared on my desk a beautiful handpainted picture of a desk – complete with color, dimensions, everything. Attached to the picture was a "buck-slip" (a piece of paper routing the picture to various generals) with signatures indicating that the picture had been inspected by each general. The picture was making the rounds with everyone adding their comments. It had gone from Gen. Casey to Gen. Akin with a note "What do you think of this as a desk for the new receptionist?"

Gen. Akin said "Well, looks OK to me." Several other generals had commented on the color. Finally, the paper was marked "Send to Headquarters Commandant for action."

It was a beautiful desk, but my word, I didn't feel we needed another new desk and another construction cycle. Now, mind you I still have the carpenter working for me. He has never made it back to the hospital.

I went in to see Gen Stivers, "General, this thing has got to end somewhere! The Headquarters can't just work for this bitch." She was screwing General Sutherland when he was in town, and when he was not there, she was screwing a different general. I don't know how far down the ranks she got? Yes, it was unbelievable! I knew what was going on. I wasn't stupid.

And here she is – has a three-year-old kid and has not seen her husband in many years. Her husband was in one of those English Mustache Brigades over in Singapore and now a Japanese Prisoner of War.

Well, we built the third desk. It was good looking. The carpenter was skilled and did a good job.

The Engineer Colonel said "You know it is a crying shame we are trying to fight a war. We have to take our carpenter off building a hospital to build a desk for this Aussie that doesn't contribute anything to the war effort."

"Colonel, don't say too much because you and I will both get fired," I said.

He said "I can't stand it!"

"You'll stand it. Don't worry about it," I said.

29.2.   The Third Desk & Mrs. Clarke's Final Tantrum – March 1943

March 1943

The third desk was finished on Monday. That was the day the shit hit the fan. Bessie-Marie came into my office and said, "Major, you know I have to have the glass cut again."

I could feel my face in full bloom and the steam rising. All I could do was take a deep breath and try to calm myself down. "I can't promise you anything, but I will do the best I can."

I called the glass cutter. I told him we had another job for him and asked when he could get it done. The glass cutter, in his calm Aussie way, said, "Well, it will be another two weeks before I can get to you."

"Alright, do the best you can," I said.

I went down the stairs and told Bessie-Marie what the glass cutter had said. She jumped up like a three-year-old throwing a temper tantrum. She waved her arms and started stomping her feet on the floor. "I won't stand for it. I won't stand for it," she shouted.

Bingo! She marched straight to the elevator, and off to Gen Sutherland's office on the Eighth Floor. I went back to my office and sat down. Mind you, she is a 28-year-old female Australian civilian with no official power.

About an hour later, I get a call from Gen Stivers, "You mind stepping down this way," the General said.

"I'll be right down, Sir," I replied.

I went into his office. He was sitting behind his desk. As I walked into the room the first thing he said was "Are you alright?"

"Yes sir," I said.

Gen. Stivers said, "I don't know what you have done, but I got orders from the Chief of Staff to relieve you."

"Good! Good! Where am I going and how soon can I go? I have had enough," I said.

Gen. Stivers said, "You know, I guess that's politics, but there is nothing I can do about it in this case."

"That's OK, Sir. I don't want you to do anything about it. Just get my ass out of here," I said. *The Texas country boy was fed up with the Australian socialite.*

29.3.   Major Day Relieved as Headquarters Commandant – 23 March 1943

<u>23 March 1943</u>

I was relieved of duties as Headquarters Commandant for GHQ. About nine months after Bessie-Marie started work, I was replaced by Col. Thomas, a full colonel with 26 years of service in the Army. Col. Thomas was made Headquarters Commandant, and initially I remained the Assistant Commandant and Company Commander of Headquarters Company GHQ.

When Col. Thomas arrived, I said "Colonel, glad to see you, here is my desk, you take it."

"No, no, you stay right there!" said Col. Thomas. "Get me a desk beside yours, and let's operate together for a while. I want to learn what you do."

"OK, which businesses do you want to take over?" I asked. "Do you want the whiskey business? How about the PX? The Mess? The Motor Pool? Or some other area?"

"No, nothing," he said. "I am going to watch." He sat down at a desk right beside mine, but nothing else changed. I made all the decisions just like before. He would ask questions – Where is this? How do you do that? He learned that I had a lot of different operations that had to be tended. He kept me at the same desk for the next three months.

General Sutherland, the Chief of Staff, would call down periodically to Col. Thomas. I was sitting right beside him so I could hear the conversations. Thomas was saying, "No, Sir." "No Sir." "Not yet, Sir."

I knew Gen. Sutherland was asking him, "When are you going to let Day go?"

After three months Col. Thomas had increased his staff to about 38 officers plus me – helping him do the same job I had done with five officers. He said, "There is no way you could do all these jobs you have with the staff you had." By this time I had over 1,000 troops in Headquarters Company.

Finally, when the third call came in from the Chief of Staff, Col. Thomas was told he had had enough time. Gen. Sutherland told him to let me go. Figuratively, I could hear Bessie-Marie whispering in General Sutherland's ear.

30.   POLIO OUTBREAK AT HOME IN TEXAS – 13 Aug 1943

August 13, 1943 - Infantile Paralysis

> Dearest Mother and Dad:
>
> Just received a letter from Cile last night where she said that polio, I took her to mean infantile paralysis, was so bad, and she was scared about Johnnie. She had thought maybe she had better clear away from Bonham. I wrote her back to come to the ranch for a while. I hope she does, as she said some lady that had a couple of children, one of whom had polio, and the other was being moved to Bonham to get away from Dallas. She wanted her healthy child and Johnnie to play together. I wrote Cile under no circumstances to let them see each other. Surely she can tell her where to head. My God, such nerve! I wish you would write Cile if you have not heard from her to come out to the ranch for a while. I'm worried about it if there are some cases there. You never see any country kids with polio.

31.   NEW GUINEA, HERE I COME

31.1.   Major Day Reassigned to Gen. Casey & USASOS – 23 Jun 1943

It was time for me to go, so I called Gen Fitch, the AG. I said, "Give me some orders. Get me on my way."

Fitch told me to come to his office. He said, "I've gone to a lot of trouble to get you a good assignment."

"Well, that is very nice of you," I replied. Of all people to do me a favor, I never expected it from Fitch.

Fitch said, "Gen Casey is going to head up an operation going into Lae, New Guinea. We are going to make a landing there very soon. He wants you to help him. With your experience, you can help him get all the supplies together he will need for the invasion. Go see Gen Casey."

I went to see Gen Casey. He said, "I have a Dutch ship in Sydney, 800 feet long, got a Javanese crew with some Greek mixed in, I want you to put enough stuff on there to set up a new headquarters of 600 men and be ready to sail in two or three weeks."

"Where do I get all this stuff?" I asked.

"Go down to Sydney, and see the Base Commander. Tell him what you need and what you're going to do with it. He will take care of you. In the meantime, I will get you a few more people," said Gen. Casey.

31.1.1.   Assigned to 23rd Port Headquarters USASOS

*Major Day's new assignment was **Headquarters Commandant. 23rd Port Headquarters, USASOS.** The 23rd Port Headquarters, originally Port Detachment C, had been activated in Sydney in Sept 1942 for training and preparation to set up advanced headquarters in a combat zone. In May 1943 the unit was assigned the mission of establishing a [supply] Base at Lae, New Guinea after its capture from the enemy. On 5 Aug 1943 by order of USASOS, the Port Detachment C was renamed the 23rd Port Headquarters. This activity was a part of Operation Cartwheel, and Major Day would remain with Gen. Casey through Operation King II, the invasion of Leyte, and the subsequent invasion of Lingayan Gulf.*

31.2.   USASOS Reorganization — 3 Sep 1943

Beginning in September 1943, the tempo of the war in the Southwest Pacific Area increased substantially, which placed greater demands on USASOS.

USASOS underwent a major reorganization with the objective to provide greater support to combat operations outside mainland Australia. USASOS Headquarters had remained in Sydney up to this time in order to be closely tied to Australian procurement. Now the offensive activities were moving up the north coast of New Guinea. USASOS Headquarters was moved from Sydney to Brisbane to be closer to the combat planning personnel in order to get earlier notice of the location of future military operations. Only a Rear Echelon remained in Sydney which included an Engineering Depot for procuring bulk engineering supplies and construction equipment in Australia and the nucleus of the Procurement Division, USASOS.

Maj. Gen. R. J. Marshall remained in command until 3 Sep 1943. At that time Brig. General J. L. Frink received his second star and assumed command of USASOS from Gen. Marshall who became Gen. Sutherland's Chief of Staff.[261]

A key element of the USASOS reorganization was to separate planning for new bases from the operation of existing bases. Greater emphasis was placed on planning because lead time for supplies in New Guinea was extremely long. Supply ships had to cross the Pacific from the United States. Ordnance and ammunition was coming from San Francisco. Not only were their issues due to the length of the supply lines, there were major deficiencies in the infrastructure of New Guinea, where there was great need for heavy construction – docks, roads, and airdromes. Heavy construction required heavy engineering equipment and construction Matéris to be brought from Australia. This meant larger ships and special docks in both Australia and New Guinea.

A network of future supply bases was planned for the New Guinea campaign. Future base commanders were appointed before the Allies controlled each site and became part of the planning process. Multiple bases were developed simultaneously.

The established supply bases had to continue operation while new bases were constructed. Control for the existing bases was decentralized to give more autonomy to the Base Commanders. The Base Section Commanders were made responsible for:

- *Servicing troops – administration, quarters, supplies, hospitalization, evacuation, medical services, engineering, morale, mail, chaplain, etc. for all troops in his area.*

---

[261] OCMH "History of USASOS and AFWESPAC", unpublished Manuscript, file 8-5.8 AA V.1, p.31. General Orders No. 48, Hdq USASOS, 3 Sep 1943.

- *Providing shelter, buildings, and grounds staging areas, rations, and safe drinking water.*
- *Receiving and delivering supplies and equipment for the troops meant port operations, storage, and distribution.*
- *Issuing and carrying out troop movement orders as directed by USAFIA.*

The Base Commander was not responsible for the tactical training or tactical mission performance of the troops that passed through each Base.

New Guinea Bases established in 1942-1944 were the following:

- *Port Detachment A – Port Moresby – arrived 6 Jun 1942*
- *Port Detachment E – Milne Bay – arrived 25 Jun 1942 - 12 Dec 1942*

- *Advance Sub-Base A – Milne Bay – 21 Apr 1943 (name change only)*
- *Advance Sub-Base B – Oro Bay – 21 Apr 1943*
- *Advance Sub-Base C – Islands of Goodenough, Kiriwina, & Woodlark – 27 Apr 1943 (closed 14 Aug 1943)*
- *Advance Sub-Base D – Port Moresby – 31 May 1943*

On 14 Aug 1943, Advanced Sub-Bases became Advance Bases in Advance Section, USASOS, and responsibilities were clarified by orders of 3 Sep 1943. Advanced headquarters was moved from Milne Bay to Port Moresby on 16 Sep 1943.

New bases established in 1943-1944 included:

- *Base E – Lae – 15 Nov 1943*
- *Base F – Finschhafen – 15 Nov 1943*
- *Base G – Hollandia – Mar 1944*
- *Base K – Leyte, PI – Oct 1944*
- *Base M – Lingayan, PI – Dec 1944*

As the combat zone moved north, so did the boundary between the Advanced Echelon and the Intermediate Echelon. Personnel from bases away from the combat zone would be regularly transferred forward to more advance bases. In Sep 1943 Advanced Echelon was moved from Milne Bay to Port Moresby. On 13 Feb 1944, Base E (Lae) passed from the control of the Advanced Section to the Intermediate Section. Base F (Finschhafen) remained in Advanced Echelon for a few more months.

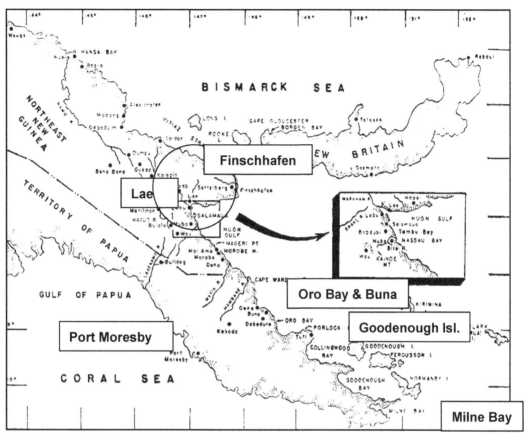

Figure 110 - ArmyAirForce-IV-9 Lae NG Map 1943

32.   THE LAE INVASION & BASE E – 4 Sep 1943

32.1.   New Guinea Geography

Lae is the second largest city in New Guinea, located about 200 miles north of Port Moresby beyond the Owen Stanley Range in the territory that in 1942 was called Northeast New Guinea. The Owen Stanley Range, with peaks up to 13,000 feet[262], provides a formidable barrier between the northeast (Australian Protectorate of New Guinea) and southwest (Australian Colony of Papua). There is no road through the mountains connecting the two regions. One either flew over or sailed around the mountains.[263]   The city of Lae is located six degrees south of the Equator and receives 180 inches of tropical rain every year. It has two nicknames – "Rainy Lae" and "Pothole City." Lae is located near the mouth of the Markham River. The river drains a large fertile interior valley that reminds this American very much of the Sacramento Valley of California.

Originally part of the German Protectorate, Northeast New Guinea was settled in the late 19th century by Lutheran missionaries. Governance for the north coast passed from Germany to Britain as part of the Versailles Treaty following World War I. When gold was discovered between 1920 and 1930, Lae and Salamaua quickly became the ports that served the gold mines in Wau, Bulolo, and the interior Highlands. With no roads, mining interests were the first to develop a network of primitive airstrips and rugged bush aircraft to deliver men and machinery to the interior. Lae grew around the airstrip that became the principal supply line serving the interior with supplies shipped in from the outside world.

From the beach at Lae the ocean floor drops off very rapidly, creating a deep-water port suitable for heavy cargo ships. In 2010 the city reminds a visitor of the Port of Oakland or the Port of Long Beach from the large number of container ships regularly arriving and departing its docks. In 1942 the docks were much more primitive.

The central Lae airfield was made famous by Amelia Earhart during her 1937 attempt to fly around the world. Lae was her last refueling stop before she disappeared on the next leg of her journey from Lae to Howland Island in the central Pacific. In 2010, the old airfield remained abandoned in the center of downtown Lae not far from the docks.

---

[262] New Guinea has the tallest mountains in the world between the Himalayas and the Andes.
[263] In 2012 there is still no road through the mountains between the two regions. The regions are connected only by air or water transportation.

The Japanese invaded Lae on 8 March 1942 and made it a major regional supply center with improved docks and warehouses. The Japanese military spread into the interior and down the coast to Salamaua and Buna/Oro Bay in anticipation of crossing the mountains to capture Port Moresby.

32.2.   Sydney Preparation for the Lae Invasion – The Chickens

So I went down to Sydney and saw the Base Commander. They put me up in a hotel in the heart of downtown Sydney. I found the ship called the *Van Outhoorn* and went to work. Now Dalgety's wharfs were not far away.

From 1884 until World War II, Dalgety plc was the principal general merchandise supplier to rural Australia, including sheep stations (ranches) and mining interests in the Australian outback and Papua New Guinea. A trading company, they imported merchandise from around the world to supply the outback settlers in exchange for their wool, minerals, and other products for export. They were one of the world's largest traders in wool and at one time were included in the London FTSE 100 stock index. They also imported scotch whiskey from Scotland and repackaged it for the Australian market.

I stashed a footlocker and a suitcase at Dalgety's warehouse because I knew I could not take them with me to New Guinea. I thought I was storing them for the duration of the war. I did not think I would ever get down to Sydney again. This way I thought if something happened to me, my footlocker might still get home.

In a few days more people were assigned to me and we began to get organized. I had a first sergeant who helped assign the different jobs. There were many things to do before we could ship out in a few weeks.

There was one unusual thing I did in Sydney that never happened again. I went down to the Red Cross and talked to them about my plan and asked for their help. They approved my plan, so I went back to Dalgety. I explained "I want 1,000 Red-Headed Leghorn chickens – mature and laying eggs. I want them in chicken coops two or three levels high. Get them ready, and I will be down here to tell you where and when to load them on a ship."

"Who's is going to pay for them?" asked the Dalgety agent.

I said, "Who do you think is going to pay for them? The Red Cross is going to pay for them, and I'm going to take them away." I wanted some fresh eggs up the line. I also arranged for chicken feed to be shipped to us every month.

So lo and behold, a Dalgety truck came down to the dock hauling the chickens. They were in chicken coops that were strong enough to hold a tiger. Each cage must have been a couple of feet wide and three or four levels high, filled with chickens and ready to load on the ship. They were stacked eight to ten feet high and were secured on the top side of the aft deck.

From the moment the chickens arrived, I had a man with a machine gun guarding the chickens. There was always someone who wanted to steal eggs. We only had so many eggs a day. I had 1,000 chickens, but we were getting perhaps 800 eggs every day. We were always fighting off people from the ship. The cook was always trying to steal eggs. I had a sergeant in charge of the chickens, collecting the eggs, crating them, and saving them until we rationed them out. We always kept the guard there, but we still caught all sorts of people stealing. I caught one corporal with eggs in his hands.

The rest of the supplies for the coming invasion came from the Quartermaster. He produced all sorts of supplies, including tents, sheets, blankets, silverware, cook stoves, K-Rations, you can't imagine the stuff we accumulated. I had no idea where we were going, only north. What I was going to do with all the materiel, I was not sure.

32.3.   *Van Outhoorn* Sails for Oro Bay, New Guinea – 20 Aug 1943

The Commanding Officer and his staff officers departed from Sydney by air about 15 August. I was lucky and got to fly up to Port Moresby, New Guinea and then over to Buna. The ship would catch up with us after we landed in Lae.

The Van Outhoorn loaded the rest of the officers and men on the evening of 19 Aug 1943. The ship sailed at 7 AM on 20 Aug 1943. It was small, crowded, and had poor living accommodations. There were mattresses on the floor in the low-ceiling mid-deck. As the ship sailed north toward the equator, the weather became hotter, so it became almost impossible to stay below deck. The aroma of the chickens on the aft deck added to the natural smells of the native crew, which made for a most unpleasant passage for all onboard.[264]

---

[264] Military History of the U.S. Army Services of Supply in the Southwest Pacific, Chapter 18: Base at Lae Until March 1944, *Historical Manuscripts Collection (HMC)* under file number 8-5.8 AA vol. 19, 30 June 1946, National Archives and Records Administration, College Park, MD.

Figure 111 - Voyage of the Van Outhoorn - Sydney to Oro Bay - 20 Aug to 9 Sep 1943

As the ship sailed around Australia and headed north, it was joined by two ships at Newcastle, and then on 23 Aug 1943 outside Brisbane, it joined a 16-ship convoy, arriving in Bowen on 26 Aug 1943 to take on coal before arriving in Townsville on 28 Aug. The troops were allowed off the ship until the next convoy for New Guinea could be assembled. After the convoy sailed from Townsville, the ships were divided into two sections, one section went to Port Moresby and the other section (including the Van Outhoorn) paused briefly at Milne Bay on 8 Sept 1943 before proceeding on to dock in Oro Bay at 3 PM on 9 Sept 1943. A few days later it proceeded to Lae.

There had been a terrible fight at Buna, and the Japanese were still in the jungle. Evidence of the war was everywhere. The tops of all the coconut trees were shot off. The Japs tied their snipers to the trees on suicide missions. They would never surrender and remained until they were killed.

Oro Bay is the port for Buna and only a few miles away. We were using Oro Bay as a supply Base and staging area to prepare to go into Lae. We remained in Oro Bay for only a few weeks before we had to move out north for the invasion. This was an amphibious landing, and we were going in on LSTs. [265]

---

[265] LST is abbreviation for a Landing Ship, Tank.

32.4.   Lae Assault and Nadzab Air Drop – 5 Sep 1943

The assault on Lae was a pincer maneuver, that is, multiple coordinated attacks from different directions. The first attack was by the Australian 9ᵗʰ Infantry Division that made an amphibious landing about 20 miles east of Lae on 4 Sept 1943. The next day (5 Sep 1943) the U.S. Army's 503ʳᵈ Paratroop Regiment dropped 1,700 paratroopers with their equipment from 96 C-47 transports in the first major airborne assault of the Pacific war at Nadzab. Gen. MacArthur himself observed the action from a command B-17 flying overhead.

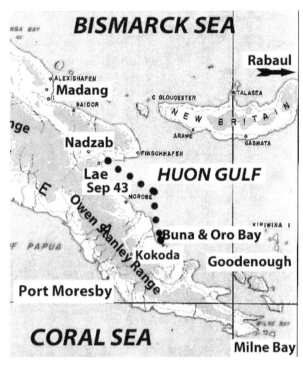

Figure 112 – Lae Amphibious Landing 19 Sep 1943

Nadzab was a pre-war emergency landing field located 20 miles inland from Lae in the Markham Valley. A coastal range keeps the heavy tropical storms near the coastline, so that the weather at the inland airfield is clear more often than at the beach where there is far more rain. The seldom-used airstrip was covered by Kunai grass that grows abundantly in the jungle to heights greater than a man with stalks the size of a finger. After the paratroopers secured the area, the grass was cleared from the landing strip with flame throwers and the airfield was made ready for the arrival the next day of C-47s carrying the Australian 7ᵗʰ Infantry Division. The Aussies attacked Lae from the west. The city of Lae was officially declared "pacified" on 16 Sep 1943.

32.5.   Amphibious Landing of the 23ʳᵈ Port Headquarters – 19 Sep 1943

I don't remember exactly when we left Oro Bay, but we had to land in Lae about 11 PM [*19 Sep 1943*]. We loaded up the LSTs and went into the Lae beach. We were told the landing ships had to pull away from the beach about 2 AM before first light to avoid being sighted by Jap aircraft. If we didn't get our stuff off the ship, the ships would leave with it.

September is the beginning of the heavy rains for Lae. It rained so much that the mud was knee deep on the beach. The beach was littered with the wreckage of Japanese landing barges, barbed wire entanglements, and bomb craters. You could hardly walk away from the water. "The sand was from six inches to eighteen inches deep."[266] We had to lay down steel landing mats in strips for the first 200 yards from the beach before vehicles could reach firm ground and drive away. As it was, trucks were stuck in the sand, and we had to get an Australian bulldozer to pull the trucks out. The sun was beginning to come up, and we were still unloading the LSTs. We worked feverishly to get the materiel off the ship, but with all the mud, we could not get everything off the beach. The LST delayed departing until 3 AM by which time we had emptied the ship. The muddiest pile of stuff you could imagine was still sitting on the beach. Everything was a mess.

In the middle of the confusion, we put up a portable latrine on the beach. Then, ping-ping, a Japanese sniper started taking shots in the dark. All of sudden we had 500 people with rifles who were looking for someone to shoot at, but it was still dark and no one knew who to shoot. I tried to get everyone to calm down and not shoot each other. Don't shoot unless you know what you are shooting.

We came ashore on the beach not far from the main airfield. After days of fighting by the infantry, most of the Japs had left Lae. There were only two Japs that had not gotten out of our sector. In about 15 minutes everyone started shooting. One Jap was killed, and one escaped into the jungle. After that, every day we would see two to four more stray Japanese soldiers. We never could be sure if they were going to try to kill us or surrender.

A convoy of three or four LSTs continued to come in to the beach every night, landing about 11 PM and departing about 4 AM after unloading their cargo.

> "*…on the second night after arrival, a Japanese Medium bomber came over and dropped a bomb close to a Japanese vessel scuttled on the LST beach. It was a very near miss. Later it was learned that an amount of valuable steel netting and other stevedore supplies were on the vessel, which the Japanese evidently did not want to have captured in condition to be used. However, everything of value on this vessel was salvaged and put to use.*"[267]

---

[266] Military History of the U.S. Army Services of Supply in the Southwest Pacific, Chapter 18: Base at Lae Until March 1944, *Historical Manuscripts Collection (HMC)* under file number 8-5.8 AA vol. 19, 30 June 1946, National Archives and Records Administration, College Park, MD. Page 5
[267] Ibid. Page 5.

32.5.1.   Lae Sniper Story[268]

We were moving our headquarters off the beach and about three or four miles up the line toward Lae. The Infantry told us it was all clear. On the right side, there was a rice field, and beyond there was a hill, maybe 1,000 feet tall, not real high [*probably Mt. Lunaman*]. Some Japs were still held up in the hill. The dive bombers were trying to get them out of that hill. Plane after plane came in. It took a little longer to get through than we expected.

Finally, the Sergeant and I went up to the area where we were planning to move the Headquarters. We were standing beside the jeep, not very far apart. I am looking into the bush when I heard "Ping."

The Sergeant standing beside me fell immediately to the ground. He was hit. A Jap sniper was still in the trees. I did not know exactly where the shot came from, so I got down behind the jeep. I pulled the sergeant around to me. He was dead. Three natives came out of the bush. They must have been guerrillas. They were yelling, "We'll get him! We'll get him!" and they ran off looking for the sniper.

They found him and killed him. The sniper was another tied to a tree. He fell after they killed him. The Japanese left a few soldiers here and there to harass and do what damage they could do. That was the closest I came to being shot.

When advancing on a road, soldiers preferred to walk in the tracks behind an Armored Personal Carrier (APC) rather than the adjacent soft mud. We were moving down the road where we came upon one APC that had 50 dead Japs around it. All three Americans in the APC were dead. They had put up quite a fight. The roads were narrow with only one-way passage so the APC was blocked and could not withdraw. We quickly squeezed by on foot for fear there were still more Japs in the area.

---

[268] Clip 3-27 1943 NG – Lae Sniper Story (4:44:38:14)

33.   MARSHALL AND MACARTHUR MEETING – 13 Dec 1943

Gen. George C. Marshall, the U.S. Army Chief of Staff, paid his one and only wartime visit to Gen. Douglas MacArthur and the Southwest Pacific Area on 13 Dec 1943. Marshall had been attending the Tehran Conference[269], the first meeting of the "Big Three Powers" – Roosevelt, Churchill, and Stalin. The U.S. and Great Britain had agreed at the conference to open a second front in Europe against the Nazis by invading France in the spring of 1944.

Marshall was returning to Washington, D.C. by way of Asia because he felt it was very important to have a personal meeting with Gen. MacArthur. They met on Goodenough Island, the headquarters of the Sixth Army off the east coast of New Guinea. Gen. Marshall and Gen. MacArthur had known each other for over 30 years during their overlapping military careers, but their relationship was strained, at best. Their relationship was perhaps colored by the role reversal of their careers. MacArthur was first the Chief of Staff over Marshall, and then ten years later Marshall was the Chief of Staff over MacArthur. One can only speculate on how MacArthur felt about reporting to a man who had previously been his subordinate.

The two generals were in many respects like the fabled tortoise and hare. Both were born in the same year (1880), but their personalities and military careers were polar opposites. Douglas MacArthur, the proverbial hare, was the son of an Army major general and graduated from West Point in 1903, ranking first in his class of 93 cadets. MacArthur was considered brilliant and a man of action. He earned the third highest academic record ever achieved in the 200-year history of the institution. By tradition, the highest academic West Point graduates join the Army Corps of Engineers, and MacArthur was no exception. He served in the Philippines in 1903, supervising construction projects across the islands.[270] As a junior officer, MacArthur traveled extensively in Asia including Japan, China, India, the Dutch East Indies, and Singapore.

In 1906, he returned to Washington where his social skills, extensive travel, and natural charisma led him to be invited by President Theodore Roosevelt to be "an aide to assist White House functions." In 1914, MacArthur was sent by President Woodrow Wilson with a military expeditionary force to occupy Veracruz, Mexico. In a combat situation at great peril to his own life, MacArthur killed several Mexicans while saving the lives of his fellow soldiers. For his bravery under fire, he was nominated for the Congressional Medal of Honor, but because of circumstances surrounding the mission, he was never awarded the medal. During World War I, however, he distinguished himself as the combat commander of the 42nd Rainbow Division. For his combat

---

[269] Tehran Conference held Teheran, Iran, 28 Nov 43 to 1 Dec 43

[270] Among his many construction project sites was one at Tacloban, the site that would later become his invasion site for the Leyte invasion.

exploits, he was decorated with two Distinguished Service Crosses, three Silver Stars, and two French Croix de Guerre. By the end of the war, he was a brigadier general and a war hero. By 1930, MacArthur was elevated to Army Chief of Staff, the highest ranking officer in the U.S. military.

George Marshall, the proverbial tortoise, was the son of a middle-class Pennsylvania coal businessman. He graduated number 15 in a class of 34 at Virginia Military Institute (VMI) in 1901. A shy, analytical, and unassuming person, Marshall was strongly committed to a military career. Because VMI graduates were not automatically granted Army commissions upon graduation, Marshall entered the Army through competitive examination. He was commissioned in January 1902 and served during the Philippines insurrection and World War I. In contrast to MacArthur, Marshall's military career was primarily as a staff officer with a specialty in logistics. He won high praise as G-3 for his planning for the St. Mihiel and Meuse-Argonne offensives and was elevated to Chief of Staff, Eighth Army Corps. Although Marshall was a respected planner, he never commanded troops in combat and at the end of World War I remained as only a captain. After the war, he served as Gen. George Pershing's aide-de-camp, and was later assigned to China.

During World War I, there had been a battlefield incident for which MacArthur blamed Marshall for a logistical problem that caused trouble for his Rainbow Division. This led to a personal rift between the two men, and in 1933, when MacArthur was U.S. Army Chief of Staff, Col. Marshall was assigned to the Illinois National Guard and later the Vancouver (WA) barracks, postings that were considered career ending assignments. Marshall was promoted to brigadier general in 1936, 18 years after MacArthur reached that rank. MacArthur retired in 1937 to take the position of Military Advisor to the Philippine Commonwealth. The next year, Marshall returned to Washington and was assigned to the powerful War Plans Office. Although most observers thought Marshall's career had ended, President Roosevelt was particularly impressed by Marshall's recommendations with respect to logistical support for Great Britain. It was Roosevelt who elevated Marshall to U.S. Army Chief of Staff in 1939, jumping him from one to four stars in a single promotion. Marshall remained the Army Chief of Staff until the war ended in 1945.

Churchill called George C. Marshall "the Architect of Victory" in World War II. Marshall became U.S. Secretary of State in 1947, Time Magazine's Man of the Year in 1947, author of the Marshall Plan for European economic recovery, and winner of the Nobel Peace Prize in 1953.

Gen. Marshall was described as quiet, reserved, and cerebral – the type of person who liked thoughtful written communications. MacArthur preferred oral communications – a brilliant conversationalist, an eloquent orator with a huge vocabulary, and amazing powers of personal persuasion. Ironically, it was Marshall who wrote the recommendation to President Roosevelt to award the Congressional Medal of Honor to MacArthur after he escaped from the Philippines to Australia. Marshall compared the non-combat award to MacArthur as similar to the non-combat award of the same medal to Charles Lindberg after his flight across the Atlantic. Marshall felt the medal would strengthen national resolve to resist the Japanese and reassure the Australians of U.S. support for MacArthur to lead the counteroffensive.

The Marshall/MacArthur luncheon on Goodenough Island included a review of the war strategy. Marshall restated the "Europe First" global strategy and informed MacArthur that the coming invasion of France was the reason why MacArthur would not be receiving increased supplies. Dwight Eisenhower would be appointed the European Supreme Commander later that month. Eisenhower had served as MacArthur's Chief of Staff before the war and had been fired by MacArthur. MacArthur gave faint praise to Eisenhower, declaring he was the "best damn clerk I ever had."

"At one point during their Goodenough lunch, MacArthur began a sentence, "My staff ....." and Marshall cut him short, saying "You don't have a staff, General. You have a court."[271]

With respect to the Pacific conflict, MacArthur was pleading his case for more troops and supplies for SWPA. He felt the best strategy to defeat Japan was to follow a path of conquest through the Philippines to the Japanese homeland. The Navy was advocating a path across the Central Pacific through the Mariana Islands. MacArthur doubted the Japanese would ever capitulate and argued that the Philippine route would save lives and matériel. Washington was always planning massive aerial bombing of Japan from China; however, there was a growing concern in 1943 about the ability of Chiang Kai-shek to maintain control of airbases in China that were within bombing range of Japan. The Pacific strategy would continue to be debated for another six months.

---

[271] Quotation from William Manchester, *American Caesar, Douglas MacArthur 1880-1964*, Back Bay Books, Little Brown and Company, New York, 1978, p.352.

34.   LAE AREA COMMANDER, BASE E – Jan 44 to Aug 44

I was initially the Headquarters Commandant for the Port of Lae. In Jan 1944 I became Area Commander (Base E), where I remained until August 1944.

In Lae, I had a job similar to what I had in Brisbane at GHQ, only in the combat zone with a lot fewer generals. I had Gen. Casey and an Air Force Brigadier General [*Brig. Gen. C. W. Connell, Commanding General Air Services, Southwest Pacific*], and the Adjutant General who was a colonel. Initially, I reported to the Commanding Officer of Base E [*Col. E. Jeff Barnette*] before I replaced him.

Lae, along with Finschhafen, became major supply ports for war matériel coming by sea into New Guinea to support the offensive along the north coast, the Admiralties, Cape Gloucester, and New Britain Island. Lae had two major purposes: first to supply the Nadzab Airbase with fuel and ammunition, and second to be a staging area for the troops preparing to move forward into the combat zone up the north coast, first to Finschhafen and Madang, and later, Aitape and Hollandia. Finschhafen fell on 2 Oct 1943. Finschhafen had a deeper water port than Lae so after its capture, Base F was set up to share the staging area responsibilities with Lae.

The Engineers had the Nadzab airport operating in 36 hours. The first planes to arrive brought in heavy construction equipment for the Engineers. During the next week, the single existing runway was lengthened to handle heavier planes and six new runways were added.

Nadzab Airbase became the principal Army airbase for the Southwest Pacific and home of the Fifth Air Force. The En-

Figure 113 - Headquarters, Base E, Lae, NG 1943
Observe water puddles on the road. – John Day

gineers built the first ever 25-mile all-weather road through the jungle from Lae to Nadzab Airport. The road opened December 15, 1943, essentially 60 days after the invasion.[272] *At the Port the Engineers built two new pile docks and one floating dock to receive arriving Liberty Ships and cargo. A fuel pipeline was constructed from the docks to the airbase. Two new hospitals and storage facilities for the Engineer, Signal and Ordnance Corps were added in the next month.*[273] *Advance Base E was formally established on 15 Nov 1943.*

My job was to feed and re-equip the American troops moving forward. Any time a new unit arrived in Lae, they had to report to me, and I would assign them a place to set up their camp. Units were spread all over the area. We had to build mess halls to feed all the officers and enlisted personnel in the Base, including both Army and Air Corps.

In the beginning, Lae was less than 100 miles from a Japanese fighter squadron. They hit us every morning, and we tried to hit them every morning. This went on for quite a spell until we finally got them knocked out.

Sept 26, 1943

Sunday Night, 19 days after the invasion
A handwritten letter:
Dearest Mother and Dad:

I have seen quite a few very interesting things in the last couple of months. Many things, such as scenery, it would be impossible to describe. You have to see it to enjoy it and imagine what it is like – the most rugged country you could imagine. If you get off the road at all, the Kunai grass grows about five feet tall and is almost everywhere. The natives use it for thatching roofs but for us, it hides the Japs.

There are lots of trees and undergrowth that begins about five feet from the waters edge and requires a lot of work to clear. After the grass is cleared, you have to burn the ground to kill the bugs, ticks, and spiders before you can pitch a tent.

I have a few men with scrub typhus. The doctors are better able to control it now than they were when we first arrived; however, we still have quite a few who die from it. The ticks in the grass seem to be the cause.

---

[272] Seventy years later Nadzab continues to be the main airport for the city of Lae. The road to the airport remains the main connection to Lae and is notorious for potholes. The modern continuation of the road beyond the airport leads to the interior Highlands. On that road a visitor still crosses streams on U.S. Army Corps of Engineer Bailey Bridges remaining from WWII.
[273] Military History of USASOS, p6.

I have just killed another big spider in my tent. He was about two inches across. Last night I killed one about twice that size. There was also a big red wasp that was bothering me, so I killed him too. Of course you try not to let the small bugs worry you, as you just have to get used to them.

We killed a six-foot (baby) boa or python today. He was under a stump that was plowed up while we were doing road work. I never seem to have my camera when I need it.

One of the interesting things is to watch the natives climbing the coconut trees to pick coconuts. They seem to walk up the trees. Lots of the natives have ring worms all over their bodies. Women wear just a little more than the men.

The natives like the Americans because we build roads and have lots of machinery. They want two bob (*shillings*) for most everything. So far, I have no souvenirs from the natives for fear I might catch something.

Will close for tonight with all my love,
    John

34.1.   The Chickens Arrive

It wasn't long before we had the harbor facilities operating and ready to receive ships. The *Van Outhoorn* arrived with the chickens and our other supplies. One day a full colonel came out to the ship and said "We are coming out tomorrow to get the chickens."

I said "Says who?" He said he wanted them for the hospital.

I said "You know where we got these chickens? We brought them up here for our unit. You get your own eggs."

The colonel said "Well, we will see about that."

Figure 114 - Natives working on the road drainage - 1943

I said, "Well, if you don't like it, why don't you talk to the general!"

"You don't have a general," he replied.

"The hell I don't," I said. "And he has two stars too – Gen. Casey." The colonel didn't have the nerve to go talk to the general, so that stopped him.

I kept the chickens. Among the hens, we had 25 roosters that we did not want since they don't lay eggs. I told the cook, "If you can find something to do with those roosters, do it." So he killed one of the roosters to see what he could fix. The cook tried to broil him, baked him, and stew him, but he was still too tough for good eating. So we gave the roosters away to the natives. We had arranged for grain to be shipped up every month for chicken feed, and the roosters just took feed away from the hens.

Oct 5, 1943

> Handwritten Letter
> AT SEA[274] - Tuesday
> Dearest Mother and Dad:
>
> Have not had time to write very much of late. Have hopes of being caught up before too long. As I have to make a few trips here and there for a while, I will continue to be on the go – Will be so glad to get settled for a while.
>
> Really have very little news – probably to tell you that the Americans have in a very short while made roads and so many other improvements where the jungle was previously – Really amazing – Even the chickens I brought with me, being the first chickens in New Guinea[275], have caused quite a sensation here. They have been doing well too.
>
> For the first time in quite some time, I had a good shower last night – washed my head and changed clothes. Could not change pants because the other pair I had in my bag was dirty too. Due to the usual rush of late, I was unable to have everything as I wanted it.
>
> I have a "poncho" which is an almost square piece of rain coat with a hole for my head – It really is much better than a rain coat. Never thought I would like one before. Of

---

[274] "At Sea" is a mystery to the author. I have no explanation of frequent trips he is making unless it is in the Crash Boat on one of his trips to trade for fresh vegetables, but this is only a guess. It could also have been a supply trip back to Oro Bay?

[275] The editor has not been able to verify if this statement is true. In 2010 there are chickens all over New Guinea.

course the poncho and my boots are below deck today and I cannot get them now –
even though it Is raining hard.

Have been looking at magazines this morning – Most of them are a couple of months
old or more but new to me. I would like this trip to last a long time so I can rest for a
while – Sure a lot nicer than being on the ground – No dust flies or mosquitoes and you
can stay clean –

Will close for now & try to get this mailed in a few days
                          Your loving son
                          John Frank

November 22, 1943   3:30 PM

Monday Eve
First New Guinea typed letter

Dearest Mother and Dad:
    I have nothing new to report only things still going on the hum. Understand that
some of us after being in a certain place for six months may get a fifteen-day leave provided we have not been to the mainland on temporary duty during the time. Of course
that is just something to joke about.

    It has started raining and is now only 4 PM. Maybe it will just settle the dust. You
see it can rain like the devil for a while and in no time the dust will be blowing.

    I have a floor in my tent now and things look a lot better. I even have electric lights
and a nice bed, so the jungle could be worse. Part of the routine of keeping busy is finding ways to make living somewhat better.

    I now have an assistant and have turned the company over to another officer who
has a couple of officers, one of which has also been designated as another assistant to
me so I can now use him too in addition to his other duties. I have more of a supervisory
job than I have had and think it will be much easier than before. That is what it was supposed to be.

I received a letter from Jo Ann[276] today, and she thinks Gilbert will remain there for the time, at least as he will have plenty of work there. I guess he is doing fine and know he is proud of Jo Ann as anyone could be. I sure bet she is pretty now. I think Jo Ann is going to be a prize, partly due to my mother and the principles she instilled into her. Jo Ann has been swell in that she has constantly written – never a week passes but what I don't have a letter from her. I answer very few as I do not have the time. I do appreciate them very much and am sure they help Gilbert as he does not have much time to write.

The water pump broke yesterday and since then we have not been able to get water for bathing. I will have to go to the creek for a bath this evening.

This is about all I know at the present so will stop again. I will too for the present anyway.

Your loving son,
John

34.2.   The Negro Division - 1943

While we were in New Guinea, the Army shipped a Negro Division over to MacArthur. He had not requested it, as in that day Negroes were not held in high regard. Our General promptly divided up the division and assigned the soldiers to the port unloading ships, driving trucks, and doing jobs that had to be done at the docks. The unit was located about a mile from my office.

One day when I was inspecting the unit, I observed the mess crew was dumping garbage in a hole in the mess hall floor. There was a loose board that opened to reveal a garbage container down below. You can imagine what it smelled like – terrible, flies all around. That was the first thing I saw. Then in back of the mess hall I came across three or four barrels of mash, fruit juice, and grain. They had emptied gallon cans of peaches, prunes, or anything you could imagine into the barrels – it was fermenting. They were stealing all this from the docks.

When I found it, I summoned the Company Commander. He had not been there with me when I found it initially, but he got down there real quick. I said "You are supposed to be the Company Commander and you allow this? You know they have a still down there. Do you ever get out of your tent? Ever look around this place?"

---

[276] Jo Ann Day [Freeman], John's niece, was 16-years-old in 1943 and the daughter of Gilbert, John's brother. Jo Ann's mother died when she was two, and she was raised by her grandmother, Flora Gray Day.

I turned over a couple of barrels of mash, just poured it out on the ground. The damn thing should never be. I turned to the officer, and said "First thing, you are fired as Company Commander. You are through. You will report to the General and tell him why I sent you. Who is your next in command? Get him over here!"

The next in command was a young lieutenant. When he arrived, I said "Lieutenant, you are now the Commanding Officer of this company. I want to show you what I have been showing the captain. You had to know this already, but you didn't do anything about it either. First thing you do is take that mess hall sergeant and mess hall crew, and before they serve another meal, they are to come out here and clean up this area. I want that floor nailed up, and the whole place cleaned up – dig a hole and put all this stuff in it before they serve another meal.

"You bust the Mess Sergeant one grade immediately. Whether he stays on the job as Mess Sergeant is up to you, but I will be back in one week. If I find any more of this going on, there is going to be some very serious trouble."

At that time there was a full colonel I reported to [*Col. Barnette*]. I told him what I did. He said, "Give them a week and follow up. Tell me the name of the officer you busted."

While this was going on, one morning I heard lots of shooting from the nigger[277] camp site, so I got in my jeep and drove over to where I heard the shots to see what it was all about. Two nigger sergeants from the unit were having a fight, chasing each other around the camp. Finally one sergeant took his rifle and shot the other sergeant. Then he took his knife and cut the dead soldier's heart out. He shouted, "I told the son of a bitch I would get him."

Now the nigger that cut the other man's heart out was arrested, put in jail, tried at a General Court, and sentenced to death by hanging. To hang a man, they had to find a professional Australian Hangman, and have him fly up from Melbourne. The Hangman was paid $1,000 to do the job. A scaffold was built out in Nadzab near the airfield. The day they hung him, you couldn't see a nigger for miles. Nobody was around to watch him hang. That was the only hanging they did in Nadzab.

---

[277] The word "nigger" is perhaps the most controversial word in the English language. In modern lexicon it is considered a derogatory or disparaging word, however, in the 1940s the word was in common usage and is used here to reflect the language of the period.

That was the second nigger to get hung in New Guinea, however. The first one was down in Port Moresby, but I don't know what they hung him for.

34.3.   The Medical Battalion

Meantime, I had a battalion of medical troops arrive, and I had to put them somewhere. About two days later, I went down to visit the medical troops. There in a tent I came across a lieutenant, a young doctor, sitting there with a bunch of tubes inside his tent. I said "What you doing?"

He said "I have a still going. What is wrong?"

I said "Before you get put in jail, you get rid of that right now! You are an officer, and if you don't know you are not supposed to have a still, you may cease being an officer very soon. Better stop."

I told my Sergeant "You stay here until this is cleaned up, and then come tell me. They heard me telling the Sergeant, so there were no more problems.

34.4.   Trade with Native Villages - 1944

Our trade with the natives started after we had been in Lae for a while.[278] The war was working its way farther up the north coast toward Hollandia, so we were less worried about running into Japanese if we wandered up the coast unescorted. The Air Corps had a crash boat for pilot rescue in case a plane came down in the water along the coast. A crash boat is a PT boat without torpedoes, about 35 feet long and very fast. The Air Corps used the boat for whatever they wanted.

One day I asked the Air Corps officer in charge of the boat if they were interested in going up the coast to the native villages to see if we could swap some food rations for vegetables. I was responsible for the mess hall where everyone ate – Air Corps and Army alike. The Air Corps officer agreed, so we started by taking a case or two of woolly beef, K-Rations, and whatever food was available, putting it in the boat, and heading up the coast. Maybe 10 miles up the beach we came to a place where we could tell we were close to a bunch of native villages. There was a small cove there, but we couldn't take the crash boat all the way to shore because of coral. We could only get within about 100 yards, so we anchored the boat.

---

[278] 1943-44 Movies of Crash Boat – NG Native Village, Clip 3-29b 4:49:54:00

We were not sure what to expect – having heard all the stories about headhunters and cannibals. The first time we went up the coast, we had to swim in to the beach, no guns or weapons, nothing. You can't go into the water with a pistol hanging around your neck.

Figure 116 - PNG Intense Cultivation - 2010

Figure 115 - New Guinea Village and Farm - 2010

It just ruins the pistol. Anyway we stripped down to our shorts and swam in. When we got to shore, we looked for the village chief. You don't know who the village chief is, but you can tell him by what he wears. He had a peculiar hat, smoked a cigar, or had something that identified him.

New Guinea has over 1,000 languages. The natives have trouble talking between villages because of language differences, but they have a language called Tok Pisin (also called Pidgin or Tok Boi) that they use between villages. There are two kinds of Pidgin – Pidgin English in the south which was settled by the British and Pidgin German in the north which was settled by German missionaries. In modern PNG, the language is a hybrid of Pidgin English and Pidgin German.

Figure 117 – Tribal Chief, PNG Tambul Province 2010

We asked their leader if he was the Big Chief. Now, of course he didn't speak a word of English, and we didn't understand anything he said either, but there was a lot of arm waving, pointing, and nodding such that we knew that's who he was.

I brought out the woolly beef. It is high in nutrition, something like K-Rations, but not as good as K-Rations. It probably was less expensive than K-Rations, but I don't know.

What is woolly beef? Woolly beef is a processed type of beef that is preserved in a can, like Spam. It is beef that has been cooked in a broth to a gelatin-like consistency and canned for long-term preservation without refrigeration. One can was normally divided among four men. The word "woolly" is used in the sense that it is without any recognizable shape or identifiable form that one would ever think is beef. Like Spam, it is canned food you can carry in your pocket and eat when you want.

Now first thing I did was give them five cans of woolly beef. He understood we wanted to swap some food with him. So he said something to one of the other people, and the next thing we knew a bunch of native women appeared with knit bags hanging from their heads down their backs carrying fresh vegetables.

Figure 118 - Native Pineapple Vendor - 2010

At each village there was one boss man for six or seven clans. Each clan had its own plot of land that they had been gardening for thousands of years. Once the chief gave his approval, word was passed to the lower boss men, and the women appeared from different directions bringing pineapple, papaya, bananas, beans, sweet potatoes, carrots, and whatever they had to offer. Well, we took it all. Whatever they offered was better in our eyes than woolly beef.

We got a few pineapples, not many, mostly papaya, watermelon, broccoli, and greens. They have a bean over there that comes in a pod that is about 15 inches long. One pod will produce eight or ten beans that will fill up a coffee cup. They were good eating. I found them at only one village, but I got a few. Most of what we got was papaya, but we would take as many as we could carry.

Figure 119 - Long bean pods - 2010

We started making regular trading runs up the coast. After the first trip, we took a skiff boat with us. The skiff was a 10-foot-long flat-bottom boat that we could pull behind the crash boat. We would load up the skiff to the gunnels with fruits and vegetables. Then everyone, natives and soldiers alike, would push the load out to our boat. We would tie it behind the boat and go home.

We would get the crash boat really flying, and that skiff would plane behind the boat, riding up high above the wake. We got back to Lae without spilling the skiff all but one time.[279] We thought it could not turn over, but it did flip once. We were going about 30-35 miles per hour and the rope twisted. Anyway we had papaya all over the ocean. We could not round them all up, so we decided to have target practice on the remaining papaya. We were shooting papaya and sharks all over the place. We had a lot of fun out of it, but lost a lot of food.

We would take the vegetables back to the mess hall, give them to the Mess Sergeant, and he would prepare them as best he could for everyone.

After the word spread around camp about the trips, everyone wanted to go and visit the village. It was always a lot of fun too. It was recreation for those that were selected to go, and I was the "boss man" that determined who got to go. I tried to spread the fun around, so each time I would designate which units got to send one or two soldiers. Regardless of who went, everyone had a ball. The weather was hotter than hell, but the speed of the boat created a breeze that cooled everyone down.

Well, after a while the trade went beyond food. There were grass skirts, knives, stone axes, and, as Johnnie knows, I brought back one shrunken head. These were stone-age people who had to trade for metal objects.

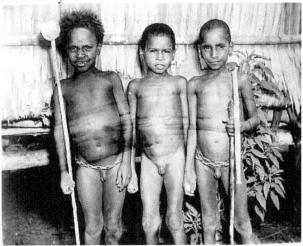

Figure 120 - Pygmy warriors - 1944

In the villages all the men slept in one building and the women and children slept in another. They don't sleep together. They have lots of kids somehow, as there were plenty of them. They are just not conceived in the houses. There must be a lot of creation going on out in the gardens.

---

[279] Video reference: 4:55:23:22

The women go topless; they wear nothing up above. The men wear a little patch or a penis gourd over their privates. Some wear absolutely nothing.

Postmark 17 Jan 1944, APO 713

Handwritten letter from Major Day
Saturday January 8, 1944
Dearest Mother and Dad

I have your Dec 21st letter and enjoyed it very much – I have not received as yet the Christmas box you mentioned. It will possibly come later. Thanks anyway.

Have just seen something whereby some will get to go home. I know there will be plenty who will apply but will be some time before all with 18 months will get to go. Some with key jobs may not get to come for a while. Only the quota may go now. I have an idea I will get to come within the year. I don't want to get Cile upset or alarmed thinking I will come anytime soon so will not say much about it to her, only that things look more favorable.

It is still hot and very little news to tell – always plenty to do in the day and hard trying to get enough sleep. As yet I have not started wearing glasses again and have done fine without them for about 3 or 4 months.

Have been unable to get any airmail envelops so have to use plain – Hope they are not too long in reaching you. I have not had a letter from Cile since her 21st Dec but should have one in a few days.

I know Johnnie had a big Christmas as usual. With all the people that give him things, he could not do otherwise – I sent him a wrist watch that cost about $26 but in the states they say it sells for about $50 or $60. We, of course, get them when available and at more reasonable prices I am sure. It had 17 jewels. Am sure it is far too nice for him at his age but maybe he will take care of it—

It is almost time for supper so will close – don't mention it but am thinking of sending Jo Ann a hundred dollars toward her college education – It is very little but will help – Don't tell her cause I may forget for a while –
            Love
            John

34.5.   The Lae Officers Club – Shooting Dice

While I was in Lae, I was one of a group that had a little shack built down the beach about a quarter of a mile from our base. We called it the "Officers Club." We got the natives to build a small traditional structure with a thatched-roof that was good rain or shine. We wanted a place to shoot craps.[280]

While the natives were building the house, a big rat ran across the floor. It was about a foot long with a big long tail. One of the natives chased after that rat with his machete. He finally caught the rat, lifted it up by the tail, took his machete, and split open its belly. He held the rat up by the tail and proceeded to put the rat down his throat like a sword swallower. He ate the rat right there and then pulled out the bones and the head from his throat. It was just like that. I almost got sick at my stomach.

Shooting craps in Lae was the regular recreational activity for the officers. Remember, we were paid in Australian pounds, not dollars, and there was no place to spend the money. So we shot craps.

As a Major, I was paid about $450 per month plus a 10 percent overseas allowance. In 1943 $6,000 per year was good money.[281] I had a regular allotment from my pay of about $300 per month that went directly to Cile at home. That left me with about $150 for craps. For about a year, I consistently sent home an additional $300 per month from my gambling winnings.[282]

I figured I would never lose at dice. Then periodically we had a colonel from the Air Corps join our game, and he seemed to always lose. He would borrow £100 from me, and every time he did, I would start losing. The colonel always paid me back the next day, but my luck rolling the dice would go away. Finally, I told him "You have to borrow from someone else, because every time I loan you money, I lose." When I quit loaning him money, I quit losing.

I was trying to make as much money as I could to send home. Cile and I had been through some hard times before the war, and we did not know what to expect after the

---

[280] Video reference 4:57:21:21.

[281] A Major (O-4) in the U.S. Army with 12-years of service in 2012 has a base salary of $75,000 per year plus $20,000 housing allowance plus overseas combat premium, roughly $110,000 per year for comparison.

[282] In 1943, $600 was enough to buy a new car.

war. The money was wired home by Western Union, and they required cash "on the barrelhead." There were no banks, no credit, and no checks.

I was always upset that Cile was not saving more of the money I sent her.[283]

34.6.   Lae Staging Area - Day's Watering Place – 11 Apr 1944

War is serious business. In 1944 the Japanese were very much a force with which to be reckoned. They held most of New Guinea and were fighting to the death. The combat front was working slowly up the north coast as the American Sixth Army (Alamo Force) repeated a series of leap-frog amphibious landings on the road to the Philippines. The next eight landings were as follows:

- *22 Sep 1943 – Finschhafen and the Huon Peninsula*
- *2 Jan 1944 – Saidor behind the Japanese lines*
- *29 Feb 1944 – Admiralty Islands invasion*
- *9 Mar 1944 – Cape Gloucester and New Britain Island*
- *22 Apr 1944 – Aitape, Hollandia*
- *26 Apr 1944 – Madang*
- *17 May 1944 – Wakde Island*
- *27 May 1944 – Biak Island*

Figure 121 - Maj. Day with Lae Staging Area Sign – Lae, NG - 1944

Before each amphibious landing, troops would gather at a staging area where soldiers prepare for the next attack. In a staging area, each soldier checks all his gear -- rifle, ammunition, rations, medical supplies, and canteen. He checks his unit's equipment, such as radios, machine guns, and explosives. He is resupplied with anything he requires. Orders are reviewed and assignments are confirmed. This is the last chance to get supplies and make sure everyone and everything is ready to go. This is also the last place where he has safe drinking water to fill his canteen. This is all

---

[283] I found out later that Cile paid for some of the Hackley house remodeling, as well as her share of living expenses. I thought somewhere in the middle of the war, she gave money to Lucille for the store, but Lucille never said anything about it.

done before loading into the landing boats for the assault. Since these were amphibious assaults, once in the boat the next stop was usually the beach and the battle. Military records indicate that Lae beaches were used for practice by the Alamo force before the Hollandia attack.

Every month we saw another wave of troops pass through the Staging Area before moving up the coast to the next fighting zone. I had a sign painted to mark our Staging Area. It was a little GI humor. We called it Uncle Sam's Sweat Shop. It showed two contrasting views of New Guinea – one, the Hollywood View and the other, the GI's View. Day's Watering Place was a "tongue-in-cheek" statement since fresh water was a treasure in New Guinea and that was all that was available. Make no mistake, there was no alcohol. We had a lot of laughs out of the sign. The sunken ship (on right) was in Lae harbor.

**Figure 122 - Lae Staging Area, Day's Watering Place
Uncle Sam's Sweat Shop
Hollywood View vs. the GI View**

A letter from Major John F. Day Jr.; APO 713 – [Lae NG]

<u>April 11 [1944]</u> – Tuesday Night 11 PM,
Dearest Mother and Dad, Carl and especially Hazel Dawn:

By golly, what do you think, but I really have a full life-size letter from Hazel Dawn. Thanks a million and hope to have many more. I finished court tonight about ten and then came down and thought I would write a couple of letters. I have not had time during the day. I know I should have written many recently, but I just have not had the time.

Suppose by now you have the money I sent to you - $300 and a letter to explain. Let me know when you have it. Glad Gilbert R. and Carl E. are doing nicely. I suppose I will have to get reacquainted with my relatives after the war is over. Too bad about all the colds, I have been very lucky and have not had one in a long time. I feel very good and have had plenty of pep. Of course, had I not, I would not have been able to keep up.

Finally, I am getting more help and should be able to do better. I have a leave coming of some kind. As soon as I can get my new assistant to take over, I think I will ask for a rest. I will have five officers I hope very soon. At present, I have one besides myself, and he has been here only a few days.

Another hint concerning Cile's medical problems:

I have a letter from Cile and she says her trouble seems to be that her stomach had dropped almost to her hips or hip bone. I don't know what to tell her, only that she might go to Temple[284] and see what should be done. I know this $3 doctor stuff will not do a bit of good except drain the pocketbook. I suggested that and told her to do what she thought best.

Based on 2012 medical knowledge, these symptoms appear to indicate a possible diagnosis of ovarian cancer. Later in 1944, Cile underwent a Radical Mastectomy for breast cancer. Breast cancer and ovarian cancer sometimes accompany each other. Cile never told her husband of the full extent of her medical problems. He would only learn of the severity of her medical situation from his father nine-months later at Christmas 1944. He did not learn of Cile's considerable medical expenses until after the war.

Mother, you should see my botanical garden. Gosh, I have transplanted so much stuff and have the prettiest place in New Guinea, I guess. I had a cute sign just painted and will try to have some pictures made to send to you. I even have a fence around the place.

I have been involved in so much "fix-up" stuff lately. I seem to be getting all the assignments of that nature from the colonel. He has turned 20 natives over to me to take care of the odd jobs around the base. I have a sergeant who deals with them. I just tell my Sergeant what to have the natives do next, and he tells the "Number One Boy." That takes care of them.

I hope Cile and Johnnie do come out to the Ranch this summer to see you. I have said nothing to her about it.

I have no idea when I will be home. Of course anything could happen – possibly late fall or maybe early next year. I told Cile it might be early next year. Well, when the time

---

[284] Temple, Texas is the location of a major medical complex for central Texas, and the home of Texas A&M Medical School.

comes, the only way you would know would be when I arrive there. I feel I have spent enough Christmas and New Years away.

It's getting late and I must close for now. All my love and kisses,
John

34.7.   Aussie Jeep Theft

We had a number of Australian troops in the area. We thought we were losing jeeps and didn't know why. When the Aussies began loading the ships to move forward toward Finschhafen, we put some Americans MPs on the dock to inspect the Australian vehicles. As the MPs inspected, anytime they saw a jeep serial number that looked like it had a little scrape or something irregular, they would set the jeep off to the side. We went through the selected jeeps very carefully and found over 100 jeeps that the Australians had stolen.

Sounds funny, I know, but they would scrape the serial numbers, repaint the jeeps with Australian colors, and add Aussie serial numbers. They were taking our jeeps forward if we didn't notice the altered numbers and catch them. We broke that up, but I don't know how many jeeps they got away with before we discovered what was happening.

34.8.   Native Sing-Sing - 1944

Outside of Lae, I attended a big native dance celebration called a Sing-Sing.[285] The natives paint themselves all over, white here, black here, hair, feathers, and have much dancing. I bought a grass skirt at one celebration. I got in there and danced with them for one or two dances to have my picture taken with them. This celebration was a big deal.

Sing-Sing is a Pidgin word for a "large musical gathering." Music in New Guinea is mostly kudu drums, chanting, and jumping around. A Sing-Sing is a gathering of a number of villages on certain festival days. It is like a harvest celebration or an American Indian powwow where families mix and the young bucks check out their neighboring villages for wives. Each village has its own special costume and dances. Kudu drums are everywhere.

---

[285] Video reference 4:57:21:21

Figure 123 – Major Day in Lae - 1944

Figure 124 - Wudux Tribe, Sing-Sing Mt. Hagen, PNG 2010

Thought to be from Morobe Province (Lae Area)
Observe skirt similarity.

Figure 125 - Wilfur Tribe, 2010

In the villages I saw more than one woman nursing a pig. The women would have a baby on one breast and a pig on the other breast –

Figure 126 - JKTribe, Morobe Province, 2010 Mt. Hagen Sing Sing

both nursing. They don't think a thing about nursing a pig. *Pigs are very valuable in the New Guinea culture, more valuable than children. You can't eat, sell, or trade your children. A child takes food from your family table while a pig does not.*

Pigs also have a special spiritual dimension. You must use a pig to buy a wife, appease the spirit of a deceased ancestor, or pay a great debt (for example, the killing of a person from another village). On very special occasions, for example, at a wedding or sometimes at a Sing-Sing, the village will feast on a pig that has been buried with leaves and hot rocks at what they call a "Mu-Mu," which is very much like a Hawaiian Luau. If you don't have a wife, you have to get some shoats (*a weaned piglet*). It takes two or three pigs or a goat or whatever you can come up with to buy a wife from her "old man" and her family.

Figure 127 - Diti Wata Tribe

Figure 128 - Huli Tribesman

Figure 129 - Unidentified, WHP

Figure 130 - Unidentified, WHP

Tribes of the unidentified photos are unknown to the photographer. All photos were taken at Mt. Hagen Sing-Sing in August 2010

34.9.   USO Entertainment Tour – Carole Landis Visit

In a period of about six months Lae was transformed into a small community. Base E took on the appearance of a major port town with three picture shows every week in different places around the Base. There was a PX, and the Base became a regular stopover on the USO entertainment tours with Hollywood movie stars like Gary Cooper, John Wayne, and Carole Landis passing through on morale visits.

Carole Landis was famous as both a pin-up girl and an actress. She began her acting career in 1937 after winning a number of beauty contests in the Los Angeles area. She was under contract with Hal Roach and Fox Studios and had appeared in six movies by 1942, including "I Wake Up Screaming" (1941) for which she received critical acclaim. Major Day had seen this movie three times while in Australia. Landis became a tireless song-and-dance performer for the USO troop entertainment program, traveling over 100,000 miles touring both the Atlantic and Pacific theaters. She continued her exhausting Pacific tour even after contracting ma-

Figure 131 - Carole Landis photo Major Day's 8mm 1944

laria and dysentery. She wrote a book entitled "Four Jills in a Jeep" about her USO tours with Martha Raye, Kay Francis, and Mitzi Mayfair that was turned into a 1944 movie by Fox Studios. She is said to have entertained more troops than Bob Hope. She died in 1948.

Figure 132 - Carole Landis Hollywood Pin-up Photo

Figure 133 - Carole Landis Performs in Pacific – Photo courtesy family

34.10.   Making Ice Cream

When I first went to Lae, I took along an ice cream freezer.[286] Why? I don't know? It was the old kind with a hand crank. It had a container with about a two-gallon capacity. Everybody wanted to know what I was going to do with it. I said, "I am going to make ice cream."

When we captured Lae, the Japanese had an ice house that we also captured. It was making about four pounds of ice a day, not much, but a little. The General said the ice had to go to the hospital. No one else had ice.

I learned that the Quartermaster had some cans of condensed milk, so I became friendly with the Quartermaster. With condensed milk and our fresh eggs, all we needed was sugar. We had to accumulate the sugar little by little over several weeks to get enough to make a batch of ice cream. We didn't steal the ingredients. They just somehow became available. We removed the metal container from the hand-cranked wooden ice bucket and mixed up a batch of ingredients.

Then we found a friendly pilot down at the airstrip who was interested in ice cream. The pilot would take the container in the back of his plane on one of his next flights up to 10,000-15,000 feet. You know when you get up pretty high and open up things, it gets cold quickly. It didn't take long to freeze two gallons of ice cream. When the pilot landed, we would take 90 percent of the ice cream up to the hospital, but then divide up the rest among our group. We each would have a bowl. When you haven't had any ice cream in a long time, it was great. That was our ice cream without any ice from the ice house. We laughed about that many times. The fun was in the making.

34.11.   Lae Downtown Airport - 1944

The downtown airport in Lae is shown in Figure 134, *a 1944 photograph by Maj. Day from Mt. Lunaman (a 1,000-foot hill) near the beach. The runway runs perpendicular to the beach and ends literally in the sand. This photo is looking south. The roof of the shelter beside the runway reads "LAE" and is shown in* Figure 135. *A line of C-47's are parked along the runway. Beside the runway there is a storage area. Ships are visible along the coast. Just beyond the end of the runway to the left in the sea is the hull of a sunken Japanese freighter. This hull is seen in* Figure 137.

---

[286] Clip 3-36; 5:29:40:26

Figure 134 - Lae Original Downtown Airport - 1943

Figure 135 - Lae Apron - 1943 Enlargement

Figure 136 - 2010 View of old runway from Mt. Lunaman
Pan-Pacific stadium in foreground

The ship hull at the end of the Lae runway was a sunken Japanese cargo ship, believed to be the Myoko Maru, a possible residual from the Battle of the Bismarck Sea. When the Americans landed, the Japanese bombed their own ship to prevent its cargo from falling into American hands. The Americans were able to salvage a lot of the cargo before the ship sank. The hull became a landmark for Lae.

Figure 137 - Sunken Japanese Freighter at Lae runway
1944 Photo by Maj. Day

Figure 138 - B-25C with 50-caliber machine gun in nose
Parked on Lae runway, the bow of the sunken Japanese
freighter in the background - 1944

This aircraft photo was taken in the Lae central air strip by Major Day. The sunken ship hull is clearly identifiable. This aircraft has been identified as the "Sandra Lee," a member of the 501st Bomb Squadron of the 345th Bomb Group of the Fifth Air Force.[287] The 501st Bomb Squadron was known as the "Black Panthers," which explains the nose art, a crouching black panther.

The Sandra Lee was transferred from the 22nd Bomb Group (Red Raiders) to the 345th Bomb Group (Air Apaches) on 31 Jan 44.[288] The 345th BG was stationed at Lae Nadzab Airfield Complex beginning 23 Feb 44 until 23 Jul 44, the likely period of this photograph.[289]

During WWII, 9,816 B-25s were built. This specific aircraft, Serial No. 42-53374, left for overseas duty in the Pacific (OBEY) from Hamilton AFB in California 15 Jul 1943. The aircraft was condemned to salvage 22 Dec 1944, probably due to being war weary, that is, flown on an excessive number of missions or damaged beyond reasonable repair.[290]

Figure 139 - B-25 Nose Paint
A crouching Black Panther on the
Sandra Lee

---

[287] http://en.wikipedia.org/wiki/501st_Bombardment_Squadron

[288] http://www.redraiders22bg.com/raiders.cgi?plane=B-25

[289] http://www.345thbombgroup.org/history_index.php

[290] Air Force Historical Studies Office, Individual Aircraft Record Card, Serial No. 42-53374

34.12.   P-38 Flights

After a while the P-38 Lightning began to arrive in Lae. The P-38 was a really good plane. Some thought it was a better plane than the P-51 because it could turn so sharply, which made it a lot more maneuverable in a dogfight. It was not as fast as the P-51. The P-38 had two engines and room for two people, one behind the other in the center nacelle. Several times I went up for a ride with my movie camera.

We took off over that Japanese ship. When the pilot rolled the plane, there is a lot of pressure on the passenger. We had a friendly dogfight with another plane. The pilot in the P-38 is located at the center of gravity of the plane, so when he rolls the plane, the pilot doesn't feel the pressure while the passenger can't move. I went for a ride several times.

34.13.   Sharks

At Lae the water drops off fast from the beach. The Engineers had built three piers at the dock, two on piles and a third that actually floated. We had a shark that lived near the pier. Every day one could go down to the pier any time of day and there was the shark. He stayed next to the pier. He was not afraid. We dropped rocks toward him, but he would not leave.

For entertainment we would go out in a boat and shoot sharks. Maybe two miles off shore the sharks were everywhere – some ten or fifteen feet long. Initially it was fun to dump the garbage in the water and watch them fight over the garbage. Then we started shooting at them with a carbine, but that carbine would not kill them. If you hit one, they never rolled over dead.

When we went into Java, we actually saw schools of sharks, perhaps 4 or 5 miles out.

34.14.   The Food Trip to Australia - Sydney and Dalgety's - 1944

My big problem in New Guinea was getting enough food to feed the troops. I had to fight for food; I mean really hustle to keep rounding up enough grub. The Quartermaster could get K-rations, but you need more variety. We needed fresh food. We dealt with the natives, but we still needed more. I wanted to fly down to Brisbane to see if we could pick up some fresh food. The colonel finally gave me permission to go to Brisbane.

Since I was going south, they had five prisoners of war they wanted taken to Headquarters. They said, "You take them down there."

When I got on the plane, there was the pilot, the five prisoners, a young lieutenant, and me. I asked the lieutenant, "What is your mission?"

"I have to take the prisoners somewhere," the lieutenant said.

I said, "You are taking them to Brisbane, and they are all yours." So I went up to the front and sat in the copilot's seat next to the pilot. We took off and were heading straight out of Port Moresby toward Townsville.

Todd, the pilot, said, "Take over for me, Major, I want to take a snooze." So I started flying the plane. It didn't seem that difficult, and the pilot went to sleep. Looking down, the coral reef off the coast of New Guinea is beautiful, so after a while I decided to take the plane down to about 500 feet to get a better look.

The pilot woke up, looked out the window, and with a startle said, "Hey, what are you doing?"

I said, "We are looking at this beautiful coral reef."

"Don't get so close to it," he said, and he took the controls back. That ended my flying career!

We flew into Townsville, where we gassed up before flying on to Brisbane. When we arrived, the lieutenant took the POWs down to Gen. Willoughby (GHQ G-2 Intelligence) where his men were hot to interview any prisoners. If they didn't have prisoners, they had nothing to do and had to imagine things. I was glad to be done with all of them.

The pilot and I went to the Officers Club and had dinner. While we were eating, the pilot said, "I am going on to Sydney. Want to come?"

Well, I saw this as my chance to get down to Sydney and pick up my two pieces of luggage at Dalgety's. When we left Sydney for the invasion of Lae, I stored a footlocker and suitcase at Dalgety's with a lot of things that I thought I would not need in New Guinea. The pilot didn't care, but I didn't have permission to go to Sydney. So what did I do? Well, I thought a moment and decided I would go ahead.

The plane landed at the Sydney airport, and everybody got off the plane but me. The Military Police asked, "All out?"

The others said, "All gone."

I stayed in back of the plane as they inspected it. Then the pilot said, "All out," and everyone started walking toward the gate. I just stepped in with them and went through the gate like everyone else. Once you are through the gate, you are OK. I went with the pilot downtown where I got myself a hotel room. I paid my own hotel bill, since I was not supposed to be there.

I knew the Adjutant at the base, so the next morning, I went to see him and told him why I was there. He said, "You will be crucified if they catch you down here."

"I don't know why," I said, "I am getting my luggage and I am going right back."

He said "Tell you what I'll do, let me send a wire to your Commander in Lae telling him that you were here because the pilot had to fly down here rather than to Brisbane, as though he didn't intend going here." Well, the pilot always was going to Sydney because that was where the Air Force Recreation Center was located, and that was where he was heading.

The Adjutant sent a message to Lae saying the plane had a technical problem so the pilot had to go to Sydney. He added, "Major Day had to come also. He has to have your OK to bring back his gear in addition to the other stuff you told him to get."

The Commanding Officer sent back a wire and said OK. So I had a free rein until I was ready to return to New Guinea. I went down to Dalgety's and collected my footlocker and suitcase. After I got my bags, I sat for a moment with my friends at Dalgety's for what I thought would be a brief conversation. I had been dealing with Dalgety's since I was at GHQ in Brisbane. From my dealings with the chickens and getting supplies for the New Guinea invasion, I had made a number of friends on their staff – one of whom was the Chief Liquor Taster.

A lot of the whiskey that goes into the Far East passes through Australia and Dalgety's. Dalgety's was receiving barrels of whiskey from Scotland, and repackaging it in smaller retail-sized bottles. They had an official "liquor taster," who tasted everything that came in the door to make sure it was what it was supposed to be. He approved it before Dalgety's accepted and paid for it. He invited me to go down into the basement with him for a wee bit of tasting.

So we went down among the barrels of Scotch whiskey. He had this small dram on the end of a stick that could go down inside the barrel and pull up a sample. He would take a taste. I would take a taste. We would discuss the merits of each barrel before moving on to the next barrel. Mostly, we tasted Scotch, but there was also some Irish whisky. We spent most of the afternoon in the basement with the barrels. I don't remember how long we were down there, but it was long enough for both us to get half lit.

I had a list of things to bring back to Lae. I arranged for a whole beef packed in several boxes and all frozen. I was sneaking it into New Guinea, as I had no permission to bring it in. I just told everybody the General told me to bring back a beef. I also had a bunch of other stuff the Quartermaster had given me, mostly food. In total, I damn near filled up two truckloads with stuff. Well, it was time for me to head back up to Lae, but I had to hitch a ride on a "space available" basis. I wasn't sure how I was going to get everything back. I had to find a pilot that could fit me and my cargo into his plane. It wasn't too much trouble to find a plane heading north, since there were planes going every day. The problem was weight, space, or destination. I wanted someone who was going all the way to Lae, not terminating in between. Here I was with a complete frozen beef, trying to hitchhike before it thawed. One plane was stopping in Brisbane, but I was afraid my beef would thaw. Some planes could not take the weight. Another plane felt my cargo was too bulky. Anyway I was in Sydney for almost a week trying to hitch a ride. Meantime, I kept sending messages to the office saying I was getting the stuff together.

Finally, I found a plane that could carry all my stuff and was heading straight through to Lae. The plane didn't land in Brisbane but refueled at some military air base up the York Peninsula. When we arrived in Nadzab (*Lae*), I called the office and told them to send a couple of trucks down to pick me up.

In New Guinea, there was no refrigeration and very little ice. The trip from Sydney had taken a number of hours, such that what was frozen in Sydney was thawing when we arrived in Lae. I was trying to find a place to store the beef overnight before someone could steal it. We put the beef in a tent with a guard. With no ice, it would not keep. We knew we had to eat it soon. The next day the entire camp had real beef for the first time in many months.

That night with my luggage back, I started looking through the footlocker to see what I had stored. There were winter uniforms, dress uniforms, and well, there was really nothing I needed. I had everything I could use already. It was more a matter of principle.

35.   HOLLANDIA – 22 APR 1944

35.1.   The War Strategy Debate: Luzon vs. Formosa – 14 Mar 1944

MacArthur's Southwest Pacific forces were moving up the north coast of New Guinea. Halsey's South Pacific forces were moving up the Solomon Islands. Nimitz's Central Pacific forces were moving across the Gilbert and Marshall Islands. The momentum of the war was shifting to the US, but the Japanese were a long way from defeated. The Japanese Navy was strong, and their Army controlled eastern China, the Dutch East Indies, the Philippines, and many of the islands of the Pacific.

Operation Cartwheel was working successfully. Rabaul was being neutralized without a direct military land attack. MacArthur had successfully executed over 35 amphibious attacks while avoiding excessively fortified Japanese installations. He was determined to avoid another bloody Buna-type battle.

The American amphibious landings on the north New Guinea coast continued in early 1944:

- *2 Jan 1944 – Saidor behind the Japanese lines*
- *29 Feb 1944 – Admiralty Islands invasion*
- *9 Mar 1944 – Cape Gloucester and New Britain Island*

The new American long-range bomber, the B-29 Superfortress, began to roll out of American factories in September 1943. The American strategy had always included the destruction of Japan by massive aerial bombing from China. In November 1943 American planners became concerned that Chiang Kai-shek and the Nationalist Chinese would not be able to defend air bases in eastern China from which the B-29 could attack the Japanese mainland. The American alternative to air bases in China would be airbases on islands in the Pacific. To secure air bases in the central Pacific, the Americans first had to secure their flank in the west, which meant they needed to control either Formosa or Luzon.

Both Luzon and Formosa are strategically located to cut the Japanese supply lines from Southeast Asia. Cutting off raw materials, particularly oil, rubber, tin, and rice, was a key step to bringing down Japan's industrial war machine. Formosa is closer to Japan than Luzon. However, if Formosa were captured first, supply lines to Formosa would be vulnerable to attack from the Japanese-controlled Philippines and Japanese-controlled China. The Philippines faces the open sea and would be easier to resupply. The Philippines was also U.S. Territory, so there were political reasons for invading the Philippines first.

To capture either island, there were two alternative paths – one path hopping between airbases up the north coast of New Guinea or a second path hopping between islands across the central Pacific. Any plan across the central Pacific would have to be done without the support of land-based aircraft, and carrier operations would be very costly in men and equipment. Following the path up New Guinea could be done with ground-based air support and should prove less costly in lives and matériel.

The US Navy favored the central Pacific route to Formosa, while the US Army favored the New Guinea path to the Philippines. There was professional competition between the Army and the Navy to reach Japan first. MacArthur was anxious to move quickly to outpace Nimitz and the Central Pacific Command that was advancing across the Gilbert and Marshall Islands. Both Nimitz and MacArthur made strong proposals to the Joint Chiefs for their command to be the single focus of Pacific resources. In the end, the Joint Chiefs decided to do both – MacArthur would continue up the north coast of New Guinea to the Philippines and Nimitz would proceed across the Pacific from the Caroline Islands north toward the Marianas and west toward the Palau island chain. Palau was considered necessary to secure the eastern flank for the invasion of the Philippines.

On 14 Mar 1944 the Joint Chiefs of Staff approved the plan to invade the Philippine Island of Mindanao on 15 Nov 1944. The same directive instructed Nimitz to capture the Marianas on 15 June 1944 and the Palau by 15 Sept 1944.

The Navy would continue to question this decision until President Roosevelt traveled by ship to Hawaii, where he met with Gen. MacArthur and Adm. Nimitz on 21 July 1944 to discuss strategy in the Pacific. This meeting finally produced the unanimous decision to attack the Philippines, rather than Formosa.

35.2. Hollandia, Dutch New Guinea

35.2.1. Strategic Location

Hollandia[291] was on the north coast of New Guinea in the territory of the Dutch East Indies. The former colonial capital of Dutch New Guinea, Hollandia is three degrees south of the equator and

---

[291] Dutch New Guinea remained under Dutch rule until 1963, even though Indonesia won its independence from Holland in 1948. After annexation to Indonesia, Hollandia was renamed Jayapura, and by 2012 the city had an estimated population of 200,000 people. In 1969 following annexation, the Indonesians renamed Dutch New Guinea as "Irian" and later "Irian Jaya," which means roughly "beautiful Irian" in Indonesian. In 2002 the name was officially changed to Papua because the Melanesian natives prefer to be called Papuans.

characterized by a hot and humid tropical climate. Heavy annual rainfall varies between 100 and 130 inches per year, providing abundant fresh water, although it still had to be boiled to be safe to drink. Beaches are narrow and often quickly turn into mangrove swamps. The coastline is marked by two large deep-water harbors – Humboldt Bay on the south and Tanahmerah Bay on the north – separated by about 25 miles. The harbors are the only deep-water ports for 500 miles in either direction. The two harbors are connected by an inland valley that is protected from the ocean by the coastal Cyclops Mountains, which have peaks over 7,000 feet. The interior valley has good flying weather, such that the Japanese had built three airdromes and had a fourth under construction on the valley plain north of Lake Sentani, a 15-mile-long lake in the valley.

Cool evening breezes flowing down off the Cyclops Mountains provide a natural air conditioning to Hollandia. The village Hollandia was active in the 1920's as an exporter of bird-of-paradise plumes for women's hats, but with the change in fashion for women's hats, there was little of commercial value in Hollandia before the war.

Forty miles to the interior from the coast is territory that in 1944 had never been mapped by Europeans. The stone-age native tribes that populated the interior had virtually no contact with Europeans and had histories of cannibalism and headhunting.[292]

Hollandia is strategically located, half-way between Brisbane and Manila.[293] Brisbane is 1,900 miles to the southeast, while Mindanao is 1,200 miles northwest

Figure 140 – Brisbane to Hollandia, Dutch East Indies

---

[292] The 2011 book "Lost in Shangri-La" by Mitchell Zuckoff deals with a crashed airplane flying out of Hollandia in May 1945.

[293] Hollandia is 1,200 miles from Mindanao and 1,800 miles from Manila.

across an open sea. Tacloban, Leyte is 1,400 miles away. Hollandia would become the last stop for many troops before the Philippine invasion. It is one of the last deep-water ports before the Philippines.

35.2.2.   Hollandia and Aitape Invasion – 22-26 Apr 1944

MacArthur was leapfrogging up the north coast of New Guinea with a series of amphibious attacks, each landing separated by about 120 to 200 miles. The separation distance of each attack was determined by the maximum range of his new P-38 fighters that provided air cover for his bombers. Each leap was arranged to capture another airdrome; the aircraft would be moved forward to the new airdrome and the process repeated. From Saidor and Finschhafen, the normal step would have been Hansa Bay, and indeed Hansa Bay was targeted by the Americans. The Japanese base at Hollandia was 475 miles from Saidor and Nadzab, well beyond the traditional range of the Fifth Air Force fighters. Air support over such a distance could only be provided by Navy carrier support. MacArthur's requests for carrier support had been constantly denied.

Nimitz was trying to fit "support for New Guinea" in between his own attacks on the Marianas and Palau islands. If MacArthur was to be given carrier support for only one attack in April, it made sense to skip Hansa Bay and jump as far as possible to Hollandia.

For Hollandia, the Joint Chiefs instructed Nimitz to provide the carrier air coverage to MacArthur. When MacArthur and Nimitz met in Brisbane on 25 Mar 1944, Nimitz agreed to loan seven smaller carriers (CVE - Carrier Escorts[294]) for the Hollandia attack but for <u>only</u> "eight days." Nimitz was justly concerned about the threat to his Escort Carriers presented by 300 Japanese aircraft stationed at Wewak, 125 miles east of Hollandia. The Japanese felt secure at Wewak because it was beyond the range of the American fighters and therefore safe from American bombers. Nimitz also had his own commitments for invasions in the Central Pacific.

MacArthur was concerned about continuing air support for his ground troops if the Navy carriers withdrew early. Aitape offered a nearby airdrome for ground-based air support for the Hollandia assault if it could be captured quickly before the Navy carriers withdrew, so it was added

---

[294] Carrier Escorts, sometime called by the Navy as "Jeep Carriers" or "Baby Carriers," were about half the size of a regular carrier and carried one-third as many aircraft as a regular carrier. Their attraction during WWII was that they could be built very quickly at a time when the US Navy was desperate for carriers. They had poor defense armaments and a number were sunk during WWII with great loss of life.

to the invasion plan.

Fortuitously, at this time the Fifth Air Force received 58 new P-38s, each with an extra 300-gallon fuel tank. Gen. Kenney ordered the immediate modification of his older P-38s to add extra fuel tanks, such that he was able to launch 80 P-38s with extended range, which brought Wewak into target distance. Hollandia remained outside target distance. With the element of surprise on his side and P-38 protection, the American bombers attacked Wewak and destroyed a total of 293 of the 300 Japanese aircraft stationed there. This virtually ended the Japanese air force in New Guinea, and cleared the way for the Hollandia attack. The air threat to the carriers was gone, and the carriers were safely deployed to support MacArthur's landing.

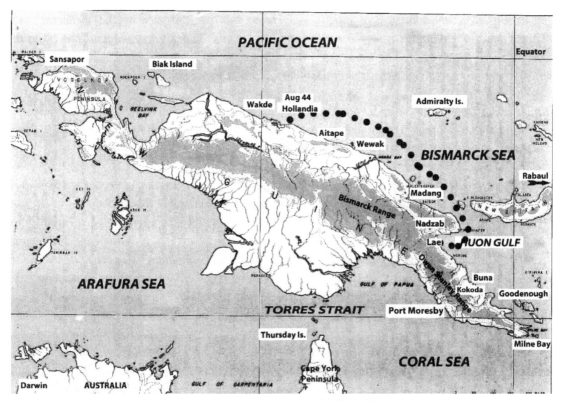

Figure 141 - Day Route - Lae to Hollandia Aug 44

The invasion of Hollandia on 22 Apr 1944 caught the Japanese by total surprise. Gen. Adachi, the commander of the Japanese 18th Army, had been withdrawing from Madang. He fully expected the Allies to attack Hansa Bay, with only a small chance that a secondary target might be Wewak. Gen. Adachi felt Hollandia was beyond the range of the Americans and had prepared very little defense. The Navy carriers made the difference. MacArthur arrived with a force of 84,000 troops, the largest amphibious landing in the Pacific to that date. American intelligence had over-

estimated the Japanese strength, as the Japanese troops in Hollandia were primarily service troops with very limited combat training. Hollandia fell in four days with light American casualties. By 6 Jun1944, American casualties were reported to be 124 killed and 1,057 wounded. The Japanese had 3,300 killed and 660 captured. Reports estimated that over 30,000 Japanese troops escaped from Wewak, Aitape, and Hollandia into the surrounding jungles where they remained for over one year until Australian forces took their final surrender near Wewak at the end of the war in August 1945. More than half of the Japanese troops that escaped into the jungle died from starvation and disease before surrender.

MacArthur continued his march up the north coast of New Guinea:

- *26 April 1944 – Madang invaded by land*
- *17 May 1944 – Wakde Island*
- *27 May 1944 – Biak Island*

35.2.3.   Supply Base G – Hollandia

With its two large harbors and four airstrips, Hollandia became the principle staging area for the invasion of the Philippines.

Hollandia was designated to become the major military headquarters and a supply center for moving personnel north. It was designated USASOS Advanced Section, Supply Base G. Between 25 Jul 1944 and 24 Aug 1944, new headquarters moving into Hollandia included:

- *General Headquarters of the Southwest Pacific Area (GHQ)*
- *United States Army Forces in the Far East (USAFFE)*
- *Alamo Force (Sixth Army)*
- *US Army Services of Supply (USASOS)*
- *Army Services Command (ASCOM)*
- *Fifth Air Force*
- *US Eighth Army*
- *US Seventh Fleet*
- *Allied Control Bureau*
  - *Allied Air Force*
  - *Allied Land Forces*
- *Royal Netherlands Indies Army*
- *Land Headquarters (Australia).*

Beyond housing, offices, food, medical supplies and POL for these headquarters, Base G was charged with providing a Staging Area to accommodate 150,000 combat troops at one time for the coming Philippine invasion. The Engineers had to create the infrastructure for a "temporary" city with a population approaching 200,000 people in four short months.

The Engineer Brigade went to work immediately to improve the roads, port, and storage facilities. Airdromes had to be improved with additional runways and longer runways. New hospitals were built. The area was a beehive of construction activity. By August, the Engineers had two saw mills operating around the clock 7 days a week, each averaging 25,000 board-feet per day output. The entire output of one sawmill was devoted the new GHQ headquarters for Gen. MacArthur, while 15,000 board-feet of the second mill went to the Far East Air Force. This left insufficient volume for all the rest of Base G.[295]

When GHQ moved forward to Hollandia, Brisbane became the Rear Echelon. In Sep 1944, MacArthur divided his Advanced Echelon into two segments. He planned to take personal charge of the advanced segment, the forces going into the Philippines. The second segment would remain in Hollandia under Gen. Sutherland and his staff.

The new complex of buildings for the Hollandia GHQ headquarters was located up the inland mountains on a prominence "overlooking beautiful Lake Sentani against the backdrop of the towering Cyclops Mountains."[296] The Engineer Battalion referred to the site as "Eagle's Nest." The Engineers had to build a winding road up the mountains to the overlook of this picturesque valley. The site included buildings patterned after Government House in Port Moresby, which would serve as both office and residence for the General Staff.

35.3.   Capt. Elaine Clarke (Bessie Marie) Appears in Hollandia – March 1944

*Paul Rodgers, in Volume II: **MacArthur and Sutherland: The Bitter Years**, deals with three issues facing Sutherland in early 1944 as he was preparing to move GHQ forward into New Guinea.[297] First, the shortage of manpower led to the consideration of using members of the Women's Army Corp (WAC) in non-combat positions. Second, there were questions on whether Australian women would be allowed to join the U.S. Army to ease transportation costs and delays for moving WAC's from the States. Third, if Australian women were allowed, there was an*

---

[295] History of USASOS, "Base G at Hollandia from Founding, March 1944 to May 1945". Historical Manuscript File 8-5.8 SO No. 780-21 (1947) AA V. 21, p 66. Also Linda Mayo, US Army in World War II, Technical Services, Ordnance, Chap. XX, The Philippines: Leyte, p387.

[296] Ibid p388.

[297] Rodgers, Paul P. Green Library, Stanford University Praeger Publishers, One Madison Ave., New York, NY 10010, Greenwood Publishing Group, Copyright 1990, published 1991, p66-67,

issue of deploying Australian women outside of mainland Australia. These three issues faced serious scrutiny in both Washington and Canberra.

The first issue, the use of WAC's, caused logistic problems involved in separate housing and security. The second issue of recruiting Australian women was apparently restricted to enlisted women only. The Washington commander of WAC's, Col. Oveta Culp Hobby, strongly opposed bringing Australian women into American ranks. Australia was also experiencing a labor shortage for their defense work and was just beginning to bring women into its own defense industry. How Sutherland pulled it off is unknown to Rogers, but there appears to have been no restriction on recruiting "a few" Australian women as officers. Third, concerning deployment outside of Australia, there was an understanding between Curtin and the US Army that Australian women would not be deployed outside of Australia. Sutherland managed to obtain approval to move three Australian and English women to New Guinea: Elaine Bessemer-Clarke (Gen. Sutherland's friend), Mrs. Meryl Stevenson (Gen. Kenney's friend), and Mrs. Louise Mouatt (Gen. Marshall's friend). Later this understanding would be modified to say Australian women would not be assigned north of the equator, which would permit them to serve in Hollandia.

Rogers states there were sound arguments for the generals having stenographers in the forward headquarters. There were also good arguments why the stenographers accompanying the generals should have officer rank.[298]   Rather than face criticism about the matter, there was an aggressive publicity campaign by GHQ to promote the event.

MRS BESSEMER CLARKE CAPTAIN IN AMERICAN WAC

From FRANK DEXTER, "Argus" War Correspondent, with Gen MacArthur's HQ.

Mrs Elaine Bessemer Clarke, daughter of Sir Norman and Lady Brookes, of Melbourne, is one of 3 British women commissioned as officers in the US Women's Army Corps.

Mrs Bessemer Clarke, who has been acting as receptionist at GHQ, has been given the rank of captain. Others commissioned are Mrs Beryl Stephenson and Mrs Mowat, both with the rank of lieutenant. Mrs Stephenson, a native of Scotland, is secretary to Lt-Gen George Kenny, Commander Allied Air Forces, SW Pacific, and Mrs Mowat, an Englishwoman, is secretary to Maj-Gen Richard Marshall, deputy Chief of Staff to Gen MacArthur.

The appointments have been approved by Washington and London. Mrs Mowat's husband, a British Army officer, was captured in Malaya.

National Library of Australia

Figure 142 - Bessemer-Clarke Promoted in USWAC
The Argus (Melbourne, Victoria) Monday, 27 Mar 1944, page 6

Mrs. Elaine Clarke (Bessie-Marie) was commissioned as a Captain and Assistant to the GHQ Headquarters Commandant. It is worth observing that the pay of a U.S. Army Captain in 1944 was higher than an Australian Brigadier.

---

[298] Ibid. p. 66-67

In 1944 Beryl Spiers Stevenson was commissioned a Lieutenant in the U.S. Army and rose to the rank of Major before war's end.[299] She continued with GHQ as it moved forward from Brisbane to Port Moresby to Hollandia and the Philippines, regularly with Gen. Kenney. At war's end she was decorated with the highest medal the U.S. can grant to a non-citizen for meritorious non-combat service to the military.[300]

Mrs. Louise Mouatt, the stenographer for Gen. Richard Marshall, remained with the U.S. Army through the war, and reached the grade of Captain.

35.3.1.　Mrs. Clarke Causes Hollandia Engineer Brigade War Bond Protest

The 5201 Engineer Construction Brigade was hard at work on the new Hollandia buildings that were expected to become the next Advanced Headquarters for GHQ. The Engineers assumed that in time these would become the living quarters for Gen. MacArthur, although they knew Gen. Sutherland would likely become the first occupant.

The buildings were in a late stage of construction when Capt. Elaine Clarke flew into Hollandia and "took charge of Eagle's Nest." I was told she arrived with a pink-colored bathtub and a pink commode and began directing the soldiers on how she wanted everything arranged, especially the location of her bathtub. She was riding high.

Figure 143 - Bessemer Clark, Melbourne Argus News, 27 Mar 44

On a military base, it doesn't take long before rumors spread among a bunch of soldiers. All it took was to have one or two soldiers see the tub, and the word spread like wildfire. Soon everyone knew about the pink bathtub.

When the colonel that commanded the Engineer Brigade found out Bessie-Marie was up the hill, he was furious. He verified the story from his troops that she was telling everyone how she wanted everything rearranged, including her pink bathtub. Well, this really did a job on the colonel. "Here we are trying to fight a war, and some bitch is shipping in a pink bathtub." But in the Army, you obey the orders of your Commanding Officer, and Gen. Sutherland was in charge. Construction continued.

---

[299] The Sydney Morning Herald, March 27, 1944, p6.
[300] Dunn, Peter, Australia @ War, Ibid.

This incident led to a not-so-silent protest. War bonds and stamps were a big deal during the war. The government financed the war with war bonds and controlled inflation by price controls and rationing. It was common and patriotic for all soldiers to place an allotment from every paycheck into a savings account that purchased war bonds. Shortly after the word got out about the pink bathtub for "Eagles' Nest,"

**Figure 144 – Aerial Photo of Gen. Douglas MacArthur House
Hollandia, Dutch New Guinea - U.S. Signal Corps – 11 Nov 1944**

every soldier in the Engineer Brigade "went on a War Stamp Strike." They dropped all their donations for government bonds as a form of protest against what was going on "up the hill." This was done with great fanfare, and I was told it was publicized in the press back in the United States.

MacArthur got to "Eagle's Nest" for only a few nights, as far as I know. The quarters on the hill became a private love nest for Gen. Sutherland and his *fem fatale*, Capt. Elaine Clarke, as they were left behind in Hollandia when MacArthur moved forward to the Philippines.

36.   LEYTE INVASION & ASCOM – 20 AUG 1944

36.1.   Army Services Command (ASCOM) Organized – 23 Jul 1944

Following the March 1944 decision by the Joint Chiefs to invade the Philippines, preparation for the invasion began immediately. The Joint Chiefs appointed General MacArthur to be the Supreme Commander of Land, Sea, and Air for the invasion. Vice Adm. Thomas Kinkaid and the Seventh Fleet would transport and support the Sixth Army which was under command of Lt. Gen. Walter Krueger.

Airdromes in New Guinea were 1,200 miles from the Philippines – too far for bombers of the Army Air Corps to reach Philippine targets. Air cover for the Army amphibious landing would have to be provided by Adm. William Halsey's Third Fleet which included four carrier task forces. Halsey was to remain on the line until the Army could establish ground-based air fields and bring aircraft forward. In a concession to the Navy, Adm. Halsey remained under the command of Adm. Nimitz of the Central Pacific Command, __not__ under MacArthur. This split Command would prove almost disastrous to the entire Philippine invasion operation.

Figure 145 - Army Services Forces Insignia – Red Border with Blue Star

The Japanese had a formidable garrison of over 180,000 troops stationed in the Philippines, divided primarily between the northern island of Luzon and the southern island of Mindanao.[301] The Americans hoped to divide the two Japanese troop concentrations by landing in between the two major islands in Leyte.

The Philippine invasion would be entirely American troops. The Australian Army, which had played an important role in the New Guinea campaign, would relieve Americans of further combat actions in New Guinea, New Britain, and the Dutch East Indies. The Australians would focus on "clean-up" of remaining Japanese resistance in the Dutch East Indies.

The Philippine invasion would be significantly larger than any Task Force in the Pacific to that point – approaching the scale of the Normandy invasion on D-Day in Europe. Up to this point, logistics were handled by the United States Army Services of Supply (USASOS-SWPA). How-

---

[301] M. Hamlin Cannon, *The Return to the Philippines*, US Army in World War II, The War in the Pacific, Office Of The Chief Of Military History, Department Of The Army, Center for Military History, Washington, D.C., 1954, CMH Pub 5-9-1, p.22.

ever, Gen. Chamberlain recommended a reorganization of USASOS to deal with the larger scale of the Philippine operation. The USASOS Advanced Echelon was designated Army Services Command (ASCOM) and was focused exclusively on the Philippine invasion. The unit was attached to the Sixth Army.

The poor infrastructure of Leyte, including airdromes, roads, and port facilities dictated that ASCOM would be largely an engineer outfit. Maj. Gen. Hugh J. Casey, MacArthur's chief engineer, was assigned as Commanding Officer and placed on detached service from GHQ for this assignment. Gen. Jack Sverdrup, Casey's Deputy, became Acting Chief Engineer for GHQ.

USASOS – SWPA (Southwest Pacific Area) remained in the rear echelon of Brisbane and was headed by Maj. Gen. James L. Frink, who reported directly to Gen. MacArthur and was responsible for everything except the Philippines.

Army Services Command (ASCOM) was established in Brisbane on 23 July 1944 but would move forward to New Guinea quickly.[302] For non-military readers, the scope of ASCOM activities can often be underestimated. ASCOM was responsible for all logistical support services to the combat arms, including engineering, quartermaster, medical, signal, transportation, chaplain, finance, and a variety of other specialty activities. ASCOM was given a dual mission, as follows:

- "To prepare and execute plans for the establishment and development of new bases in accordance with USASOS Directives and Logistic Instructions. (These bases would be similar to Lae, Finschhafen, and Hollandia, but in the Philippines.)

- "To plan and execute the immediate combat logistical support of Army Task Forces to which it may be attached, as directed by Commanding General Sixth Army."[303]   (This meant combat support to Gen. Krueger and the full Sixth Army.)

ASCOM was organized[304] into five sections as follows:

- G-1 – Administration and Personnel Section
- G-2 – Intelligence Section: To collect and disseminate maps, photos, intelligence, and reference data and maintain reference library.
- G-3 – Troop Unit Section: To coordinate service troop requirements with the other staff sections; and, by liaison with Task Force Commanders, to maintain station lists of ASCOM troops, to issue warning and movement orders, and arrange for transportation.

---

[302] ASCOM General Order 132 of 23 July 1944.

[303] USASOS Letter, Basic Organizational Directive, 25 Jul 1944.

[304] ASCOM General Order No. 3, 15 Aug 1944.

- *G-4 – <u>Base Development Section</u>: To plan and organize new bases, set requirements for supply, equipment, and personnel, and organize and absorb personnel*
- *<u>Construction Section</u>: To plan construction for each objective area, set requirements, and organize and absorb key construction supervisory personnel.*

During August 1944, the immediate needs of ASCOM for personnel and supplies were submitted to USASOS. By 31 Aug 1944 the unit had 25 officers assigned and 19 attached. The headquarters company had 101 enlisted men.[305] The first personnel assigned to ASCOM included:

- *Col. Elmer F. Wallender, Inf – Dep. Commander & Chief Base Development*
- *Col. Edward C. Harwood, CE – Chief of Staff*
- *Col. Charles R. Dawley, Inf – Asst Chief of Staff*
- *Lt. Col. Merle A. Sparks, AGD – Chief of Administration (G-1)*
- *Maj. George H. Adams, CE – Chief of Intelligence Sec. (G-2)*
- **Lt. Col. John Day, FA – Chief of Troop Section (G-3)**
- *Col. Kilbourne Johnston, BSC – Exec of Base Development (G-4)*
- *Col. Thomas F. Kern, CE – Act Chief of Construction Sec*
- *Col Reginald L Dean, CE – Exec of Construction*

ASCOM arrived at Hollandia from Brisbane on 5 Sept 1944. General Casey set up headquarters at Hol-La-Kang, adjacent to Sixth Army Headquarters. By 14 September his planning was nearly complete for KING I (the Mindanao landing) scheduled for 15 October and KING II (Leyte), scheduled for 20 December.[306]

Luzon was the ultimate target. Mindanao was a stepping stone to Leyte before striking Luzon. In early September, Halsey did a carrier reconnoiter of the Leyte coast which revealed the weakness of Japanese defenses for the island. Upon Halsey's recommendation, the invasion of Mindanao was cancelled in favor of an early invasion of Leyte on 20 Oct 1944.

On 15 September, the day ASCOM was attached to Sixth Army, the KING I (K-1) operation was canceled and the date of KING II (K-2) was advanced to 20 October 1944.[307] K-1 plans were immediately set aside and K-2 planning accelerated. Gen. Casey conferred with Gen. Krueger and GHQ, as the change of date caused many major problems, especially for the engineers.

K-2 was a larger action with many more heavy construction projects due to the lack of infrastructure on Leyte. October is the beginning of the cyclone rainy season, one of the worst times of the

---

[305] OCMH History of USASOS, File 8-5.8, AA, Vol. 8, p. 3-4.

[306] Ibid. p. 3.

[307] Ibid. p.4.

year for construction. Requisitioning heavy construction equipment for SWPA required Washington, D.C. advanced approval on an operation-by-operation basis. Plans had been submitted to Washington on the basis of the December KING-II date. When the invasion was moved forward, there was insufficient time for construction equipment to arrive in the theater before the invasion date. SWPA would have to get by with the much lighter equipment planned for KING-I.

One special equipment shortage between KING-I and KING-II that would cause major problems was the limited number of pontoon docks for KING-II to handle the volume of supplies. The coral along the Leyte beach prevented landing craft from getting closer than about 600 feet off the beach. This forced the construction of a pontoon dock out to the landing craft. This would lead to a major bottleneck for supplies on the beaches making them vulnerable to aerial attack.

With bad weather and equipment shortages, there were serious engineering problems facing the construction projects planned for Leyte, specifically airdromes, highways, and piers. Airdrome construction was urgent in order to bring forward the Army Air Force before the departure of the Navy aircraft carriers. Speed for this was considered paramount. In addition to a shortage of heavy construction equipment, there was also a shortage of construction rock on Leyte.

Col. William J. Ely, the Exec Officer for the Sixth Army Engineers, formally protested through proper channels about the unreasonably short construction period, and asked for a doubling of military engineer personnel or a lengthening of construction time. All his requests were denied. His protests would prove prophetic.

Construction labor was also a concern. The Engineers planned to hire native labor, but there were questions about the willingness of native labor to work in a combat zone, when faced with Japanese air raids and enemy strafing attacks. The Civil Affairs Officer was assigned to ASCOM to work with the Filipinos.

On 16 Sep 1944, ASCOM began organizing Headquarters, Base K, the supply base at Leyte.[308] Headquarters, Base M, the base for Luzon-Lingayan Gulf, began organizing on 25 Sep 1944.

One manpower problem quickly arose as a result of the invasion date being moved forward. There was insufficient time for the Australian troops to relieve MacArthur's US 27th and 40th Infantry Divisions from their combat activities in New Guinea and New Britain in order for them to participate in the Leyte invasion. To substitute for these units, the Central Pacific Command (Nimitz) made available his XXIV Corps with its 7th and 96th Infantry Divisions from Hawaii and

---

[308] Linda Mayo, *The Ordnance Department: On Beachhead and Battlefront*, United States Army in World War II, The Technical Services, Office of The Chief Of Military History, Department Of The Army, Center for Military History, Washington, D.C., 1968, CMH Pub 10-11, 1968, p.387.

Guam. The Central Pacific Command combat troops were welcome, but they came with supplies and equipment already loaded for landing on a coral atoll, equipment that was totally inadequate for the tropical rain forest of Leyte. Equipping these units further complicated the supply problem.

The Leyte invasion was the first time troops from two Pacific Commands would fight together under a single commander, Gen. Douglas MacArthur, that is, everything was under one commander except Halsey's Third Fleet, the split command.

36.2.   Major Day Promoted to Lt. Col. & Assigned ASCOM G-3 – 20 Aug 1944

On 20 Aug 1944 I received my promotion to Lieutenant Colonel and was assigned **ASCOM G-3, Asst. Chief of Staff and Chief of the Troop Section,** reporting to Major General Hugh J. Casey, Commanding General; ASCOM. I joined Gen. Casey in Hollandia on 5 Sep 1944.

For the Philippine invasion, we were landing 202,000 troops in three days with all their supplies for the first ninety days.

My job was to assign and coordinate all the Service Troops for the Sixth Army. Before it was all over, I did both the invasion on Leyte and the invasion on Luzon at Lingayan Gulf. I got together with the G-3 of Sixth Army and we worked out

Figure 146 - Lt. Col. J.F. Day, 1944
ASCOM, Hollandia or Tacloban, PI

the loading of all the Service Troops. For the Philippine invasion, we had MacArthur's troops coming from Hollandia, Finschhafen, Admiralty Islands, Manus Islands, and Sydney. Nimitz's XXIV Corps was coming from Guam, Hawaii, and the Solomon Islands. We had supplies coming from Australia – well, essentially we had troops coming from all over the Pacific. *We had 24 ships carrying ordinance and ammunition coming from San Francisco.* All the orders had to be cut, including ship assignments, loading instructions for the supplies, food, ammunition, POL,[309] medical supplies, everything. Troops had to be told where to go to board the ship, what ship to board, what to bring, how many rations to bring, what to pack, how much ammo, how much medical supplies, when to expect to sail, and so on. They all had to arrive at their assigned beaches at the assigned times to avoid a traffic jam.

We worked every night until three or four in the morning, writing the orders. Getting the job done required so many details to work out. We had to adjust the load of every ship. You can't overload any ship. You must have enough ships to get all the supplies to the beach. The order in which the supplies arrive on the beach is very important. The next day's supplies have to be covered every day. This was what planning for an invasion is all about. *[There were 823 supply ships involved in the invasion.]*

We tried to tell people to take only what they needed, and we specified what was needed – the list was endless. Don't take anything extra. Some of the units were making two-wheeled buggies to make carrying all the stuff easier, but there was no room for the buggies on the boats. They had to leave a lot of stuff behind. They could give it away, but there was no one to give it to. Lots of stuff was just abandoned on the docks.

When we got through, everyone had their orders. You couldn't watch everything. You just had to hope it was done right.

All this was done in an era before computers, calculators, copy machines, email, internet, voicemail, or cell phones. There were no Excel spreadsheets, no critical-path project software, no virtual meetings – all logistics were done with only pencil, paper, and telephone. The supply requirements had to be forecast, inventoried, assigned, and delivered on a timely schedule to the units that needed them. Telephones had to be secured lines, and radio communications were subject to enemy interception. All orders had to be typed on manual typewriters with multiple carbon copies for all files for every military unit, every ship, and every supply base.

The magnitude of supplies for the invasion[310] had been estimated as follows:

"The supplies required for the operation involved staggering quantities. For an invasion force of 150,000 men, the War Department figures showed that, for the landing period alone, 1,500,000

---

[309] POL – Petroleum, Oil, and Lubricants
[310] M. Hamlin Cannon, *The Return to the Philippines*, US Army in World War II, The War in the Pacific, Office Of The Chief Of Military History, Department Of The Army, Center for Military History, Washington, D.C., 1954, CMH Pub 5-9-1, p.36-39.

tons of general equipment, 235,000 tons of combat vehicles, 200,000 tons of ammunition, and 200,000 tons of medical supplies were required.

Thereafter, 332,000 tons of equipment would be required every thirty days. According to the final plan, issued by General Krueger on 30 September 1944, the units of the Sixth Army, X Corps, and Sixth Army Service Command, under General Casey, which were to arrive at Leyte between 20 and 30 October were to take ashore a minimum of ten days' supply of all classes (except engineer supplies, which were to be for at least thirty days), and two units of fire. In this way the strain on ASCOM supply units would be lessened, and ASCOM, it was hoped, would have time to establish dumps and make the necessary supply installations.

In addition to supplies accompanying the assault troops, sufficient quantities were to be brought into Leyte by 30 October to bring the total supplies for the troops to the following levels (expressed in days): thirty days of food, clothing, and equipment; fifteen days of motor transport fuel and distillate; and thirty days of other petroleum products. There were also to be five units of fire for combat troops and three for service troops. The original plan had called for a thirty-day supply of all petroleum products to be brought in by A+10."[311]

36.3.   D- Day vs. A-Day Comparison – 6 Jun 1944 vs. 20 Oct 1944

MacArthur wanted to make a clear distinction between the European Normandy invasion and his Asiatic Philippine invasion, so the designation for the invasion of the Philippines was A-Day [Asiatic Day?[312]]. The American press and popular movies have reported extensively about D-Day, but much less about A-Day – yet the two invasions were very similar in scale, but quite different in geography.

To put the scale of these two campaigns in perspective, the Allied invasion of Europe, D-Day, occurred on 6 June 1944 when 156,000 troops from America, Britain, and Canada were landed on a 50-mile beach in France. The invading force came from England and had to cross the 20-mile-wide English Channel. Their supply line was 20-miles long from English docks to French docks.

The American invasion of the Philippine Islands, A-Day, occurred on 20 Oct 1944, when 202,500 troops from America landed on a 20-mile beach on Leyte Island. The invading force came from at least six different island groups and had crossed several thousand miles of Pacific Ocean with synchronized timing to reach the Leyte beach on a prescribed schedule. Secondary ordinance

---

[311] Ibid.

[312] The author is not clear on the reason for the selection of the letter "A."

supply for the Leyte invasion came aboard a fleet of 22 to 24 ships that traveled directly from San Francisco without intermediate stops – over 7,000 miles.

The invasion of Leyte was the largest amphibious landing in the Pacific to that date. The ground assault forces were the Sixth Army under Lt. Gen Walter Krueger. Krueger had 202,500 troops under his command. The troops were transported to Leyte by Vice Adm. Thomas Kincaid and the Seventh Fleet, which consisted of 701 ships including 157 warships.

Invasion Comparison Chart

	Hollandia	Leyte	Normandy[313]
Date	22 Apr 1944	20 Oct 1944	6 Jun 1944
Length of Beach		20 miles	50 miles
Combat ground troops	50,000		
Service troops	23,000		
Air Force troops	12,000		
Total	84,000		
American Troops		150,000[314]	57,500
British & Canadian Troops			75,215
Ground Sub-total			132,715
American Paratroops			15,500
British Paratroops			7,900
Paratroops Sub-total			23,400
Grand Total – first day		202,500[315]	156,115
Supplies & Equipment	58,100 tons		289,927 tons by 30 Jun 1944 off-loaded at beach
General Equipment		1,500,000 tons[316]	

---

[313] Official British Military History, British Archives, UK

[314] Different number from different source.

[315] Gen. Krueger commanded 202,500 troops that landed over a three day period.

[316] US Army Center of Military History, "Leyte: The Return to the Philippines," p. 36-37.

Combat vehicles		235,000 tons	
Ammunition		200,000 tons	
Medical supplies		200,000 tons	
			British Port Problems
Ships		823 supply ships[317] (or 738 ships)[318]	7BS, 5Cru, 17 Light Cru, 135 Destroyer, 352 other war-ships
			Over 5,000 ships
After first days, each day needed			
Supplies			56,200 tons
Vehicles			20,000
Troops per day			180,000

36.4. ASCOM Landing in Leyte

36.4.1. Leyte Invasion Orders (KING-2) – 3 Oct 1944

ASCOM Field Order 1, dated 29 Sep 1944, for K-2 operations was distributed on 3 Oct 1944. I was assigned to the Advanced Echelon of ASCOM, which was ordered to embark Hollandia on 15 Oct 1944 in order to arrive in Leyte on A+2 Day, or S day (22 Oct 1944). Base K personnel were separated from ASCOM Headquarters on 10 Oct and staged in a different area (Base G). *Gen. E. F. Wallender, Commanding General, Base K, would sail on 18 Oct to arrive in Leyte on A+4 Day.*

---

[317] Office of the Center of Military History, Ft. McNair, DC.

[318] Different number from different source.

36.4.2.   Hollandia Departure – 15 Oct 1944

We sailed for Leyte. I got on board an LST in Hollandia, but other troops were coming into Leyte from all over – Solomon Islands, Brisbane, Admiralty Islands, New Guinea, Guam, and even Hawaii - all sorts of islands around the Pacific.

Fighting troops had certain days to land, and when the combat units go in, the service troops go with them.

We were on the LST for a week traveling from Hollandia to Leyte. Day after day, we played "Rat Poker." There were about six of us, I don't remember who. You deal five or six cards, everybody puts in a buck, and the idea is to get the best poker hand. You pass some cards, but everyone has to draw and discard one time. After you have gone around one time, you can knock. I forgot the rules, but it's a little like Hearts. You play each player

**Figure 147 - Invasion Voyage, Hollandia to Leyte
15-22 Oct 1944**

individually. If you beat one, he gives you his money. If you lose, you have to pay everybody. That is what we did on the boat while waiting.

36.4.3.   Leyte Beach Landing – 20 Oct 1944 (A-Day)

Palo Beach is where MacArthur landed on Leyte, and said "I have returned." You have seen the picture many times on the newsreels. They filmed it about three times (Figure 148). They kept going back and taking it again, because he wanted to make sure they got a good shot of it.

We arrived on shore two days after MacArthur's first visit. MacArthur had arrived and then departed again.

ASCOM Advanced Echelon landed at White Beach on the morning of A+2 (22 Oct 1944). The site originally designated for ASCOM at Palo Beach was still under Jap control, so we picked out another place for ASCOM Headquarters. About 6 to 8 hours later, before we moved in, we were told we are not going there either because that was where MacAr-

Figure 148 – MacArthur lands on Palo Beach, Leyte
Near Tacloban 20 Oct 1944

thur was going to put his headquarters. So we went down the beach further and found another place.

The next day ASCOM Headquarters was setup in a large house on the outskirts of Tacloban. We set up a campsite on the grounds of the house. Civil Affairs and Base K were set up next door.

By this time the Japanese air force had recovered from its initial surprise of our landing and started frequent air raids against us (A+5). During the initial bombings, no damage was done to ASCOM HQ, but Civil Affairs (next door) had one killed and five wounded (25 Oct 1944 – A+5).

Where we landed, there was a partial airfield right there just off the beach. It was not too good an airfield because it was short. *The Japanese had lighter planes than the Americans, so*

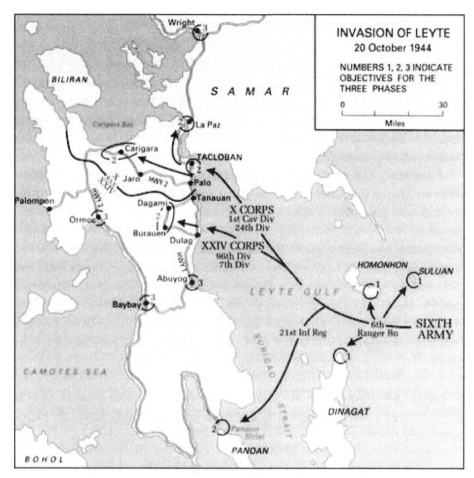

Figure 149 - Leyte Invasion Plan - 20 Oct 1944; US Army

they did not need as long or as wide an airstrip as the American aircraft. When our planes were having trouble, they might land early. We lost many people who ended up in the rice fields next to the airfield. They couldn't get to the airfield, either the plane was crippled, or they missed the runway, I couldn't tell. Pilots would set their planes down in a rice field, get out of the plane, go over to the road and bum a ride back to their unit, leaving the plane in the field. Within three days the natives had stripped the radios or anything of value they wanted out of the planes. The planes became empty shells.

The Engineers began on A+1 to repair and extend that landing strip. They managed to complete a 5,100-foot steel-mat runway by A+5. They continued to work until they had a 6,900-foot runway two days later. Afterward, the Air Force gave the Engineer unit a Meritorious Citation for outstanding achievement.[319]

---

[319] Ibid. p10

36.4.4.   Gen. Casey Arrives in Leyte

*Gen. Casey arrived off Leyte on A-day aboard the **Blue Ridge**, Adm. Daniel E. Barbey's command ship. However, on board the ship, Gen. Casey had experienced a sacroiliac injury, a cracked vertebra, such that he could not stand or walk. The doctor wanted to return him to Hollandia for X-rays and treatment, but Casey refused. He had left the Philippines two-and-a-half years earlier on a PT boat with MacArthur, and under no circumstances was he going to miss this invasion. He remained on the ship until A+3, when the medics shot him with morphine, bound his back in a corset, and put him on a stretcher to be carried ashore. He commented in his memoir that he was the only stretcher going ashore as all the other stretchers were departing with the wounded. Casey wore the corset for at least the next three months.*

When Casey came ashore he was quartered initially in the GHQ building while he recovered. He was brought to the ASCOM building on A+6 and participated in a number of conferences regarding unit area assignments. Many of the areas selected in advance for unit campsites proved to be unsuitable due to swampland, irregular topography, and the tactical combat situation. On 27 Oct (A+7) the Commanding Officer for the 5201 Engineer Construction Brigade presented a proposed reallocation of areas, which ASCOM submitted to Sixth Army and GHQ after obtaining comments.

The areas suitable for construction of the hospital and Base K storage areas were occupied by GHQ and other headquarters. Finally Brig. Gen. Baker was brought in from Hollandia to deal with the beach area assignments.

One key change was that the Navy agreed to relocate their docks and repair facilities from west of Tacloban to across the bay to Samar Island. The Navy had been assigned an area in Tacloban that

proved unsuitable. They called their new base "Philippine Frontier Base."[320] Captain R.M Fortson of the Navy Service Command was probably very relieved to get out of the crowded Tacloban area. The Navy would build a new airdrome at Tolo-

Figure 150 - Leyte Supply Ships - 1944, ww2.wwarii.com

---

[320] Ibid. p 8.

sa. Until the new airdrome could be constructed, Air Force agreed to allow the Navy to temporarily use their airdromes in Dulag and Buri to land and stage their aircraft. This relocation opened more dock space for Base K to unload ships, which greatly relieved a serious supply bottleneck.

36.4.5.   Kamikaze Attacks and Missing Personal Movies

Leyte was the first time we encountered *kamikaze* attacks *[translated divine wind]*. These were suicide pilots who intentionally guided their armed aircraft directly into Allied ships.

The Battle of the Philippines was the first major confrontation that the Japanese made extensive use of kamikaze. The first official kamikaze "kill" was on October 25 in Leyte Gulf. At that time a kamikaze sunk an Escort Carrier, St. Lo. There were three other kamikaze hits that day. The use of kamikaze was a direct result of their shortage of trained pilots, as well as a shortage of combat aircraft. Kamikaze use was evidence of the Japanese determination to defend the Philippines at all cost. The kamikaze proved a very destructive force in Leyte and especially in Luzon-Lingayen Gulf.

Many people are amazed by the suicide act of these pilots, but their act was no different than the behavior of many Japanese soldiers who dug into the mountain caves in machine-gun pill boxes until they were killed.

I was watching one Jap plane *(kamikaze)* after another diving into our ships. I saw an American LST and two or three more ships hit. One crewman was killed when his turret gun was hit – cutting iron and steel all over the place. I had my movie camera, and photographed four American planes shooting down twelve Japanese bombers over my head. I sent the film into Kodak with instructions to hold for duration of the war, but they developed the roll and censored all but one plane getting shot down.

36.5.   Battle of Leyte Gulf – 24 to 27 Oct 1944 (A+4 to A+7)

36.5.1.   Japanese Strategic Defense Plan – the Big Picture

Before the Philippine invasion, the Japanese Central Command was not sure where the next American attack would come. To cover all possibilities, the Japanese developed four separate defense plans for four possible targets – Showa-1 (Philippines defense), Showa-2 (Formosa defense), Showa-3 (Kyushu defense), and Showa-4 (Hokkaido defense). Regardless of the target, these defense plans were an all-out desperation effort by the Japanese to win a decisive battle with the Americans.

After the Battle of the Marianas, the Japanese Navy air force was a shell of its former self. The Japanese program for pilot training could not supply enough replacements to cover the losses their carriers had experienced. Their most experienced pilots had been lost in combat, and they were short of instructors and training planes for replacement pilots. They also did not have enough military aircraft to fully equip their large carriers. Their planners decided to use their large carrier with very few airplanes as a decoy to lure Adm. Halsey and the 3rd Fleet completely away from the Philippines and out of position in the hope that another force could destroy MacArthur's invasion forces. The Japanese had correctly read Arm. Halsey's aggressive personality, and their plan worked to a point. Adm. Halsey took the bait and abandoned his tactical position protecting MacArthur's troops. His movement came close to costing the Americans the invasion of the Philippines.

36.5.2.   The Naval Battle Line for Leyte[321]

The Japanese naval battle line for Leyte was divided into three forces:

1. *The Northern Force – Adm. Ozawa had a decoy fleet of 116 ships to bait Halsey and his 3rd Fleet away from the Leyte invasion troops.*
2. *The Central Force – Adm. Kurita had five battleships, ten heavy cruisers, and a host of supporting ships, intended to slip through the Philippines from the west through the San Bernardino Strait, and after Halsey pulled out, to strike the MacArthur Leyte beach invasion force from the north. They almost succeeded.*
3. *The Southern Force – Adm. Nishimura and Adm. Shima intended to slip through Surigao Strait from the west and strike the Leyte invasion force from the south.*

The American naval battle line consisted of the following:

1. *7th Fleet – Adm Kinkiad, MacArthur's Navy*
   - *Responsible for delivering the invasion force of 150,000 troops on 738 ships, with over one million tons of supplies*
   - *Charged with providing aerial support to the ground troops invading Leyte*
   - *Equipped with 12 smaller Carriers (CVE – called "Jeep" Carriers) armed for ground support warfare with anti-personnel and anti-tank weapons, not anti-ship weaponry.*
   - *Finally had to face off with the Japanese Central Force.*
2. *7th Fleet Bombardment and Fire Support Group – Adm. Oldenberg*

---

[321] James D. Hornfischer, *The Last Stand of the Tin Can Sailors*, Bantam Books, 2004.

- *Equipped with six battleships, including five salvaged veterans of Pearl Harbor, plus eight cruisers, 22 destroyers, and a fleet of PT boats which confronted the Japanese Southern Force*

3. *3rd Fleet – Adm. Halsey, reporting to Adm. Nimitz in the Central Pacific*
   - *Responsible for protecting the invasion force from the Philippine Sea*
   - *Three fast Fleet Carrier Task Forces (CV), including 17 carriers and six battleships, plus an armada of additional war ships*
   - *Geared for naval warfare – armor piercing anti-ship bombs to protect the invasion force from the sea.*
   - *Lots of airplanes*

The American command situation

1. *The Split Command – Halsey reported to Nimitz, not MacArthur. Nimitz orders allowed Halsey to abandon MacArthur's invasion force*
2. *Tired of "baby sitting" MacArthur when there were Japanese aircraft carriers north, Halsey "took the bait" and headed north.*
3. *Halsey did not notify the 7th Fleet (Adm. Kinkaid) that he was leaving.*

Halsey's departure and miscommunication left the San Bernardino Strait unguarded and opened the door for the Japanese Central Force to get 23 warships through the channel without any resistance.

Leyte Gulf Naval Battle timeline:

- *20 Oct (A-Day) – Leyte Invasion – 6th Army goes ashore*
- *22 Oct (A+2) – Japanese Naval forces sail from Borneo and the Japanese Inland Sea for the counter attack. Showa-1 is activated.*
- *24 Oct (A+4) – Japanese Central Force loses three cruisers by American submarine attack. A major battleship succumbs to an air attack by the 3rd Fleet. Still 23 warships in 10-mile long column march through the San Bernardino Strait around the island of Samar north and into Leyte Gulf.*
- *24 Oct (A+5) – Halsey "takes the bait," abandons MacArthur's invasion force, and heads north for Ozawa's decoy aircraft carriers without notifying Adm. Kinkaid and the 7th Fleet.*
- *24-25 Oct (A+4 to A+5) – The Japanese Southern Force is confronted by Adm. Oldenberg in Surigao Strait in a monumental night battle that destroys the Japanese.*
- *25 Oct (A+5) – Planned Japanese rendezvous off Leyte at 9 AM*

- *25-26 Oct (A+5 to A+6) – Battle of Samar – With the San Bernardino Strait unguarded, Adm. Kurita's Central Force enters the Leyte Gulf in a surprise attack. Thus began the largest Naval surface battle of the war in which the out-gunned American fleet of 12 small ships, including six small CVE jeep carriers and their destroyer screen from the 7th Fleet, fought gallantly against 23 of the largest ships in the Japanese Navy, including the Yamoto, the largest battleship in the war from either side. Aircraft aboard the CVE were not armed with anti-ship armor piercing bombs but were armed for infantry support anti-personnel warfare. As a result, the CVE aircraft could not attack the Japanese warships. The Americans lost two CVE and three destroyers to successful kamikaze attacks.*
- *27 Oct (A+7) – For reasons not fully understood, when the Japanese appear to be gaining the upper hand in the battle, Adm. Kurita withdrew to the north.*
- *27 Oct (A+7) –Kinkaid's mission to support MacArthur with close air support and to protect his supply lines from Japanese submarines delayed recovery efforts of the battle survivors in the Leyte Gulf. This delay led to a tragedy for the American navy with loss of life from hypothermia, dehydration, and sharks.*

The Showa-1 Plan to defend the Philippines was a brilliant plan. The Japanese came within 20 minutes of defeating the Leyte operation, but for reasons unknown, they disengaged at the last moment.

Halsey never appeared before the engagement ended. Perhaps the largest naval surface battle of the Pacific War was withheld from the American public for a long period. The Battle of Leyte Gulf was probably the "biggest cover up" of the Pacific War in order to hide a big mistake made by Adm. Halsey, a hero. The battle involved more ships and staggering American losses which would have embarrassed the American Navy.

36.5.3.　Day's Oral History

The ground war was being fought in Leyte and that was our focus.[322] I was in Tacloban, but out in the Gulf of Leyte there was a real fight going on with the Japanese Navy. I was not in it, but I was like everyone else, glued to the radio listening to the pilots to learn whatever we could. That was the only way you knew the latest happenings. You couldn't listen too long because you had your own work to do, but we knew the battle was really rough.

Halsey went off north hunting for the Japanese big boys (*aircraft carriers*). He left the invasion force protection to old battleships and smaller destroyers in the Gulf of Leyte, but

---

[322] Video location: 5:50:40:19

the Japanese surprised him and came in around the back door from the western side of the Philippines passing through Straits north and south of Leyte. The Japs were shooting up the Americans pretty badly. The Navy Commander was calling for all the ground-based planes we could muster to come down there and help him.

This was a real tough day for the Navy. The Japs almost got us, as we had 700 to 800 un-protected supply ships unloading in Leyte Gulf. The Japs could have had a real "turkey shoot" if they had gotten in there, as there were no American warships near the beaches. The Japs were shooting carriers out from under the planes, so Navy planes were landing on land runways anywhere they could. We had several planes come into Tacloban for fuel and bombs. One landed in a rice patty.

This battle went on for a couple of days. There was a lot of fighting, and it was rough, but our boys held on, and fought them off.

Halsey got the word, but it was too late. He was too far away to get back in time to do any good. Halsey was wrong. Anyway that was the Battle of Leyte Gulf.

36.6.   Leyte – On the Ground

36.6.1.   Tacloban (Leyte) Defense

The battle line was not far from Tacloban, as our combat troops were having problems. The Japanese were bringing in reinforcements. There was fear that small bands of Japs could slip through the lines and pose a real danger to the Headquarters. I was placed in charge of headquarters defense.[323]   The ASCOM Headquarters office staff was not trained as infantry, so we had a couple of emergency training drills and instruction in defensive tactics for everyone.

We had 125mm anti-aircraft guns. The shells went up and then came back down. One of our own shells came down through the cylinder block of a jeep. Fortunately; it didn't hit anybody, but it sure killed the jeep.

On 25 Nov 1944, a Japanese bomber attacked Base K, about 100 yards from ASCOM Headquarters, killing 12 soldiers and wounding 30. The bombs ignited the gasoline dump, so the engineers had to lay a new oil pipeline from the dock to the airdrome.

---

[323] ASCOM Field Order 2, 26 Oct 1944.

The next night three planeloads of Jap soldiers crash-landed in the Dulag area, and we thought they were planning a large counterattack. ASCOM Headquarters immediately dug in additional defensive positions around the Headquarters area and had another defense drill for the office staff. Fortunately, no Jap soldiers appeared.

On 7 Dec 1944 about 300 Japanese paratroopers dropped into the Buri airstrip. They caused some damage and casualties, actually taking control of one end of the airstrip before they were destroyed. It certainly disrupted construction.

On 10 Dec, about 90 tons of plastic explosive was ignited at the Red Beach engineer dump, destroying 75% of the Army-Navy POL tank farm in Palo. It appeared that Japanese paratroopers had slipped in and done the job.

36.6.2.   Mud

During the first month after landing, Leyte was hit by a "triple typhoon." There were 23.5 inches of rain, which meant that mud was a constant problem. Roads were breaking down due to mud and heavy use by military and construction traffic. Hauling construction matériel for the airdromes was very difficult. Moving supplies from the docks to storage was a problem. Constant rain created a nightmare for construction crews as men and equipment were constantly being diverted from construction to clearing roads and extracting stuck vehicles. Traffic control was implemented to reduce the traffic, but the engineers were always fighting mud. The Japanese infiltrators also interrupted construction from time to time as engineers had to take up defensive arms.

The rain did not slow up until about mid-December. About then the amount of gravel we could obtain from the local quarries increased, so the muddy road situation slowly got better.

36.6.3.   Construction Problems

The 5201st Engineer Construction Brigade was divided into three groups:

- *1113th Engineer Construction Group – Tacloban Sector*
- *1129th Engineer Construction Group – Palo Sector*
- *112th Engineer Construction Group – Dulag Sector*

Before landing, the engineers had planned one runway in the center of Leyte. Upon physical inspection, the site was found unsuitable to bear the weight of aircraft. A replacement site was found in Tanausan on the beach that was more amenable for construction. Japanese-built run-

ways usually ran perpendicular to the beach. American engineers usually found it more expedient to build their runways parallel to the beach. There were problems, however. A very high hill was located at one end of the Tanausan runway that caused Gen. Kenney to object to the site. The location also was the exact place where Gen. Krueger had located his Sixth Army Headquarters. Finally, Krueger and Kenney both yielded because of the urgency to get ground-based aircraft to Leyte, and Tanausan was approved. Krueger moved his Sixth Army Headquarters.

The engineers were building two docks for Liberty ships, one floating dock, one barge jetty and two hospitals, but they were delayed as heavy construction materials (large timbers) were diverted to forward combat areas. The Japanese were offering stronger resistance than we expected, so some engineer units were diverted to tactical combat support duty. The engineers also had to repair the Tacloban city water system, the power plant, and the ice plant.

The problem of recruiting local construction workers created a crisis. Civil Affairs sought the support of the Governor of Leyte, the Mayor of Tacloban, and the local priests but the number of workers recruited was far below the need. Premium pay was offered, but the natives found they could make good money selling souvenirs to the Americans. By 31 October (A+10) the engineers had 2,500 workers engaged, but that was still too few. The periodic Japanese air raids were discouraging recruitment of the Filipinos, but by three weeks later (19 Nov 1944), there were 18,652 Filipinos registered to work on Leyte construction sites, including 13,270 in the Tacloban-Palo-Tanausan area and 5,382 in the Dulag-Burauen area. Being registered as a worker was different that showing up to work. On 19 Nov there were about 11,300 on the job. Worker attendance greatly improved when the payroll was shifted from daily to weekly. [324]

36.6.4.   Wrong Knock at the Door

We had most of our combat troops going forward getting up into Leyte, but in the rear we had service troops and police who stay behind to keep things in order

One night one of the colored boys got in bed with a Japanese girl, and about 2 AM, who comes to the front door but a Japanese soldier who had come back home to get his wife. He had slipped through the lines, and when he got into his home, he was surprised to find this black man in bed with his wife. The black man did not have a gun, but he did have a knife. He was so scared to see an unexpected Japanese soldier that he took his knife and chopped up that Japanese soldier before the Jap could shoot him. Then he ran out the door yelling that the Japanese were back. He was so scared.

---

[324] Ibid. p13

36.6.5.   Purple Heart Taken from a Major

We had an Adjutant General in Headquarters, a Major, assigned to writing orders for others, doing only paper work. One evening he was in the office during an air raid, got scared, bumped into a light bulb, and cut his finger. He put himself in for a Purple Heart, and somehow it was approved. When the medal arrived, they ask the General to present it. The General asked how the wound had happened?

When the General was told the story, he hit the roof. He took the medal away from the Major, and said "Tomorrow I want him shipped out of here back to the States." He was released from the Army.

36.6.6.   Malaria with Complications of Yellow Jaundice

I got very sick in Leyte. I came down with malaria and had complications of yellow jaundice. Malaria can come and go, so no one knew I had it at the beginning. I had been vomiting like hell, couldn't keep anything down. I thought some fresh eggs might help. We had nothing fresh, and so I told the Sergeant to go outside town and find some Filipino farmer with chickens, and bring me back two fresh eggs. He got the eggs and took them to the cook. The cook fixed the eggs for me along with some bacon and toast to settle my stomach. I drank a little coffee, but I hadn't taken five steps, and I started vomiting again. I felt like I had to go to the toilet, started going and could not stop. It was coming out both ends. I was getting weaker and weaker.

The Doctor gave me some pills. I lay down for a while, but still couldn't keep anything down. After a few days, the medicine began to help. I had spells that returned periodically for some time before I got home. When I got back to the States, I was put in the hospital for three weeks trying to get control of my body again. I have not been allowed to give blood for a transfusion since then. That was as sick as I have ever been.

Figure 151 - Lt. Col. J.F. Day – 1944
Hollandia or Tacloban

MALARIA WITH YELLOW JAUNDICE - The malaria parasite develops inside red blood cells. When it is mature, it breaks the cell apart and swims off in the blood. Bilirubin, a yellow substance, is a byproduct of the breakdown of hemoglobin within red blood cells. When enough cells burst at once, yellow jaundice may result from the large amount of bilirubin. This substance is normally cleansed from the blood stream by the liver, and discharged as bile. When the liver is unable to cleanse the blood, the person's skin and the whites of the eyes turn yellow. The pigment may reach the urine in sufficient quantities to cause "black-water fever," an often lethal form of malaria. Source: Free On-Line Medical Dictionary.

36.6.7.   Twists of Fate

Major Sawyer had shot down 75 Jap planes and was ready to rotate home. He wanted to get one more before he returned home. He was up there coming home late from his last mission and started chasing a Japanese plane over our base when our anti-aircraft fire shot him down. Another pilot who was with him got home OK with the anti-aircraft shooting all around him, but Major Sawyer never made it.

P38 was a really good plane, some thought better than P51, because it could really turn sharply. It knocked down a lot of Japanese planes.

36.7.   Relieved from Leyte to Prepare for Luzon Invasion

On 25 Dec 1944, the Eighth Army relieved the Sixth Army from the battle lines in Leyte. The Sixth Army was pulled out to rest and stage in preparation to invade northern Luzon at the Lingayen Gulf. This was to open a second front with the Japanese and begin a pincer movement on Manila. About 68,000 troops entered the beaches in northern Luzon, less than half of the number that went ashore in Leyte, but not far from the number that invaded Hollandia.

ASCOM remained attached to the Sixth Army, so they also were relieved in Leyte. Again, they provided the Services support for the next invasion, and again Lt. Col. Day, as G-3, was providing the Services troop scheduling and logistics.

36.7.1.   Sights and Sounds of Rural Leyte

<u>Postmark: Jan 27, 1945</u>

Lt Col John F. Day Jr.
ASCOM APO 358

Saturday Eve 27 January 1945[325]
Dear Mother and Dad:
I have so little actually to write that I should not attempt, however, I think it has been some time since I wrote so will at least tell you that I am OK. Things I could write about I cannot write, as you may understand.

However, the Filipino people are always interesting to watch and observe their characteristics. To watch them fish is a treat. The other day I was watching some of them in a puddle of water with a net. Each and all were in a line as though they were running all the fish to one end of the pool. The nets they had are small and why a fish could not get thru I do not know, but they do come out with some fish.

Here they have so many fish ponds which are merely parts of some creek that is dammed up or water run to a nearby place that has been dammed up. The ponds have outlets for the water which prevent the fish from leaving. When the water gets low, they go in and net the fish that are there. Most of the time the fish are small, like mullet, in fact that is what most of them are. I would not like to eat much if any of the fish because of the water. To us it would be like catching fish from a stale pond. Also their ponds are used to spread fertilizer (animal waste) to make the vegetation grow faster and fish get fatter in a shorter time[326]. We do that of course in places, mostly in Minnesota, but the fish always have to be cooked before eating. You know some people eat raw fish, but there is a tape worm that is in fish (here as well as Minnesota). The tape worm is what you are likely to get if fish are eaten raw. You know some Jews eat fish raw too.

All of the vegetables are supposed to be boiled, as they were in Java for similar reasons. So far we have not seen many fresh fruits or vegetables. We have seen some small eggplant that we fried. Also, saw some bananas and coconut. That's about the extent of fresh stuff if you would call it fresh. Seems to me that I have eaten bananas now for a long time, they also have papaya which is the same as what we called pawpaw in New Guinea. They are fairly good – especially with ice cream if you have any.

---

[325] Letter file name: 1945-01-27 358 PI-fishing-airplane noise-rice farming.doc
[326] Animal waste can lead to e coli in the vegetables.

The lands here are mostly low lands and used mainly for rice farming. It rains during certain parts of the year; thank goodness that this is not that part. There is lots of sugar cane. The fields as I started to say are very clean. They use the water buffalo with their crude plow and after that they pick by hand all the grass that is in the field. Not even a weed stands. They then wait for the water and then the water buffalo starts tromping around in the mud and makes the land very mushy before planting. The planting is all done by hand too, so that is the main reason we do not care to raise a lot of rice due to labor. The farm families are so large, in fact a new baby each year. Naturally a large family makes quite a sizable number of workers. Many of the Filipinos are mixed race with Chinese, and usually those are the ones that have the money. The Filipinos are not as anxious to have the dough, or should I say not so ambitious. There is a limit on the amount of land one man can own, so that keeps the land ownership divided into small farms. However, one can still own enough land to make a sizeable income.

Each Barrio is under a certain provincial capital, which rules to a certain extent. The mayor of the place seems to have the main say about the affairs of his people – he is the judge and the jury, so to say. I think the people look to him for that.

The climate here at night is good for sleeping, if it were not for all the noises we make ourselves. During the day we have all our vehicles moving, and at night and early in the morning, it is our planes taking off and landing. We do not notice the planes as much during the day, but at 5AM you cannot help but notice. I must close for now.
Your loving son
          John

37.   CILE'S MEDICAL PROBLEM REVEALED – 25 DEC 1944

For over two years Major Day was aware that Cile was having medical problems. However, his requests for information concerning the matter directly to Cile went unanswered. Finally, in December 1944, Major Day's father told him the gravity of situation. Cile had undergone a Radical Mastectomy for breast cancer.

25 Dec 1944, (Tacloban, PI) – A Christmas Present?

ASCOM APO 358
Lt Col John F Day Jr.

25 December 1944[327]
Xmas Day
Dearest Mother and Dad: Carl and Hazel Dawn:

    Mother, I have your letter of Dec 1 which I received last night along with three from Cile. First letter I had had from her for some time. *Cile said Mr. Nail, who was formerly from Eden and is now in El Paso has sent Johnnie another letter telling him he wanted to buy another ten thousand dollars of war bonds you know Johnnie has already sold him about that amount. He saw Johnnie's name in the paper a long time ago and then bought his first five thousand.[328] Also told Cile that he had known me for a long time etc. I could not imagine it and not entirely able to yet.* He must be doing good [sic] since he left Eden. Have you heard anything about Mr. Nail since then?

    I have not heard from Gilbert but feel sure there will be a letter here soon or on the way. I don't know what he makes a month but feel sure it costs something for him to live, no doubt they do not have a lot as it is.

    I asked you I believe what money you sent Cile sometime back. I will wait for an answer. If I have additional money in Roswell, buy another heifer red face if you can. Go ahead and buy what it will buy, may as well get it busy. If you think best save for what is necessary for feed. How did you come out this year Dad? Have you cut your indebtedness down, I think you are about clear except for the two. Is that right or do you owe more. I would like to see you clear of course.

---

[327] Letter file name: 1944-12-25 358 ASCOM War Bonds-Cile Illness-P38 pilots ; Enclosed in envelope dated 25 Dec 1944

[328] We have no accurate accounting about Johnnie's war bond sales, but family lore let us to believe Johnnie sold more than $30,000 in bonds before the end of the war.

If you had not told me I guess I would never have known what was wrong with Cile. She has not told me yet even though I have asked her. She always overlooks it.

We had a little help with our fireworks last night, saw one cluster go down. It does disturb your sleep at times you know. A couple of *P*-38 pilots that I had not seen for some time came in yesterday morn and stayed most of the day. They want to take me out to their camp for dinner tonight and I will probably go.

I have lost several pounds since being here and my pants seem a bit large. No doubt that will continue for some time yet.

By the time you get this, I hope things have made more progress than before and that the war will end just twice as fast. Things here are going swell.
Your loving son
John

OBSERVATION: Cile said nothing in her letters to John about her cancer problems, and John said nothing to Cile about his malaria and yellow jaundice problems. John's weight loss was a direct result of his bout with malaria.

38.   LUZON INVASION - 9 JAN 1945

38.1.   War Strategy – Why Luzon

The Joint Chiefs continued to debate the next target to follow the conquest of Leyte. MacArthur advocated an immediate invasion of Luzon, but there were still Navy doubters who thought Luzon could be bypassed with a direct attack on Formosa. MacArthur felt Formosa could never be secure without full control of Luzon.

MacArthur felt any attack on Formosa would be precarious since there were no supply bases close to Formosa. There was a major shortage of service troops in the Pacific theater, such that MacArthur had difficulty finding supply troops to support his existing operations, much less an operation in Formosa. In the Philippines he relied heavily on friendly Filipino populations for service troops, such as construction workers on runways, stevedores at the docks, and drivers in supply bases. This friendly labor pool could not be assured on Formosa. SWPA could not spare service troops to support a Formosa operation and it was not clear where these service troops could be obtained. Finally, on 3 Oct 1944, the Joint Chiefs of Staff approved the SWPA "Musketeer III" plan, which called for the invasion of Luzon with occupation by 20 Dec 1944. This plan included Operation Love, the preliminary strike on Mindoro and Aparri, and Operation Mike, the main strike on the Lingayen Gulf.[329]

Combat in Leyte continued. US troops were behind schedule due to both Japanese resistance and the weather. Before an invasion of Luzon could be executed, air superiority had to be established. Key to air superiority was the establishment of airdromes on the southern tip of Mindoro, an island off the southeast coast of Luzon. Mindoro became the last necessary stepping stone for an invasion of the Lingayen Gulf.

The weather played a major role in determining the route of the invasion convoy from Leyte. The shortest route from Leyte to the Lingayen Gulf followed south of Leyte through the Surigao Strait, around the Visayans, across the Sulu Sea and up the western side of the Philippines past Mindoro to Lingayen. The Navy was worried about kamikaze attacks along the southern route because the convoy would pass through narrow channels and close to islands under Japanese control. The Navy advocated the longer route up the eastern coast around the north end of Luzon, which could be more distant from land and therefore less vulnerable to kamikaze aircraft. The stormy weather prospects in the China Sea, however, finally persuaded the leadership to use the southern route.

---

[329] U.S. Government, Reports of General MacArthur, *The Campaigns of MacArthur in the Pacific, Volume I*, Prepared by his General Staff, 1966, p.242.

The invasion of Mindoro was scheduled for 5 Dec 44, but continuing operational problems on Leyte caused a delay. New airdrome construction on Leyte was behind schedule, so a planned airborne assault on Mindoro had to be cancelled due to inadequate airstrips on Leyte to support the operation. The airborne troops were switched to amphibious landing craft instead. The weather on Leyte also plagued air cover for the Mindoro invasion force. All things considered, the Mindoro assault was delayed to 15 Dec, which pushed the Lingayan invasion from 20 Dec 44 to 9 Jan 45.

Figure 152 - Luzon Invasion Route - Leyte to Luzon 9 Jan 1945

Operation Mike I, the main thrust into the Luzon, called for General Walter Krueger to land the Sixth Army, a force of 68,000 troops (two corps including four combat divisions), in the Lingayen Gulf and advance on Manila from the north. This was approximately one-third of the troops MacArthur had in Leyte. The Eighth Army would invade southern Luzon and advance on Manila from the south and east, creating a pincer on the City of Manila.

The extreme weather impacted planning for the invasion of Luzon. Seasonal fog and overcast skies prevented reconnaissance aircraft from photographing landing sites and airdrome construction sites, which delayed planning.

High seas made naval operations north and east of Luzon very difficult. A typhoon struck in early January in the middle of the Lingayen invasion, preventing operation of carrier-based aircraft and compromising the effectiveness of naval surface artillery. Two US destroyers were lost in the storm. The weather impact on Navy air operations north of Luzon caused MacArthur to send elements of the Third Fleet to attack Formosa airdromes where the Japanese still had good weather conditions for flying in order to prevent the Japanese Formosa aircraft from attacking Luzon.

38.2.   ASCOM Landing in Luzon – 9 Jan 45

38.2.1.   ASCOM Base M-1 (Luzon) Planning[330]

ASCOM had been divided into two echelons – the Advanced Echelon focused on Leyte and the Rear Echelon focused on Luzon. By 18 Oct 44, the Advanced Echelon had departed Hollandia for Leyte. ASCOM total troop compliment at this time was as follows:

ASCOM Troops	Date	Officers	Enlisted Men
Total Compliment	15 Oct 44	63	174
Adv Echelon – Leyte		24	108
Rear Echelon – Hollandia	31 Oct 44	37	84
Total Complement	31 Dec 44	37+29 attached	120+38attached

On 1 Nov 44 Base M-1, destined for Lingayen Gulf, was organized in Hollandia with Col. Herbert D. Vogel, CE, as Commanding Officer. Col. Vogel and the ASCOM Rear Echelon left Hollandia on 4 Nov 44 and arrived in Leyte 11 Nov 44. They set up their tents adjacent to ASCOM in Tacloban.

Planning for M-1 was delayed because of a shortage of maps and aerial photographs of the landing site and of the major construction sites. ASCOM planned to build two new air strips, a new port facility, an improved communication center, and a supply depot in Lingayan. There were continuing delays caused by problems at Base K supporting Leyte combat operations. Resources intended for M-1 had to be redirected on 5 Dec 44 to establish a Sub-Base K at Tanauan (Tolosa) to alleviate a serious problem of getting supplies to the Leyte combat lines.

On 24 Dec 44 Operation KING-II (the Leyte invasion) was officially declared complete and terminated. There was a physical change of personnel at Tacloban. ASCOM personnel were pulled out and USASOS personnel took over the ASCOM desks. ASCOM shipped out with the Sixth Army to invade Luzon.

---

[330] Edgar M. Howell, Historian, OCMH, Volume III – USASOS Operations During Initial Phase of Invasion and Re-Conquest of Luzon, PI (Base M – Lingayan Gulf (26 Dec 1944-13 Feb 1945), Document dated 12 May 1949, p.5. Office of the Chief of Military History, Department of the Army, Fort McNair, Washington, D.C. 20315, Historical Manuscript File, Historical Section, Army Forces Western Pacific, *History of the USASOS* (U.S. Army Services of Supply Southwest Pacific) and AFWESPAC (Army Forces Western Pacific) 1941 to June 1946. The following are unpublished manuscripts located in File Call Number 8-5.8; AA; F.1, Copy 2 (Fort McNair). OCMH Form 10, dated 1 Jun 62.

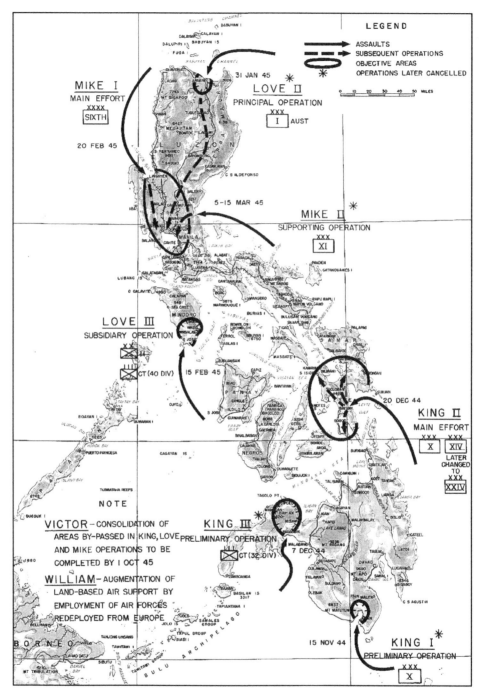

Figure 153 - Musketeer II Plan for the Conquest of the Philippines
MacArthur Staff Report, US Government Report, 1966, Page 171.

As of 31 Dec 44, key personnel[331] for ASCOM, including Construction Force, Civil Affairs, and Base M were as follows:
Command Section:

      Commanding General, Major General Hugh J. Casey, USA
      Chief of Staff, Col. Edward C. Harwood, CE
      Commanding General's Aide, Capt. Cruikahank, CAC
      Adjutant General, Lt. Col. Merle A. Sparks, AGD
      Intelligence Section, Major George K. Adams, GSC
      Troops Section, Lt. Col. John F. Day, GSC
      Civil Affairs Section, Col. Narciso L. Manzano, CE
      Construction Section, Col. Reginald L. Dean, CE

Base M:

      Base Commander, Col. H. D. Vogel
      Executive Officer, Col. K. Johnston
      Asst. Executive, Lt. Col. R. B. Arnold
      S-2, Major Riley F. McKoy
      S-3, Col. R. C. Holliday
      S-4, Major W. I. English
      Fort Commander, Lt. Col. S. E. Walker
      Service Center Commander, Col. R. W. Bond
      Area Commander, Lt. Col. C. L. Winkel
      Adjutant General, Lt. Col. J. N. Shigley
      I&E Officer, Lt. Moss
      Finance Officer, Lt. Col. Miller
      Provost Marshal, Lt. Col. J. V. Mueller
      Chaplain, Lt. Col. Hardegree
      Headquarters. Commandant, Major Cowgill
      Special Service Officer, Lt. Col. Clapp
      Inspector General, Major W. H. Hall
      Civil Affairs Liaison Officer, Lt. Col. Beale
      Control Officer, Major Cook
      Director, American Red Cross, Mr. Baldwin

---

[331] John Musacchio, 1st. Lt., C.A.C., Historian. Unpublished manuscripts dated 12 May 1949, Found in Office of the Chief of Military History (OCMH), Department of the Army, Fort McNair, Washington, D.C. 20315, Historical Manuscript File, Historical Section, Army Forces Western Pacific, *History of the USASOS* (U.S. Army Services of Supply Southwest Pacific) and AFWESPAC (Army Forces Western Pacific) 1941 to June 1946. Document located in File Call Number 8-5.8; AA; F.1, Volume III – USASOS Operations During Initial Phase of Invasion and Re-Conquest of Luzon, PI (Base M – Lingayan Gulf (26 Dec 1944-13 Feb 1945), p.9.

38.2.2.   ASCOM Lingayen Landing – 26 Days in January 1945

The original schedule for the invasion of Luzon (codenamed S-Day) at Lingayen Gulf (20 Dec 1944) had been moved back to 9 Jan 1945. The ASCOM Commanding General and his Commanding Section were to land on the beach on S-Day along with the US Sixth Army.

Due to a shortage of LSTs, ASCOM personnel and supplies were distributed among convoys arriving on S-Day, S+1, S+2, S+4, and S+12. The distribution of troops among echelons was Lt. Col. Day's responsibility. The General Staff arrived on S-Day, but General Casey and his aide, Capt. Cruishank, arrived at Crimson Beach (Lingayen) on S+1 at 1600 hours aboard the destroyer, USS Smith. The USS Smith had been detached from the S-Day convoy to escort a crippled Carrier Escort (CVE). The Lingayen beach map is found in Figure 154 .

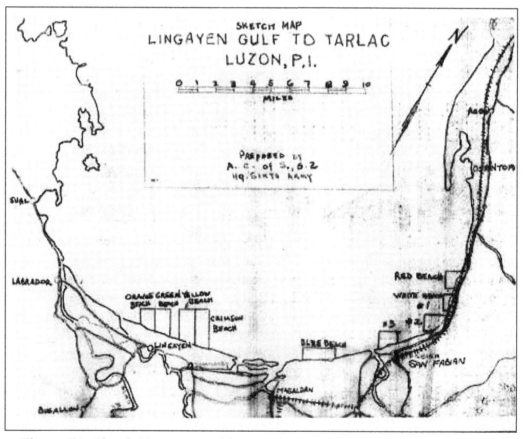

Figure 154 - Sketch Map – Mangaldan, Pangasinan Province, Philippine Islands
Lingayen Gulf to Tarlac Jan 1945

The US Navy fleet supporting the Lingayen invasion experienced heavy losses from the largest Japanese kamikaze attack of the war to date. During the eight-day period [4-12 Jan 1944] the Allies had 24 ships sunk and 67 ships damaged from kamikaze attacks, including three battleships, two cruisers, and two destroyers.

On S-Day (9 Jan 45), Col. Harwood, ASCOM Chief of Staff, along with the Command Section (which included Lt. Col. Day), came ashore at Blue Beach. After the first night inland from Blue Beach, they made a short reconnaissance trip to Mangaldan and took possession of a school building in the center of the town for the ASCOM Headquarters.[332] When Col. Vogel came ashore on S+4, Base M headquarters was established at San Fernando and a supply point at Sual.

38.2.3.   Supply and Reconstruction – An Engineer's Story

The main S+1 supply Echelon landed at White Beach No. 2 at 1900 hours and unloaded their supplies at night. They came under enemy artillery fire, and one man was wounded. The S+2 Echelon landed on Blue Beach and moved quickly to Mangaldan, Pangasinan Province where thanks to plentiful Filipino labor, a new supply depot was constructed.

The attitude of the Filipinos in the area was most cooperative. They did everything in their power to help the Americans. Civilian labor proved most important in building the airstrip in such a short time period. One unconfirmed report indicated that as the Navy cannons were beginning their shelling of the landing site, the ships learned that the Filipinos of the village of Lingayen were preparing a victory parade and were in the streets with American and Filipino flags. The gunners very quickly redirected their fire away from the village. When the Americans moved on shore, there was no resistance in that area.

The Construction Battalion went to work on the Lingayen airstrip. Lt. Col. Pickard and Major Walters evaluated two possible locations for a second strip, and selected a site near Blue Beach.[333] The original requirement of two all-weather airstrips was abandoned after consultation with GHQ, the Army, and the Air Force. Since the tactical situation was going better than expected and the weather appeared to be improving, Command decided that two dry-weather airstrips available four days earlier were better than one all-weather strip later. The target for a steel-mat airstrip at Lingayen was moved up to S+6 (15 Jan 45). In spite of delays in unloading and poor beach conditions, the engineers laid 5,000 feet of steel mat at Lingayen by 2230 hours on S+6. The next morning at 0930, two P-38s landed, and by 1 pm, C-47s started landing. Between 40 and 50 C-47s landed that first day.

---

[332] OCMH, Unpublished historical manuscript, SOS Oper. During Initial Phase of Invasion and Reconquest of Luzon, 26 Dec 44 to 13 Feb 1944, file 8-5.8, AA V 3 p11.
[333] Ibid. p11.

Lt. Col. Christianson of ASCOM Construction was in charge of railway rehabilitation. He found the railroad roadbed in fair condition and located a locomotive at Dagupan and 23 flat cars near San Fabian. Within a few days, some 400 experienced civilian railway men were hired to start repairing the rail bed and rail stock. Several rail bridges were out and had to be repaired. There were a number of direct hits on the tracks around Dagupan and San Fabian that had to be repaired, but generally repairs were well underway.[334]

By S+5, the next two engineer units arrived and began work on the second landing strip. Again, the help of the locals was invaluable. The area for the landing strip was cleared by Filipinos using only hand tools until S+7 when the heavy equipment from the engineers arrived.

By S+6, work was moving forward for construction of a 270-foot wharf near the mouth of the Dagupan River. A shortage of structural timbers delayed progress, but an oil jetty was started at Blue Beach that would feed an oil pipeline to the Lingayen air strip.

By S+7 at Lingayen, the air strip extension to 6,000 feet was almost complete, and the field had been oiled down to control dust.

On S+8 (17 Jan 1945) a third airstrip was started near Dagupan. The site, selected by Gen. Casey, was judged to be superior to either of the other airstrip sites. This was to be a dry-weather strip and to be constructed with all possible speed.

Pockets of heavy Japanese resistance were encountered as US troops moved inland. The 1896th Engineer Aviation Battalion, which landed on S+4, was ambushed while en route to their inland objective area and sustained 66 men killed, 46 MIA, and 23 injured. All the injured had to be evacuated.

On S+9 (18 Jan 45), General Casey held his first full staff meeting at Mangaldan. All sections were represented including Capt. Webb, Commander of the Naval Service Command, and the Commanding General of the 4th Engineer Service Brigade. The issues discussed included:[335]

a. ASCOM troops should carry arms and helmets at all time since Japanese infiltration was still present.

b. Care should be exercised in giving food to civilians. It had been proved at Leyte that indiscriminate distribution of food created a labor problem, as most Filipinos would not work as long as they had plenty of food.

---

[334] Ibid. p11-12.

[335] Ibid. p19.

c. *ASCOM assumed all unloading responsibilities on S+10 and assigned that to Base M.*

d. *Meetings were to be held twice each week, Monday and Thursday, to determine unloading priorities. Initially bridge timbers and structural timbers had first priority.*

e. *Naval Service Command needed a Naval Ship Repair installation. San Tomas was to be that site. Also an advanced PT base was to be located at Sual. Navy Seabees would start construction S+12.*

f. *Airdromes, POL, and railroad situations were discussed.*

g. *The status of roads and bridges and the availability of gravel and local timber was discussed.*

h. *Gen. Casey emphasized the importance of coordination and cooperation between units so that idle equipment and labor could be minimized.*

On S+10 (19 Jan 45), when Base M took over unloading responsibility from the Sixth Army, they unloaded 6,113 tons of supplies in 42 hours under unfavorable conditions of sea and beach. This was 50% above the amount scheduled by Sixth Army.[336]

On S+13 (22 Jan 45), General Casey and Colonel Calkins, representing the Sixth Army, witnessed the formal opening ceremony of the railroad from Dagupan to Bayambang. The first train consisted of seven loaded flatcars carrying 230 tons of matériel to the Bayambang railhead 25 miles to the south destined for the XIV Corps. The rail line to the north was also ready for use.[337]

38.2.4.   ASCOM to Become LUBSEC (LUzon Base SECtion)

On S+6 (15 Jan 45) Headquarters USASOS issued an order entitled, *Enlarge Functions of ASCOM*. ASCOM was to be reorganized for the *Assumption of Logistic Responsibility for Luzon[338]*.

On S+8 (17 Jan 45) the letter was received at ASCOM indicating that the ASCOM was moving under the command of USASOS as of S+35 (13 Feb 1945), and would be given a new enlarged mission to serve all Luzon.

---

[336] Ibid. p20.

[337] Ibid. p22.

[338] ASCOM GO No. 5 dated 28 Jan 1945 entitled "Reorganization for the Assumption of Logistic Responsibility of Luzon." OCMH Ibid. Vol.3 Appendix.

The enlarged mission included the following:[339]

    a. *Continue the establishment and development of Base M and logistic support of current tactical operations.*

    b. *Execute all engineer construction on Luzon, except that undertaken by tactical forces incidental to their operations.*

    c. *Organize and develop an operating Transportation Command for Luzon, which will operate the railway, long-distance highway transportation, and water trans-shipment between the Luzon bases.*

    d. *Organize, develop, and operate USASOS bases to be established on Luzon (including Manila, Legaspi and others, as required)*

    e. *Prepare for the continued performance of the foregoing missions, the release of such missions as may be directed by Headquarters, USASOS, prepare for functioning as Advance Section I, and prepare for merging with the Manila Base; the foregoing alternative developments being dependent on the magnitude of the logistic problem in Luzon and other circumstances not yet foreseeable.*

The enlarged mission added responsibility for Manila and all of Luzon. The first order of business was the continued logistic supply of tactical operations, including Base M operations. This included the planning and development of additional supply bases, as required, including Bicol in Legaspi (about 300 miles south of Manila).

The Luzon Engineer District was established to support Manila city utilities, public transportation, railroads, highways and bridges, the port of Manila, including construction of hospitals, airdromes, staging and other military facilities throughout Luzon.

Civil Affairs Services continued to recruit local construction labor, maintain liaison with the civil governments, and provide civilian relief as directed.

The Transportation Command took responsibility for the railways, the long-distance highways and water transport within Luzon. The Port Command took responsibility for the Port of Manila and all subports in the Manila area.

On S+13 (22 Jan 45) only five days after construction of the Mangaldan airstrip began, the first plane landed. In three hours there were 120 planes on the strip. The ASCOM Construction Section was commended.

---

[339] Ibid.

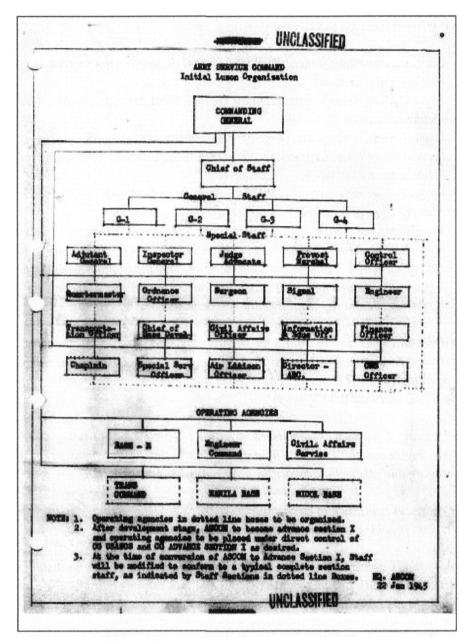

Figure 155 – HQ. ASCOM Organization Chart - LUBSEC - 22 Jan 1945
Attachment to ASCOM General Order No. 5 dated 28 Jan 1945

On S+14 (23 Jan 45), General Frink, CG of USASOS, arrived with part of his staff. He attended the ASCOM staff meeting and discussed the coming reorganization with expanded responsibilities for ASCOM. Under the new organization, ASCOM was to have a General Staff, a special staff composed of Chiefs of Services, and was to control operating agencies including Base B, the

Engineer Command, the Civil Affairs Service, the Transportation Command, the Manila Base, and the Bicol Base. General Frink returned to Tacloban on S+16.

Personnel for the enlarged organization arrived through the latter part of January and early February:[340]

- *Lt. Col. Black, G-1 arrived on 28 Jan 45*
- *Col. Falkner, G-4, on 29 January.*
- *Major Adams of the Intelligence Section became G-2*
- ***Lt. Col. Day of the Troops Section became G-3***
- *General Baker, prospective Commanding General of the Manila Base, arrived at Mangaldan on 4 Feb 45.*

On S+18 (27 Jan 45), two additional combat divisions arrived and were unloaded. One of these divisions was the 1st Cavalry Division.

By S+25 (3 Feb 45), construction progress was reported as follows:

			Percent Complete
a.	*Mangaldan Airdrome*		*100%*
b.	*Lingayen Airdrome*		*70%*
	a.	*1,000 foot extension of strip*	*22%*
	b.	*Two scramble alert areas*	*65%*
	c.	*43 hardstands on North taxiway*	*55%*
	d.	*32 hardstands on North taxiway*	*91%*
	e.	*50 reveted bomb bays*	*100%*
	f.	*20 Avgas bays*	*100%*
	g.	*Fighter Sector*	*70%*
	h.	*Alert hut*	*93%*
c.	*Hospitals*		
	a.	*Lingayen Hospital*	*80%*
	b.	*San Fabian 1000-bed Hospital*	*12%*
	c.	*Calasiao 500-bed Hospital*	*35%*
d.	*Railroads*		
	a.	*San Fabian to Alacan*	*20%*
	b.	*Restoration of 2500-foot spur from jetty to mainline*	*15%*
e.	*Jetties*		
	a.	*20 LST slots at San Fabian*	*25%*
	b.	*Water and oil jetty*	*50%*

---

[340] Ibid. OCMH Vol. 3 p.27.

c.	RR jetty	18%
f.	Hydrographic survey of Dagupan River	100%
g.	Pugmill, rock crusher, gravel pit and three clay pits	100%
h.	Total tonnage unloaded for 24-hour period 3 Feb 45	10,100 tons

ASCOM was noted for collecting statistical information to improve efficiency in different operations. ASCOM was working harder to build tighter coordination with the Navy to reduce lost time unloading LSTs.

38.3.   The Sixth Army in Luzon – Manila Campaign

Lingayen is approximately 120 miles north of Manila on the north end of the central plain of Luzon. There are two main Highways from northern Luzon into Manila – Highway No. 3 and Highway No. 5. After invading Lingayen on 9 Jan 1945, General Krueger's plan was to send Maj. Gen. Innis Swift and I Corps down the eastern side of the valley following Highway No. 3. Lt. Gen. Oscar Griswold and XIV Corps would go down the western side of the valley following Highway No. 5. The two Corps would converge in Manila.

By 27 Jan 45, the 37th Division (part of I Corps) had covered over 75 miles and reached Clark Air Force Base at Ft. Stotsenburg, which fell on 29 Jan 45.

On 31 Jan 1945 the Eighth Army under Gen. Robert L. Eichelberger opened up a new front south of Manila with an amphibious landing at Nasugbu. A parachute landing at Tagaytay followed on 3 Feb 1945. The Eighth Army began to advance on Manila from the south and east. Manila was in the jaws of a north-south pincer maneuver.

The 1st Cavalry Division had been brought into Lingayen Gulf on 27 Jan 45 and attached to XIV Corps. On 1 Feb 45 the 1st Cavalry Division moved out from their staging area at Guimba and headed south down Highway No. 5 toward Manila on the left flank of the 37th Division.

The 1st Cavalry Brigade, a unit of the 1st Cav. Division, teamed up with the 44th Tank Battalion to form a "flying column" that became a mechanized wedge to advance quickly down Highway No. 5. The speed of their advance surprised and overran many Japanese defenders. The column arrived at a key bridge across the Pampanga River before the Japanese had ignited the 3,000-pounds of dynamite wired on the bridge. With Japanese mortar rounds falling near the bridge, Americans ran on the bridge and threw the armed charges into the river. Saving this bridge was extremely important to speed the column to Manila. After the bridge was crossed, there was only token Japanese resistance before the "flying column" joined up with the 37th Infantry in Plaridel.

The 37th Division encountered many more destroyed bridges than the 1st Cavalry which delayed its advanced south down Highway No. 3 arriving 2 Feb 1945.

38.3.1.   The "Flying Column" and the First Prisoner Rescue – 3 Feb 1945

In the evening of 2 Feb 45 news was brought to the Americans by Filipino guerillas that there were 4,000 captives and civilian internees inside Santo Tomas University and possibly more at Malacanan Palace. There was fear that these internees might be harmed during the coming battle for Manila. At dawn the next morning, the same "flying column" of the 1st Brigade and the 44th Tank Battalion left their camp at Santa Maria on a focused rescue mission lead by two Filipino guerillas into the heart of Manila.

The "flying column" crossed the bridge across the Tuliahan River at Novaliches just in time to extinguish the burning fuses of the Japanese demolitions. This bridge was the city limits of the City of Manila. Beyond the bridge several small groups of Japanese soldiers tried to ambush the advancing column with small arms fire, but the "flying column" viewed these attacks as only "distractions" and continued into the city. The unit sped directly down Rizal Avenue to the main gate of Santo Tomas University, where thanks to a tank, the main gate was breached. The infantry entered, and most of the Japanese were destroyed. The Japanese had turned Santo Tomas into a prison for civilians and nurses of the Army and Navy, and approximately 3,700 internees were freed. At the end of the battle, a unit of 47 Japanese soldiers managed to hold 221 internees as human hostages, demanding safe passage to the Japanese lines in exchange for the lives of their hostages. The exchange was accepted by the Americans, and the hostages were released the next day. The Japanese soldiers were released at their selected location, however, this location had fallen into Allied hands the preceding day, such that these Japanese soldiers were later either killed or captured.

A platoon of the 1st Calvary was diverted to Malacanan Palace but found only Filipino guards and no internees.

While the "flying column" was engaged at Santo Tomas, the Japanese demolition people managed to destroy the bridge across Tuliahan River, so the "flying column" was stymied without gasoline supplies until the US engineers could repair the bridge.

The next day, 4 Feb 45, the 37th Infantry Division came into Manila and affected their own rescue mission at Bilibid Prison where 800 Prisoners Of War and 500 civilian internees, including women and children, were liberated. The combination of Santo Tomas and Bilibid Prison totaled 5,000 internees -- 4,000 Americans and 1,000 British, Australian, and other nationalities.[341]

---

[341] Campaigns of MacArthur, Report of his Staff, Volume 1, 1966, p. 276.

38.3.2.   ASCOM Manila Reconnaissance Detachment – 6 to 12 Feb 1945

On 8 Feb 1945 (S+30) at the ASCOM staff meeting, General Casey indicated concern for the condition of the many bridges. Most of the bridges had been hastily constructed to enable the troops to move forward and were temporary in nature. He felt many would be washed out when the Philippine wet season returned. Casey instructed Col. Pickard to set up a schedule to replace these bridges.

On 10 Feb 1945 (S+35), a radiogram sent by USASOS stated that ASCOM would revert to USASOS control as of 0001 hours 13 Feb 1945.[342]

In expectation of taking logistical command for Manila, ASCOM Headquarters organized a special detachment of 17 officers and 14 enlisted men under the command of Lt. Col. Ernest O. Black to enter the Manila combat zone and assess the physical condition of the facilities that could be used by ASCOM. The detachment needed to determine the condition of the port for unloading activities, to identify city areas and buildings suitable for supply storage, to assess the condition of the city water supply and utility facilities for power and sanitation, to assess the structural integrity of buildings as possible sites for ASCOM headquarters and Base M headquarters, to locate a site for a major depot, and to assess the condition of the railroad, highways and major bridges. They were charged with delivering a report describing needed repairs within two days of their return.

The detachment was warned that many of the facilities they were to inspect were booby-trapped. They were to remain armed at all times and exercise extreme caution. They were instructed to work closely with their tactical counterparts in the combat arms who were still fighting in the city.

The ASCOM detachment departed for Manila on the morning of S+28 (6 Feb 1945) traveling by convoy. They expected to arrive in Manila that same evening however, because of bridge destruction, heavy traffic, Japanese infiltration, and an impending Japanese counterattack, their journey required an extra day. They arrived on the evening of S+29 (7 Feb 1945).

---

[342] Ibid. OCMH Volume III – USASOS Operations During Initial Phase of Invasion and Re-Conquest of Luzon, PI (Base M – Lingayan Gulf (26 Dec 1944-13 Feb 1945) (Appendix enclosure No. 23)

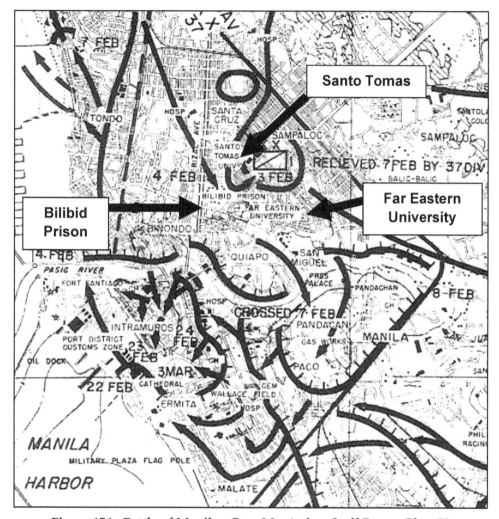

Figure 156 - Battle of Manila - Gen. MacArthur Staff Report Plate 78

The detachment had expected to find most of the city clear of Japanese. That was not the case. The battle for Manila was just beginning. Japanese soldiers still controlled large neighborhoods, especially south of the Pasig River. After a couple of days, the fighting let up enough for the detachment to begin their work.

- *The Far Eastern University was selected at the site for ASCOM headquarters.*
- *The Quezon City area and the Dilliman estate were selected for the General Depot.*
- *The north piers, warehouses, sheds and railways leading to the piers were found in good condition.*

General Casey flew into Manila from Mangaldan on S+31 (9 Feb 1945) where he reviewed and approved the recommendations of the Reconnaissance Detachment. He remained with the detachment for 48 hours, after which he left to attend a meeting at GHQ.

On S+34 (12 Feb 1945), Col. Dean, Lt. Col. Solluhub, and Maj. Adams returned to Mangaldan to submit their formal report and recommendations to General Casey.

38.3.3.   ASCOM Final Report – 13 Feb 1945

*On S+35 (13 Feb 1945), ASCOM was redesignated LUBSEC (**Lu**zon **B**ase **Sec**tion)[343] and transferred back to USASOS. The General Staff and Base M personnel retained their positions at LUBSEC. To the soldiers of ASCOM, it was only a change in name. All standing orders were unchanged.*

During the 25 days of responsibility for the Lingayen Gulf Area, ASCOM had performed a herculean feat of both supply and construction. ASCOM had:

- *Provided logistic support for approximately 215,000 troops.*
- *Unloaded about 250,000 tons of supplies and equipment in the 25-day period from S+6 (15 Jan 45) to S+35 (13 Feb 45). The highest single day was 11,995 tons on S+34 (12 Feb 45).*
- *Established Base M at San Fabian with three subbases at Dagupan, Sual, and White Beach.*
- *Increased total tonnage unloaded to 11,800 tons daily, almost double the tonnage unloaded on S+10.*

The engineer units completed major military construction including:

- *Two airdromes*
- *40 miles of roads*
- *Two wharves*
- *35 miles of railroad*
- *Oil and water jetties at San Fabian*
- *Work on the reconstruction of the railroad from Bayambang to Tarlac*
- *Three hospitals were under construction*
- *Hydrographic survey of Dagupan River complete*
- *Pugmill rock crusher, gravel pit, and three clay pits complete*

---

[343] USASOS GO No.42 dated 11 Feb 1945 entitled "Redesignation of Army Services Command" OCMH Ibid Vol. 3, Appendix.

All of this was accomplished in spite of Japanese air attacks and infiltration, adverse surf conditions, shortages of equipment, and transportation difficulties.

ASCOM personnel completed many construction projects well in advance of the proposed scheduled by working 24 hours per day. The unit kept in step with the advancing US combat forces. ASCOM contributed to the tactical and strategic success of the operation.

On S+35 (13 Feb 1945) Major General Hugh J. Casey was relieved of his "Temporary Duty" assignment as Command of ASCOM and returned to his permanent position as GHQ Chief Engineer on Gen. MacArthur's staff.

On 15 Feb 1945, Brig. Gen. Frayne Baker[344] was assigned as Commanding General for Luzon Base Section (LUBSEC). He had previously been designated Base "X" Commander, which meant he was in line for the next Base Command to be established.

General Krueger, Commanding General, Sixth Army, issued a unit commendation to ASCOM for outstanding performance and many of the ASCOM staff officers received Medals of Commendation, including Lt. Col. John Day.

38.4.   LUBSEC Moves into Manila[345] – 13 Feb 1945

The ASCOM Advanced Reconnaissance Detachment had arrived in Manila 6 Feb 1945. Now LUBSEC established its own Advanced Reconnaissance Party under the command of Colonel H. A. Cavanaugh, which arrived at Far Eastern University, Manila, on 14 Feb 1945. The unit reported in to Lt. Gen. Oscar Griswold, the Commanding General of XIV Corps, the combat arm in northern Manila, and proceeded to the ASCOM facility.

At this time, the North Harbor area and the area south of the Pasig River were still in control of the Japanese, so the first areas reconnoitered were the northern suburbs of the city. LUBSEC allocated the various Services into the northern sector according to their requirements for transportation or special facilities. Despite combat conditions, the first Liberty ship landed and unloaded its cargo in the North Harbor on 2 Mar 1945, sixteen days after the Advanced Party arrival in Manila. More supplies were brought in overland on 11 Mar 1945. South Beach was the next area to be cleared of rubble, land mines and booby traps.

---

[344] Brigadier General Frayne Baker, 0134923, USA.

[345] OCMH Historical Manuscript File No. 8-5 SO, CC. No. 780-20: Unpublished Manuscript, "History of USASOS AND AFWESPAC, Luzon Base Section USASOS for 13 Feb to 1 Apr 1945," Vol. XVIII, 24 Jun 1947, p1-76. pages are unnumbered

On 13 Mar 45 the location of LUBSEC Headquarters was moved to the Customs Building, Port Area, Manila, to be closer to the docks. The Engineer Construction Section set up offices one block away in the Manila Port Terminal Building. The docks had been devastated by the Japanese before they withdrew. Extensive repairs had to be done.

Col. D. G. McGregor was appointed Manila Area Commander, and handled the area allocations, billeting of senior officers, operation of a Casual Camp, inspections, morale, supervision of the Headquarters Commandant, the provost marshal, the Chaplin and the special services officer.

The Billeting Section of the Area Command began operating actively on 3 Mar 1945. Within ten days they were housing sixteen generals, two admirals, 215 colonels and lieutenant colonels, and an intermediate number of female officers and Red Cross civilians.

The Survey Section began surveying the entire Greater Manila area. A major portion of downtown Manila was reduced to large-scale plot plans and checked for accuracy by aerial photography.

Troops were pouring into Manila. The Camp Control Section of Area Command handled the movement of troops into Manila area. This was coordinated with G-3 Section. Troops arrived over the beach from 48 ships. An additional 38 units arrived in the area by rail and motor transportation. The Casual Camp was initially designed to handle 2,000 Casuals and was initially located in the northern part of the city. However, it had to be relocated to make room for a Petroleum-Oil-Lubricant storage area. Casuals were moved to a location about five miles from the port in the northeastern part of the city. There were major problems feeding all the Casual troops. The camp eventually handled 4,700 Casuals, with up to 860 in one day passing through to other units.

38.4.1.   LUBSEC G-3 Organization – Lt. Col. Day

The G-3 Section was organized on 14 Feb 1945.[346] **Lieutenant Colonel J.F. Day** *was initially assigned as the Assistant Chief of Staff, G-3, but was later succeeded by Major G. H. Adams, when Lt. Col. Day departed for Command and General Staff School, Fort Leavenworth, Kansas.*

G-3 was divided into four sections:

- *Troop Movement Division*
- *Troop Location Division*

---

[346] By General Order No. 1, Headquarters LUBSEC dated 13 Feb 1945.

- *Training and Service Inspections Division*
- *Administrative Division*

The Troop Movement Division prepared assignment and attachment orders for all LUBSEC units. It prepared movement orders and coordinated moves of all units moving to Manila. An information card file system set up for LUBSEC units showed locations by coordinates, unit strength, table of organization and equipment, and other data.

The Troop Location Division initiated a project in pin-pointing on maps the location of all units on Luzon, information being received from the Area Command, Unit Commanders, Sixth Army, XIV Corps, Engineer Construction Command, Base M, Debarkation letters, Status of Troop Movement and Signals. This division prepared all letters, orders and necessary follow-ups on all General Orders from Headquarters, USASOS, reorganizing and redesignating USASOS units attached to LUBSEC.

The Training and Service Inspection Division prepared plans for inspection teams whose duty would be inspect all LUBSEC units. The Inspection Section was mainly concerned about proper sanitation, construction for housekeeping facilities, personnel staffing levels to perform operations and improve troop camping areas.

The Administrative Division was established to represent the Base Motor Command for Manila. This Division was concerned with personnel who were assigned to the Port Command. By the end of March the Port Command had grown to 112 officers, 124 enlisted men, and 724 civilians.

38.4.2.   Entering Manila

When we came down through Manila, the battle lines were very jagged. There were a lot of Japanese suicide missions left behind. I don't know if you can call it suicide missions because ALL the Japanese were that way. They did not value their lives. *They were trained in the Japanese code of Bushido, a military code that taught the soldier to never become a Prisoner of War.* They were trained to fight to the death. They would keep a hand grenade, and when Americans came to capture them, they would pull the pin and try to kill some Americans with themselves. They thought if they died in battle, they would go to heaven.

The First Cavalry Division kept telling their troops "Don't make that mistake. If a Jap is holding his hands close, he probably has a grenade. If one wants to surrender, have them strip naked before you get close. If they don't strip, shoot them."

When the Japs were in caves, I guess the thing they feared the most were the flame throwers. Everyone was glad to have those things around. I never had one nor fired one, but I was close enough when one was fired to feel the heat.

38.4.3.   Battle of Manila – 4 Feb 1945 to 4 March 1945

By 4 Feb 45 the Pasig River had become the battle front. The Japanese controlled the southern bank of the river while the Americans controlled the northern bank. The Battle for the City of Manila had begun and would continue for one month. The battle was recorded as the bloodiest urban battle of the Pacific War. American losses included over 1,010 dead and 5,565 wounded. Filipino civilian losses have been estimated at 100,000.[347]   Japanese losses were estimated at 190,000. The City, including many historic Spanish structures, was virtually destroyed by collateral damage from the conflict,.

One of the cultural treasures of Manila before the war was the 16th-century Spanish walled city, Intramuros, the original Spanish settlement of Manila established in 1571. The name, Intramuros, is Latin for "within the walls" and describes a district of about 160 acres[348] which is completely surrounded by a three-mile-long stone wall, estimated to be 40-feet thick at the base and 20-feet thick at the top. Intramuros is located south of the river near the confluence of the Pasig River and Manila Bay. Original construction had begun in 1571 by the Spanish, but over its 300-year history the stone citadel had been renovated several times.

Intramuros contained civil, military, ecclesiastical, and commercial centers. There was a public plaza and market, eight churches, including the Manila Cathedral, Fort Santiago, military barracks, and two universities. The buildings were all laced with underground stone structures that provided strong defense against modern bombardment.

The Japanese troops that occupied the fortress were committed to never surrender. They held over 4,000 internees as prisoners. On 23 Feb 45 the Japanese released 3,000 women and children, the last people to leave the walled city alive.

To breech the walls, the Americans brought in their heaviest field artillery - 105mm, 155mm, and even 240mm howitzers. Cannon trailers were elevated so the artillery could fire with no elevation at point-blank range as close as 250 yards. Round after round was necessary to penetrate the

---

[347] David Horner, Australian military historian, reported in his book The Second World War, Vol 1: The Pacific, 2003, p60, that the Sixth Army lost 8,000 killed and 30,000 wounded, compared to 190,000 dead for Japan.

[348] About a-quarter-of-a-square-mile.

stone walls. In the late stage of the battle, the Japanese commander executed 1,000 prisoners, including women and children, who had survived the American shelling.

Figure 157 shows General MacArthur with his staff in the ruins of MacArthur's pre-war Manila home during a tour of the city. The photo was taken on 1 Mar 1945. The nine men identified by asterisk had accompanied Gen. MacArthur when he evacuated Corregidor by PT boat on 11 Mar1942. This is often called the "I have returned" photo. (L-R) Generals LeGrande Diller* (1901 - 1987), Public Information Officer; Charles P. Stivers* (1891 -), G-1; Charles A. Willoughby* (born Adolf Tscheppe-Weidenbach, 1890 - 1972), G-2; Spencer Akin* (1889 - 1973), Chief Signal Officer; Richard K. Sutherland*

Figure 157 - General Douglas MacArthur and his Staff - 1 March 1945

(1893 - 1966), Chief of Staff; General MacArthur, Richard K. Marshall* (1895 - 1973), Deputy Chief of Staff; Hugh J. (Pat) Casey* (1898 - 1981), Chief Engineer; Colonel Sidney Huff,* Aide de Camp; Major General William Marquat* (1894 - 1960), Anti-Aircraft Officer; and Lieutenant Colonel Joseph McMicking (1908 - 1990). This photo was taken by Carl Mydans of Time Life Pictures.

When the battle ended on 4 Mar 45, a total 16,650 Japanese dead were counted within the walls. Intramuros was in ruin.[349]

38.4.4. Filipino Vigilante Justice

I never will forget one scene – it was as bad as anything I saw. I was in Manila at the Pasig River Hotel one night when I received a call about 11 PM. They called me to come down. Now I am G-3 for LUBSEC, so I wasn't supposed to be fighting. I coordinated everything. Well, apparently they had a bunch of 155mm's banked and shooting across the river. The Japanese were shooting back. The Americans had some problems and wanted an artillery officer to come down.

I got me a driver and we started working our way through the crowded streets down to the river. The streets were filled with people wandering aimlessly about. With so much destruction, most people were homeless. They did not know where to turn. All were in a total daze. Down at the river bank, I saw twenty or twenty-five Filipinos pushing and shoving one man they had tied up. They walked him down to the river, shot him, and pushed him in the water. That was it! If the Filipinos thought a man was a collaborator with the Japanese, they killed him. There was no trial. He was dead. There was no excuse. Sometimes they killed innocent people who had not helped the Japs. The guerillas were more interested in revenge than justice.

We supplied the guerrillas with guns, ammunition, and food. The only problem was you had to be sure you were dealing with a "patriot" guerrilla, and not a "hoodlum." The guerrillas had a badge with a big label and traveled in groups of three to six. The guerrillas were a lot of help because they could speak the local dialect, but I am sure there were some thugs mixed in.

---

[349] In 1951 Intramuros was declared a Philippine National Treasure, and the government, with a very limited budget, began a long slow process of restoring Intramuros. In 1950s, the Manila Cathedral was rebuilt. In 1979 a government agency started restoring the walls to control urban encroachment, but results have been slow. In 2010, Intramuros was identified by the Global Heritage Fund as one of twelve worldwide heritage sites that are in danger of being irreparably lost.

39.   COMMAND AND GENERAL STAFF SCHOOL (C&GS)

The Command and General Staff School (C&GS) is the mid-career graduate school for professional military officers to train to become field grade commanders or staff officers. Sometimes referred to as the Major's School, attending C&GS was and is a career requirement for promotion to higher rank.

39.1.   Orders to the United States – 7 Mar 1945

My orders came in for a "Temporary Duty" assignment to attend the US Army Command and General Staff School (C&GS) at Fort Leavenworth, Kansas. After attending school, I would return to GHQ for a new assignment. It meant I was returning to the States – at least temporarily.

I guess the General figured after being a General Staff Officer through the invasions of Leyte and the Lingayen Gulf, it was time for me to learn how to do it right before we hit Japan. We were all beginning to look beyond Manila and knew the invasion of Japan was on the horizon.

I was thrilled to be going home. After 39 months in the South Pacific, I was ready for a break. My orders were to proceed to Tacloban on Leyte for Military Air Transport Service back to San Francisco. The Army gave me twelve days to get from Manila to Kansas, including five days of travel and a week of Leave. I had to be at Ft. Leavenworth by 19 Mar 1945. I would finally see Cile.

39.1.1.   "Mrs. Clarke is Arriving?"

I flew down to Tacloban from Manila. When I arrived in Leyte, I was swapping stories in the waiting room with two guys I knew, when a third guy came in and said, "Hey, Bessie-Marie is coming in tonight and will be landing shortly."

When I left GHQ (Brisbane), I was followed as Headquarters Commandant by a Colonel Thomas. Col. Thomas was there about a year when he also had a run-in with Bessie Marie and was fired by Gen. Sutherland. Later they brought in a Brigadier General as Headquarters Commandant. In March 1944 Gen. Sutherland had made Mrs. Clarke a member of the American Army, so now this Australian woman wore an American Army uniform and carried the rank of a Captain.

For about a year I had not heard any more about Mrs. Clarke. When I was in Hollandia, I learned about her pink bathtub escapade at "Eagle's Nest." Then in the Philippines, the rumor circulated that General Sutherland had sent "Bessie Marie" and two lieutenants back to San Francisco on a procurement trip to purchase fresh fruits and vegetables for the Pacific and for MacArthur's headquarters.

When I learned about Bessie Marie's imminent arrival in Tacloban, returning from San Francisco, I was astonished and said, "She is?"

I got on the phone and called Col. Roger O. Egeberg, General MacArthur's Aide and Doctor, who I still knew from Brisbane. I said "Colonel, I just arrived in Tacloban going back to the States to attend the Command and General Staff School, and I learned something that I am sure you will be interested in knowing. Bessie Marie is coming into Leyte on a plane tonight and will be arriving here shortly."

Col. Egeberg shouted into the phone, "WHAT!!"

"They tell me she is arriving with her pink bathtub, commode, and all," I said jokingly.

He said, "Where is she going to land?"

"Tacloban, Sir," I said.

"When?" he asked.

"I was told it would be in another hour," I said.

Col. Egeberg said, "Somebody is going to hear about this."

My plane for the States left shortly thereafter, so I had no more direct knowledge of events related to Bessie Marie. I was told that Col. Egeberg went to General MacArthur. "General, did you know Mrs. Clarke is coming into Tacloban?"

General MacArthur apparently called in Sutherland and said, "I understand Mrs. Clarke is coming into Leyte."

"Yes, Sir," said General Sutherland. "She is supposed to report in."

General MacArthur is said to have said, "I tell you what I want you to do. I want her out of here before sunrise, bathtub and all, and I want you to report to me that she is gone."

When her plane landed in Tacloban, Mrs. Clarke got off the plane long enough to go to the bathroom, but then boarded another special plane arranged for her by Sutherland to fly to Australia. She was out of Tacloban before sunrise and never returned.

MacArthur had an agreement with Australian P.M. Curtin that no Australian women were to go north of the equator. That meant no Australian was to be north of Hollandia. Sutherland had violated this understanding.

MacArthur relieved Sutherland a few months after that incident and got himself a new Chief of Staff. On 2 Sep 45, Sutherland was on board the battleship Missouri in Tokyo Bay for the surrender ceremony, but Sutherland was sent back home very soon afterward. In time, he retired from the military and moved to Florida.[350]

That was the end for the saga of Bessie Marie.

After the war I ran into Col. Thomas at Ft. Sam Houston Officers Club. We laughed about the saga of Bessie Marie. We were the two SOBs that got fired first by her. Col. Thomas said "You know, we ought to get together and write a book."

I said, "Boy, if we did, we would both get shot, not fired, shot!"

39.1.2.   The Flight to United States – 9-13 Mar 1945

The flight back to the States across the Pacific by military air was a true experience. From Tacloban, Leyte P.I. to Travis Air Force Base near San Francisco in 1945 required five legs, or hops, each between eight and sixteen hours. The total passage took four days, but air travel was much preferred over a ship that required a month.

The military air transport workhorse was the Douglas C-54 Skymaster, a military version of the 1942 DC-4. The plane carried a crew of six and between 50 and 86 soldiers in the unpressurized military passenger version. The craft had four radial-powered propeller engines with a normal cruising speed of 227 miles per hour and a range of 2,500 miles flying between 10,000 and 12,000 feet. [351]

The military practice was to take the passengers off the aircraft after each landing while the plane was refueled and serviced. The passengers were bused to a mess hall where they were fed a hot

---

[350] See Paul P. Rogers, *The Bitter Years: MacArthur and Sutherland*, Prager Publishers, NY, NY, 1991 for an extensive discussion of Mrs. Clarke and her activities.

[351] *American Museum of Aviation*, www.prop-liners.com/dc4tech.htm

meal and given a chance to walk around for a while before reboarding the aircraft for the continuation of the journey. On board the food consisted of K-Rations. If you were fortunate, you might see a box lunch consisting of a sandwich and some fruit.

The individual flight leg durations were very dependent upon the weather, particularly head winds. Col. Day's flights were as follows:

- *9 Mar 45 – Depart Tacloban, Leyte P.I.*
- *10 Mar 45 – Guam – 8 to 11 hours flight time*
- *11 Mar 45 – Kwajalein Island – 11 or 14 hours flight time*
- *11 Mar 45 – Johnson Island – 10 to 13 hours flight time*
- *12 Mar 45 – Hickam AFB, Hawaii – 9 to 12 hours flight time*
- *13 Mar 45 – Travis AFB, California – 14 to 16 hours flight time*

After arrival at Travis, passengers were taken to a barracks where they could sleep on a cot to recover.

39.1.3.   Command & General Staff School –19 Mar 45 – 26 May 45

Lt. Col. Day attended Command and General Staff School, Class #23, at Fort Leavenworth, Kansas (19 Mar 1945 to 26 May 1945). Cile and Johnnie joined him at Fort Leavenworth. This eleven-week program had a curriculum built around planning for the invasion of Japan.

40.   PLANNING THE INVASION OF JAPAN

40.1.   US Army Forces, Pacific (AFPAC) – 6 Apr 45

On 6 Apr 45, the Joint Chiefs appointed MacArthur as Supreme Commander for US Army Forces, Pacific. This brought Okinawa and the Central Pacific Area, along with the Philippines and SWPA, under his purview for the first time. The Joint Chiefs instructed MacArthur to complete the conquest of Luzon and the remainder of the Philippines, to prepare to occupy Northern Borneo, and to make plans for the campaign in Japan

The General Staff was turning their thoughts toward the invasion of Japan. The Allies were planning on the assumption that Germany would fall by July 1945. The consensus opinion of the General Staff was that 18 additional months after the defeat of Germany would be required to defeat Japan.

40.2.   The Battle for Okinawa – 1 Apr 1945 – 22 Jun 1945

The battle for Okinawa was fought under the direction of Adm. Nimitz. On 1 April 45, the US Army landed on Okinawa to begin an 81-day campaign for the Ryukyu Islands. The battle was one of the bloodiest battles in the Pacific, and was a stepping stone to the Japanese mainland. In this battle Americans had casualties of over 12,000 killed and 39,000 wounded. The casualties in Okinawa approached the 14,000 killed in all of the Philippine Islands. This fact was one reason why General MacArthur took issue with the tactics of Nimitz, feeling it was not necessary to clear all the Japanese from an island. Rather, MacArthur wanted to capture the airfields, and then take a defensive position to isolate and starve out the remaining Japanese.

40.3.   Operation "DOWNFALL" – 1 Dec 45

Planning for the invasion of Japan, Operation DOWNFALL, was begun immediately. DOWNFALL had two parts: "Operation Olympic" and "Operation Coronet." Olympic was to be the first strike on the southern island of Kyushu lead by Gen. Krueger and the US Sixth Army, veterans of New Guinea and the Philippines. Operation Olympic was to involve fourteen divisions and was scheduled for 1 Dec 45. Operation Coronet, the major strike on Honshu would follow in three months (1 Mar 46) and would involve three Armies with a total of twenty-five divisions. Troops for Coronet were to come from Okinawa, Hawaii, and Europe. Follow-up reinforcements would come from the redeployment of troops from Europe. The invasion for Japan would be the largest military force in the history of the world.[352] *Marshal reported to President Roosevelt at*

---

[352] U.S. Government, Reports of General MacArthur, *The Campaigns of MacArthur in the Pacific, Volume I*, Prepared by his General Staff, 1966, p.395.

the Potsdam Conference that fourteen divisions would be required for DOWNFALL, compared with nine that were used in the Normandy invasion.

What did you know about the invasion of Japan?
I knew the plan. We were going into Kyushu, the Southern island of Japan. We planned five or six divisions for the initial landing, followed by many more. I don't remember the number, but perhaps 600,000 troops. I would probably be with the Sixth Army again. A second landing on Honshu would have been even larger, maybe one million troops.

How many would have died?
Millions! Dying for the Japs was nothing. Very few ashes got back to Japan. If a Jap died for his country, he would go to heaven. If we had invaded Japan, we would have lost millions of troops.

I always say Harry Truman did a great job. He was one of the best Presidents we ever had. He had the guts to say what he felt.

40.4.   Preparing to Return to the Pacific – 6 Aug 1945

I had completed C&GS, enjoyed a home leave, become reacquainted with my family, visited my folks, and driven back to San Francisco with Cile and Johnnie. I was waiting to be assigned to a troop ship to return to the Philippines.

On Monday morning, 6 Aug 45, *at 10:45AM in Washington, DC*, President Harry Truman announced that an "atomic bomb" of incredible strength had been dropped on Hiroshima about 16 hours earlier. Three days later there was a second atomic bomb dropped on Nagasaki.

Everyone was ecstatic. We knew that the war was over. I knew we would not have to invade Japan. From San Francisco, I sent a wire to General Fitch, Adjutant General of GHQ in Manila. I asked him "Why do I have to go back? The war is over. The Philippines are finished." I thought I had been over there enough.

Fitch sent a very short reply "No need to return." It would be a few more months before I learned that only four days later on 10 Aug 45 Fitch issued General Order No. 102 that awarded me the Legion of Merit for my service to General Casey. I don't know if that was in the works or if Fitch was saying thank you and goodbye to me. My war was over.

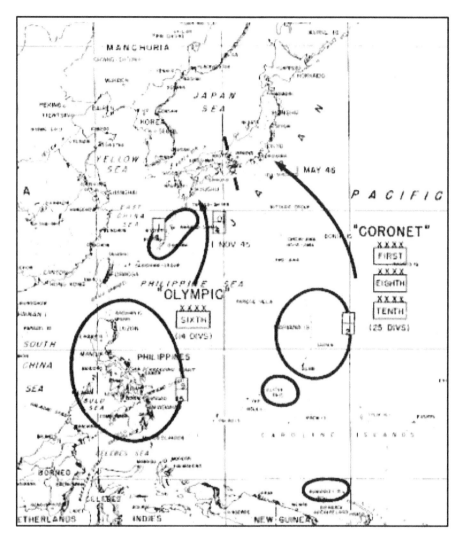

Figure 158 - *DOWNFALL* **Plan - Operation Olympic and Operation Coronet**
Report of MacArthur Staff, 1966, Plate 112, 28 May 1945, p394.

The Day family left San Francisco for the drive back to Bonham, Texas to await further orders. The final events of the war were as follows:

- 6 Aug 1945 – Hiroshima Atomic Bomb
- 9 Aug 1945 – Nagasaki Atomic Bomb
- 10 Aug 1945 – GHQ USAF, Pacific, Gen. Order No. 102, dated 10 Aug 1945 to Lieutenant Colonel John F. Day, Jr., 0271190, Field Artillery, United States Army, awarded the Legion of Merit for his service from 5 Sep 1944 to 12 Feb 1945, signed by Gen. Richard Sutherland.
- 14 Aug 1945 – Japanese accept unconditional surrender (V-J Day)
- 2 Sept 1945 – Formal surrender ceremony onboard the Battleship Missouri in Tokyo Bay

How do you feel about the Atomic Bomb?
Glad to see it was on our side. People can't appreciate the strength of those bombs. After the war, I saw three atomic bombs exploded in Las Vegas, Nevada. I am supposed to go to a hospital periodically to see if the bombs had any residual effect on me.

Everybody had a button to measure radioactivity exposure. You turned away before the bomb went off. After it went off, everything was as bright as daylight. You turned around and were hit by a shock wave that could knock you down. More stuff was picked up from the ground and went up in air. We were seven miles from where it went off. Every bomb has a Y-4.[353] You never know which way it is going to blow.

We went up there and looked at Ground Zero to see what had happened. Five miles out an airplane was parked. The concussion took one wing off but did nothing to the wing on the opposite side. Sheep tied in the area were all dead.

---

[353] Shape of the destruction pattern

41.   LEGION OF MERIT – 10 AUG 1945

The Legion of Merit was established in 1942 by Congress as the fourth highest military decoration of the United States military and the highest award granted for non-combat performance during the Second World War. It was awarded to General and Colonel Staff Officers for meritorious service. The following is the Citation for Lt. Col. Day:

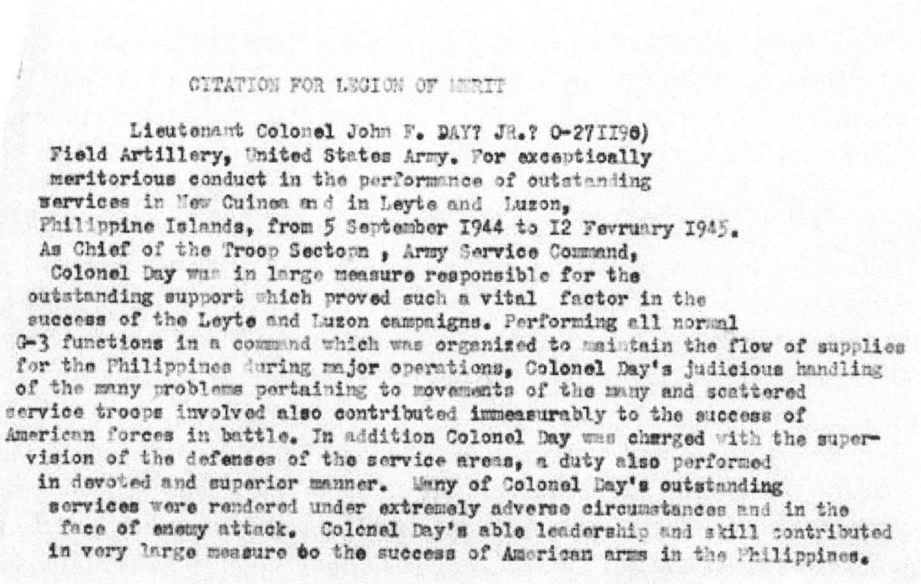

CITATION FOR LEGION OF MERIT

Lieutenant Colonel John F. DAY? JR.? O-271198)
Field Artillery, United States Army. For exceptionally
meritorious conduct in the performance of outstanding
services in New Guinea and in Leyte and Luzon,
Philippine Islands, from 5 September 1944 to 12 Fevruary 1945.
As Chief of the Troop Sectorn , Army Service Command,
Colonel Day was in large measure responsible for the
outstanding support which proved such a vital factor in the
success of the Leyte and Luzon campaigns. Performing all normal
G-3 functions in a command which was organized to maintain the flow of supplies
for the Philippines during major operations, Colonel Day's judicious handling
of the many problems pertaining to movements of the many and scattered
service troops involved also contributed immeasurably to the success of
American forces in battle. In addition Colonel Day was charged with the supervision of the defenses of the service areas, a duty also performed
in devoted and superior manner. Many of Colonel Day's outstanding
services were rendered under extremely adverse circumstances and in the
face of enemy attack. Colonel Day's able leadership and skill contributed
in very large measure to the success of American arms in the Philippines.

Figure 159 - Original Citation - 1945

Figure 160 - Legion of Merit

Figure 161 - Lt. Col. Day receives the Legion of Merit

42.   EPILOGUE

War is not fun. Everyone experiences their own war. Everyone has their own job to do, and that is the war to him. Your job depends on everybody else doing their job; everybody else depends on you. It is a collective effort. Each person had their own experiences, and those experiences were the war to them.

I was lucky. I was in some good places. I got through some tight places. Every night when the Japanese came over dropping bombs or strafing, you got in a hole. Any bomb could get you. It was just a matter of chance if you got hit or if the fellow next to you got hit. I was lucky and did not get hit. Many others got hit.

17 Oct 1947 – *Lt. Col. John F. Day Jr. accepted a Recess Appointment into the Regular Army by SO No. 17. There are two types of Army Commissions – Reserve Army and Regular Army. This Regular Army Commission enabled Col. Day to remain on active duty until 1960 when he retired at the rank of full Colonel with credit for 30 years of service [Regular Army Serial number was 051502. Reserve Army Serial Number was 0271190].*

Spring 1948 – *Cile had a second major operation, said to have been for lung cancer. She was definitely a smoker. When the surgeon opened her body, he found it to be filled with an abundance of cancer polyps throughout. The surgeon informed Col. Day, who was present in the operating room, that there was no hope to save Cile by doing major lung surgery. The best course of action was to close the body to minimize trauma and try to speed recovery. Future actions should be taken to provide a reasonable quality of life for the balance of her days. This was done. Medical understanding in 2012 suggests that her symptoms and these polyps might be symptoms of ovarian cancer rather than lung cancer.*

13 Nov 1948 - *Cile Day died at Brooks Army Medical Center, Fort Sam Houston, Texas. She was 33 years old.*

18 Jun 1950 – *Lt. Col. Day married Josephine Polito Carsten at Fort Sill, OK on 18 Jun 1950. They had two sons, Robert Francis Day and James Russell Day. Col. Day also adopted Ellen Jane Carsten, Josephine's daughter by a previous marriage to Capt. Frank Carsten. Capt Carsten died in 1943.*

30 Sep 1960 – *Colonel Day retired from active military service. He moved to North Palm Beach, Florida where he became a stock broker for over 25 years. He enjoyed golf and fishing for the rest of his life.*

<u>14-16 Feb 1988</u> – *Col. Day recorded his memoirs of the Southwest Pacific Area in eight hours of video in North Palm Beach, Florida. These tapes were used in the preparation of this book.*

<u>26 Oct 2000</u> – *John F. Day Jr. died at the age of 91 in North Palm Beach, Florida, where he had lived for 40 years. On 1 Nov 2000, at his request, he was buried in his uniform with full military honors at Willow Wild Cemetery in Bonham, Texas in a family plot next to the grave of Cile.*

<u>8 Jan 2004</u> – *Josephine Mary Polito Carsten Day died at the age of 85 in West Palm Beach, Florida and was buried at the Royal Palm Memorial Garden.*

<u>1947</u> - *Elaine Bessemer-Clarke returned to England after the war where in 1947 she was divorced by Reginald Bessemer-Clarke.*[354] *In 1948 she was living at No. 1, Park Village, Regent's Park, London. Her son, Anthony Bessemer-Clarke was attending "a near-by prep school."*[355]

<u>Jun 1949</u> – *Elaine Clarke married Frederick G. Roe (born 22 May 1904).*[356] *Elaine (born 2 Jan 1914) and her new husband traveled extensively on the Queen Mary, all recorded in the database of Ancestry.com. Elaine Gertrude Roe died in January 1986 at the age of 71 in the Poole District, Dorset, UK.*[357] *Her son, Anthony Bessemer-Clarke died in 1996.*

---

[354] National Archives, Kew U.K., Piece Reference J77/4078, Bessemer-Clark EGB & RF, Former reference (Department 8749) Public Record, Dates: 1/1/1947 – 31/12/1947, with photographs.

[355] The Argus (Melbourne, Victoria) 7 Jan 1948, p5.

[356] England & Wales Marriage Index, Ancestry.com. The marriage was recorded in the June quarter 1949 in the St. Pancras District, Middlesex, Vol. 5d, p.1038.

[357] England & Wales Death Index (1916-2005), June 1986, Poole District, Dorsett, U.K. Recorded Vol. 23, p.638. Ancestry.com

War Time Service Record for John F. Day Jr.

1st.Lt/Capt.	Btry Commander	38th FA Bn., Hq. Btr.	Nov 1940 – Nov 1941
Capt.	Btry Commander	26th FA Bgd., Hq. Btr.	Jan 1942 – Apr 1942
Capt./Maj.	Hdq Commandant	USAFFE	3 Apr 1942 – 31 Dec 1942
Maj.	Hdq Commandant	GHQ SWPA	1 Jan 1943 – 24 Feb 1943
Maj.	Asst Hdq Commandant	GHQ SWPA	25 Feb 1943 – 21 Jun 1943
Maj.	Hdq. Commander	23 Post Hdq. (USASOS)	22 Jun 1943 – 23 Dec 1943
Maj.	Base Area Commander	Base E (USASOS)	24 Dec 1943 – 26 Aug 1944
Maj./Lt.Col.	Chief of Troops Sec. (G-3)	Hq. ASCOM (Sixth Army)	27 Aug 1944 – 12 Feb 1945
Lt.Col.	G-3, Troops Section	LUBSEC (USASOS)	13 Feb 1945 – 7 Mar 45

43. BIBLIOGRAPHY

43.1.   General Douglas MacArthur

- Roger Olaf Egeberg, *The General, MacArthur and the Man He Called 'Doc'*, (New York: Hippocrene Books, 1983).

- Doris Clayton James, *The Years of MacArthur*, (New York: Houghton Mifflin, 1975) vol. 2, 1941-1945.

- William Manchester, *American Caesar*, Douglas MacArthur 1880-1964, (New York: Back Bay Books, Little, Brown and Company, 1978).

43.2.   Pacific Passage

- John F. Day Jr., *World War II Diary and Letters of John F. Day Jr.*, 21 Nov 1941 to 4 Dec 1942, The Pacific Theater, Compiled by John F. Day III, (2006).

- John F. Day Jr., *World War II Memories: An Oral History*, Video Transcription, original recording 15 Apr 1988.

- Glen Williford, *Racing the Sunrise, Reinforcing America's Pacific Outposts, 1941-1942*, (Annapolis, MD 21402: Naval Institute Press, 2010).

43.3.   Seeds of Pearl Harbor Attack

- *Yuichi Arima, The Way to Pearl Harbor: US vs. Japan*, Inventory of Conflict and Environment (ICE), Trade and Environment Case Studies (TED), ICE Case Study Number 118, December, 2003. - http://www1.american.edu/TED/ice/ice.htm

- Sadao Asada, *Japan and the World, 1853-1952*. (New York: Columbia University Press, 1989).

- Robert Dallek, *Franklin D. Roosevelt and American Foreign Policy, 1932-1945*. (New York: Oxford University Press, 1979).

- Justus D. Doenecke and John E. Wilz. *From Isolation to War, 1931-1941*. (Arlington Heights, Illinois: Harlan Davidson, 1991).

- Cordell Hull, *The Memoirs of Cordell Hull, vol.2*. (New York: Macmillan, 1948).

- Saburo Ienaga, *The Pacific War, 1931-1945: A Critical Perspective on Japan's Role in World War II.* (New York: Pantheon Books, 1978).

- Edwin T. Layton, with Roger Pineau, and John Costello. *"I Was There" Pearl Harbor and Midway – Breaking the Secrets.* (New York, William Morrow and Company, Inc., 1985).

- Donald G. McCloud, *Southeast Asia: Tradition and Modernity in the Contemporary World.* (Boulder, Colorado: Westview Press, 1995).

- Daniel Marston (Editor), *The Pacific War Companion, From Pearl Harbor to Hiroshima.* (Oxford, UK: Osprey Publishing Ltd., 2005).

- Michael Montgomery, *Imperialist Japan: The Yen to Dominate.* (New York: St. Martin's Press, 1988).

- Naval History and Heritage Command, U.S. Navy
http://www.history.navy.mil/photos/events/wwii-pac/pearlhbr/ph-ja1.htm

- Scott D. Sagan, *The Origins of the Pacific War*, (Journal of Interdisciplinary History: Spring 1988).

- Mitsuo Fuchida, *For That One Day: The Memoirs of Mitsuo Fuchida, the Commander of the Attack on Pearl Harbor.* Translated by: Douglas T. Shinsato and Tadanori Urbe, (Kamuela, HI: eXperience Inc. 2011).

- Robert Smith. Thompson, *Empires on the Pacific: World War II and the Struggle for the Mastery of Asia.* (New York: Basic Books, 2001).

- Peter Wetzler, *Hirohito and War,* (Honolulu, Hawaii: University of Hawai'i Press, 1998).

- Roland H. Worth, Jr., *No Choice But War: the United States Embargo Against Japan and the Eruption of War in the Pacific.* (Jefferson, North Carolina: McFarland, 1995).

43.4. Brisbane, Australia

- Peter Dunn, *Australia at War,* www.oz@war.com, Brisbane, Australia was most generous with his time and counsel (2010).

- Karen Nunan, *Douglas MacArthur Museum Brisbane*, (Brisbane QLD, Australia, 2010). The Archives included an original telephone book, vintage photographs, and other documents that assisted this research.

43.5.   Java and the Dutch East Indies

- Kelly E. Crager, *Hell Under the Rising Sun: Texan POWs and the Building of the Burma-Thailand Death Railroad*, (Texas A&M Press: Williams-Ford Texas A&M University Military History Series, 2008).

- John F. Day Jr., *World War II Diary and Letters of John F. Day Jr.,* 21 Nov 1941 to 4 Dec 1942, The Pacific Theater, Compiled by John F. Day III (2006).

- John F. Day Jr., *World War II Memories: An Oral History*, Video Transcription, original recording 15 Apr 1988.

- Walter D. Edmonds, *They Fought with What They Had: The Story of the Army Air Forces in the Southwest Pacific,* 1941-1942: (Boston: Little, Brown and Co., 1951), pp. 409-415.

- Mitsuo Fuchida, Captain, and Masatake Okumiya, Commander, *The Battle that Doomed Japan – Midway*, by two Japanese Officers, (New York, Ballantine Books, 1958), p.49.

- James D. Hornfischer, *Ship of Ghosts*, (New York: A Bantam Book, A Division of Random House, Inc., (2006).

- Kirk, *Website: www.msAbbekerk.nl*

- Nederlands Instituut voor Militaire Historie (The Netherland's Institute for Military History) at The Hague, Bronbeek Museum (Dutch Indies Military Museum). http://www.defensie.nl/cdc/bronbeek/museum/kenniscentrum/

- U.S. Government, *Reports of General MacArthur, The Campaigns of MacArthur in the Pacific*, Volume I, Prepared by his General Staff, (U.S. Government Printing Office, 1966).

- Robert Sherman La Forte, Ronald E. Marcello, *Building the death railway: the ordeal of American POWs in Burma, 1942-1945,* (New York: Rowman & Littlefield Publishers, 1993).

- Noel Tunny, *Winning From Downunder,* (Salisbury, Brisbane, Australia: Boolarong Press, 2010).

43.6.   Escape from Java

- Kelly E. Crager, *Hell Under the Rising Sun: Texas POWs and the Building of the Burma-Thailand Death Railroad,* (University of Texas A&M Press, 2008).

- Walter D. Edmonds, *They Also Fought With What They Had,* footnote on p.410 attributed to Lt. Stewart B. Avery.

- Louis Morton, *III Reinforcement of the Philippines, The Fall of the Philippines* (U.S. Army in World War II: The War in the Pacific) (United States Army Center of Military History: CMH Pub 5-2, 1953), p.146.

- Kirk, *Website: www.msAbbekerk.nl*

43.7.   General Headquarters (GHQ)

- Hugh J. (Pat) Casey, *Engineer Memoirs, No. 7,* Office of History, US Army Corps of Engineers, Washington, DC. Edited by Dr. John T. Greenwood, then Chief of the Historical Division, (US Army Corps of Engineers, Sept 1979). Part of the US Army's commemoration of the 50th Anniversary of the war.

- Reports of General Douglas MacArthur, *The Campaigns of MacArthur in the Pacific,* Volume I, (Originally Prepared by his General Staff, Tokyo, Japan, Originally published 1950. Reprinted by U.S. Government Printing Office, LCCN 66-60005 1966). Also available online at http://www.history.army.mil/books/wwii/macarthur%20reports/macarthur%20v1/ch02.htm

- Paul P. Rogers, *The Good Years: MacArthur and Sutherland,* (New York: Praeger Publishers, 1990).

- Paul P. Rogers, *The Bitter Years: MacArthur and Sutherland,* (New York: Praeger Publishers, 1991).

43.8.   New Guinea

- David Dexter, *Australia in the War of 1939-45: The Army: The New Guinea Offensives* (Melbourne, Australia: 1961) is an excellent recounting of Australia's ground war on New Guinea.

- Edward J. Drea, *New Guinea*, U.S. Army Center of Military History, U.S. Army Campaigns of World War II, (U.S. Government CMH Pub 72-9, 2003) (Reprinted 3 Oct 2001), www.history.army.mil/brochures/new-guinea/ng.htm .

- Edward J. Drea's *MacArthur's ULTRA: Codebreaking and the War Against Japan, 1942-1945,* (Kansas: University Press of Kansas, 1992). Analyzes MacArthur's use of intelligence during the New Guinea and Philippine campaigns.

- Robert L. Eichelberger and Milton MacKaye, Our *Jungle Road to Tokyo,* (New York: Battery Press, 1950). Reprint Battery Press (1989).

- Robert L. Eichelberger, *Dear Miss Em*, Eichelberger letters published by Jay Luvaas, et.al. (1972).

- Gregory M. Franzwa & Lt. Gen. William J. Ely, *Leif Sverdrup*, (Gerald, Missouri: The Patrice Press, 1980).

- Harry A. Gailey, *MacArthur's Victory, The War in New Guinea*, 1943-1944, New York: Presidio Press , Random House Publishing Group, Ballantine Books, 2004).

- J. E. Hewitt, *Adversity in Success*, (Victoria, Australia, Langate Publishing, 1980).

- George C. Kenney, *General Kenney Reports, A Personal History of the Pacific War* (USAF Warrior Studies, Office of Air Force History, USAF, 1949) (Second edition, 1987), discuss New Guinea operations in general terms.

- Martin J. Kidston, *Poplar to Papua*, (Helena, Montana: Farcountry Press, 2004).

- Walter Krueger, *From Down Under to Nippon,* (New York: Battery Press, 1953) (Reprint 1979).

- Samuel Milner, *Victory in Papua*, US Army in World War II, The War in the Pacific, (Washington, D.C.: Office Of The Chief Of Military History, Department Of The Army, CMH Pub 5-2, 1953) (Reprint 1957)p.31.

- John Miller Jr., *CARTWHEEL: The Reduction of Rabaul*, US Army in World War II, The War in the Pacific, (Washington, D.C., Office Of The Chief Of Military History, Department Of The Army, CMH Pub 5-2, 1950) (Reprinted 1959)

- Robert Ross Smith, *The Approach to the Philippines*, US Army in World War II, The War in the Pacific, (Washington, D.C.: Office Of The Chief Of Military History, Department Of The Army, CMH Pub 5-2, 1959)

- Military History of the US Army Services of Supply (USASOS), Southwest Pacific, and Army Forces Western Pacific, 1941-1946, Chapter XVIII, *Base at Lae Until March 1944*, (Washington, D.C.: Office Of The Chief Of Military History, Department Of The Army, 24 Jun 1947) (*Historical Manuscripts Collection (HMC) under file number 8-5.8 AA vol. 19*)

43.9.   Philippine Islands

- Charles R. Anderson, *Leyte*, The Campaigns of World War II: A World War II Commemorative Series, (Washington, D.C., Office Of The Chief Of Military History, Department Of The Army, Center for Military History, CMH Pub 72-27, 1954) p.36-39.

- M. Hamlin Cannon, *The Return to the Philippines*, US Army in World War II, The War in the Pacific, (Washington, D.C., Office Of The Chief Of Military History, Department Of The Army, Center for Military History, CMH Pub 5-9-1, 1954) p.36-39.

- James D. Hornfischer, *The Last Stand of the Tin Can Sailors*, (New York: A Bantam Book, A Division of Random House, Inc., New York, 2004).

- Linda Mayo, *The Ordnance Department: On Beachhead and Battlefront*, United States Army in World War II, The Technical Services, (Washington, D.C., Office of The Chief Of Military History, Department Of The Army, Center for Military History, CMH Pub 10-11, 1968) p.387.

- Robert Ross Smith, The US Army in World War II: The War in the Pacific, "The Approach to the Philippines," (Washington, D.C.: US Army Center of Military History, 1952)

- Robert Ross Smith, *Luzon Versus Formosa"* the strategic debate about the targets of the Western Pacific (Washington, D.C.: US Army Center of Military History, 1952).

43.10.   Army Services Command (ASCOM)

The following is a direct quotation from M. Hamlin Cannon's *The Return to the Philippines"*:

> "The "history" of the Sixth Army Services Command is poor and there are few records of ASCOM in the Historical Records Section, Adjutant General's Office."

This statement is not consistent with the extant records of the U.S. Army Historical Division, Center of Military History (U.S. Army CMH), Ft. McNair, DC in 2012. CMH has unpublished Historical Manuscripts that were prepared in 1949-1951 entitled *History of ASCOM* and other titles dealing with ASCOM and USASOS. These manuscripts were clearly prepared with the intention of publishing a history of the role of ASCOM in the invasion of the Philippines however, the project was never completed. The matériel is incomplete but divided into unnumbered chapters. These papers were copied by the author, arranged in chronological order, and used extensively in the preparation of this book. The original papers are located in File Drawer 8-5.8, AA. The author thanks the librarian, James Tobias, Archivist, for assistance in locating these documents.

- Hugh J. (Pat) Casey, *Engineer Memoirs, No. 7*, Office of History, US Army Corps of Engineers, Washington, DC. Edited by Dr. John T. Greenwood, then Chief of the Historical Division, US Army Corps of Engineers (Sept 1979). Part of the US Army's commemoration of the 50th Anniversary of the war.

Cover Photograph: 8 Jan 1945, Gen. Douglas MacArthur smoking corn cob pipe on deck of ship w. aide Col. Lloyd Lehrbas, en route to USAF landing site at Lingayen Gulf in victorious (I Shall Return) WWII return to Philippine Islands site of earlier defeat. (Photo by Carl Mydans//Time Life Pictures/Getty Images)

44.   INDEX

45.　　ABOUT THE AUTHOR

John F. Day III lived in Bonham, Texas during World War II with his mother and grandparents while his father was on Gen. MacArthur's staff in the Southwest Pacific. When the war ended, the family moved to Ft. Sam Houston, Texas and later Ft. Bragg, North Carolina. Day attended the Massachusetts Institute of Technology where he earned both a B.S. in physics and an M.S. in mechanical engineering (thermodynamics). Upon graduation, he received an ROTC commission and served his obligation in the U.S. Army Corps of Engineers, reaching the rank of captain.

After discharge, Day worked as an engineer on several classified military airborne and satellite reconnaissance systems. He returned to school at the Stanford Graduate School of Business where he received an M.B.A. He enjoyed a 35-year career as a marketing executive, entrepreneur, and publisher. His publishing company produced technology newsletters, market reports, seminars, and conventions for the semiconductor industry for 22 years. He retired in 2001.

In retirement, Day has pursued his interest in genealogy, history, and DNA. His genealogy interests led him to publish a family story in the Magazine of Albemarle History (Virginia). His fascination with World War II led to an extensive investigation into his father's World War II experiences, travel to Australia and Asia, and eventually this book. He is also the worldwide coordinator for the Day family DNA project at Family Tree DNA.

Day lives in Los Altos, California with Stephanie, his wife of 55 years. They have two adult children and four grandchildren.

CPSIA information can be obtained at www.ICGtesting.com
Printed in the USA
BVOW09s0700020814

360838BV00002B/7/P